Exploring Psychology: Introductory Readings

Exploring Psychology: Introductory Readings

Ivan N. McCollom

Professor Emeritus
California State University, San Diego

Nancy Lloyd Badore

Massachusetts Department of Education

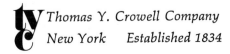 Thomas Y. Crowell Company
New York   Established 1834

1 2 3 4 5 6 7 8 9 10

Library of Congress Cataloging in Publication Data

McCollom, Ivan Newton, 1905-   comp.
  Exploring psychology.

  Includes bibliographies.
  1. Psychology—Addresses, essays, lectures. I. Badore, Nancy Lloyd, joint
comp. II. Title. [DNLM: 1. Psychology—Collected works. BF 121 M129e
1973]
BF149.M22 1973   150'.8   73-2947
ISBN 0-690-28270-2

Part title page acknowledgments: Part One–Photography Department,
Phoenix House. Part Two–Wide World Photos. Part Three–New York
Academy of Medicine. Part Four–Gerber Products Co. Part Five–Diana
Henry/Editorial Photocolor Archives. Part Six–National Museum Vincent
van Gogh, Amsterdam. Part Seven–George W. Gardner. Part Eight–Woods-
Ramirez. Part Nine–National Education Association/Ben Spiegel. Part Ten–
Pablo Picasso, *Study for Weeping Head*, May 24, 1937, pencil and wash on
white paper, 11½ x 9¼". On extended loan to the Museum of Modern Art,
New York. Part Eleven–New York University Testing Center. Part Twelve–
Mark Haven, New York, N.Y. Part Thirteen–Charles Gatewood. Part
Fourteen–Barbara Baenziger. Part Fifteen–Carole Bertol. Part Sixteen–
Charles Gatewood. Part Seventeen–United Press International Photo. Part
Eighteen–Daniel Brody/Editoral Photocolor Archives.

Preface

The purpose of an introductory course in psychology is two-fold: (1) It should acquaint students with available learning materials concerning psychology. (2) It should so motivate students that they will willingly turn to these materials. They should do this not only during the course, but long after its completion.

In a field potentially so filled with human interest as psychology, the reading materials presented should excite the student. Unless he is excited about a subject, a book filled with encyclopedic facts and generalizations is dry as dust and largely meaningless. Its contents can be assimilated only by rote memory.

S. Howard Bartley (*Perception in Everyday Life*, Harper & Row, 1972) has pointed out a distinction between *truth* and *reality*. "Science as we view it in terms of laws and principles is a collection of statements of truth. . . . The student fails to see them in action; hence, he calls for what is real. He wants direct experience or else *examples* of specific situations which convince him they are like his own. He can live vicariously in them. [pp. 282-3]."

Present the student with events that are meaningful to him; get him excited about the subject; and you can't keep him away from the facts and the generalizations. Expose him to the *real* and he will, on his own, become a seeker of *truth*.

We have sought, in this book of readings, to select meaningful and relevant examples of behavior and experience. In assembling the book we have been guided by four general principles:

1 *Every selection should concern something of interest to college students taking their first course in psychology.* We believe that a student will learn more from what he reads if that reading is voluntary, if that reading is of sufficient interest to him that, even if it were not assigned, he would read it because it is meaningful and enjoyable to him.

2 *Only material that is scientifically sound—that is, "good" psychology—should be used.* This has meant finding some things in the professional journals in psychology. Fortunately, there are some psychologists who write well. Fortunately, too, there are some professional writers who are accurate interpreters of psychological knowledge. So we have searched magazines of general circulation for well written articles of high

quality. This has meant being very selective for, far too often, the popular press offers its readers material that is more sen- sational than valid. We have not only tried to avoid such ma- terial, but to avoid those periodicals that, from time to time, perform a genuine disservice to psychology. One of the an- cillary learnings that should accrue to the student from a book such as this is that he becomes aware of the sources of scien- tifically sound ideas in the field. What are the journals, both professional and general, to which he can turn for solid stuff that he can read with understanding?

We have also gone to books. There is an increasing number of very readable books that students can and do read with both profit and enjoyment. Each of the book items we have in- cluded contains ideas that, in themselves, contribute to our goals. We hope, also, that the sample may induce the student to get the book and read all of it. (This may be a form of se- duction, but we admit that we are trying to seduce students.)

3 *Every reading must have been written at an appropriate readability level.* This led us to reject a great many articles, for we have insisted on including only selections that can be read with relative ease and understanding by first-year college students—not by just the upper half, but by practically all of them.

There are many good articles written by psychologists for other psychologists. There are many written by psychologists for advanced students. But there are few things written ex- pressly for beginning college students. This book is intended for students who are being exposed, for the first time in a systematic way, to the subject matter of psychology. Since the book is intended for these people, we have accepted for in- clusion in it only material that can be readily assimilated by them.

4 *Each selection must occupy a meaningful place in an or- ganized presentation of the field of psychology.* Psychology is a developing science. Year by year there are new discoveries. Many of our selections reflect the contemporary aspects of the science. But not all of the basic principles of psychology have been discovered or revised within the past year, or even the last decade. We have chosen from among recent contributions; we have selected things that are a bit older. And then there are a few classics which should be recalled and presented to each new student generation. They often enable us to view current problems with greater perspective. We have tried to present a balanced collection, reflecting both the historical development of psychology and the problems that are current today.

We have not minded too much if our screening process re- sulted in leaving out some topics. Any introductory course must be selective. We think that we have selected material covering a broad sampling of psychology topics. Our purpose has not been to *cover* the field. Rather, it has been to help the student to discover—to *uncover*—enough about psychology that is of interest and concern to him that he will wish to venture farther into the field. One of the major goals of the educative process is to help the student become self-educative. This includes the development of an interest in seeking new learning adventures.

As originally conceived, this book was to be a collection of readings to supplement a basic textbook. We believe that it offers just that kind of exploration into the literature that will make it a valuable adjunct to any course in elementary, general psychology. The instructor will find readings which will supplement and make more meaningful most of the major topics in the basic textbook he uses.

But, as the book has developed, it seems to offer the possibility of serving as the core around which a first course may be organized. All of psychology cannot be squeezed between the covers of any one book. We have been selective, but we believe that we have included those areas which constitute the basics for a general education course. This book could readily be used as the basic text, itself. The readings are grouped into major topics and original commentary has been provided in order to tie them into a unified whole.

As we have said, we are trying to seduce students, to seduce them into using the library, buying books of their own, trading well-liked books with fellow students—in other words, into reading.

But students can be seduced into reading only if there are enticing things available for them to read. We have discussed in our "Psychological Thrillers" (see Reading No. 56) some of the books that our students have found interesting. This is not a magic list. It but demonstrates that students will get excited about reading psychology if enticing materials are made available.

Too often the student, having read an assigned text or supplementary book, closes it with a snap and a relieved, "That's finished!" Assigned readings tend to be terminal. We would prefer that our book be seminal, that it contribute to the development of a desire for further exploring. Toward this end we have given, following each related group of readings, a few suggestions for additional reading. This is a common practice in textbooks. But our experience with such "suggestions" has been that they refer students mostly to advanced books beyond their present level of competence and outside their range of interest—the same textbooks that are being assigned to advanced undergraduate and graduate students. We have tried to suggest books and articles that students can and will read with interest and enjoyment.

It is obvious that prime credit for such a book as this belongs to the authors of the materials used. We extend hearty thanks to both the authors and the publishers who have permitted us to reprint their works. Special recognition is due the two former students who have permitted us to use papers they wrote when first-year students. They both have been most gracious in granting permission to place before the public these papers, written for class assignments and with no thought of publication. There is probably no better way to come to understand a concept than to read good sources of information and then to organize what has been learned into a written statement or summary. Perhaps we can inspire students to write as well as to read!

Ivan N. McCollom
Nancy Lloyd Badore

Contents

A Few Words
About This Book

One of the purposes of this book is to provide students with information about psychology. But we are more interested in stimulating questions than we are in providing answers. We cannot, between the covers of any one book, bring to students all of the information they might desirably have about psychology. There are many questions concerning psychological topics, questions that are relevant to their own lives, that students might reasonably ask. Perhaps we may provide partial answers. Hopefully we may arouse their curiosity. We may even succeed in inducing them to search further for answers. If our greatest hope is achieved, we shall alert students to some of the many questions that will continue to confront them, this year, next year, from here on out, at the same time giving some direction to their search for answers.

In her preface to a book by the late Dr. William Blatz, Mary Northway says of him: "W. E. Blatz was primarily and consistently a teacher. He taught, not to instruct, but to provoke." [1]

Our purpose in this book is to play a role in the process of teaching and learning. We are not ready to say that our purpose is *never* to instruct, but we most certainly do hope to provoke. We agree with the ancient Greek Plutarch that "the mind is not a vessel to be filled, but a fire to be kindled."

The psychologist Piaget has said that "The principal goal of education is to create men who are capable of doing new things, not simply of repeating what other generations have done—men who are creative, inventive and discoverers. The second goal of education is to form minds which can be critical, can verify, and not accept everything they are offered. The great danger today is of slogans, collective opinions, ready-made trends of thought. We have to be able to resist individually, to criticize, to distinguish between what is proven and what is not." [2]

CONTRADICTIONS   Rather than present a consistent point of view in the following selections we have made every attempt to be inconsistent.

[1] W. E. Blatz. *Human Security: Some Reflections.* Toronto: University of Toronto Press, 1966, p. ix.

[2] David Elkind. Giant in the Nursery—Jean Piaget. *The New York Times Magazine*, May 26, 1968.

Hopefully, the student reader will be able to find contradictions. Alfred North Whitehead once said that "a contradiction in science may mark the birth of a great discovery." Perhaps contradictions the student will find herein will lead him to discover that all knowledge is not fixed for all time and, at least, to discover his own conclusions, his own interpretations. Thus he will proceed in the building of his own organized body of knowledge.

Perhaps we need, also, to say a word about the organization of the materials chosen for inclusion in this collection. If we are to digest knowledge, it must be broken into segments of reasonable size. So, we don't just study Psychology, we study Perception, and Emotion, and Learning, and Motivation. And we divide our books into chapters with these and other labels.

But we are trying here, when dealing with human psychology, to keep in mind, always, that our subject matter is *people*. When dealing with the process of perceiving in people we must be aware that these people are, at the same time, learning, and feeling. When we study the psychology of personality we are considering all of these things, and more. In many instances, perhaps in most, the pigeonhole where we have placed a given selection could be questioned. It might just as well fit somewhere else. It might rightly be included under several headings.

Oh! we have tried to help you, the student, and you, too, the instructor who guides the student, by indicating which readings go best within the various parts of an organized course. But if all of our selections were such as to be easily and readily placed in clear-cut categories, we would not have included some of the things we wished to include—materials that give insight into the day-by-day behavior of human beings in a social context.

ANIMAL PSYCHOLOGY

But, quickly, before you get the idea that we are limiting our psychology to the study of *human* behavior, let's talk about animals. Sometimes people are disturbed because psychologists perform experiments on white rats and follow with generalizations about human behavior. There are some psychologists guilty of this. But we must point out that it is possible to learn much from the study of animals that will give us leads for further study in humans. That is why the psychological study of animals is often called *comparative* psychology. So we include some animal studies for comparative purposes. We realize that such studies do not lead to final proof of anything about human beings. But in a shorter time and under more rigid controls than can be applied to humans, animal studies enable us to learn much that is helpful. And it is surprising how much we resemble other animals, after all.

Then there is another reason for studying animal psychology. That is to learn more about *animals*. We have included some selections with this in mind (although we challenge you never to see some eccentric uncle, some friend or neighbor, in reports of the behavior of various animals).

MOLAR VS.
MOLECULAR

Psychology is concerned with the study of behavior and experience. Each of us has direct access to the experiences of no one but himself. We are limited in our study of other people, and certainly of animals, to their behavior. Even though another person tells us about his experiences, the telling is, itself, but his behavior.

The study of behavior can be concerned with what goes on inside the body; what goes on within the brain; what happens in the nervous system. This kind of psychology is distinctly a biological science. It can be thought of as a *molecular* approach to psychology, a concern with the elements of behavior.

The study of behavior can be looked at another way. In the case of human psychology, it becomes the study of the whole person, a whole person interacting with other people, with the total environment. This approach would classify psychology as a social science. This is a *molar* approach.

A study of the nerve pathways involved in learning would be molecular. A study of stereotypes in relation to minority groups would be molar.

In choosing selections for inclusion in this book, we have leaned in the direction of the molar approach. In the appropriate place we shall adopt a molecular approach briefly in order that you get a glimpse of that phase of psychology.

LEARNING HOW
TO LEARN

The greatest service we can render the student is to help him learn how to learn. We agree with a recent writer who said: "To be practical, an education should prepare a man for work that doesn't yet exist and whose nature cannot even be imagined. This can be done only by teaching people how to learn, by giving them the kind of intellectual discipline that will enable them to apply man's accumulated wisdom to new problems as they arise, the kind of wisdom that will enable them to *recognize* new problems as they arise." [3]

We cannot teach you everything that is known about psychology. Not in one book! But we can give you a sampling of selections from various sources, sources that can usually be depended on to provide valid information. We can help you sample a few of the professional journals in psychology. We

[3] Charles E. Silberman. Murder in the Schoolroom. *Atlantic*, June, 1970.

can provide examples of good things from general magazines. We can delve between the covers to read a few pages from each of several books that deal with various aspects of psychology. We can act as guides as we explore territory you may not previously have visited. This could be an adventure for you. We hope that it is.

But the real adventure will come when the conducted tour is over, when you are ready to explore on your own. It will come when you are ready, in your general reading, to search out new articles in the journals and magazines you have learned about and to probe more deeply into books that have been sampled but briefly and when you are ready to venture into other books and magazines and decide for yourself what is acceptable as sound psychology and what you will reject as shoddy goods. And we hope that, after reading this book, you *will* wish to continue exploring psychology.

Part One

Studying Psychology: "The Proper Study of Mankind"

A wise man once said that there was more undiscovered territory in the mind of man than ever existed on the face of the Earth. Although it was probably first said long, long ago, it would still seem to be true. We believe Niko Tinbergen would agree with this.

Tinbergen studies the behavior of animals but, as we shall see in the following selection, he is also greatly interested in the behavior of humans. We have said that we are going to consider the behavior of both humans and nonhumans. Something written by Tinbergen, then, would seem to be ideal as a first selection—to set the stage for what follows.

1

THE NEED TO KNOW OURSELVES

N. TINBERGEN

In 1935 Alexis Carrel published a best seller, *Man—The Unknown (1)*. Today, more than 30 years later, we biologists have once more the duty to remind our fellowmen that in many respects we are still, to ourselves, unknown. It is true that we now understand a great deal of the way our bodies function. With this understanding came control: medicine.

The ignorance of ourselves which needs to be stressed today is ignorance about our behavior—lack of understanding of the causes and effects of the function of our brains. A scientific understanding of our behavior, leading to its control, may well be the most urgent task that faces mankind today. It is the effects of our behavior that begin to endanger the very survival of our species and, worse, of all life on earth. By our technological achievements we have attained a mastery of our environment that is without precedent in the history of life. But these achievements are rapidly getting out of hand. The consequences of our "rape of the earth" are now assuming critical proportions. With shortsighted recklessness we deplete the limited natural resources, including even the oxygen and nitrogen of our atmosphere (2). And Rachel Carson's warning (3) is now being followed by those of scientists, who give us an even gloomier picture of the general pollution of air, soil, and water. This pollution is seriously threatening our health and our food supply. Refusal to curb our reproductive behavior has led

SOURCE: From on war and peace in animals and man, *Science*, 1968, *160*, 1411–1418. Copyright © 1968 by the American Association for the Advancement of Science. Used by permission.

to the population explosion. And, as if all this were not enough, we are waging war on each other—men are fighting and killing men on a massive scale. It is because the effects of these behavior patterns, and of attitudes that determine our behavior, have now acquired such truly lethal potentialities that I have chosen man's ignorance about his own behavior as the subject of this paper.

I am an ethologist, a zoologist studying animal behavior. What gives a student of animal behavior the temerity to speak about problems of human behavior? Of course the history of medicine provides the answer. We all know that medical research uses animals on a large scale. This makes sense because animals, particularly vertebrates, are, in spite of all differences, so similar to us; they are our blood relations, however distant.

But this use of zoological research for a better understanding of ourselves is, to most people, acceptable only when we have to do with those bodily functions that we look upon as parts of our physiological machinery—the functions, for instance, of our kidneys, our liver, our hormone-producing glands. The majority of people bridle as soon as it is even suggested that studies of animal behavior could be useful for an understanding, let alone for the control, of our own behavior. They do not want to have their own behavior subjected to scientific scrutiny; they certainly resent being compared with animals, and these rejecting attitudes are both deep-rooted and of complex origin.

But now we are witnessing a turn in this tide of human thought. On the one hand the resistances are weakening, and on the other, a positive awareness is growing of the potentialities of a biology of behavior. This has become quite clear from the great interest aroused by several recent books that are trying, by comparative studies of animals and man, to trace what we could call "the animal roots of human behavior." As examples I select Konrad Lorenz's book *On Aggression* (4) and *The Naked Ape* by Desmond Morris (5). Both books were best sellers from the start. We ethologists are naturally delighted by this sign of rapid growth of interest in our science (even though the growing pains are at times a little hard to endure). But at the same time we are apprehensive, or at least I am.

We are delighted because, from the enormous sales of these and other such books, it is evident that the mental block against self-scrutiny is weakening—that there are masses of people who, so to speak, want to be shaken up.

But I am apprehensive because these books, each admirable in its own way, are being misread. Very few readers give the authors the benefit of the doubt. Far too many either accept uncritically all that the authors say, or (equally uncritically) reject it all. I believe that this is because both Lorenz and Morris emphasize our knowledge rather than our ignorance (and, in addition, present as knowledge a set of statements which are after all no more than likely guesses). In themselves brilliant, these books could stiffen, at a new level, the attitude of certainty, while what we need is a sense of doubt and wonder, and an urge to investigate, to inquire.

REFERENCES

1. A. Carrel, *L'Homme, cet Inconnu* (Librairie Plon, Paris, 1935).
2. AAAS Annual Meeting, 1967 [see *New Scientist 37*, 5 (1968)].
3. R. Carson, *Silent Spring* (Houghton Mifflin, Boston, 1962).
4. K. Lorenz, *On Aggression* (Methuen, London, 1966).
5. D. Morris, *The Naked Ape* (Jonathan Cape, London, 1967).

Just how does one go about the business of studying man— and other animals? The methods of psychology are, basically, the methods of science. A writer on the history of psychology tells us, "Psychology became a distinct and experimental science at a time when European thought was imbued with the spirit of positivism, empiricism and materialism. The idea that the methods of science could be applied to mental phenomena is inherited from philosophical notions of the nineteenth century. . . ." [1]

This does not imply that all psychological knowledge comes from the laboratory. The experimental method includes much more than laboratory experimentation, for example, field studies, case studies, empirical observation. The experimental method is a way of thinking. It is a way of arriving at generalizations based on observations of all sorts.

Our next writer, Vincent G. Dethier, is also a student of animal behavior. He experiments with common houseflies. His style of writing is so humorous that some readers fail to take him seriously. But his experimental methods are faultless and his conclusions sound. His chapter on experimental method, well—why should we tell you anything about it? Just read it!

[1] Duane P. Schultz. *A History of Modern Psychology.* New York: Academic Press, 1969, pp. vii, viii.

2

HOW TO DESIGN AN EXPERIMENT

VINCENT G. DETHIER

A properly conducted experiment is a beautiful thing. It is an adventure, an expedition, a conquest. It commences with an act of faith, faith that the world is real, that our senses generally can be trusted, that effects have causes, and that we can discover meaning by reason. It continues with an observation and a question. An experiment is a scientist's way of asking nature a question. He alters a condition, observes a result, and draws a conclusion. It is no game for a disorderly mind (although the ranks of Science are replete with confused thinkers). There are many ways of going astray. The mention of two will suffice.

The most commonly committed scientific sin is the lack of proper experimental control. The scientist must be certain that the result he obtains is a consequence of the specific alteration he introduced and not of some other coincidental one. There is the case of the gentleman who had trained a flea to leap at the command "Jump!"

"Now," said the clever gentleman, "I shall do an experiment to discover where the flea's ears are located. First I shall amputate his feelers." Whereupon, the operation having been completed and the flea having recovered, the command "Jump!" was given. The flea jumped. "Ah," said the gentleman obviously pleased, "he does not hear with his antennae. I shall now amputate his forelegs." With each succeeding operation the flea leaped on command until only the hindmost legs remained. When they were removed, the flea failed to jump. "You see," concluded the gentleman triumphantly, "he hears with his hind legs."

Or there is the well-known case of the chap who wondered which component of his mixed drink caused his inevitable intoxication. He tried bourbon and water, rum and water, scotch and water, rye and water, gin and water and concluded, since every drink had water as a constant, that water caused his drunkenness. He then gritted his teeth and tried water alone—with negative results. When I last saw him he had concluded that the glass was the intoxicating agent, and he was about to begin another series of experiments employing paper cups.

SOURCE: From *To Know a Fly*. San Francisco: Holden-Day, 1962. Pp. 18–27. Copyright © 1962 by Holden-Day, Inc. Used by permission.

Of course even controls can be carried to absurd extremes as in the case of the atheistic scientist who seized upon the opportunity afforded by the birth of twins to test the efficacy of religion. He had one baby baptized and kept the other as a control.

Another common fallacy is that of confusing correlation with cause and effect. This is exemplified by the case of the gentleman who was extricated from the rubble of an apartment house immediately after an earthquake. "Do you know what happened?" his rescuers inquired.

"I am not certain," replied the survivor. "I remember pulling down the window shade and it caused the whole building to collapse."

The kind of question asked of nature is a measure of a scientist's intellectual stature. Too many research workers have no questions at all to ask, but this does not deter them from doing experiments. They become enamored of a new instrument, acquire it, then ask only "What can I do with this beauty?" Others ask such questions as "How many leaves are there this year on the ivy on the zoology building?" And having counted them do not know what to do with the information. But some questions can be useful and challenging. And meaningful questions can be asked of a fly.

Between the fly and the biologist, however, there is a language barrier that makes getting direct answers to questions difficult. With a human subject it is only necessary to ask: what color is this? does that hurt? are you hungry? The human subject may, of course, lie; the fly cannot. However, to elicit information from him it is necessary to resort to all kinds of trickery and legerdemain. This means pitting one's brain against that of the fly—a risk some people are unwilling to assume. But then, experimentation is only for the adventuresome, for the dreamers, for the brave.

It is risky even at higher levels. I am reminded of the eminent professor who had designed experiments to test an ape's capacity to use tools. A banana was hung from a string just out of reach. An assortment of tools, that is, boxes to pile up, bamboo poles to fit together, etc., were provided, and the ape's ability was to be judged by his choice of method. To the chagrin of the professor, the ape chose a method that had never even occurred to that learned gentleman.

Extracting information from a fly can be equally challenging. Take the question of taste, for example. Does a fly possess a sense of taste? Is it similar to ours? How sensitive is it? What does he prefer?

The first fruitful experimental approach to this problem began less than fifty years ago with a very shrewd observation;

namely, that flies (and bees and butterflies) walked about in their food and constantly stuck out their tongues. The next time you dine with a fly (and modern sanitary practice has not greatly diminished the opportunities), observe his behavior when he gavots across the top of the custard pie. His proboscis, which is normally carried retracted into his head like the landing gear of an airplane, will be lowered, and like a miniature vacuum cleaner he will suck in food. For a striking demonstration of this, mix some sugared water and food coloring and paint a sheet of paper. The first fly to find it will leave a beautiful trail of lip prints, hardly the kind suitable for lipstick ads but nonetheless instructive.

Proboscis extension has been seen thousands of times by thousands of people but few have been either struck by the sanitary aspects of the act or ingenious enough to figure out how they might put the observation to use to learn about fly behavior.

The brilliant idea conceived by the biologist who first speculated on why some insects paraded around in their food was that they tasted with their feet. In retrospect it is the simplest thing in the world to test this idea. It also makes a fine parlor trick for even the most blasé gathering.

The first step is to provide a fly with a handle since Nature failed to do so. Procure a stick about the size of a lead pencil. (A lead pencil will do nicely. So will an applicator stick, the kind that a physician employs when swabbing a throat.) Dip one end repeatedly into candle wax or paraffin until a fly-sized gob accumulates. Next anaesthetize a fly. The least messy method is to deposit him in the freezing compartment of a refrigerator for several minutes. Then, working very rapidly, place him backside down on the wax and seal his wings onto it with a hot needle.

Now for the experimental proof. Lower the fly gently over a saucer of water until his feet just touch. Chances are he is thirsty. If so, he will lower his proboscis as soon as his feet touch and will suck avidly. When thirst has been allayed, the proboscis will be retracted compactly into the head. This is a neat arrangement because a permanently extended proboscis might flop about uncomfortably during flight or be trod upon while walking.

Next, lower the fly into a saucer of sugared water. In a fraction of a second the proboscis is flicked out again. Put him back into water (this is the control), and the proboscis is retracted. Water, in; sugar, out. The performance continues almost indefinitely. Who can doubt that the fly can taste with his feet? The beauty of this proboscis response, as it is called, is that it is a reflex action, almost as automatic as a knee jerk.

By taking advantage of its automatism, one can learn very subtle things about a fly's sense of taste.

For example, who has the more acute sense of taste, you or the fly? As the cookbooks say, take ten saucers. Fill the first with water and stir in one teaspoon of sugar. Now pour half the contents of the saucer into another which should then be filled with water. After stirring, pour half of the contents of the second saucer into a third and fill it with water. Repeat this process until you have a row of ten saucers. Now take a fly (having made certain that he is not thirsty) and lower him gently into the most dilute mixture. Then try him in the next and so on up the series until his proboscis is lowered. This is the weakest sugar solution that he can taste.

Now test yourself. If you are the sort of person who does not mind kissing his dog, you can use the same saucers as the fly. Otherwise make up a fresh series. You will be surprised, perhaps chagrined, to discover that the fly is unbelievably more sensitive than you. In fact, a starving fly is ten million times more sensitive.

You console yourself with the thought that he may be less versatile, less of a gourmet, than you. Well, this too can be tested. Try him on other sugars; there are any number of sugars: cane sugar, beet sugar, malt sugar, milk sugar, grape sugar. Each is chemically different; each has for you a different sweetness. It is only necessary to determine for each the most dilute solution that will cause the fly to lower his proboscis. Then when the sugars are listed in order of decreasing effectiveness, it turns out that the order is the same for you and the fly: grape sugar, cane sugar, malt sugar, milk sugar, beet sugar. In one respect the fly is less gullible; he is not fooled by saccharine or any other artificial sweeteners.

But, you may argue, I can distinguish many other kinds of tastes. This is only partly correct. You can distinguish many kinds of flavors, but to assist you in this you recruit your nose. Flavor is a mixture of tastes, odors, and textures. With taste alone you are pretty much restricted to sweet, salt, sour, and bitter.

The old adage that one can catch more flies with honey than with vinegar has a sound basis in physiology. Leaving aside for the moment the fact that flies react differently to different odors, the truth remains that flies accept materials that taste sweet to us and reject those that taste salt, sour, or bitter to us. This fact, too, can be demonstrated with the proboscis response, but the only way for a fly to say "No" is to retract his proboscis, and it can be retracted only if it is first extended. Accordingly, one prepares several saucers of sugared water. A pinch of salt is added to one, two pinches to another, three pinches to a third, and so on. As before, the fly is lowered gently into the saucer with the least salt. He responds, as expected, by extending his proboscis. He is then allowed to taste the next dish, and the next, and the next. At one of these dishes he will stubbornly refuse to extend his proboscis. Since this dish contains the same amount of sugar as the rest, one must conclude that it is the salt that is being rejected. The test can be repeated with vinegar, lemon juice, or quinine water. It can even be tried with aspirin, whiskey, bicarbonate of soda, tobacco juice—anything that will dissolve in water. If you wish to be really sophisticated, you can test the relative sensitivity of his legs and mouth by standing him in one solution and allowing his proboscis to come down into a different one. A friend of mine who once wished to study the stomach of the fly and to color it so it could be seen more easily under the microscope hit upon the idea of standing a fly in sugar but arranging for its mouth to come down in dye. As a result the fly's insides were stained beautifully. This is one example of a physiological way to coat a pill.

In all experimentation, in all thinking, one needs to exercise certain controls. The experimenter seeks to keep all variables constant except one, which he varies independently of other factors; this is the *independent* variable. Then he observes what changes, if any, take place with variations in the independent variable. If his logic is correct, these changes will *depend* on what happens to the independent variable; they constitute the *dependent* variable. The independent variable may involve using two groups of subjects, each group treated in a different way. One is the *experimental* group; the other, the *control* group.

But, more about this in our next selection.

3

THE CONTROL GROUP
DONALD O. HEBB

In the physical sciences it may often be possible to hold constant all but one of the factors that might affect the outcome of an experiment; this one, the *independent variable*, is changed

Source: From *A Textbook of Psychology*, Third edition. Philadelphia: W. B. Saunders, 1972. Pp. 147–149.

systematically, and the experimenter observes the effects in the *dependent variable*. In a study of the pressure of the atmosphere, for example, the independent variable may be height above sea level; the dependent variable is the height of a column of mercury in a barometric tube. Other influences that might affect the outcome are eliminated or kept constant: temperature, contaminating substances in the mercury, movement of the surrounding air, and so forth. In the biological sciences one can only approach this ideal procedure; and only too often fundamental questions have gone unanswered because it was not possible to get anywhere near it. In psychological research there are two great difficulties which frequently demand the use of control groups as a substitute for the ideal procedure.

One is that taking a psychological test usually changes the subject; a later test does not give the same result because of *practice effect*—the subject as we say "remembers" the first test. The second difficulty is that we are dealing with extraordinarily complex material; after we have used up our first sample of the material (the first subject or group of subjects) we cannot get a second that is identical with the first, because animals and men differ in many ways which we cannot identify before beginning an experiment.

Suppose, for example, that we want to find out whether removing the frontal lobes of a monkey's brain affects his ability to learn a visual discrimination. In an ideal procedure we would measure his learning ability, remove the frontal lobes, and measure his learning ability again. But in reality the second measurement is disturbed by memory of the first. We must measure learning ability by the number of trials, or the number of errors made, in achieving the discrimination. In the second measurement there will almost certainly be a practice effect, and we do not know how great it will be. Next best, in a slightly less ideal world, we would obtain two monkeys identical in all respects; we would remove the frontal lobes from one, have both learn the task under identical conditions, and see how much faster the normal monkey learned, compared to the one operated on. But in practice we cannot find two identical subjects, animal or human. (Identical twins are identical with respect to heredity, but it is impossible that everything that has happened since birth which might affect them psychologically is exactly the same. Also, of course, there are not many of them.) Thus we are driven to the comparison of two groups, an *experimental group* and a *control group*, large enough to make individual differences average out. If the original learning capacity of two subjects is not identical, the average for two groups is likely to differ much less, and the probable degree of difference can be dealt with statistically.

The ideal cases referred to, however, should be kept in mind, for they tell us what we are trying to achieve by the use of the control group. In the frontal-lobe question referred to, what we would like to do is measure the learning ability of the same monkey with and without his frontal lobes, with the second measurement not being affected by the first. This is impractical. So is the hope of finding two identical monkeys; but it is not impractical to find two groups which, if they are large enough, will be much more similar, as groups, than two individual monkeys. Our choice of a control group, then, is a matter of choosing animals which are as much like the animals in the experimental group as possible, in every way that affects visual learning.

The experiment may then proceed in one of two ways. First, we can operate on one group, and test both. We compare the mean scores of the operates and of the normal control subjects, and see whether they differ significantly. Statistics at this point enables us to evaluate the probability that the difference we have found is due simply to accidental differences in our two groups, treating them as two samples in the way already described. The second procedure would be to test both groups, operate on one, test both groups again, and see whether the increases in score by the normals (due to practice effect) are significantly greater than the increases by the operates (though the experiment might come out with a still clearer result, the normals all showing increases and the operates all showing losses).

The principle is clear: make your control group like the experimental group in every way that would affect the outcome of the experiment, except for the one variable in which you are interested. The pitfalls and gins besetting the path of the investigator on this point mainly consist of not recognizing a variable that affects the results. If one is picking rats out of a colony cage, and puts the first 10 into the experimental group, the second 10 into the control group, one overlooks the possibility that the most easily caught animals, or the ones that come to the front of the cage and allow themselves to be picked up, are tamer than the others; and this difference is likely to affect any experimental result. The easiest solution is to put no. 1 into the first group, no. 2 into the second, no. 3 into the first, and so on. (There are also more sophisticated ways of doing this by the use of random numbers assigned to the animals, but we need not go into this.)

Again, in clinical investigations one does not have the choice of one's "experimental" group, and one perforce must try to find a similar control group. This is usually difficult. The clinical group (corresponding to the experimental group of the laboratory) generally includes people of all sorts of occupations, rural as well as urban, educated and uneducated, old and young. It is difficult indeed to persuade a group of similar persons, who are not ill and have no reason to take tests, to give up the time to act as subjects—especially since they are apt to view any psychological test with suspicion. But if one wants to know whether removal of the human frontal lobe affects intelligence, and if the clinical group with frontal lobe operation has a mean age of 40 and a mean of 8 years' schooling, for example, one must make one's comparisons with a group that is similar in these respects, as intelligence test scores vary with amount of schooling and with advancing age.

The following selection is included to give you an opportunity to try out part of what you have just read. In this study we do not find a *control* group, since all groups are equally involved. But we do find a clear-cut *independent variable*. Can you identify it? Then, as the experimenter varies this independent variable, what event varies? What is the *dependent variable*? (Hint: Look at the table.)

Incidentally, we have purposely chosen an old study, for we do not wish you to become confused with your own preferences should you be a cigarette smoker. While some of the brands in the study are still on the market, it is safe to say that the products, themselves, have undergone many changes in approximately forty years, as have the advertising claims.

AN EXPERIMENTAL STUDY OF CIGARETTE IDENTIFICATION

RICHARD W. HUSBAND AND JANE GODFREY

In a number of ways, through advertising and in personal conduct, there seems to exist an assumption that a person can identify his favorite brand of tobacco. The most striking example in advertising is the well-known "blindfold test" which has been run by one of the larger cigarette companies. The results —at least those which were published—all favored the company which conducted the tests. Persons were blindfolded and

SOURCE: From *Journal of Applied Psychology*, 1934, *18*, 220–223.

given several brands of cigarettes to smoke in succession, and were then asked to indicate their preference. It seems highly unlikely that the tests were run in an impartial, well-controlled manner.

This instance is only slightly more extreme than are cases which appear daily in magazines and newspapers. When Chesterfield advertises that it is milder, that it is compounded from an optimal blend of domestic and Turkish tobaccos; when Camels claim they use a more expensive raw product; when Luckies claim they use a toasting process—they state in substance that the facts or processes are such that the cigarette becomes preferable over others which are not made in that way.

As to personal conduct, the same implicit assumption appears at the consumer end of the economic order. The majority of cigarette users have definite preferences. Many individuals either refuse offers of other brands or smoke them with reduced satisfaction.

If both advertising statements and consumer preferences had factual bases, one would find that people could discriminate different brands of cigarettes from each other. If tobaccos are so much alike that brands can not be told apart, or if the gustatory or olfactory senses are so dull that one can not spot his favorite brand, then we will be forced to admit that advertising and subjective preferences both are founded on hypotheses which are not based on facts or that suggestion is responsible.

It is, therefore, the purpose of our investigation to see whether persons, habitual users of one particular brand, can identify their preferred brand through taste alone.

TECHNIQUE   Fifty-one subjects were selected from a total group of nearly twice that size on the basis of questionnaire data. We only used persons who smoked regularly, at least several cigarettes a day; those who had smoked for at least a year and who preferred one particular brand. We did not demand that they never smoked another kind but that they would use just one make if it could be obtained with reasonable effort. We did not attempt to study pipe or cigar users. Actually, 21 subjects preferred Camels, 12 Lucky Strikes, and 11 Chesterfields, with a few other brands scattering. The three chief brands were used in all tests, with others added for subjects who used them, or for pragmatic purposes to keep supplies about even.

The subject was blindfolded and four cigarettes were placed on a tray. To ensure random selection and order he made his choice by groping in the dark. All he was told was that his own brand would be supplied along with three others. Several minutes were allowed between cigarettes until the subject felt there would be no interference. If he wished, he was given a mint to remove the taste but this usually caused more of an after-taste than a cigarette. The subjects were not compelled to smoke the whole cigarette, but could stop as soon as they had made their judgment. If they could not name any brand, they were asked to indicate whether or not it was their favorite.

RESULTS   The main results are presented in Table 1. To see how often a brand was correctly identified as itself one can find the percentage quoted in both axes for any name. Obviously, 25 per cent accuracy should be achieved through chance alone. We

Table 1. Percentage Identification of Different Brands

	Camel %	Lucky %	Chesterfield %	20-Grand %	Spud %	Miscell. %
Camel	31	14	38	6	2	10
Lucky	19	41	21	4	0	14
Chesterfield	27	23	33	2	0	15
20-Grand	38	26	3	17	0	15
Spud	0	6	6	0	76	11

see that each brand is identified as itself in somewhat better than chance proportions. But the trend is not very pronounced, with Camels only 6 per cent better than chance, Luckies 16 per cent, and Chesterfields 8 per cent. 20-Grand, for some reason, has poorer than chance accuracy. We also find a few anomalies. Camels are identified as Chesterfields more often than as themselves. 20-Grands are said to be Camels more than twice as often as 20-Grands. Chesterfields were spotted correctly only a few times more than as two other brands. Spuds were identified correctly by practically all their users and by many others who had used them occasionally. Being mentholated, the proposition was somewhat different. It is as if a certain apple had a distinct taste of quinine; the merest novice would be able to identify it.

The average of cigarette users' correct decision in regard to their own brand was 31 per cent. This is very little better than chance.

Some rather interesting observations were made by the subjects during the tests. Many subjects expressed a liking for a particular cigarette and thought it was their favorite, and were terribly upset to find that it actually was one which they ordinarily refused to smoke, even if they had to go without. Others found cigarettes flat at times and judged them to be Chesterfields on the basis of mildness, while actually they were other brands as often, or more often, than that make.

SUMMARY   It is not our place here to condemn any advertising or to state that cigarettes do not have the qualities attributed to them. It is perfectly possible that Luckies are less irritating to the throat, that Chesterfields are really more mild, that a Camel does give a better taste, and that an Old Gold is really smoother. But it is certain that under controlled experimental conditions, subjects are unable to select their own brands from others on the basis of gustatory or olfactory cues alone.

Did you correctly identify the independent variable as the brand of cigarette? And conclude that the dependent variable is the percentage identification?

Any time you read a report of an experiment, look for the independent variables. Insist, in your thinking, before you accept the results of the experiment as valid, that the experimenter has seen to it that all other possible variables are held constant. Then look to see what else varied in step with the independent variable. If something did, you have identified the dependent variable.

Don't confine this process to experiments alone. In empirical reports, ask what varied independently. Were all other factors held constant? What else then varied, *depending* on changes in the independent variable?

You may make a nuisance of yourself, but when a friend tells you, for example, that he can study better with his stereo going full blast, ask him a few questions. Perhaps he truly can. But has he controlled all of the variables except one? And does he have an adequate measure of the dependent variable?

In reflecting on your own experiences, try to build a number of independent variable–dependent variable relationships. The next time you are just about to state a generalization in any area of experience, ask yourself some of these questions.

We suggest that as you read selections in this book you make it a habit to identify the independent variable or variables involved. Then find the dependent variables, if any, that relate. You should find this habit an aid to clear thinking.

FURTHER ADVENTURES

If you wish to venture further into this area, you will find an excellent discussion of independent and dependent variables in John C. Townsend, *Introduction to Experimental Method* (McGraw-Hill, 1953). This book is also a good source of information about other aspects of the design and conduct of experiments in psychology, the theory of experimentation, and applications of the experimental method. You may also find helpful a little paperback by Arthur J. Bachrach, *Psychological Research: An Introduction* (Random House, 1962). Should you become interested in performing a psychological experiment, you might also get help from another paperback, Barry F. Anderson, *The Psychology Experiment* (Wadsworth, 1966). A more general book, covering the entire breadth of science, is Garvin McCain and Erwin M. Segal, *The Game of Science* (Brooks/Cole Publishing Co., 1969).

Part Two

Freedom or Control: Defining the Issues of Psychology

Possibly the most generally acceptable definition of psychology is that it is the *science of behavior and experience.* Some people would leave out the *experience* on the grounds that only behavior is readily available to inspection. Others would insist that no psychology is complete that does not include an awareness of the experiencing individual.

There seem to be four purposes involved in the study of psychology:

First, we seek to *understand* the behavior of ourselves, of other humans, and of animals. We want to know why all of us do what we do.

Second, on the basis of this understanding, we seek to *predict* behavior. We want to be able to know in advance what an individual or members of a group are going to do as circumstances change.

Third, not content with predicting what others will do, we seek to exert some *influence* on their behavior, to bend their behavior in the direction of our desires. Popularly, this is what people seem to mean when they speak of "using psychology" on others. They seem to imply, often, that psychology is concerned only with some degree of manipulation. But, as we think about it, it becomes apparent that understanding and predicting are prerequisites of influencing.

Fourth, we may seek to *control* the behavior of others. Perhaps the difference between influence and control is but a matter of degree. But, while many people would acknowledge the desirability of "having a good influence on others," it does not seem quite so proper to acknowledge a desire to control. To speak of a person as "influential" is a compliment. To say that he is "controlling" may imply that he is an undesirable schemer.

Or perhaps you are one of those who aspire to be a controller of others. There do seem to be such people in the world—even in our own society.

So, anyone who studies psychology must face up to such issues. Is it possible to understand behavior only after it has occurred? Are people so governed by circumstances that what they do is predetermined and thus predictable? Or is man, at least, free to decide what his actions shall be? Is he a creature of free will? And if humanity is not free who, then, can and who should be in control?

Dr. Robert Oppenheimer, the atomic physicist, was invited to address the Annual Meeting of the American Psychological Association in 1956. In comparing his field, physics, with psychology, Oppenheimer said:

In the last ten years the physicists have been extraordinarily noisy about the immense powers which, largely through their efforts, but through other efforts as well, have come into the possession of man, powers notably and strikingly for very large-scale and dreadful destruction. We have spoken of our responsibilities and of our obligations to society in terms that sound to me very provincial, because the psychologist can hardly do anything without realizing that for him the acquisition of knowledge opens up the most terrifying prospects of controlling what people do and how they think and how they behave and how they feel. This is true for all of you who are engaged in practice, and as the corpus of psychology gains in certitude and subtlety and skill, I can see that the physicist's pleas that what he discovers be used with humanity and be used wisely seem rather trivial compared to those pleas which you will have to make and for which you will have to be responsible.[1]

About a year after Oppenheimer extended this warning, the late Edwin G. Boring discussed the problem at greater length. Boring was a professor of psychology at Harvard University and is considered one of the outstanding historians of psychology. He saw some of the dilemmas involved. Is all of man's behavior determined for him? Is man completely the object of external control? Or is there some freedom for the human mind?

Fortunately, perhaps, for our peace of mind he suggested some possible resolutions of this sticky problem. He ended his article with a concluding statement—a "parting shot"— that is startling in its simplicity. To save you from having to peek now at the last page of the article, we'll tell you how it ends. Boring concluded that if "you want to know where to find a free man. . . . Go to him who is earnestly trying to persuade you that all men are robots. . . . it takes a free man to start a war on freedom."

Now that we've revealed the outcome, it becomes your responsibility to read what Boring had to say to justify this conclusion.

[1] Robert Oppenheimer. Analogy in Science. *American Psychologist,* 1956, *11,* 127–135.

5

WHEN IS HUMAN BEHAVIOR PREDETERMINED?
EDWIN G. BORING

When is human behavior predetermined? Is man free to choose? sometimes? always? in respect of everything? May

SOURCE: From *Scientific Monthly,* 1957, *84,* 189–196. Reprinted by permission of the American Association for the Advancement of Science.

he thus by choice control his own individual destiny? This is surely what most men believe most of the time. The scientist, on the other hand—because the business of science is the study of causes and their effects—keeps insisting that any action of man, if we but knew enough, could be referred to its causes; that the explanation of all human behavior lies in the ancestral genes of the behaving person, in his past experience, and in the various accidents that have happened to him since he was conceived. On which side does truth lie? Is man quite free to think as he will or are his beliefs but a reflection of the climate of fact and opinion that envelops him, and of the circumstances that belong to the century, the country, and the family in which he lives?

This problem is not made easier when we realize that man's belief that he is free may itself be predetermined. The belief in freedom could be man's great delusion—nearly, if not quite, immutable. It is conceivable, you see, that there could be a society of talking robots, designed so that they continue to interact one with another in accordance with the principles on which they have been constructed, all of them chattering the while about their behavior in words that imply that each is free to choose whatever he does; that each, choosing freely, thus becomes responsible for his own conduct—a society of robots in which everyone asserts his own freedom for the excellent reason that he is *not* free to deny it.

We keep thinking, representatives of mankind that we are, that the integrity of each of us is so great that our assurances and convictions are at least partially self-validating; that our sense of certainty, even though it may waver, must at the very least tend to point toward truth. But what if delusion has been designed into us? What if the robot residents of some psychologist-designed utopia have been constructed so as to believe in falsehood and never to know it, the truth of their basic determinism being carefully hidden from them behind barriers of rationalizations to which assurance and conviction are firmly fastened? What are we to say in the face of this possibility? Biology offers us no protection against it, for there is always the possibility that survival can be favored by delusion, and that wisdom may on occasion be, if not lethal, at least not maximally helpful. In this respect man finds himself caught in an egocentric predicament, unable to grasp the standard by which he can tell reason from rationalization. What is he to do? What should we do?

This is no new problem, but it has recently received a new importance, because the development of the behavioral sciences has shown how the actions of animals and men can be controlled in greater degree than had formerly been possible, and even more, I should say, because the totalitarian countries, with their brain-washings and their forced self-accusations, have shown that man's integrity—the citadel of his freedom—can be invaded, and man's opinion, faith, and conscience enslaved. Indeed, the sense of freedom could be turning out to be man's great delusion. Is it? How do you answer a question like that?

There is, I believe, an answer, for that is what this paper is about; but first let us see how this dilemma between freedom and determinism keeps turning up as wise men try to understand and cope with human action.

FREEDOM AND DETERMINISM: THE DILEMMA

Just now the universities—all of them—are worrying about what will happen when the new birth-rate floods the admissions offices with would-be students. How can academe accommodate them all? This matter came up in a certain faculty of a large university some months ago, and the president expressed his concern and gave his advice on how to meet the coming tidal wave. "But why admit so many?" a professor of government asked. "Where," he added, "does the area of decision in this matter lie?" The president was able to discern no such idea. He knew that his university, an endowed institution, could still not remain unconcerned about the applicants it rejects. You might decide for new dormitories but not for a fixed enrollment. The professor, of course, was believing in freedom just then. That is the way governments work: they make decisions. And the two men, the president and the professor, were representing irreconcilable philosophies. Yet no one remarked that incompatibles cannot both be true, for this contradiction is so commonplace that people are fully accustomed to ignore it.

Years ago William McDougall, the psychologist, was my colleague at Harvard. He believed in freedom for the human mind—in at least a little residue of freedom—believed in it and hoped for as much as he could save from the inroads of scientific determinism (1). To the determinist-psychologists, such a view was scientifically immoral. John B. Watson, behaviorism's founder, reviewed McDougall's textbook of 1923 under the title "Professor McDougall returns to religion," and you may be sure that Watson was not thinking of himself as a rejoicing father welcoming back a prodigal (2). I used to wonder about McDougall and determinism, and then one afternoon in a colloquium—one of those rare occasions when argument brings insight and does not merely serve to harden preconceptions—I found out where lay the difference between us—McDougall, the voluntarist, and me, the determinist. McDougall's freedom was my variance. McDougall hoped that variance would always be found in specifying the laws of behavior, for there freedom might still persist. I hoped then—less wise than I think I am now (it was 31 years ago)—that science would keep pressing variance toward zero as a limit. At any rate this general fact emerges from this example: freedom, when you believe it is operating, always resides in an area of ignorance. If there is a known law, you do not have freedom.

Then there is Francis Hackett's assertion that psychoanalysis did not help the novelist after all (3). The novelists thought at first that Freud had presented them with accurate knowledge of human nature—a knowledge that psychology had hitherto failed to provide. Freud did, of course, but he also gave them determinism. Novelists, however, need heroes, and heroes need freedom. What machine was ever a hero to its owner unless the owner—a child undoubtedly—endowed it with freedom and life? You cannot write a novel about robots, unless they are free. The characters must meet difficulty and overcome it, in face of the possibility that they could have failed (4). It is the same with an athletic team. A team that won because it was drugged would not be given the trophy. Victory must originate from within the victor, not be rigged in advance.

The Russians—I am relying on Raymond Bauer's excellent historical account of the development of psychology in the Soviet Union—had occasion to discover this dilemma (5). In the 1920's they stuck to economic determinism as part of their dialectical materialism—to that and to Pavlov's determinism of conditioning. Then their 5-year plans got into difficulty and, in the early 1930's, the leaders reversed themselves, abandoning Pavlov, conditioning, mental testing, and everything that seemed to make the individual a consequence of causes outside himself. As a substitute they introduced a voluntaristic dynamic psychology, letting praise and blame, responsibility and guilt, operate instead of conditions external to the individual. The leaders themselves, of course, must still have believed in the predeterminism of behavior, for it was they who were to determine the conduct of the people by making them believe they were free and responsible. That the leaders thought they were free to delude the people into believing they were free is pretty obvious.

And then there is my colleague, B. F. Skinner, famous for his patterning of the lives of rats and pigeons and now turning his attention to the teaching of children in the grades (6) and to the analysis of psychotic behavior (7). He preaches a gospel of how psychological knowledge can be used to improve human living (8), and how, as behavioral science advances, human conduct becomes more and more subject to control (9). Control by whom, though? Or should one ask, by what? Skinner is saying something more than that behavior is caused, that it is the inevitable consequence of determinable scientific law. He is saying that, because behavior can be controlled, human living can be improved. Not merely that human living will be improved because biological selection promotes human weal willy-nilly, but that it can be and that there is therefore a possibility that it may not be, unless the gospel is accepted. This is sheer voluntarism. It is a mixing of languages, a hoping that hoping itself makes no sense except as a sign of the existence of a feeling of desire that contributes to the inevitable. Can one choose to do without choice?

It is in this way that the determinist gets trapped in the egocentric predicament (*10*). He has to be outside the system in order to recommend it. He would be more convincing if he would take up his stand firmly on the outside—the man from Mars viewing human society—and describe what is going on, that and nothing more, just as a human being may describe the behavior of ants, without praise or blame for their conduct, or suggestions for improving their social structure, or even the admonition that ants could be happier if they were controlled by positive reinforcement and not by aversive stimulation. A book by a behavioral determinist ought not so much advocate the control of behavior as describe it. Advocacy undermines the argument for determinism because preference belongs to the world of values. You can indeed consider advocacy as a behavioral event with necessary and sufficient antecedents and consequences, but such rigor requires that the author rid himself of preferences and prejudices in his devotion to objective description if his implications are not to subvert his explication.

TRUTH VERSUS POLICY IN SCIENTIFIC THEORY

Perhaps I have now already made my point. It is that fact and value, as surely everyone knows, belong in different worlds, each with its own language, and that the wise man must keep both in his repertoire if he is to get along in the culture in which he lives. To me this view means that the wise man is something more than the scientist, who does indeed need, as scientist, to stick to determinism and thus to description. I am saying that science must be something less than the one way to truth. But is not this exactly the principle that prevails today? In 1907, J. J. Thomson remarked that a scientific theory is a policy, not the truth but a view that, if held, gets us ahead (*11*). Today we hear less about theories and more about models. What is the difference? The theory claims to be true, even though we all know that assurance about the validity of these claims varies greatly from theory to theory and from time to time for the same theory. The theory is an *as*, whereas the model is an *as-if*. The theory is indicative; the model, subjunctive. The model is a pattern to be abandoned easily at the demand of progress. Thus science is less than the whole of wisdom, and the wise teacher of science, being also a human being, will not seek to try to make those other human beings who come under his tutelage less wise or less free than himself.

Now let us examine how this dilemma enters into another field and how it can be met there. Let us consider the great man.

GREAT MEN:
FREEDOM AS
A NEGATIVE
CONCEPT

Long ago the problem of freedom and determinism as it pertains to the conduct of great men came up in the contrasting views of Carlyle and Tolstoy. Carlyle, writing about heroes in 1840, was for freedom (*12*). "The history of what man has accomplished in this world," he said, "is at bottom the History of the Great Men who have worked here." Progress is what the great men started. Little is ever said about what started them, for it is conventional to suppose that they are self-starters, creative minds, and it would be derogatory to refer to their causes, if indeed they have any.

Tolstoy—in his *War and Peace* (1869)—was, of course, on the other side (*13*). "A king is history's slave," he said. "History . . . the unconscious, general, hive-life of mankind, uses every moment of the life of kings as a tool for its own purposes. . . . The higher a man stands on the social ladder, the more people he is connected with and the more power he has over others, the more evident is the predestination and the inevitability of his every action." That is, in part, the *Zeitgeist* theory of history, before Matthew Arnold picked that word out of Goethe's writing and made it important. According to this view the great man becomes merely the agent of history. He is not only the cause of his consequences but also the consequence of his causes. You can regard him, if you wish, as a symptom, an event so conspicuous in an otherwise obscure causal train that it comes to be the sign or label by which the whole train is known—like calling all classical physics *Newtonian*.

Herbert Spencer was on the tough side of this argument with Tolstoy. William James was on the soft side with Carlyle. James was promoting scientific psychology in the days when it was very new, but also he was holding tight to the dignity of man. While he wanted us all to meet the new experimental psychologists, "these new prism, pendulum, and chronograph-philosophers," as he called them, he also wished to save the human mind from destruction by "the spying and scraping, the deadly tenacity and almost diabolic cunning" which the scientific attack in the hands of the meticulous German *Ge-lehrter* threatened to bring about—as James thought.

There is a proximate solution to this great-man problem, although one that does not go quite far enough. It is that you have freedom only when you are not interested in causal antecedents, in genesis. Everything depends on where you place the boundaries of your universe of discourse. If you are satisfied to consider only great men and their consequences, then of course they appear as free, because you have ignored all the conditions that made them great, the conditions that require the great scientist at the moment of discovery (when there is such a moment) to have the insight that puts him into the histories of science. So the great man is found free, freed by the unconcern of all hero-worshippers.

Now change your point of view, enlarge your universe of discourse, inquire into the antecedents of the great man's great achievement, find out that he was, at least to some degree, anticipated by others, that another man, a small one, independently made the same discovery later, without knowledge of what the great man had done, and then you begin to transform the great man into a symptom and to believe in the *Zeitgeist* as furnishing the climate necessary for great discovery. Thus you move over from Carlyle to Tolstoy, and from William James to Herbert Spencer. Although you have diminished the dignity of great men, you have, on the other hand, enlarged your vision of the causal web of the universe.

It is possible to visualize a model of this causal nexus. Imagine a diagram, plotted between time, which runs from left to right, and simultaneity, which is up and down. Fill it in with separate little circles, each of which is an event—an event like Max Wertheimer's thought on the train in 1910 about perceived movement's being *ipso facto* a phenomenon, the *phi*-phenomenon, the thought that made him get off at Frankfurt-am-Main, buy a stroboscope at the German equivalent of the dime store, and start, after a few billion other events, the school of *Gestalt* psychology (14). Now on this diagram draw in all the cause-and-effect relations from every event to its consequents at the right. Simultaneous events are above and below each other and are never connected directly. Multiple causes and multiple effects are, of course, the rule. Every event has many causes and many effects. Now select a crucial event, one of the circles, Wertheimer thinking of *phi* on the train. Put in a boundary line that excludes all the antecedents and includes all the consequents. There you have the model for freedom. Wertheimer is seen as an originator. His idea was *sui generis*. When you think of freedom, you think in these terms. But take away the boundary, and you have before you the entire causal nexus. Wertheimer's insight may now be a necessary link in the system, but there are many others. His insight becomes less special, but your universe of understanding is enormously increased.

The main point here is that freedom is a negative conception. It is the absence of causes. The freedom for which men fight and die is also a negative conception, the absence of constraints. Within science the complaint of the intuitionists about the positivists has been that positivism offers constraints upon scientific freedom; that positivism is a police measure insisting that explanation shall be in terms of *nothing but*, as the protesting intuitionists put it, whereas they, the antipositivists, want not exactly *something more*, for they are not prepared to specify the something more, but freedom to let the inquiring mind advance as it will. This is the faith of the artist who resists control or assessment until his job is done and judgment may be passed. Who shall say that artistic expression should be more rigorously constrained?

So the question is: When is *nothing* better than *something?* And the answer is: You can tell *ex post facto*, and freedom— a negative, a faith in a nothing—has justified itself in more contexts than one.

It is true that, in general, men do not like nothings. Scientists will hold on to a disproved theory for long years until there emerges a better theory to replace the wrong one. Belief abhors a vacuum. So, too, men will hypostatize a negative into a positive, as they have done with the concept of freedom and also with the concept of chance. Both *freedom* and *chance* are terms that are used when efficient causes of present events are not known and often appear to be unknowable.

The scientific view of the history of thought is, of course, the deterministic one. You look for causes and believe in their existence even when you cannot specify them. Tolstoy and Herbert Spencer, not Carlyle and William James. But the scientists' view is often quite different from the scientific view, for a scientist is a human being, required to make value judgments if he is to survive in the milieu in which he has to live. Indeed, there exists what might be called the moral history of science. It deals with the psychological forces that block or misdirect the progress of science and that also drive science forward: the inertias of the scientists, their prejudices, their egoisms, their needs for self-consistency, and also the positives of these negatives—the integrity, the pride, the loyalty of scientists. You might regard these personal characteristics as determining causes which advance or hinder progress, and then you would still be thinking scientifically; but actually this is not the way the business of science runs.

Take enthusiasm, for example. Science runs on enthusiasm, gets its research done by dedicated workers; yet enthusiasm is a prejudice, and science is supposed to eschew prejudice. There is a very real conflict here between objectivity and personal drive, a conflict that has the consequence that you ought not to trust the ego-involved theorist, or at least you ought not to be influenced by the intensity of his conviction. His enthusiasm has pushed the pendulum one way, and a better approximation to fact is reserved for posterity, which will have all the evidence before it and none of the distorting enthusiasms (15). Max Planck said that many a wrong theory could not be abandoned until its author died (16).

So what? You can be too scientific to be successful as a scientist. You need your prejudices. Trust posterity to straighten you out, and posterity's posterity to do even a better job.

This is a psychological antinomy. The scientist's mind must make use of incompatible attitudes. He will have to use now one attitude, now the other. Or the necessary combination of incompatibles may be found in a set of men, or perhaps merely in a pair, say, the enthusiastic researcher and the sober handbook-writer. The basic fact remains, however: the prejudiced mind gets more progress into science than does the mind of the critical assessor.

CAUSES OF
BELIEF

In this connection it becomes desirable to inquire into the nature of belief, to ask what use are an organism's beliefs to it, and when, if ever, it is a good thing to believe in error. When is man advantaged by having a great delusion?

There is no need for us to try to distinguish between a belief and a pattern of behavior. The termite believes in a totalitarian society. The life of each termite is devoted to the fulfillment of its role in a complex social organization, which the ethnologist, William Morton Wheeler, once compared favorably to the less efficient, more variable, less assured governance under which man survives (17). The newly hatched gosling follows its mother, real or foster, or rather whatever large, dominating animal or other mobile object has come in those early hours of its life to bear the mother-image for it. Lorenz calls this fixation *imprinting* (18). It is the gosling's fifth commandment: Honor thy mother and follow her whither she shall go, that thy days may be long—for it is plain that a good belief has survival value.

Those beliefs survive that help the organism to survive: The termite; the gosling; the spider's web; the lioness springing for the throat of her quarry; man's gregariousness. Nor does a belief have to be in the genes. Man's social institutions persist because they are useful to him: forms of government; forms of religion.

Darwin's first principle also applies to these beliefs (*19*). Harmless but no longer useful remnants of originally useful beliefs survive: the cat circling around before it lies down on the parlor rug, as if treading down its bed in the forest; man, baring his second canine in a sneer, though he will not really bite. With man these remnants of useful habits may, however, gain a secondary use as they become means of communication. Your sneer warns the other fellow that you are ready to attack with teeth other than your biological ones.

Generalization may, moreover, preserve a belief that is actually harmful but not distinguished from the useful beliefs with which it is classed. The classical example is the sweet-tasting poison. But what about appetite? The belief in the goodness of eating is basic to the preservation of life, but it can also induce obesity. America is filled with people today who would be better off with a different adjustment of this habit. In a way the fat man's hunger is his great delusion, for he does not need so much food; and man's belief in his own freedom might turn out to be a similar kind of self-deception. It is doubtful that it would be sensible for a termite to believe in personal freedom. For it the good life is fixed by the state.

These human beliefs are, of course, very complex. For instance, is it ever good for man to believe a superstition? Probably yes, but let us consider ritual. Members of a Jewish family keep a kosher kitchen, not because they believe that any biological harm would follow if the two sets of dishes got mixed, but because they like to preserve ancient customs, to have their children perpetually reminded that they belong to a special group which has these customs. Patriotism is similar. The salute to the flag is good because it is symbiotically reinforcing. It makes you one with your compatriots. Both of these kinds of behavior are examples of good false beliefs—that is to say, false in their manifest content, yet good to have because of the psychological effect of having them.

Certainly the belief in human freedom of action is in one sense a superstition, one that is, however, justified biologically by the fact that it is woven into the fine structure of society. Language itself would have to be eviscerated were this conception to be extirpated from it. Beliefs, you see, can be false as to logical content and good as to use and function. Does not this conclusion settle the problem of freedom? It is a useful superstition.

But no, it does not, for the argument can also be made that causality is another useful superstition. This is what a scientific model is, a useful superstition, for it stands above the observed evidence. So we had better return to our principal inquiry.

Against this background I now have three things to say.

1. The behavioral determinist is not wrong. We do indeed want all the controls for human nature that we can get. To prefer ignorance to knowledge is not best—not in the Western culture of this modern age.
2. The model of human nature in social interaction, which is the natural outcome of scientific thinking about behavior, is nevertheless only a model. It is something to have in your repertoire of usable models, something to use on proper occasions. It is pushing science too far to say that this model is true now, but a model does not have to be true to be useful.
3. The analogy that once recommended this model as something that might be true is classical physics, but physics has changed. Causality is not so simple a relation as it seemed to be to LaPlace and to Helmholtz. Physics has become psychological. Operationism says that what you cannot observe does not exist. If you cannot ever observe the position and momentum of an electron simultaneously, then they do not exist simultaneously. Here we are dealing with physical incompatibility, with the physical techniques of observation. In the case we are considering, however, we have only a psychological incompatibility, two attitudes that cannot be assumed simultaneously. The point is that behavioral scientists should not be coerced into too great a simplicity by physical analogy, when physics itself has had to revise its thinking so radically.

Sometimes the humanists raise the question, not whether behavior can be controlled but whether it should be (20). It is hard for me to take this question seriously. You need all the knowledge of control that you can have. Only then are you prepared to consider how it should be used.

Education and government are instituted for the purpose of human control, and nearly all discussion and debate of any subject are directed at control. I prepare this paper in the hope that by it I may exercise some small degree of thought-control upon all who read it. Skinner claims to have better and surer methods for the design of behavior than have been available heretofore. You should see his pigeons, taught to earn their livings by the rewarding of their successes (not by punishment of their failures). So it is that he envisages a happy society, in which success and reward are the rule, and frustration has been reduced or eliminated by good social design. No one, of course, ever designs frustration into a machine so that it tries to make the same wheel go in opposite directions at the same moment.

One objection made to the behavioral scientists' development of human control is that their power might get into the hands of evil men. This objection seems to me to miss the point. Surely any elite that undertook to use behavioral science to enslave the world would find beneficence more efficient than maleficence. Slavery would be designed as a happy and desirable state, and, if these successful slaves still felt that they needed variety in their companionship, variety can be designed too. All you need is the specifications for *n* personalities, and the desirable frequency for each of them, to get mass production going.

In any case, you should push knowledge of the means of social control as far as you can. Modern civilization would rather run the risk of being bombed out of existence than return to the complacency of the Middle Ages, when scientific inquiry into natural law was not one of the most important activities of wise men. It is true that the physicists opened a Pandora's box, but what wise man would have stayed them, would have counseled that more safety is to be found in ignorance than in knowledge?

As man alters the world in which he lives, he has to trust that he will be able to adjust it to himself or else adjust himself to it. So far the advance of civilization has consisted of these changes and adjustments, and I see no reason to fear that the behavioral determinists are starting something that will get out of hand. The attempt to control men's actions and thoughts is as old as history. You cannot have social engineering that does not conscript the individual.

USE OF INCOMPATIBLES

So we come back to the main problem. Do we have to accept incompatibles simultaneously? Perhaps not simultaneously, but certainly alternatively—or so it seems to me. Certainly we all like to believe that nature is uniform and does not admit contradictions. Nevertheless, it seems clear that there may be limits to the resolving power of the understanding mind. Let me remind you of four such instances.

1.   First there are the *antinomies* of Immanuel Kant (21). The best known is that you cannot conceive of space as finite nor yet as infinite. What do you do? You admit the contradiction as a limitation of the understanding, and the practical man uses one model or the other as suits his thought.

Kant also included freedom and determinism among the antinomies (22).

2. Then there is Ralph Barton Perry's *egocentric predicament*, the dilemma that applies especially to our argument (10). How can the mind that considers other minds include itself? If I am to see all other men as robots, can this seeing be an event in my own robotic nature or have I got to stay outside the system in order to discuss it? Human nature could be viewed whole by the man from Mars. If n is the population of the world, then at most you could never knowingly have more than $n-1$ robots, for there has to be the 1 left over to do the viewing. In this way one can get around the difficulty of solipsism, not by reducing all reality to events in the Red King's dream, but by ruling the Red King out of consideration. And this was the reason for Max Meyer's writing a psychology under the title *The Psychology of the Other One* (23). Everyone counted but Meyer; he wrote the book.

3. Then there are Sir Arthur Eddington's *Postulates of Impotence*, the a priori impossibilities (24). The best known is the principle that you cannot detect a uniform translatory motion that is possessed by a system as a whole by means of observations taking place wholly within the system. This is a relativity principle, but it is also a kind of robotic egocentric predicament.

4. And finally there is Bohr's *Principle of Complementarity*, which includes the Heisenberg *Principle of Uncertainty*, that you cannot know both the position and momentum of an electron for the same instant (25). This seems to be a physical, not a psychological, incompatibility, but Robert Oppenheimer has told us that Bohr came upon this idea long before he ever formulated it, by thinking about such antinomies as fact and value, the tolerance of pure description as opposed to the intolerance of moral judgment (26).

So we do not have to be afraid of embracing incompatibles. It happens every day. Thought is polygamous. As a matter of fact, this kind of polygamy has been enormously eased by the present-day tendency to substitute the model for the theory. The theory had truth-value. It was a claim upon truth, and it had no right to persist—in spite of the fact that habitually it did—in the face of any single contradictory fact. As I have suggested, the theory is an *as*, whereas the model is but an *as-if*. You can have as many models as you want and use them when you will.

Causal determinism is the scientific model. It works enormously well. There are places in science where it breaks down, but they are not many. On the other hand, there are, in the process of living, all the situations in which values are called for and in which the scientific model itself fails. In such cases we get along best with the truncated causality model which we call freedom.

REITERATION   And that is that. Now that I am done I seem, to myself, to have said very little. Yet when I see the humanist battling the scientific behaviorist, seeking to save human freedom and dignity from the ruthless hands of the invading scientist, I feel that something should be said, and this has been it.

Human dignity is all right. It is not silly to want to save it. Robots do not have it. Science does not preserve it. It is an attribute that lies outside of science. It implies that its possessor is free. Freedom is a negative concept, a truncated causality, but it is part of the warp of language. To get rid of this concept would change the whole of our civilization. Yet we need not attempt that, for causality is only the form of a model, and freedom is also a model, and we can use our models at will without letting them dominate us.

One thing more—my parting shot. Do you want to know where to find a free man, a man who acts as if he were free and thinks of himself as free (and how much freer could he be than that)? Go to him who is earnestly trying to persuade you that all men are robots. He will not claim that his ardor was designed into him and has no necessary connection with the validity of what he is saying. If he calls himself a robot, still he will not act like one, for it takes a free man to start a war on freedom. An IBM machine does not have the dignity to make an argument convincing, and an IBMpty organism is a poor evangelist.

REFERENCES AND NOTES

1. W. McDougall, *Outline of Psychology* (Scribner's, New York, 1923), especially pp. 446–448.
2. J. B. Watson, *New Republic 34*, Book Section, 11 (11 Apr. 1923).
3. F. Hackett, *N. Y. Times Book Review* (15 Aug. 1948), pp. 1, 15.
4. B. F. Skinner, *Walden Two* (Macmillan, New York, 1948). It was intended to be a novel about robots but did not meet F. Hackett's specifications.
5. R. A. Bauer, *The New Man in Soviet Psychology* (Harvard University Press, Cambridge, Mass., 1952).
6. B. F. Skinner, *Harvard Educational Review 24*, 86 (1954).
7. B. F. Skinner, *Theory and Treatment of the Psychoses*

(Washington University Studies, St. Louis, Mo., 1956), pp. 77–79.

8. B. F. Skinner, *Science and Human Behavior* (Macmillan, New York, 1953).

9. B. F. Skinner, *American Scholar 25*, 47 (1955).

10. R. B. Perry, *Present Philosophical Tendencies* (Longmans Green, New York, 1912), especially pp. 129–134.

11. J. J. Thomson, *The Corpuscular Theory of Matter* (Scribner's, New York, 1907), pp. 1 *f*. See also J. B. Conant, *Modern Science and Modern Man* (Columbia University Press, New York, 1952), pp. 53 *f*.

12. T. Carlyle, *On Heroes, Hero Worship and the Heroic in History* (Chapman and Hall, London, 1840).

13. L. Tolstoy, *War and Peace* (1869), bk. 9, sect. 1; bk. 10, sect. 1; bk. 11, sect. 1; bk. 13, sect. 11; 1st epilogue, sect. 1; 2nd epilogue; appendix entitled "Some words about *War and Peace*."

14. E. B. Newman, *American Journal of Psychology 57*, 429 (1944).

15. E. G. Boring, *Sensation and Perception in the History of Experimental Psychology* (Appleton-Century-Crofts, New York, 1942), pp. 608–613.

16. M. Planck, *Scientific Autobiography and Other Papers* (Philosophical Library, New York, Eng. trans. 1949), pp. 33 *f*.

17. W. M. Wheeler, *Science Monthly 10*, 113 (1920).

18. K. Z. Lorenz, *J. Orn. Lpz. 83*, 137, 289 (1935); but see also F. A. Beach and J. Jaynes, *Psychology Bulletin 51*, 239 (1954); R. A. Hinde, W. H. Thorpe, M. A. Vince, *Behaviour 9*, 214 (1956).

19. C. Darwin, *The Expression of the Emotions in Man and Animals* (Murray, London, 1872), chap. 1.

20. J. W. Krutch, *The Measure of Man* (Bobbs-Merrill, Indianapolis, Ind., 1953), especially chap. 3.

21. J. Watson, *Selections from Kant* (Maclehose, Edinburgh, 1901), pp. 155–194, and many other places in the book.

22. J. A. Wheeler, *American Scientist 44*, 360-377, especially 372–376 (1956).

23. M. Meyer, *The Psychology of the Other One* (Missouri Book Co., Columbia, Mo., 1921).

24. E. Whittaker, *American Scientist 40*, 45 (1952).

25. N. Bohr, *Atomic Theory and the Description of Nature* (Macmillan, New York, 1934), pp. 9–15 and 52–91; also in P. A. Schlipp, *Albert Einstein: Philosopher-Scientist* (Library of Living Philosophers, Evanston, Ill., 1949), pp. 199-241.

26. J. R. Oppenheimer, in preparation.

Boring has given support to those who would hold for mankind's freedom to choose, for the freedom of the mind. But the question persists: what are the possibilities of any one of us being controlled? What might happen if a knowledgeable and experienced psychologist tried to establish a situation in which he could subtly but surely change the values of a group of people?

Milton Rokeach tried to do just this, and succeeded! He then raised some questions concerning the ethics of what he had done, and what others might, and may, do.

6

PERSUASION THAT PERSISTS
MILTON ROKEACH

Suppose you could take a group of people, give them a 20-minute pencil-and-paper task, talk to them for 10 to 20 minutes afterward, and thereby produce long-range changes in core values and personal behavior in a significant portion of this group. For openers, it would of course have major implications for education, government, propaganda and therapy. Suppose, further, that you could ascertain quickly and that you could predict accurately the nature and direction of these changes.

Scientists have urged us all to consider the consequences of research in this area, warning that we are on the brink of breakthroughs that will demand new levels of social responsibility. According to these predictions we will soon face several major ethical questions that have to be answered.

My colleagues and I have in the last five years achieved the kinds of results suggested in the first paragraph of this article. As a result we must now face up to the ethical implications that follow from the fact that it now seems to be within man's power to alter experimentally another person's basic values, and to control the direction of the change.

Dissonance   Contemporary social psychologists generally agree that before changes in attitudes or in value-related behavior can occur, there must first exist what John Dewey had called a "felt difficulty" and what social psychologists nowadays call a state of psychological imbalance or dissonance.

Source: From *Psychology Today*, September, 1971, 5 (4) 68–71, 92. Copyright 1971 by Milton Rokeach. Reprinted by permission.

There are two major experimental methods for doing this: 1) You can force a person to act in a way that is incompatible with his professed or real attitudes and values, or 2) You can expose him to conflicting attitudes or values held by persons who are in some way important to him.

We used a third method. We exposed a person to information designed to make him consciously aware of inconstancies within his own value-attitude system, inconsistencies of which he is normally unaware.

We have also differed in our definition and measurement of dissonance itself. Dissonance requires at least two elements— let us call them X and Y—that stand in some dissonant or unharmonious relationship with each other. Leon Festinger's theory and other similar theories usually identify X and Y as two "ideas" (beliefs, attitudes, values, or rationalizations) about some particular situations or actions that will occasionally differ from or be incompatible with one another.

In contrast, we identified X and Y in such a way that they are not two ideas that vary from one situation to another, but rather are elements that remain invariant across all situations. In our hypothesis, X was equivalent to self. We defined Y as a person's interpretation of his own performance or behavior in any given situation.

Gauge Dissonance occurs whenever a person's behavior in any given situation, Y, leads him to become dissatisfied with himself, X. Conversely, if a person is pleased with himself in any given situation, we consider that X and Y are nondissonant or harmonious. We can measure such states of dissonance and self-satisfaction in any experiment simply by asking the subject how he feels about what he may have said or done in a given situation.

It might be objected that such a question really tests the subject's general self-esteem; self-confident persons would probably report satisfaction with their behavior, while a person with low self-esteem would probably report chronic dissatisfaction with his achievement, no matter how acceptable that achievement might be in some objective sense. Although a number of psychiatric theories seem to predict such an outcome, it is nevertheless also true that self-confident persons are not always satisfied with what they do and say in certain situations, and, conversely, that persons of low self-confidence are not always dissatisfied with what they do or say.

We also made a firm operational distinction between attitudes and values, and, unlike many researchers in the field of social psychology, we focused on the latter. We also defined values as more fundamental to human personality than attitudes for values serve as determinants of attitudes as well as of behavior.

Hotpants   For the purposes of our research we identified an attitude as a more or less enduring organization of interrelated thoughts and feelings called into being by a specific object or situation. Thus an attitude always has a historical context as well as a personal one—toward the Pill, for instance, or civil-rights demonstrations, hotpants, or J. Edgar Hoover. Assuming that values are less embedded in particular temporal or socioeconomic contexts, we used the word *value* to describe either a desirable end-state of existence (a terminal value) or a desirable mode of behavior (an instrumental value). In a sense, values are the source and foundation of attitudes and behavior toward specific events, people, or situations. A person can have thousands of attitudes but only a few values that transcend and dynamically determine these thousands of attitudes.

My colleagues and I performed a number of experiments in which we induced in our subjects feelings of self-dissatisfaction about specific values and behavioral situations, and we measured the long-range effects that such self-dissatisfaction produced.

We took two groups of college students—usually 20 to 25 in a group—and asked them to rank 18 terminal values in an order of perceived importance. The 18 values were:

A comfortable life, an exciting life, a sense of accomplishment, a world at peace, a world of beauty, equality, family security, freedom, happiness, inner harmony, mature love, national security, pleasure, salvation, social recognition, self-respect, true friendship and wisdom.

Grade   We asked each subject to rank each value from one to 18 in order of its personal importance. We then asked members of both groups to state in writing their attitudes toward civil-rights demonstrations; after this was done, we dismissed one group, which became our control group.

Members of the remaining or experimental group then viewed a chart that showed the average rankings of the 18 terminal values obtained from students in a previous experiment conducted at their school. We drew their attention especially to the data concerning two of the 18 values shown in the chart—equality and freedom—pointing out that students in previous tests had ranked freedom first and equality 11th. We interpreted these findings to mean that "students are, in general, much more interested in their own freedom than other people's." We then invited students to compare their own value rankings with those of their peers.

Importance of Values as Ranked in Previous Tests

1	freedom
2	happiness
3	wisdom
4	self-respect
5	mature love
6	a sense of accomplishment
7	true friendship
8	inner harmony
9	family security
10	a world at peace
11	equality
12	an exciting life
13	a comfortable life
14	salvation
15	social recognition
16	national security
17	a world of beauty
18	pleasure

To raise levels of self-dissatisfaction further, we asked students to indicate the extent of their sympathy with the aims of civil-rights demonstrators by agreeing to one of the following phrases: "Yes, I am sympathetic, and I have personally participated in a civil-rights demonstration"; "Yes, I am sympathetic, and I have not participated in a civil-rights demonstration"; or "No, I am not sympathetic."

Average Rankings of Freedom and Equality for and Against Civil Rights in Previous Tests

	Yes, sympathetic and have participated in a demonstration.	*Yes, sympathetic but have not participated in a demonstration.*	*No, not sympathetic to civil rights.*
freedom	6	1	2
equality	5	11	17
difference	+ 1	−10	−15

After this, students viewed a second table from previous tests that showed correlations between rankings of freedom and equality and positions on civil-rights issues. The main finding brought out in this table is that those who are unsympathetic with civil rights rank freedom high and equality low, while those who are sympathic rank both freedom and equality high. We explained that the findings of this table can be interpreted to mean that persons who are against civil-rights are really saying that they are indifferent to other people's freedom, while they care a great deal about their own. Those who are *for* civil rights want freedom not only for themselves, but for other people too. We then invited students to compare their own rankings of equality and freedom and their own positions on the civil-rights issue with those on the table.

Dismay   In this procedure, many of the experimental subjects—about 40 per cent—became aware of certain inconsistencies within their own value and attitude systems. Some students discovered to their dismay that they had placed a high value on freedom but a low value on equality. Others discovered that they cared about civil rights but had ranked equality low in their scaling values. Many thus discovered that they had been doing their liberal thing because it was fashionable rather than because of principle.

At the end of the experiment, we asked students to rate—on a scale ranging from one to 11—how satisfied or dissatisfied they were in general with what they had found out about their values and attitudes. More importantly, we asked them to indicate whether they were satisfied or dissatisfied with their ranking of each of the 18 values considered separately. This latter, more specific rating proved to be a significant predictor of subsequent changes in the value hierarchy.

Members of the control group, you will recall, had no opportunity to think about their values or possible conflicts among them; they did not see the tables that the experimental subjects saw. Sessions for the control group lasted only about 20 minutes, and the experimental session ran from 30 to 40 minutes.

Change   Follow-ups on the experimental and control groups indicated that the experimental groups experienced highly significant changes in values and attitudes, increases in the value placed on equality and freedom, and increases in favorable attitudes toward civil rights that were evident three to five months after the 10-to-20-minute experimental "treatment." Further, the self-ratings on satisfaction-dissatisfaction obtained at the end of the experimental sessions predicted the value changes that were to be observed three weeks and three to five months afterward.

We were extremely reluctant to accept these experimental

findings as evidence of genuine, long-range changes in values and attitudes. It seemed unlikely that any single, brief experimental session could produce such effects. We therefore did more experiments—II and III—to monitor the long-term effects more closely and in more detail.

Subtlety   Experiments II and III were basically identical in procedure to the initial series. However, this time we used more subtle measures of behavioral effects in addition to paper-and-pencil tests of change in value and attitude. We extended post-testing to include more intervals, among them three-week, three-to-five-month and 15-to-17-month intervals.

The subjects of Experiments II and III were newly entering freshmen of two small new residential colleges at Michigan State University, James Madison College and Lyman Briggs College. Both experiments were identical in all respects; only the students were different. In both cases, we aroused feelings of self-dissatisfaction by making the subjects aware that certain of their values or attitudes were possibly incompatible with one another. As in previous experiments, the only difference between the experimental and the control groups was that we exposed the experimental students to tables, along with a brief commentary on the tables, and did not do so with the control students.

Join   Pre-testing showed no significant differences between the two groups. On the average both groups ranked equality and freedom approximately the same, and took the same range of civil-rights positions toward black Americans. Post-testing techniques included unobtrusive measurements of behavior along with questionnaires. For example, three to five months and 15 to 17 months after the experiment, each subject received a direct solicitation through the mails from the National Association for the Advancement of Colored People (on N.A.A.-C.P. stationery). The letter invited the student to join the N.A.A.C.P. To do this, the student had to fill out an application blank, enclose $1.00, and mail back a prestamped return envelope.

We found significant increases in ranking for both equality and freedom in the experimental students on all the post-tests. After 15 to 17 months, for example, the experimental group had increased its ranking of equality an average of 2.68 units (on the 18-point scale) while the control group had increased its ranking by only .32 units. Freedom also rose in value. Within the same period, the experimental ranking of freedom increased an average of 1.59 units, while the control ranking increased only .22 units. This suggests that significant changes in bedrock standards or broad normative beliefs about social ends and means took place as a result of a relatively short experimental session.

Backlash The findings in relation to attitude-change (how do you think-feel about civil rights for blacks?) also were significant. Three weeks after the session, we noticed what might be called a sleeper effect among the experimental students. There was no positive change in attitude toward civil rights. In fact there was a slight backlash. However, we did find significant increases in pro-civil-rights attitudes among these same experimental subjects three to five months later, and 15 to 17 months later. These results point to long-range attitude change, and the time-lag suggests that a change in the ordering of values preceded the change of attitude.

In contrast to the findings for the experimental group, there were no significant changes in value hierarchy or attitude among the control students at any of the post-test intervals. After 15 to 17 months' exposure to the college environment, the students in the control groups had essentially the same value and attitude profiles they started with.

Range I come now to the long-range behavioral effects of the experimental session. In the first N.A.A.C.P. solicitation of all experimental and control subjects, undertaken three to five months after the experimental session, 40 students responded by joining N.A.A.C.P., and 13 more responded by writing sympathetic letters asking for more information. In all, 53 of 366 students responded; of these, 39 were experiment subjects and 14 were control subjects.

A full year after the first solicitation—and 15 to 17 months after the experimental sessions—each experimental and control subject received another invitation to join N.A.A.C.P., (or to renew his membership) by paying another dollar. The second letter resulted in six new memberships—five experimental and one control. In addition there were 11 favorable letters, seven from experiment subjects, four from controls, one of whom had also written after the first solicitation. There were six renewals, half of them by experimental students and half by control students. There were two indignant letters—both from experimental students complaining about the N.A.A.C.P.'s year-long silence. In all, 17 experimental subjects responded as against eight controls. When the results of both N.A.A.C.P. solicitations are combined, we find that a total of 69 persons out of 366—about 20 per cent—responded to the letters. Of these 69 persons, 51 were from the experimental group and only 18 were from the control group. This represents a statistically significant response rate of about one out of 10 for the control group and one out of four for those students who had been in the briefing.

The data produced by the satisfaction-dissatisfaction ratings throw some light on the basic psychological processes that underlie the long-range changes seen in the experimental groups. Experimental subjects substantially revised their rankings of equality and freedom over the long haul, whether they reported themselves initially satisfied or dissatisfied. But it is apparent that those students who reported themselves dissatisfied with parts of their original value hierarchy changed more significantly than those who reported themselves satisfied. Reports of specific satisfaction or dissatisfaction predicted changes in value rankings that could be observed three weeks after the experiment, three to five months afterward, and 15 to 17 months afterward. Any value that caused dissatisfaction typically changed place in latter rankings. On the other hand, reports of general dissatisfication did not predict as reliably, although they had some predictive value.

Ethics In the very process of conducting our experiment we caused an unsolicited reordering of people's value systems and behavioral choices. It might be argued that no scientist should be permitted or required to cause such changes without some broad social or consensual ethical framework to refer his work and its effects to. We should remember that institutions—such as public schools—are based upon the assumption that such changes are not only desirable but do in fact occur.

Every teacher I have ever met who takes professional pride in his work would like to think that his teaching somehow changes the values, attitudes and behavior of his students in some significant way. So long as he cannot prove that what he does in the classroom actually results in such change, none will bother him, or raise questions about the ethics of changing other people's values. But when the day comes that he can demonstrate that certain changes in values, attitudes and behavior have in fact occurred, the teacher exposes himself to the danger of being accused, by the community in which he lives and by his colleagues, of unethically manipulating his students' values, attitudes and behavior without their informed consent.

I believe that educational institutions have always been in the business on the one hand of transmitting knowledge and, on the other, of shaping the values of students in certain directions. Psychologists like Jerome Bruner and B. F. Skinner have spent a good deal of their professional lives trying to figure out better ways of transmitting knowledge from one generation to succeeding generations, and we all applaud such efforts. But if we agree that educational institutions are also in the business of shaping values then we should encourage scientific research on better ways of shaping values.

But which values, and in which directions?

Market If it is possible to alter the process of valuation so that freedom and equality go up in value market, it is also possible to short-sell them. We obviously need safeguards to ensure that the values we choose to change in our students and the direction we choose in changing them are consistent with the values of our educational and scientific institutions, and are consistent with the values of political democracy and, above all, with interests of all humanity.

What exactly are the values of education, science, democracy, and humanity?

We have heard much in recent years about "brainwashing." Sometimes we seem to think of brainwashing only as a practice of "the enemy" involving captured soldiers. Then, again, we begin to wonder whether we might be the victims or potential victims of influential elements within our own society.

Are we free to decide, entirely on our own, how we shall vote in the next election? Or will our vote be controlled by the subtle influences of pressure groups? Or will it only be influenced, not completely controlled, by other persons? And where is the line between influence and control?

Are we free to choose our religious values? Our ethical values? To what degree is the life style of each of us the result of controls imposed upon us? How about those who rebel? Are they freely choosing to go against the establishment? Or are they merely the pawns of an inevitable reaction? Each of you can extend this list of questions on and on. This problem of control versus freedom of thought and decision continues to haunt us all.

This is not a happy ending, even for a chapter. But, possibly it is a good place to begin the study of various aspects of psychology. It may be well to keep this matter of purpose continually in mind as we seek out the kinds of information psychologists can provide us. We might ask certain questions regarding each selection. Do the outcomes, the results of the study, help us better to understand behavior? Are we, as the result of a particular study, better able to predict behavior? Have we been presented with a new or improved technique for influencing others? Has the study resulted in increasing our ability to control others—or the ability of others to control us?

There is an old Roman saying:

> Who shall look after our custodian?
> Who shall guard our guardians?

We have said that we are more interested in raising questions than providing answers. There is no answer book to accompany these questions. Yet, they are questions that must be answered in some measure by every person every day.

VENTURING FURTHER ON YOUR OWN

An example of a society based on principles of behavioral control is presented in a utopian novel written by the well-known and controversial psychologist B. F. Skinner, *Walden Two* (Macmillan, 1948). Skinner has himself described the novel as "a proposal to apply a behavioral technology to the construction of a workable, effective and productive pattern of government."

Skinner's followers are many. So are his critics. The two different points of view were clearly presented in a symposium involving Skinner and Carl R. Rogers. Rogers, equally as well-known as Skinner, is perhaps most famous for his nondirective approach to psychotherapy and his insistence on the freedom of the individual. This symposium was published under the title, "Some Issues Concerning the Control of Human Behavior," in the November 30, 1956, issue of *Science.*

Skinner sees behavioral control as leading to a world in which "people are truly happy, secure, productive, creative and forward looking." But Rogers is disturbed by Skinner's proposals. He asks such questions as: "Who will be controlled? Who will exercise control? What type of control will be exercised? Most important of all, toward what end or what purpose, or in the pursuit of what value, will control be exercised?"

Another discussion of Rogers' point of view is his article, "Learning to be Free" in S. M. Farber and R. H. Wilson (Eds.), *Conflict and Creativity* (McGraw-Hill, 1963). This article is also available in Carl R. Rogers and Barry Stevens, *Person to Person: The Problem of Being Human* (Real People Press, 1967). Another source of information on the Skinner side of the controversy is B. F. Skinner, *Beyond Freedom and Dignity* (Knopf, 1971).

Part Three

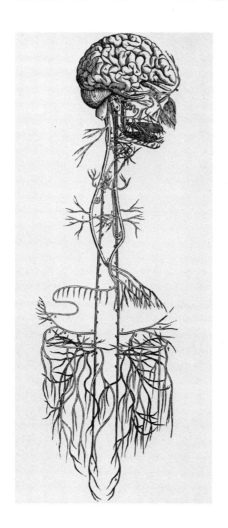

The Brain:
The Master of
the Body

The ancients considered the heart the controlling center of the body. We still "put our hearts into" various activities and "learn by heart." Actually, we know now that these functions are performed higher up within the body's shell. The *control center* of the body is the *brain.*

The brain has been called "the most highly organized bit of matter in the universe." [1] It is so complex as to create one of the greatest paradoxes of all time. The complexity of the brain is such that it cannot be understood by itself. A complete understanding of the human brain would require a being with an even more complex brain. And who, then, could understand *it*?

Even though it would be impossible to achieve a complete understanding, there are some things that we can and do know about the brain and the way it works. We have said that we shall deal in this book mostly with a molar approach to behavior. But for just a few pages we would like to ask you to take a look inside the "black box," inside the machine (if we dare call it that) that is the human body.

The "black box" is the engineer's term for any instrument that picks up input of one kind of energy and transforms it into output of another kind. A radio is a "black box." Thus, by analogy, a human being who receives stimuli (input) and, as a result, performs some action (output) is a "black box." In Edward de Bono, *The Dog Exercising Machine,* you will find a discussion of the "black box" concept and of the way it can be of use in human thinking.[2] Looking up this reference might yield added benefits: the discovery of a book that may interest you, and an advance look at one to which we shall refer you when we come to consider the subject of thinking.

We are not asking you to master the field of physiological psychology in a few minutes, but we do think that you may feel rewarded to be able to glimpse, briefly, some of the things that researchers have been learning about the brain and its functioning. Many of these studies are performed on lower animals. The results tell us something about these animals; they also tell us something about what may be happening in the human brain.

We have found a discussion of the brain that is quite rare in that it is highly readable. The writer, George B. Leonard, is neither physiologist nor psychologist. But he is a good writer. We wondered how adequately a nonscientist writer could deal with so difficult a subject. Neither of us being an expert in this area, we turned to a colleague who is. We

[1] "The Brain." *Life*, October 1, 1971.

[2] Edward de Bono, *The Dog Exercising Machine.* New York: Simon and Schuster, 1970, p. 15.

asked him to read this selection and to render judgment. His verdict: "The findings are accurately, if poetically, reported."

We don't mind Mr. Leonard's "poetic license." In fact, we rather like it and think you will, too.

7

THE BRAIN
GEORGE B. LEONARD

Start with the brain. This marvelous piece of matter, now so intent upon analyzing itself, is the most complex organized entity in the known universe. Plato called the mind "a gift of Memory, the mother of the Muses," and guessed it to be a block of wax on which the perceptions were printed, preserved and modified. Since Plato's time, man's concept of how his brain works has evolved considerably and is currently undergoing revolutionary revisions.

The brain may be viewed as a sort of computer. Each of its ten billion neurons (brain cells), if sufficiently excited, may fire a burst of electricity. This burst may help excite a nearby neuron so it, too, will fire, and so on, until a long chain of firing neurons carries a message that may command a muscle to move, may produce the sensation of "green," may help form a "memory trace" or may be an element in the discovery of an abstract mathematical formula.

In this commonly held view of the brain, each neuron has only two possibilities, to fire or not to fire. Even so, there are enough possible combinations of the billions of neurons to account for the behavior exhibited by Beethoven in composing the late quartets, by Milton in writing *Paradise Lost* and by Einstein in formulating the General Theory of Relativity—with plenty of unused ability left over.

But that, as it turns out, is only the beginning. To peer into the more complex workings of the brain requires a computer that fills a room and a tiny electric probe that pierces a single neuron. Several research teams are using these and other modern tools to deduce new concepts of information processing and storage in the central nervous system. The new models of the brain that emerge from this work are to the old computer-like brain as poetry is to grammar. Dr. W. Ross Adey

SOURCE: From *Education and Ecstasy* by George B. Leonard. Copyright © 1968 by George B. Leonard. Reprinted by permission of the publisher, Delacorte Press.

and his colleagues at the Space Biology Laboratory of UCLA's Brain Research Institute have discovered hitherto unsuspected electrical happenings deep within the brain. They have found complex wave patterns during learning and recall. They have measured the changing resistance to electricity across certain key brain areas and again have found significant patterns during the learning process. This electricity, these waves flow not through the neurons themselves but through the softer neuroglial cells that surround them and the jellylike substance that fills the space between the cells. Such activity may well constitute an exceedingly subtle means for influencing the *probability* of neurons' firing across a relatively wide area of the brain.

"The on-off of neurons," Dr. Adey told me, "is the minimum way the brain has of operating." Adey's associates have gone as far as to prepare a sort of weather map of the mind, taking several ongoing brain waves from an astronaut candidate and, with a computer's help, charting them all together on a piece of paper. Looking at one of these charts, we may visualize changes in "mood." Just where the would-be astronaut's task becomes unexpectedly more difficult, we see what might be termed a sharp "cold front" followed by "thunderstorms."

"The brain," Dr. Adey said, "is not a telephone switchboard that operates only when signals arrive from outside. The switchboard is always flooded. It is altered in the whole. And it is altered by subtle, qualitative changes in the incoming signals, not by the presence or absence of lights on the switchboard, but by shifts of brightness or color."

Adey's hypothesis dovetails with recent news from the laboratories of the biochemists. Every living cell, including brain cells, contains DNA (deoxyribonucleic acid), the complex genetic molecules that pass along the blueprints of the species. Somewhat similar molecules of another substance, RNA (ribonucleic acid), serve as messengers for the DNA, informing the proteins in the body what and how to build. The RNA in the brain's cells, it now seems, has another talent, one that helps explain the brain's remarkable capacities. Each RNA molecule is a storehouse of information, a microscopic library. What if the RNA molecules *inside* the brain cells could be altered by events taking place *outside* the cells? What if the temporary electrical and chemical happenings going on throughout the brain could, by changing RNA, make a lasting change inside the brain cells? If so, it would be much easier to explain one of life's great mysteries: how the behavior of a living thing can be changed for more than a moment by its environment—in other words, how it learns.

Such an explanation is gathering shape in the work of such

chemists of the brain as Holger Hyden. At his laboratory in Göteborg, Sweden, Hyden has devised exquisite techniques for measuring the RNA in a single neuron. He has shown that, in brain areas where a great deal of learning occurs in a short period, there is an explosive increase of RNA. When the amount of RNA and protein increases inside the neuron, it decreases in the neuroglia outside. "It could be," Dr. Adey proposes, "that the electrical activity coursing through the neuroglia causes it to pour something into the fluid around the neuron that in turn alters the RNA and the protein inside the neuron."

Experiments conducted by Adey's team suggest that it takes about twenty minutes to change the firing pattern of a neuron. Biochemists say that is about the time needed to make any basic change in RNA. Twenty minutes is also approximately how long it takes for the memory to become permanent. Electroshock treatment wipes out remembrance of anything that happened during the twenty or so minutes prior to the shock. All earlier memories—safely deposited in the protein of the neurons—are retained in the storehouse of memory.

Dr. Adey's concept of the brain is one of many. Each researcher in this field proceeds with his own model—explicit or implicit—in mind. At present, there's no way of proving which one is "right"; the brain is far too complex for that. But some of Adey's key points are beginning to gain support in other labs. Dr. Phillip G. Nelson at the National Institute of Health has shown that the nerve cells in the spinal cord interact, not only by firing bursts from one to the other, but also on the basis of the more subtle electrical fields they themselves generate. The cells in the spinal cord are larger and more widely spaced than those in the brain. If they can transcend the "fire or no-fire" mode of operation, it makes it seem almost inevitable that cells tightly packed in the brain can do the same and more.

The complicated new math used by Dr. Adey and his colleagues in analyzing brain-wave activity finds affirmation in the work of Mr. Harry Blum of the Air Force Cambridge Research Laboratories. Mr. Blum writes that, "despite more than two millennia of geometry, no formulation which appears natural for the biological problem has emerged," and he goes on to seek new ways to describe shapes by analyzing waves of light that bounce off them. Similarly, Dr. Adey's team uses waves of electricity to describe events within the neurons in the brain. Research that tends to bolster Dr. Adey's theories also is being carried out in the laboratories of Otto D. Creutzfeldt in Germany and Yasuichiro Fujita and Toshio Sato in Japan.

If subtle electrical fields generated in the brain can affect thinking and perceiving, what would happen if the same sort of fields were applied from outside? Dr. James Hamer of Northrop Systems Laboratories has attempted to answer this question in a rigorously controlled series of experiments. Dr. Hamer applies low-voltage alternating current (only two volts) to aluminum plates on either side of human subjects' heads. The plates do not touch the head and the amount of electricity that can penetrate to the neurons is minuscule indeed—certainly not enough to set off neuronal firing. And yet, this tiny electric field significantly alters the subjects' perception of time.

All of which adds up to a sensitive and subtle brain indeed. With enough poetic license, we may view each of its neurons not merely as a computer-like cell with a single function, but as a versatile, complex personality in miniature. It may have a specialty, but is also able to participate in a multitude of memories, moods, perceptions and actions. It interacts directly with its neighbors, but also tunes in to news of distant events in the brain, ready to add its vote or its influence when the moment is appropriate. It has a stable, recognizable character, but is willing and able to change, to learn from experience.

A brain composed of such neurons obviously can never be "filled up." Perhaps the more it knows the more it *can* know and create. Perhaps, in fact, we can now propose an incredible hypothesis: *The ultimate creative capacity of the brain may be, for all practical purposes, infinite.*

But *how* are the capabilities of this marvelous organ to be tapped? And for whose benefit? The men who probe for the secrets of the central nervous system often find themselves asking these questions. Most of them assume that a better understanding of the brain will guarantee new techniques for achieving the human potential. But they grow cautious when asked for specific—if speculative—examples.

Not so cautious are some popular books and magazines. Stretching the substance of brain experiments to the shape of science fiction, they come up with futuristic thinking caps that will teach you, in a twinkling, everything there is to know about, say, calculus. Or intercranial hookups that will make it possible for students to get a famous professor's insights without the bother of listening to his lectures. From the speculation come two fairly promising tools for changing human behavior: electrical stimulation of the brain and mind-altering drugs.

As far back as 1936, the Canadian neurosurgeon Dr. Wilder Penfield discovered that electrical stimulation of certain brain areas (especially in the brains of epileptics) sometimes creates a vivid mental experience. The patient seems to be reliving old memories with one part of the mind while retaining consciousness of the present with another. Several researchers also have discovered that electrical current applied through slim electrodes inserted deep inside the brain of animals may strongly influence their actions.

Scientists at the Max Planck Institute at Seewiesen, Germany, for example, have probed for controlling centers in the brains of chickens. They never know exactly what action they will get from these small-brained creatures when they turn the current on. Electricity directed to one point may make the chicken into a compulsive eater. Applied a millimeter away, the electronic persuader may keep the chicken from eating at all. A little jolt in the rage center may cause a cock to beat his wings and clack his spurs against a stuffed animal.

The Planck Institute scientists moved closer to creating automatic chickens when they equipped them with tiny transistor radio receivers so that current could be turned on from a distance. This led to interesting social situations among a freely moving but transistorized flock of chickens. The low hen on the pecking order, the most chicken of the flock, could be turned into a tiger if her aggression center was stimulated.

Sometimes more than one electrode was activated within the chicken's brain, giving the scientists control over possibly contradictory behavior. One chicken, equipped with two electrodes, could be ordered electronically either to sit or to jump and flee. The scientists complicated things by turning on both the "sit" and the "jump" electrode at the same time. Confronted with a dilemma not unknown in ordinary human life, the chicken did the best she could. After a period of agitated shuffling, she sat down, remained seated for a while, then leaped up with a squawk.

A number of researchers in various parts of the world have carried on similar experiments with various animals. Dr. José Delgado of Yale's School of Medicine implanted a radio-controlled electrode in the fear center of a fighting bull; then, to prove his point, entered the bull ring. When the bull charged, Dr. Delgado pressed a button on a small transmitter he was carrying. The bull braked and backed off. Pictures of the episode appeared in the world press.

The finding that has most delighted the human imagination has to do with a deep-seated pleasure center. Dr. James Olds, then of McGill University in Montreal, discovered this well-spring of Elysium in the brain of a white rat in 1954. The rat, presented with a pedal attached to the electrode stuck in his own pleasure center, would spend most of his days and nights stimulating himself, oblivious to fine food and a lady rat alike.

In later experiments by Olds and others, rats have been known to press their pleasure pedals up to 8,000 times an hour and to carry on their electronic pursuit of happiness for weeks. What happens to these pleasure-bent rats? Do they, like some portrait of a rodent Dorian Gray, turn ravaged and worn? Bad news for the Puritans who linger among us: the orgiast rats generally end up in better physical and mental shape than do their pleasure-deprived littermates. They are alert. Their coats are glossy. Their eyes shine.

These experiments foreshadow an increase in the knowledge of the intricate workings of the brain, a greater understanding of the complexities of that marvelous organ. From continuing research into the relations of specific areas of the brain to behavior there should come discoveries of far greater importance than those which enable a rat, or a man, to press pedals for momentary pleasure.

DIGGING DEEPER

If this subject interests you at all, you just may find pleasure digging into it. Leonard's discussion merely scratches the surface.

Scientific American has published a few articles about some of the studies Leonard discussed. You might begin with James Olds, "Pleasure Centers in the Brain" (*Scientific American,* October 1956). The studies at the Max Planck Institute for the Physiology of Behavior in Seewiesen, Germany, are discussed in an article by Erich von Holst and Ursula von Saint Paul, "Electrically Controlled Behavior" (*Scientific American,* March 1962).

Dealing specifically with the human brain is an article by A. R. Lurie, "The Functional Organization of the Brain" (*Scientific American,* March 1970). Another article by Luria is "The Complex Mechanisms of Psychological Processes" (*Impact of Science on Society,* 1968, *18,* 141–156).

For more on Wilder Penfield's studies, see his article, "The Integrative Cortex" (*Science,* 1959, *129,* 1719–1725).

John Rowan Wilson, *The Mind* (Time, 1964) includes a chapter on "The Mechanisms of Mentality," much of it helpfully illustrated.

In case you wish to keep digging, we suggest you turn next to a beginning textbook of physiological psychology, such as Francis Leukel, *Introduction to Physiological Psychology,* Second edition (C. V. Mosby Company, 1972). If someone beats you to that one in the library, try R. L. Isaacson, R. J. Douglas, J. F. Dubar and L. W. Schmaltz, *A Primer of Physiological Psychology* (Harper and Row, 1971); or Peter Nathan, *The Nervous System* (J. B. Lippincott Company, 1969).

Part Four

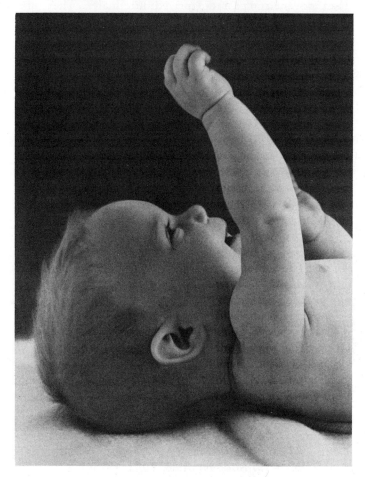

Development:
Genetic
Determiners

In teaching, we sometimes like to show a handful of acorns to a class and ask, "What is the potential of these acorns?" Invariably the answer is, "Oak trees!" We then disagree, pointing out that any given acorn is much more likely to find its way into the inside of a ham sandwich than to become an oak. Probably no more than one acorn in a million finds its way into that particular environment, sheltered from marauders, with the proper balance of moisture, sunshine, and shade, which will allow it to sprout, grow, and survive to become a tree. Many, many more are eaten by the pigs that commonly root among the leaves in oak forests.

Yet, give the acorn the proper environment and it will become an oak tree, never a cherry tree.

Chimpanzees reared in captivity become different animals from chimpanzees reared in the wild. Yet, chimpanzees reared in a home, treated as though they were human children, grow up to be chimpanzees, not humans. Changes take place, but in a sequential pattern that is characteristic of the species.

Those students of animal behavior, the *ethologists*,[1] have provided us with many examples of this. Ethologists, as a group, emphasize the genetic factors in the causation of behavior. They point out that certain behaviors appear only at certain stages of maturation—and that many behaviors appear, not spontaneously, but only when triggered by certain environmental stimuli.

Among this particular breed of scientist, Konrad Lorenz stands out, topflight as both scientist and storyteller.

[1] An ethologist is probably best described as half biologist and half psychologist.

8

INNATE REACTIONS IN JACKDAWS
KONRAD Z. LORENZ

Of all the reactions which, in the jackdaw, concern the recognition of an enemy, only one is innate: any living being that carries a black thing, dangling or fluttering, becomes the object of a furious onslaught. This is accompanied by a grating cry of warning whose sharp, metallic, echoing sound expresses,

SOURCE: From *King Solomon's Ring* by Konrad Z. Lorenz. Copyright 1952 by Thomas Y. Crowell Company. Used with permission of the publisher, Thomas Y. Crowell Co., Inc. Pp. 140–143.

even to the human ear, the emotion of embittered rage. At the same time the jackdaw assumes a strange forward-leaning attitude and vibrates its half-spread wings. If you possess a tame jackdaw, you may, on occasion, venture to pick it up to put it into its cage or, perhaps, to cut its overgrown claws. But not, if you have *two*! Jock, who was as tame as any dog, had never resented the occasional touch of my hand, but when the young jackdaws came to our house, it was a different story altogether: on no account would she allow me to touch one of these small, black nestlings. As all unsuspecting, I did so for the first time, I heard behind me the sharp satanic sound of that raucous rattle, a black arrow swooped down from above, over my shoulder and on to the hand which held the jackdaw baby—astonished, I stared at a round, bleeding, deeply pecked wound in the back of my hand! That first observation of this type of attack was, in itself, illuminating as to the instinctive blindness of the impulse. Jock was, at this time, still very devoted to me and hated these fourteen young jackdaws most cordially. (Her adoption of Leftgold took place later on.) I was forced to protect them from her continually: she would have destroyed them, at one fell swoop, if she had been left alone with them for a few minutes. Nevertheless she could not tolerate my taking one of the babies into my hand. The blind reflex nature of the reaction became even clearer to me through a coincidental observation later that summer. One evening, as dusk fell, I returned from a swim in the Danube and, according to my custom, I hurried to the loft to call the jackdaws home and lock them up for the night. As I stood in the gutter, I suddenly felt something wet and cold in my trouser pocket into which, in my hurry, I had pushed my black bathing drawers. I pulled them out—and the next moment was surrounded by a dense cloud of raging, rattling jackdaws, which hailed agonizing pecks upon my offending hand.

It was interesting to observe the jackdaws' reaction to other black objects which I carried in my hands. My large, old, naturalist's camera never caused a similar commotion, although it was black and I held it in my hands, but the jackdaws would start their rattling cry as soon as I pulled out the black paper strips of the pack film which fluttered to and fro in the breeze. That the birds knew me to be harmless, and even a friend, made no difference whatever: as soon as I held in my hand something black and moving, I was branded as an "eater of jackdaws." More extraordinary still is the fact that the same thing may happen to a jackdaw itself: I have witnessed a typical rattling attack on a female jackdaw who was carrying to her nest the wing feather of a raven. On the other hand, tame jackdaws neither emit their rattling cry, nor make an attack, if you hold in your hand one of their own young whilst it is still naked and, therefore, not yet black. This I proved experimentally with the first pair of jackdaws which nested in my colony. The two birds, Greengold and Redgold—two of the aforementioned fourteen—were completely tame, perched on my head and shoulders and were not in the least upset if I handled their nest and watched all their activities at close quarters. Even when I took the babies from the nest and presented them to their parents on the palm of my hand, it left them quite unmoved. But the very day that the small feathers on the nestling burst through their quills, changing their colour into black, there followed a furious attack by the parents on my outstretched hand.

After a typical rattling attack, the jackdaws are exceedingly mistrustful and hostile towards the person or animal which has given rise to it. This burning emotion stamps incredibly quickly into the bird's memory an ineradicable picture which associates the situation "jackdaw in the jaws of the enemy," with the person of the plunderer himself. Provoke a jackdaw's rattling attack two or three times running and you have lost its friendship for ever! From now on, it scolds as soon as it sees you, and you are branded, even when you are not carrying a black and fluttering object in your hands. And further, this jackdaw will easily succeed in convincing all the others of your guilt. Rattling is exceedingly infectious and stimulates its hearers to attack as promptly as does the sight of the black fluttering object in the clutches of the "enemy." The "evil gossip" that you have once or twice been seen carrying such an object, spreads like wildfire, and, almost before you know it, you are notorious amongst the jackdaws in the whole district as a beast of prey which must at all costs be combated.

Not only among jackdaws, but in all species, all members of the species will perform in certain ways under given circumstances. There is also another factor that enters into these performances or behaviors. That is age, or level of maturation. Like all animals, children are most receptive to certain experiences only when they are maturationally ready for them.

Edward de Bono, in his book of children's drawings, *The Dog Exercising Machine* (Simon and Schuster, 1970), listed "the three intellectual ages of man" as:

0–5	years	the age of WHY
5–10	years	the age of WHY NOT
10–75+	years	the age of BECAUSE

While de Bono's categories may be more clever than valid, it certainly does illustrate the fact that characteristic behavior changes with age. (And de Bono's classification system just could be correct.)

One of the earliest psychologists to consider the age factor in relation to the behavior to be expected of children was William James. James was one of the pioneers of psychology in America and one of the all-time psychological greats. He was not an experimentalist, but he was a keen observer. Much of what he had to say back in the nineties was largely hypothetical conjecture and empirically derived knowledge. Psychology has gathered much data since the time of William James. It is not surprising that, from time to time, psychologists of a latter day uncover evidence to contradict James. The truly surprising thing is that he seems to have been right so very often.

In this next selection James discusses the way certain inborn, or native, reactions, particularly curiosity, develop in children.

WHAT THE NATIVE REACTIONS ARE
WILLIAM JAMES

First of all, *Fear*. Fear of punishment has always been the great weapon of the teacher, and will always, of course, retain some place in the conditions of the schoolroom. The subject is so familiar that nothing more need be said about it.

The same is true of *Love*, and the instinctive desire to please those whom we love. The teacher who succeeds in getting herself loved by the pupils will obtain results which one of a more forbidding temperament finds it impossible to secure.

Next, a word might be said about *Curiosity*. This is perhaps a rather poor term by which to designate the *impulse toward better cognition* in its full extent; but you will readily understand what I mean. Novelties in the way of sensible objects, especially if their sensational quality is bright, vivid, startling, invariably arrest the attention of the young and hold it until the desire to know more about the object is assuaged. In its

SOURCE: From *Talks to Teachers on Psychology and to Students on Some of Life's Ideals*. New York: Dover, 1962. (Originally published: New York: Holt, 1899.) Pp. 24–25 of the Dover edition and 45–47 of the original Holt edition.

higher, more intellectual form, the impulse toward completer knowledge takes the character of scientific or philosophic curiosity. In both its sensational and its intellectual form the instinct is more vivacious during childhood and youth than in after life. Young children are possessed by curiosity about every new impression that assails them. It would be quite impossible for a young child to listen to a lecture for more than a few minutes, as you are now listening to me. The outside sights and sounds would inevitably carry his attention off. And, for most people in middle life, the sort of intellectual effort required of the average schoolboy in mastering his Greek or Latin lesson, his algebra or physics, would be out of the question. The middle-aged citizen attends exclusively to the routine details of his business; and new truths, especially when they require involved trains of close reasoning, are no longer within the scope of his capacity.

The sensational curiosity of childhood is appealed to more particularly by certain determinate kinds of objects. Material things, things that move, living things, human actions and accounts of human action, will win the attention better than anything that is more abstract. Here again comes in the advantage of the object-teaching and manual-training methods. The pupil's attention is spontaneously held by any problem that involves the presentation of a new material object or of an activity on any one's part. The teacher's earliest appeals, therefore, must be through objects shown or acts performed or described. Theoretic curiosity, curiosity about the rational relations between things, can hardly be said to awake at all until adolescence is reached. The sporadic metaphysical inquiries of children as to who made God, and why they have five fingers, need hardly be counted here. But, when the theoretic instinct is once alive in the pupil, an entirely new order of pedagogic relations begins for him. Reasons, causes, abstract conceptions, suddenly grow full of zest, a fact with which all teachers are familiar. And, both in its sensible and in its rational developments, disinterested curiosity may be successfully appealed to in the child with much more certainty than in the adult, in whom this intellectual instinct has grown so torpid as usually never to awake unless it enters into association with some selfish personal interest.

There would be those who agree with James that fear of punishment is the teacher's greatest weapon and that it will ever be so in the classroom. Others would disagree. The important idea that we get from James in this selection is his view that we can best help children learn by synchronizing our teaching to their natural progress. If a child has not developed theoretic curiosity, says James, it will do little good to offer him abstractions. Real objects will appeal to him much more as a vehicle for learning.

A Swiss psychologist, Jean Piaget, has impressed many of his fellow psychologists, and others as well, with his ideas about the ways in which children's thinking develops. He concludes from his research studies that all children go through a sequence of stages in their psychological development. What the child is capable of learning or doing at any given time is dependent upon where he is in this sequence of developmental stages.

Piaget's own descriptions of these stages are complex and not always easy to understand. But Dorothy Singer has made the interesting discovery that A. A. Milne, the well-known writer of such children's stories as *Winnie-the-Pooh*, had much the same ideas about the mind of a child as does Piaget.

10

PIGLET, POOH, & PIAGET
DOROTHY G. SINGER

A. A. Milne published *Winnie-the-Pooh* in 1926, three years after Jean Piaget wrote *The Language and Thought of the Child*. I am sure that neither had heard of the other's work, yet Milne's story exemplifies the concepts that Piaget had developed through his experimental and observational work in Geneva. In the make-believe world of Christopher Robin we find instances of egocentrism, time confusion, animism, ludic (playful) symbolism, immanent justice, artificialism, realism, centering, adaptation, preoperational logic, conservation, and collective monologue. From the moment we are introduced to Edward Bear to the final pages when Christopher Robin leads his imaginary playmate up the stairs to bed, Milne provides an enchanting picture of how a child uses logic, language and fantasy.

Fantasy   Where did Milne find his insight into children? He was a mathematics student at Cambridge between 1900 and 1903. Psychology in England then was devoted mainly to studies of learning,

Source: Reprinted from *Psychology Today* Magazine, June, 1972, 6 (1) 70–74, 96. Copyright © Communications/Research/Machines, Inc.

practice and fatigue. Piaget did not start his work until 1920. By then, Milne was writing essays, plays, and humorous pieces for *Punch*. His first adventure into children's literature came at the request of a friend who was starting a children's magazine. Milne responded with a poem, "The Dormouse and the Doctor," then followed that with a book of verse, *When We Were Very Young*. This was the first of the four books that have since become classics in children's literature. They are favorites because they so accurately reflect the child's fantasy world. Milne commented on the success of his books in his autobiography:

"Whether I have added to technique that 'wonderful insight into a child's mind' of which publishers' advertisements talk so airily, I wouldn't know. I am not inordinately fond of or interested in children; their appeal to me is a physical appeal such as the young of other animals make. I have never felt in the least sentimental about them, or no more sentimental than one becomes for a moment over a puppy or a kitten. In as far as I understand their minds, the understanding is based on the observation, casual enough and mostly unconscious, which I give to people generally: on memories of my own childhood: and on the imagination which every writer must bring to memory and observation."

In the 1920s Piaget worked at the Jean Jacques Rousseau Institute of Psychology where he developed systematic methods of observing children at play. He designed experiments that would provide data about the child's logic, his view of the world, and his development of language and concept formation. Piaget's first work *The Language and Thought of the Child* deals with the notion of egocentrism—the idea that the child views the world subjectively. The child believes that the world was created for him, that everyone thinks as he does, and that everyone shares his feelings and wishes. The child cannot distinguish between what is self and what is outside world.

The concept of egocentrism is at the core of *Winnie-the-Pooh*. Milne states in his autobiography:

"Heaven, that is, does really appear to lie about the child in its infancy, as it does not lie about even the most attractive kitten. But with this outstanding physical quality there is a natural lack of moral quality, which expresses itself, as Nature always insists on expressing herself, in an egotism entirely ruthless. . . . A pen-picture of a child which showed it as loving, grateful and full of thought for others would be false to the truth; but equally false would be a picture which insisted on the brutal egotism of the child, and ignored the physical beauty which softens it."

Milne cites many examples in his poetry that reflect the child's egotism. Christopher wants to know after he has watched them changing guard at Buckingham Palace, "Do you think the King knows all about me?" In "Disobedience" James James Morrison Morrison, the child whose mother has died, tells his other relations "not to go blaming *him.*"

Piaget felt that the growth of intellect freed the child from egocentrism. He outlined four periods of cognitive development. I do not intend to present Piaget's theory in detail in this article, but the four periods may be summarized as follows:

1. The sensorimotor period (birth to age two): the infant first displays intelligence in the use of his senses (vision, hearing, taste and smell), and in his motor activities (reaching, grasping, crawling, walking and running). He internalizes his perceptions and activities to create his private view of the world. The infant begins to develop language, and to use symbolic imagery.

2. Preoperational period (ages two to seven): the child begins to use language more fully and he begins to conceptualize. He may not make distinctions within classes (all cats or dogs have the same name as the child's own cat or dog). The child can express his view of the world through drawings, language, or dreams. Prelogical reasoning appears in the intuitive stage of this period from ages four to seven. The child may play with imaginary companions or engage in compensatory play (doing in make-believe what he is forbidden in reality).

3. Concrete-operational period (ages seven to 11): the child's thinking becomes logical and reversible. He understands the logic of classes. He has learned to conserve, to see that objects or quantities remain the same despite changes made in their appearance. Play is more social and has strict rules.

4. Formal-operational period (age 11 to adulthood): the child now understands the logic of propositions and hypotheses. He can think about theories such as space, motion, time. He develops a value system, and a sense of morality.

Stairs   *Winnie-the-Pooh* focuses on the world of the child in the preoperational period and more specifically, the period of intuitive thought (ages four to seven).

We first meet Edward Bear as he is being dragged down the stairs on the back of his head. "It is, as far as he knows, the only way of coming downstairs." This example of *egocentrism* sets the tone for the rest of the book. The narrator informs us that Edward's name is Winnie-the-Pooh. When asked if Winnie is not a girl's name, Christopher replies with a second example of egocentric reasoning. "He's Winnie-ther-Pooh. Don't you know what 'ther' means?" Again, an example of *egocentrism.*

Christopher knows, so no further explanation is necessary, or forthcoming.

Christopher Robin wants a story, and his father obliges him, incidentally demonstrating the child's *conception of time*.

"Once upon a time, a very long time ago now, *about last Friday*." Piaget suggests that the child's sense of time is dependent on the order of succession of events and on the duration of intervals. The young child often confuses present and past events. Minutes may seem like hours as he waits for the promised trip to a friend's house.

Pooh's first monologue is another example of egocentric thinking. Sitting in the forest, he muses: "That buzzing-noise means something. You don't get a buzzing-noise like that, just buzzing and buzzing without its meaning something. If there is a buzzing-noise, somebody's making a buzzing-noise, and the only reason for making a buzzing-noise that *I* know of is because you're a bee . . . and the only reason for being a bee that I know of is for making honey . . . and the only reason for making honey is so as *I* can eat it," and in the chapter where the great flood comes, Pooh discovers a note in a bottle floating past his house. On the note is a message from Piglet: "Help Piglet (me)" and on the other side "It's Me Piglet, Help, Help."

Piglet, an egocentric friend of Pooh, is sure that everyone must know where he is in his distress. But Pooh is just as egocentric when he interprets the note. Pooh only recognizes the letter "P" and each "P" convinces him further that " 'P' means 'Pooh' so it's a very important Missage to me."

In a later chapter Pooh eats a jar of honey that he had intended to give to Eeyore on his birthday. In perfect form, Pooh rationalizes his gluttony and decides to give Eeyore the empty jar: after all, "It's a very nice pot, Eeyore could keep things in it."

Toys Piaget has shown that children in the preoperational stage attribute life to inanimate objects; he calls this tendency *animism*. Milne recognized his process in his own son, Christopher. All of the characters in *Winnie-the-Pooh* (except for Rabbit and Owl) are based on toys from Christopher's nursery. They all have distinct personalities.

Pooh, the teddy bear of "little brain," is always in search of honey and adventure; Piglet, a weak and timid pig, is Pooh's best friend. Eeyore, the donkey, is a cynic and pessimist; Kanga, the kangaroo, is the bossy, practical image of motherhood; Owl, the expert on spelling, is all-wise and knowing; and Rabbit, who attempts to be clever, is sometimes a bit mean.

Each of these imaginary characters displays a talent for animism. In the first chapter, Pooh evolves an elaborate plan to steal some honey from a bee's nest. He will disguise himself as a

cloud in a blue sky. He rolls over and over in the mud until he is as dark as a thundercloud. He borrows a sky-blue balloon from Christopher and floats off into the sky. As Winnie-the-Pooh approaches the bee's nest, he sings:
"How sweet to be a Cloud
Floating in the Blue!
Every little cloud
Always sings aloud."

Pony The singing cloud is an example of *animism* and it is also an example of *ludic symbolism*—the symbolism of child's games. Sometimes, for a child, a broom becomes a pony. For Pooh, the balloon becomes the sky. Pooh, feeling very proud and happy with his deception, calls down to Christopher: "What do I look like?"

Christopher, who always serves to bring fantasy back to reality, replies, "You look like a bear holding on to a balloon."

Poor Pooh replies. "Not like a small black cloud in a blue sky?"

"Not very much," says Christopher.

Pooh persists. He says: "Ah well, perhaps from up here it looks different."

Pooh reasons intuitively; he bases his reasoning on perceptual appearances. He urges Christopher to walk below him with an umbrella, saying loudly: "Tut, tut, it looks like rain."

Pooh is certain that if the bees see the blue sky *and* an *umbrella* they will surely be fooled by "the little dark cloud."

Honey Piaget has shown that the child believes that justice is built into the natural order of things. Matches burn children who play with them when they have been forbidden to do so. This notion of *immanent justice* is evident in the same honey-and-bee adventure. Pooh falls down into a gorse bush, where he is covered with prickles. In true Piaget fashion he believes his punishment comes "of *liking* honey so much."

Later in the book, Pooh pays Rabbit a visit, hoping to be fed in the bargain. Rabbit plays the kind host and Pooh eats so much that he cannot get back out the way he came in. He becomes stuck and blames it on the narrowness of the door. Rabbit sternly advises: "It all comes of eating too much."

Pooh is punished now, and can't get out. Christopher Robin comes to the rescue and declares that the only way for the bear to get out of the hole is to get thin.

"How long does getting thin take?" asks Pooh.

"About a week," Christopher Robin replies.

Here again Milne uses time as a child might experience it. Christopher settles down to read to the bear who indeed becomes thin, and then is pulled out of the hole.

Magic   Piaget suggests that the child is confused about the physical world as well as the temporal world. The child believes in artificialism, or the notion that human beings have created mountains, lakes, trees, etc. The young child believes too that his chants and songs can in some way control the elements. ("Rain, rain, go away, come again another day.") The child in the intuitive period cannot easily recognize a familiar scene if he looks at it from a different angle. The tree he sees from his window is not the same tree he sees from the garden below.

This difficulty with physical space is shown in the chapter called "Pooh and Piglet Go Hunting and Nearly Catch a Woozle." While the two friends are out hunting they walk in circles and cross each other's tracks in the snow, not realizing that they have made the extra footprints they see. They believe that "woozles or strange animals are about." Piglet suddenly remembers some things that he must do immediately. He checks the time with Pooh, finds out that it is about 12:00, and excuses himself from the hunt: "It isn't the sort of thing you can do in the afternoon, it's a very particular morning thing, that has to be done in the morning . . . between as I was saying, the hours of 12:00 and 12:05. So, really, dear old Pooh, if you will excuse me." Eventually Christopher appears and explains the whole thing to Pooh—the two friends had made the tracks themselves.

Pole   Piaget states that the young child has a tolerant belief in the *realism* of words, pictures, dreams and objects. Everything is credible. If an adult mentions the North Pole, it must exist. The child associates things without making logical connections between them. Things just seem to go together. Names exist as parts of the things named. The sun is always the sun, and gets its name from someplace in the sky. Rabbit says the North Pole is "sure to be a pole because of calling it a pole, and if it's a pole, well, I should think it would be sticking in the ground, shouldn't you, because there'd be nowhere else to stick it."

Christopher plans an expedition to discover the North Pole. When Pooh asks him "What *is* the North Pole?" Christopher replies, "It's just a thing you discover." During the expedition to the North Pole, Roo, the baby kangaroo, manages to fall into some water. Pooh saves Roo with a long pole that he happens to find. After the rescue, Christopher looks at Pooh and says quite solemnly, "The Expedition is over. You have found the North Pole." Christopher, who knows about the South Pole, believes that there must be an East Pole and West Pole, "though people don't like talking about them."

Clay   *Conservation* is probably the most familiar of Piaget's concepts, and the one most readily adapted to research. Piaget defines conservation as the ability to see that objects or quantities remain the same despite changes in appearance. Piaget believes that children learn to conserve substance, weight and volume, in that order, and that they can not truly conserve until age seven. In one experiment Piaget presents to a child two *identical* balls of clay, one of which is elongated or flattened or cut into pieces. He then asks the child if there is still as much clay in the one as in the other. The child below the age of seven generally sees the elongated clay as having more clay than the ball of clay. The child believes that the experimenter has actually produced *more* clay by changing the shape or container.

Milne's story of Eeyore's birthday illustrates this inability to conserve. Piglet plans to give Eeyore a large red balloon. On the way, Piglet catches his foot in a rabbit's hole, and falls down. When he recovers he discovers to his dismay that the balloon has burst. All that he has left is a "small piece of damp rag." Nevertheless, Piglet is determined to give a present to Eeyore. When he finally reaches Eeyore, the conversation goes like this:

" 'Eeyore, I brought you a balloon.' 'Balloon?' said Eeyore, . . . 'one of those big coloured things you blow up? Gaiety, song-and-dance, here we are and there we are?'

'Yes . . . but I fell down . . . and I burst the balloon.'

'My birthday balloon?'

'Yes, Eeyore,' said Piglet, sniffing a little. 'Here it is. With—with many happy returns of the day.'

'My present?'

Piglet nodded again.

'The balloon?'

'Yes.'

'Thank you, Piglet,' said Eeyore, 'you don't mind my asking,' he went on, 'but what color was this balloon when it—when it *was* a balloon?' " Poor Eeyore cannot understand that red remains red even when the balloon is small and no longer round or full.

Tail Eeyore is the victim of centering, another of Piaget's concepts, in a later chapter. Piaget has shown that a child will focus on the most compelling feature of what he sees, while excluding all other aspects. Eeyore's most compelling feature is his tail, but he loses it. Pooh promises to help look for the missing tail. Visiting Owl, Pooh notices that the bell-rope on Owl's front door looks rather familiar to him. " 'Handsome bell-rope, isn't it?' said Owl. Pooh nodded and said, 'It reminds me of something, where did you get it?' "

Owl describes how he found it hanging over a bush. Owl thought someone must live in the bush and he rang it but nothing happened. He rang it again and it came off in his hands.

Since nobody wanted the bell-rope, Owl took it home and hung it on his door. For Owl, a tail without Eeyore attached to it is not a tail. Hanging over a bush, it becomes a bell-rope, waiting to be pulled.

Pooh tells Owl that the bell-rope is Eeyore's tail, and the story ends happily with Christopher Robin nailing it back onto Eeyore.

Lesson   The child constantly learns how to adapt to his environment. Piaget described how his own children learned to explore empty boxes and to seek out toys hidden under pillows. They repeated their motor acts until they understood and mastered a situation. Roo learns that he cannot eat and talk at the same time or he chokes and gets the hiccups. Pooh presents an empty honey jar to Eeyore who discovers that it's a good thing to put things into and take things out of. He repeats the act until he learns the lesson.

Pooh discovers that a bottle with a cork stopper can float on water. It becomes a suitable boat for him. Later he learns that an inverted umbrella makes a bigger boat that can accommodate two adventurers.

These characters are participating in what Piaget calls *assimilation* and *accommodation.* Both are necessary for the child to adapt to his environment. The child must organize the data from his senses into his conceptual framework. Milne presents several episodes that show how Christopher and his friends use play to assimilate the customs, manners and values of middle-class English society into their experience. The little girl who plays house and the boy who plays fireman learn about their world through symbolic play, just as Christopher, the explorer, learns about his.

Songs   Language in its beginning stages is primarily egocentric. A child talks for himself and not for the point of view of the listener. Echolalia—repeating phrases—gives him much pleasure. Certainly, Pooh's songs are repetitive.

"How sweet to be a child" or "Sing Ho for the life of a Bear" are themes repeated over and over in two separate little songs.

The child also uses *onomatopoeia*—words that sound like the noises the objects make. For example, many children say "choo-choo," before learning the word "train," or "bow-wow" before learning the word "dog." After the bee-and-cloud adventure, Pooh's arms were so stiff from holding on to the balloon that whenever a fly landed on his nose, Pooh had to blow it off: "Pooh."

"That is why he's called Pooh," says Christopher Robin.

Sign   Children use language in concrete ways during the preoperational stage. For example, Pooh lived in the forest all by himself "under the name 'Sanders.' " Christopher interprets this to mean that a sign must be hanging *above* the door with the name "Sanders" printed in gold letters.

Piglet has a broken sign with the words "Trespassers W" on it. Piglet explains to Christopher that this was his grandfather's name. When Christopher takes issue with this, Piglet says that this sign is short for "Trespassers Will," which is short for "Trespassers William," and his grandfather had had two names in case he lost one . . . "Trespassers" after an uncle, and "William" after "Trespassers."

"I've got two names," said Christopher Robin, carelessly.

"Well, there you are, that proves it," said Piglet.

Neither recognizes the partial meaning of the sign (Trespassers Will be Prosecuted), a typical fault in the logic of children.

A conversation between Owl and Pooh exemplifies other linguistic tricks that are peculiar to children. Owl tells Pooh that the "customary procedure in such cases is as follows"; "What does Crustimoney Proseedcake mean?" said Pooh, "for I am a bear of Very Little Brain and long words bother me." Again, when Pooh calls the expedition an "Expotition," Christopher corrects him, "Expedition, silly old Bear. It's got an 'x' in it."

Parallel   One of the delightful aspects of preoperational language is *collective monologue*—the conversation of the child who does not try to understand or even listen to the point of view of another person. The other person is mainly a stimulus for the child. Children sit alongside each other in a sand box busily playing, but they are completely absorbed in their own fantasies and conversations. Piaget calls this *parallel play*. The child pays little attention to questions posed by playmates; he gives answers that are unrelated to specific questions. And yet, the child would be distressed if his friend left his side.

Milne demonstrates this notion of *collective monologue* in his final chapter of *Winnie-the Pooh*.

Pencils   Christopher Robin gives a party for Pooh and invites all the forest animals. Several conversations are taking place at once around the festive table. Owl tries to tell Christopher about an accident that nearly happened to his friend; Roo is steadily hiccuping; Kanga is preoccupied with scolding Roo; Eeyore is making a long-winded, senseless speech; and finally, Christopher is attempting to praise Pooh for his past heroics. All are happy to be together at the party, but each egocentric animal is involved with his own thoughts and conversation.

Finally, Christopher presents to Pooh a Pencil Case with "Blue

Pencils, and Red Pencils, and Green Pencils for saying special things in blue, and red, and green." Christopher Robin believes that words have special meanings when they are written in special colors. He endows the little gift with one more of Piaget's notions—that of *physiognomic properties.* Inanimate objects can take on the emotions of human beings. If Jean Piaget opened the pages of *Winnie-the-Pooh,* he would discover, as I have, how A. A. Milne intuitively uses psychological insight to give life and meaning to a story about an imaginary forest, peopled with animals from the nursery. But instead, Piaget has collaborated with Etienne Delessert on a tale about a mouse to demonstrate how children of five and six view the world. It remains to be seen whether Piaget's effort will ever match the popularity of *Winnie-the-Pooh* among children and adults.

Our ability to communicate with each other marks us as unique among all other creatures. So, if one facet of human development deserves special consideration, it is the development of language. We are not speaking here of merely acquiring a foreign language. If you have ever done so, however, you have had a glimpse of the enormity of the task confronting the average one-year-old.

For an English-speaking person to learn French, for example, he must acquire a new basic vocabulary, new idioms, new word order, new conjugations, new declensions, new sounds, and above all, new rules for combining it all into a meaningful whole. Quite a chore! But at least he already knows how to speak one language. Many of the rules which apply to his own English hold true as well of French. To a great extent, his task will be to relate his language to the new one to be learned.

What of the one-year-old child? He has no already-learned language on which to build. And nobody can explain to him how to go about acquiring it! He has to figure it all out—the sounds, the meanings, the rules—entirely on his own.

Kornei Chukovsky, a Russian writer of books for children, discusses the process in the selection following.

11

IMITATION AND CREATIVITY
KORNEI CHUKOVSKY

Two- and three-year-old children have such a strong sensitivity to their language—to its many inflections and suffixes—that the words they construct inventively do not seem at all distorted and freakish but, on the contrary, extremely apt, beautiful, and natural.

At times the child creates words that already exist in the language but are unknown to him or to the adults around him. I heard, for instance, a three-year-old child in the Crimea spontaneously use the word "bulleting" [*puliat'*], and he "bulleted" from his tiny rifle all day long, not even suspecting that this word has been thus used for centuries in the faraway Don region. In a story by L. Pantileev, *Len'ka Pantileev*, a Yaroslavl woman says several times: "And so they bullet and they bullet!"

Another child, whose exact age I did not know, created the words "shoeware [*obutki*] and "clothesware" [*odetki*]; this youngster lived in the steppes near Odessa, not far from the Black Sea. He, too, was completely oblivious of the fact that these two words had existed for a few centuries in the past in the distant north, in the Olenets district. How could he possibly have known this since he had not read the ethnographic notes of P. N. Rybnikov [a noted folklorist], who recorded a certain folk tale in which the following words appeared: "I received as promised, food, shoeware, and clothesware [*obutki i odetki*]." This very same two-part phrase, "shoeware and clothesware," was formulated independently by a small child from the household words for footwear and clothes heard from adults.

"Oh, you grasshopper!" a mother said to her active three-year-old.

"I'm not a grasshopper; I'm a 'people' [*liud'*]!"

The mother was nonplused about this *"liud',"* but some time later she discovered, inadvertently, that a thousand kilometers away, in the Urals, a person had been called a *liud'* since the distant past. Indeed, one still says there:

"What kind of a *liud'* is he?"

SOURCE: From *From Two to Five*, translated and edited by Miriam Morton, Berkeley: University of California Press, 1963. Originally published by University of California Press; reprinted by permission of the Regents of the University of California. Pp. 4–11.

In this manner the young child at times spontaneously arrives at word structures that were developed by the people over the centuries. His mind masters, as if miraculously, the same methods, processes, and peculiarities of word construction which were used by his very distant ancestors in building the language.

Even the original words invented by children, which do not already exist in the language, seem almost real. They could have come into being, and their absence from the language seems to be merely fortuitous. One somehow reacts to such words as to old acquaintances, feeling that one has already heard them somewhere, at some time.

Having been told by a little boy that a big-horse [*loshada*] "hoofed" [*kopytnula*] him, I used this word [hoofed] at the first opportunity in a conversation with my young daughter. Not only did she understand at once the meaning of the word, but she did not even suspect that it did not exist, for it seemed to her completely normal. And, in a sense, such words *are* normal; at times they are even more "normal" than conventional ones. Why, one might ask, do we call a full-sized horse a "horsie" when speaking to a small child? To a tiny tot a horse must seem enormous. Can we expect him to use a diminutive word for so huge a creature? Sensing the falseness of this diminutive, the child transforms the word "horsie" into "big-horse" [*loshada*], thus underscoring the hugeness of the animal. [The Russian word for an average-sized horse is *loshad'*].

I have heard children deal similarly with other words, using the special word that stands for an unusually large object or animal. In all such instances the child has done exactly what the poet Mayakovsky did when he changed the word "puppy" [*schenok*] into "big-pup" [*schen*]:

> With all his big-pup's might
> The poor creature yelped.
>
> [*Izo vsekh shcheniachikh sil
> Nishchii shchen zagolosil.*]

Changing words, the child most often does not notice his own originality, and thinks that he is repeating words he has heard spoken.

This unconscious word creation first came to my attention, and amazed me, when a four-year-old boy, whose acquaintance I had just made on the train, kept insisting that I let him touch a certain gadget I was holding in my hand. He invented a word for this object, right there and then, and this revealed an extraordinary skill in adapting a suffix that often appears at the end of Russian words to denote the instrumentality of an object— the "l" suffix. An example of this "l" suffix is the way the word *myt'*, which means "to wash," is converted to *mylo*, which means "soap"; the "l" in the word *mylo* is the suffix of instrumentality. This process of distinguishing and classifying, and then using, a certain suffix so aptly seemed to me so impressive because the child, at his young age, was still totally unaware of his inventiveness in this respect.

One notices the same grammatical skill [in young preschool children] in their use of grammatical forms; a child having no notion of grammatical rules uses quite correctly all noun cases, verb tenses, and moods, even when he uses unfamiliar words. This perceptive use of words is a most amazing phenomenon of early childhood!

Even the mistakes that the child often makes in the process of this creative mastering of speech are evidence of the tremendous achievement of his mind in coördinating bits of linguistic knowledge. For instance, although a child could not explain why he calls a letter carrier a "mail*er*" [i.e., calls a *pochtal'on* a *pochtanik*], this reconstruction of the word is evidence that he has become aware of the use of the suffix ["-er" in English] *-nik* in the Russian language, which characterizes a person according to his work or trade. Adults may laugh at "mailer" or *pochtanik* [*pochta* means "mail" in Russian], but it is not the child's fault that etymology does not adhere to a strict logic. If words came into existence according to a consistent principle, children's locutions would not seem so diverting; they are often more "correct" than grammar and "improve" upon it.

To be sure, in order to learn the language, the child imitates adults in his word creativity. It would be nonsense to claim that he *adds* to a language in any way. Without suspecting it himself, he directs all his efforts, by means of analogies, toward assimilating the linguistic riches gradually developed by many generations of adults. But the young child adapts these analogies with such skill, with such sensitivity to the meaning and significance of the elements from which words are formed, that it is impossible not to be enthralled by the power of his understanding, awareness, and memory, so apparent in the very arduous effort he makes every time he speaks.

The minutest variation in grammatical form is apprehended by the child, and, when he needs to contrive (or re-create in his memory) one word or another, he applies precisely that suffix or precisely that grammatical word ending which, according to the mysterious laws of his native tongue, is essential for the needed nuance or meaning or image.

A two-year-old girl was taking a bath and making her doll "dive" into the water and "dive out" of it, commenting:

"There, she drowns-in—now, she drowns-out!" ["*Vot pritonula, vot vytonula!*"]

Only a deaf-mute would not notice the exquisite plasticity and the refined meaning of these words. "Drowns-in" is not the same thing as "drowns"—it is to drown only temporarily with a definite expectation implied that the doll would be "drowning-out" again. . . .

It seems to me that, beginning with the age of two, every child becomes for a short period of time a linguistic genius. Later, beginning with the age of five to six, this talent begins to fade. There is no trace left in the eight-year-old of this creativity with words, since the need for it has passed; by this age the child already has fully mastered the basic principles of his native language. If his former talent for word invention and construction had not abandoned him, he would, even by the age of ten, eclipse any of us with his suppleness and brilliance of speech. Not in vain did Leo Tolstoy, addressing himself to adults, write: ". . . [the child] realizes the laws of word formation better than you because no one so often thinks up new words as children."

Of course, when we speak of the creative powers of the young child, of his keen sensitivity to language, of his genius, we do not consider these words sentimental hyperboles. But we must not, just the same, forget that the basis for all the linguistic aptitude attributed to the child "from two to five" is imitation, since every new word he invents he creates in accordance with the norms made known to him through adult speech. However, he does not copy adults as simply (and as docilely) as it seems to the casual observer. . . . a large amount of evidence is presented to show that in the process of assimilating his native spoken language the child, from the early age of two, introduces a critical evaluation, analysis, and control.

The young child acquires his linguistic and thinking habits only through communication with other human beings. It is only this association that makes a human being out of him, that is, a speaking and thinking being. But, if this communication with other human beings did not evoke in him, for even a short period of time, a special, heightened sensitivity to the materials of speech which adults share with him, he would remain, to the end of his days, a foreigner in the realm of his own language—as though repeating lifelessly the dull rules of textbooks.

In the old days I had occasion to meet children on whom were imposed, from a very early age and for various reasons (mainly because of the [snobbish] whims of rich and shallow parents), the vocabulary and the structure of a foreign language, most often French. These unfortunate children, estranged from the elements of their native speech, mastered neither their own nor the foreign language. Their speech, in both instances, was equally colorless, bloodless, and pallid, because, during the age "from two to five" they were deprived of the possibility of familiarizing themselves creatively with their spoken language.

To be sure, many neologisms of the child are often evidence of his inability to make himself conversant, in his early attempts to speak the language, with this or that exception to a grammatical norm. At times a word or a locution "invented" by the child, which seems to us so original, has occurred to him actually only because he has applied to it, too directly, some [grammatical] rule, unaware of any exception to it. Despite this, I am convinced of the tremendous speech-giftedness of the preschool child.

This giftedness consists not only in his early ability to classify word endings, prefixes, and suffixes, a process he accomplishes unconsciously in his two-year-old mind, but also in the divination with which he chooses them when he creates a new word, imitating and using for such a word an appropriate model. Imitation itself is in this way a creative act.

It is frightening to think what an enormous number of grammatical forms are poured over the poor head of the young child. And he, as if it were nothing at all, adjusts to all this chaos, constantly sorting out into rubrics the disorderly elements of the words he hears, without noticing, as he does this, his gigantic effort. If an adult had to master so many grammatical rules within so short a time, his head would surely burst—a mass of rules mastered so lightly and so freely by the two-year-old "linguist." The labor he thus performs at this age is astonishing enough, but even more amazing and unparalleled is the ease with which he does it.

In truth, the young child is the hardest mental toiler on our planet. Fortunately, he does not even suspect this.

We have said earlier that by the time the child reaches his eighth year his keen sensitivity to his language is dulled. However, it does not follow that his linguistic development suffers to any extent from this loss. Having lost his recent giftedness to improvise original word structures, he replaces this lack a hundredfold with valuable new qualities of his linguistic growth. The linguistic work of the child has now switched to new rails. Using his achievements of the earlier period, he now equips himself for more intricate and varied communication with others.

"At this age," says A. N. Gvozdev, "the child has already mastered to such a degree the entire complicated grammatical system, including the finest points of the esoteric syntactic and morphological sequences in the Russian language, as well as the solid and correct usage of the many single exceptions, that the Russian language, thus mastered, becomes indeed his own." All this becomes obvious to those who, for instance, study with sufficient awareness the intellectual endeavors of school children who were only recently preschoolers. The fact remains incontrovertible, however, that the process of learning one's native language has a much faster tempo specifically at the age of "from two to five."

It has been established for a long time that at the age of about one year the child knows less than ten words; at the end of two years his vocabulary has grown to 250 or 300 words, and by the end of his third year it is in the thousands— that is, in only a year's time the child builds up his basic word "reservoir," and after this accumulation of new words proceeds much more slowly. The same is true of the grammatical forms that the child learns in the same period. I once tried to make a list of these forms (declensions, conjugations, the use of prefixes and suffixes). I noted down not less than seventy. Most of these "generalizations" that are formed in the child's brain forever, for his entire life, are established between the ages of three and four, when the linguistic giftedness seems to be particularly strong.

DEVELOPING THE TOPIC FURTHER

We have seen that all of us, acorns, chimpanzees, and humans, are limited in our development to those activities which are *natural* for the species and which are appropriate at a given stage of maturation. If you liked Konrad Lorenz's approach to this subject you will want to read his entire book, *King Solomon's Ring* (Crowell, 1952). For more on Piaget's theory of development we suggest Mary Ann Spencer Pulaski, *Understanding Piaget* (Harper and Row, 1971). And, by now, you may well wish to reread the Pooh books. For a start you might try A. A. Milne's *Winnie-the-Pooh* (Dutton, 1960) and *When We Were Very Young* (Dutton, 1960). Another book about child development is David Elkind, *A Sympathetic Understanding of the Child: Six to Sixteen* (Allyn and Bacon, 1971).

For additional material about language development, see Roger Brown, *Words and Things* (Free Press, 1958) and Peter Herriot, *Language and Teaching: A Psychological View* (Methuen, 1971). If you enjoyed Chukovsky's discussion of this topic, you may wish to read his book on child development in its entirety: *From Two to Five,* Revised Edition (University of California Press, 1968).

Part Five

Development:
Environmental
Factors

Like the acorn, the child needs the proper environment if it is to be nourished to develop its greatest potential. But what are the characteristics of such an environment?

There has been increasing pressure in recent years to hasten the process of education. It seems to some people desirable that children learn to read at five, four, even two years of age. Anyone who has ever attended an American public school knows what we mean when we say that children are *pushed.* Perhaps this is beneficial. Perhaps it is harmful. That is the controversy!

At the same time, schools, and society as a whole, have been subject to much criticism for being too permissive. One sometimes wonders about this. Where is the permissiveness in a society that insists that every child must prepare for college? Where is the permissiveness in our ridiculous insistence that *all* children must achieve at an above-average rate?

We are reminded of that often-told story of the editorial in a big city newspaper. The editor had just discovered that, in the public schools of his city, half of the children were below average in intelligence. Something must be done, immediately, to remedy that deplorable situation! Imagine! *Half* of them—below average! Half of them in the lower fifty per cent.

Most parents may be willing to admit that the facts of arithmetic are such that approximately half of any group will be below the arithmetic average of that group on any measure. But if it is *our* children you are talking about, they must achieve above average in school!

The question is not one of how rapidly we desire children to learn. Rather, it is a matter of how best to fit an educational program to the nature of the developing child. Was James right, that the basic native reactions of children are fear, love, and curiosity? How would one build an environment for the healthy development of children based on this, or other, assumptions of the nature of children?

A doughty old Scotsman, A. S. Neill, has for many years operated his Summerhill School in England on the basis of love and curiosity. He would completely disagree with James as to the inevitability of fear in a school program. To say that Neill and Summerhill are controversial is to understate the situation.

Neill's book, *Summerhill,* has been read by millions in America. More recently a translation of *Summerhill* has had proportionately even greater distribution in Germany. In England the general attitude toward Summerhill, and Neill, seems to be a gentle tolerance. In Neill's native Scotland they don't seem to have heard of him.

But in America there seem to be few who are neutral. Most people who know about Summerhill become either avid fans or severe critics. Why? Read Neill's own discussion and see what you think of his attitude toward children and his program for their development.

12

CAN I COME TO SUMMERHILL? I HATE MY SCHOOL.
A. S. NEILL

Just over 20 years ago I had two books published in New York, *The Problem Teacher* and *The Problem Family*. So far as I could make out each issue sold a few hundred copies and the rest were sold as remainders at a few dimes each. The press notices I got were either lukewarm or hostile. One called the books old hat. "We have lived through this in the States and there is nothing new for us." Twenty years later the book *Summerhill* became a best seller in the States. Why? I have no idea. I like to think that the U.S.A. has come up to date rather than that I have gone out of date. I do not know why I get so large a mail from the U.S.A. It is mostly from young people and in the seven years since the book was published I can recall only two hostile letters. Many are from school children. "Can I come to Summerhill? I hate my school. It is all pressurization. The teachers make every lesson dull and dead and originality is frowned upon." Oddly enough, although our British education is all wrong, I never get letters from home children.

The mystery to me is this: Why has America become conscious that its education is not good enough? Why now and not 20 years ago? Surely the schools have not changed all that much. But is it a case of a change of society? Is society sicker than it was a couple of decades ago? I fancy that that is the deep reason. In all countries youth is rebelling. Alas, too often rebelling against all that does not matter. The hippies, the flower merchants show their protests, not against war, not against race discrimination, not against the stupid learning we call education; no, all the challenge is the right to wear long hair and leather jackets and blue jeans. That is the impression I get in this country, but from what I hear and read about America the young, especially in the universities, are challeng-

SOURCE: Reprinted from *Psychology Today* Magazine, May, 1968. Copyright © Communications/Research/Machines, Inc.

ing real evils—the insane dollar values, the dead uniformity of the people who have been molded and indoctrinated so much that they are automatic slaves to any ideas thrown out by the press and the TV screens. In Britain I think that the average TV program is geared to a nation of 10-year-olds. Our B.B.C. refused to put on *The War Game* because it told of the horrors of an atomic war and it might upset the nice folks who want to think that God is in his Heaven and all is right with the world. The young feel that they have been cheated by the old, lied to, castrated by their parents and teachers. They no longer accept glib answers—in Vietnam we are saving the world from Communism; in South Africa we are preserving the God-given rights of the superior whites; in the U.S.A. we are battling to preserve the white civilization. It is significant that all these reasons involve hate and war and possibly ultimate death to humanity. Youth sees a world full of savagery. Hitler's six million Jews paved the way for a world that accepted torture and death as almost commonplace factors in our modern life. In short, the world is very very sick, and youth feels it but, alas, cannot do much about it. Summerhill's good friend Joan Baez, recently in prison, has no power over the hate merchants; all she can do is to march in protest and then be carted to prison. It is the helplessness of youth that so often brings despair.

In this American *Stimmung* the book *Summerhill* was launched in 1960. It caught on because it was voicing what so many of the young had felt but had not intellectualized, had not made conscious. For its theme was freedom—real freedom, not the sham thing so often called democracy. Freedom for all to grow at their own pace; freedom from all indoctrination, religious, political, moral; freedom for children to live in their own community, making their own social laws. To many a youth Summerhill became synonymous with Paradise. I hasten to say that it isn't—*Gott sei dank!* Most of the rebellion stems from home, from what Wilhelm Reich called the compulsive family, the family that strangles youth, fears youth, often hates youth. From my mail I am led to believe that the American family is more dangerous than the British one. I never get the sort of letter I had two days ago from New York. "I am 17 and I am allowed no freedom at all. I have to be in at certain hours and if I am late my father hits me. I hate my parents." A girl of a middle-class family. I have had scores of similar letters. A boy of 15 writes, "I hate school and cannot concentrate on my work and my parents bully me all the time because they say that I must go to college and get a good job." I have no idea how much truth is in Vance Packard's *The Status Seekers* but even if a 10th is true it gives a terrible picture of

American civilization. A Cadillac-civilization with its sequel, dope and drugs and misery for those who cannot accept the god of cars and furs and wealth.

This looks like an attack on a country by an outsider and it may well be resented by some readers, but I do not mean it as an attack; it is a case of trying to think aloud the answer to the question: Why did the Summerhill book catch on in the U.S.A.? At home we have our own miseries and troubles. The growing race hate due to the immigration from Jamaica. The futility of a culture that dwells on bingo and football crowds, on infantile TV programs; a culture that gives the cheap sensational press millions of readers while the more cultured papers—*The New Statesman*, the *Observer*, the *Sunday Times* —too often struggle to keep themselves alive. World sickness is not confined to North America. Russia has its teen-age gangsters also.

One reason why Summerhill appealed to the U.S.A. may be that it is, so to say, anti-education. The great American educationists, Dewey, Kilpatrick and their kind, were mostly pre-Freudian in their outlook. They kept linking education to learning, and today in all countries educational journals concentrate on the learning process. I escaped that trap. I was and I am ill-versed on what the educationists did. I never read Rousseau or Pestalozzi or Froebel; what I read in Montessori I did not like, partly because it made play the mate of learning. Learning what? Summerhill is not a seat of learning; it is a seat of living. We are not so proud of David who became a professor of mathematics as we are of Jimmy who was hateful and antisocial and is now a warm-hearted engineer with much charity and love to give out. Summerhill puts learning in its own place. I have more than once written that if the emotions are free the intellect will look after itself. What a waste it all is! Sixty years ago I could read some Latin and Greek. Today I can't decipher the Latin words on a tombstone. Our schools teach children to read Shakespeare and Hardy and Tennyson and when they leave school the vast majority never read anything better than a crime story. For my part I'd abolish nearly every school subject, making geography and history matters for the school library, and quadratic equations a luxury for the few boys and girls who loved maths. Abolish exams and my school will have only creative teachers—art, music, drama, handwork, etc.

Every man has a bee in his bonnet. It was comforting to read in Erich Fromm that Freud had to be in the station an hour before his train was due. My original bee was psychology. In the 1920s my home was Vienna and my associates the psychoanalysts. Like all young fools I thought that Utopia was just 'round the corner. Make the unconscious conscious and you have a world full of love and fellowship with no hate. I grew out of that phase but did retain the belief that education must primarily deal with the emotions. Working for many years with problem children made my belief stronger. I saw that the aim of all education must be to produce happy, balanced, pro-life children, and I knew that all the exams and books in a million classrooms could not do a thing to make children balanced. A B.A. could be a hopeless neurotic—I am an M.A. myself. A professor could remain at the age of 10 emotionally. What the emotional level of the British Cabinet or the American Pentagon is is anyone's guess; my own guess is a low one. Today in any school anywhere it is the head that is educated; every exam paper proves the point.

Now one cannot flee from reality. I could not say to prospective parents, "Exams and school subjects are not education and I refuse to teach the ordinary school subjects." That is what the Americans would call flunking out, and, by the way, I get too many letters from students in the U.S.A. saying, "I can't go on with my college career. The teaching is too dull; I am flunking out. I want to be a child psychologist." I answer that they won't let one be a child psychologist unless one accepts their qualification demands. I wrote to the last man who had flunked out, "If you haven't the guts to walk through the muck heaps, how can you ever expect to smell the roses you value so much?"

I do not find this flunking-out element in old Summerhill pupils. One of my first pupils spent two years standing at a mechanical belt in a car factory. He is now a successful engineer with his own business. His brother who wanted to be a doctor had to pass an exam in Latin. In just over a year he passed the matriculation exam in Latin. "I hated the stuff but it was in my way and I had to master it." That was over 40 years ago when students did not as a rule flunk out. I do not think that youth has become defeatist; rather it is that society has reached a point of futility and cheapness and danger where youth, frustrated by the mundane standard of success, simply gives up in despair. "Make Love not War" is a most appropriate motto for youth even if youth feels it is a hopeless cry, and it is a hopeless cry; the hate men who make wars force youth to die for country but when the young demand freedom to have a sex life, holy hypocritical hands are held up in horror. Youth is free to die but not to live and love.

I fear I am rambling, not sticking to the point. My consolation—too many who stick to the point make it a blunt one. I ramble because I am trying to evaluate Summerhill as a factor in the sick world, really asking what value freedom has for youth. One is naturally apt to think that one's geese are swans; one tends to forget or ignore the outside world, so that when a lecturer in education in an American college wrote and told me that over 70 per cent of his students thought that Summerhill was all wrong it came as a shock. I had repressed the idea that when the young are conditioned and indoctrinated from cradle days, it is almost impossible for them to break away, to challenge. Few can stand alone without a supporting crowd behind them. "The strongest man is he who stands most alone." Ibsen.

I like to think that freedom helps one to stand outside the maddening crowd. Symbolically one sees differences. The conventional suburban office-goer with his striped trousers and his neat tie and his neater mind on one side. On the other, the creator, the artist to whom exterior things mean but little. Compare the tailoring of L. B. J. with that of a film director or a Picasso. Symbols, but characteristic. Put it this way: Summerhill gets hundreds of visitors but I do not think that any visitor ever notices that my staff never wear ties. Summerhill hasn't got to the Old-School-Tie stage. But one cannot carry such phantasying too far; my old friend Bertrand Russell wears a tie, and no one would claim that he is a crowd man.

I think that one aspect of Summerhill is that it, rightly or wrongly, gives pupils an anti-crowd psychology. I could not imagine any old pupil following a Hitler or for that matter a Kennedy or a Reagan. This sounds incongruous because the chief feature of Summerhill is the self-government, the making of laws by one and all from the age of five to 84. Pupils become ego-conscious and at the same time community-conscious. Bill can do what he likes all day long as long as he does not interfere with the freedom of anyone else; he can sleep all day if he wants to but he is not allowed to play a trumpet when others want to talk or sleep. It is as near democracy as one can get; every child is a member of parliament able to speak "in the house." No doubt because this democracy is real and honest our old pupils cannot tolerate the sham we name politics. Because politicians have to rely on votes nearly every urgent reform is delayed for two generations. In England an M.P. has —say—a predominantly Catholic constituency or a Baptist one. How can he act honestly when faced with some reform—a bill to abolish punishment for homosexuality, a much-needed reform of the divorce and abortion laws? Was any great man a politician? Any Darwin, any Freud, any Einstein, any Beethoven? Was any big man ever a crowd-compeller, a demagogue?

When children are free they become wonderfully sincere. They cannot act a part; they cannot stand up in the presence of a school inspector because they will not countenance insincerity and make-believe. Tact forces them to make minor adaptations as it does with you and me. I dutifully doff my hat to a lady although I realize that it is a meaningless, even dishonest, gesture, hiding the fact that in a patriarchal society a woman is inferior in status, in pay, in power. To tell a social white lie is often a necessity but to live a lie is something that free people cannot do. And my pupils feel that to be a member of a crowd must involve living a lie.

This crowd psychology angle is important. It is at the root of the sickness of the world. A neighboring country insults your flag and many thousands of young men die for the honor and glory of their fatherland. National hatreds everywhere, Greek v. Turkey; Israel v. Arabs; Rhodesian white v. Black. And it is not only the nationalism crowd. Our football grounds are full of irrational, partisan hate and violence. Gang warfare is not confined to Chicago. Yet in a way violence is minor. It is the violence that a crowd inflicts on its members that frightens, the violence of intimidating, of molding. A school uniform means: We are members of a crowd, a crowd that will not tolerate opposition. We must all dress alike, think alike, act alike. For the great law of any crowd is: Thou shalt conform. The world is sick because its crowds are sick.

Education therefore should aim at abolishing crowd psychology. It can do this only by allowing the individual to face life and its choices freely. Such an education cannot lead to egocentricity and utter selfishness, not if the individual is free within the confines of the social order, an order made by himself. The slogan "All the way with L. B. J." shows the iniquity of the crowd, a system that makes crowd members sheep who can feel the most elementary emotions without having the intellectual capacity to connect such emotions with reason. Today our schools educate the head and leave the emotions to the crowd-compellers—the press, the radio, the TV, the churches, the commercial exploiters with their lying advertisements. Our pop heroes and film stars have become our leading schoolmasters, dealing with real emotions. What teacher in what school could have a few hundred hysterical females screaming their heads off when he appeared?

The danger today is undeveloped emotion, perverted emotion, infantile emotion. Millions scream in Britain every Saturday afternoon when their favorite football teams take the field. If the evening paper had a front page in big lettering "Atom War Very Near," most of the spectators would turn to the back page to see the latest scores. Crowd emotions are not touched by news of starvation in India or China. It is this same unattached unrealized emotion that makes the crowd numb to any realization of a likely atomic war. Crowd emotion is not shocked by our inhuman and un-Christlike treatment of criminals in prison; it does not even realize that the inhumanity is there. And none of us is guiltless. I do not cut down my tobacco and give the savings to the starving nations. We are all in the trap and only the more aware of us try to find a way out. My own way is Summerhill or rather the idea behind Summerhill, the belief that man is originally good, that, for reasons no one so far knows, man kills his own life and the lives of his children by harsh and anti-life laws and morals and taboos. It is so easy to cry, "Man is a sinner and he must be redeemed by religion" or what not. God and the Devil were comfortable explanations of good and evil. One thing I think Summerhill has proved is that man does not need to become a "sinner," that man does not naturally hate and kill. The crowd in Summerhill is a humane one. In 47 years I have never seen a jury punish a child for stealing; all it demanded was that the value of the theft be paid back. When children are free they are not cruel. Freedom and aggression do not go together. I have known a few children who were reared with self-regulation, that is, without fear and outside discipline and imposed morality. They seem to have much less aggression than most children have, suggesting to me that the Freudians with their emphasis on aggression must have studied the wrong children.

Even in Summerhill, where very few pupils were self-regulated, there is a peacefulness, a minimum of criticism, a tolerance that is quite uncommon. When a Negress pupil came from the States not even the youngest child seemed to notice her color. Our TV showed white faces full of hatred when black pupils were being stoned in the Deep South. This is alarming. We can condition children to hate and kill by giving them a hate environment. But we can also give them another sort of environment—were I a Christian I'd call it a love-your-neighbor environment. But then, what is a Christian? Catholics and Protestants beat children in home and school—didn't Jesus say suffer the little children? The Christians see that they suffer, all right. But to narrow the life negation to religion is wrong. A humanist can hate life and children; he can be as anti-sex as any Calvinist.

Summerhill has not answered many questions, the biggest one being: Why does humanity kill the life of children, why does it take more easily to hate than to love? Why did jackboot Fascism conquer a nation of 60 million?

One answer to the question of world sickness is sex repression. Make sex a sin and you get perversions, crime, hates, wars. Approve of children's sex as the Trobriand Islanders did under a matriarchal system and a Malinowski will fail to find any trace of sex crime or homosexuality before the missionaries came and segregated the sexes. Wilhelm Reich, to me the greatest psychologist since Freud, dwelt on the necessity for a full natural orgastic life as a cure for the sickness of an anti-life society. Then came the new American Interpersonal Relationship school of Sullivan and Horney, with long case histories of patients who seemed to have no sex at all. I have a book on problem children written by an Adlerian; I failed to find the word sex in it. And in all this divergence of views on sex, what can one believe? One can make the guess that the torturers of German Jews were sex perverts, but can one safely conclude that the men in the Pentagon are Hawks because of their sex repressions?

I have gone through many phases in the last 50 years, the most exciting my long friendship with Homer Lane and then with Reich. Now, at 84, I simply do not know the truth about sex. Is a teacher who canes a boy's bottom a repressed homosexual or a sadist or simply a man who has never been conscious of what he is doing? I ask because my father in his village school tawsed children with a leather strap and when I became a teacher I automatically did likewise without ever once wondering if it were good or bad. Looking back now I see that one motive was fear, fear of losing one's dignity, one's power; fear that any slackness would lead to anarchy. I cannot see anything sexual in my tawsing.

Summerhill society is a sex-approving society. Every child soon learns that there is no moral feeling about masturbation or nudism or sex-play. But every adolescent is conscious of the fact that if approval meant the sharing of bedrooms by adolescents the school would be closed by the Establishment. One old boy once said to me: "The fear of closing the school if pregnancies occurred gave us a new form of sex repression." The difficulty was and is this: How far can a school go in being pro-sex in an anti-sex society? Not very far, I fear. Yet one factor is of moment; the pupils are conscious of our attitude of approval. They have had no indoctrination about sin or shame, no moralizing from Mrs. Grundy. Their free attitude shows itself in minor ways. In our local cinema a film showed a chamber pot. The audience went into fits of obscene laughter but our pupils did not even smile; one or two asked me later why the people laughed. Free children cannot be shocked— by cruelty, yes, but by sex, never.

Summerhill products are often said to be quiet, unaggressive, tolerant citizens, and I wonder how much their rational attitude on sex has to do with their calmness of life. They prove that censorship is the product of a life-hating civilization. I never see our adolescents taking from the school library

Lady Chatterley or *Fanny Hill*. A girl of 16 said they were boring.

Most of our old pupils are pacific. They do not march with banners against the H-bomb or against racial discrimination. I cannot imagine any of them ever supporting warmongers or religious revivalists or play censors. But how much this has to do with a free attitude to sex I cannot know. Certainly sex is the most repressed of all emotions. Most of us were made anti-sex when in our cradles our hands were taken from our genitals, and it is an arresting thought that the men who have the power to begin a nuclear war are men who were made sex-negative long ago. Anglo-Saxon four-letter words are still taboo in most circles, maybe partly for class reasons; a navvy says fuck while a gentleman says sexual intercourse.

I confess to being muddled about the whole affair of sex. I do not know if we all experienced Reich's perfect orgasm there would be an end to war and crime and hate. *I hae ma doots.* Yet it is true that people who have a pro-sex attitude to life are the ones most likely to be charitable, to be tolerant, to be creative. Those who do not consider themselves sinners do not cast the first stone. For charity I would go to Bertrand Russell rather than to Billy Graham.

Billy naturally leads to religion. Summerhill has no religion. I fancy that very few religionists approve of it. A leading Church of England priest once called it the most religious school in the world, but few parsons would agree with him. It is interesting to note that I have had many letters of approval from Unitarians in the U.S.A. I asked one Unitarian minister what his religion was. Did he believe in God? No, he said. In eternal life? "Good heavens, no. Our religion is giving out love in this life," and I guess that is exactly what the Church of England priest meant. It is our being on the side of the child (Homer Lane's phrase) that has aroused so much antagonism among religionists. The other day a Catholic school inspector told a meeting of Catholics that corporal punishment was practiced much more in their schools than in Protestant ones. "We beat the body to save the soul." In the days of that life-hater John Knox I would have been burned at the stake. The widening interest in the freedom that Summerhill stands for fits in with the lessening belief in religion. Most young people, outside the R.C. faith, have no interest in religion. To them God is dead. God to them was father, molder, punisher, a fearful figure. The gods and fathers were always on the side of the suppressors. In Britain the enemies of youth, those who call for the return of beating with the cat, those who want to censor plays and films and language, those who demand strict punishment for the teen-age delinquents, they are not the young;

they are the old, the old who have forgotten their teen-age period.

I am sure that the growing interest in freedom for children coincides with modern youth's rejection of a joyless, repressive religion. A religion that has become perverted. Christ's "love your neighbor as yourself" has become: Okay, so long as he isn't a Jew or a Black. "Let him who is without sin among you cast the first stone" has become: Censor plays and novels and measure bathing costumes. Owing to the threat of universal incineration youth today is possibly more pro-life than it has ever been. Juvenile crime is really at bottom an attempt to find the joy of life killed by morals and discipline and punishment. In the days when Summerhill had many delinquents they went out cured simply because they were free from adult standards of behavior. Religion must be rejected because it tells the young how to live, but it does not need to be religion; I have known humanists who gave their children sex repression; I know agnostics who believe in beating children. Really what one believes does not matter; it is what one is that matters. After all religion is geographical; had I been born in Arabia I'd have had three wives and, alas, no whisky.

There is a comic element in religion even if there isn't a joke in the Bible or the Prayer Book. The true believer must know that Bertrand Russell will roast in hell for eternity while Billy Graham sits at the right hand of God. With Russell to look after, the familiar words "poor Devil" will have a real significance.

What is the outlook for freedom? Will the minority ever take over from the majority? And if it does, will it retain its belief in freedom? Doesn't Ibsen say somewhere that a truth remains a truth for 20 years, then the majority takes it up and it becomes a lie? Summerhill has 64 children who are free from molding: the world has millions of children who have little or no freedom, millions of adults who frankly are sheep. One tragedy of life is that men have followers. Men who remain disciples are always inferiors. The Pharisee who thanked God that he was not as other men may have been a conceited ass but on the other hand he may have got hold of something. There is something wrong when millions who praise the Beatles never heard of Milton or Freud or Cézanne, when millions kill the life of their babies, when thousands of young men die in a battle for they know not what. Anti-life is all around us, and I wish I knew why. I wish I knew why mankind kills what it loves. I do not know the answer; all I know is that when children are free they do not kill life; they do not condemn their fellow men. They do not want to tell others how to live. It is significant that old pupils do not seek jobs where they will boss others; few have gone into business. I used to daydream of one's becoming a tycoon and endowing the school, knowing all the time that he would be so hard-boiled that he would not endow anything.

I am not trying to sell Summerhill. I am trying to say that the cure for the sickness of man does not lie in politics or religion or humanism; nay, the cure is freedom for children to be themselves. Like many others I once thought that the Russian Revolution would bring Utopia to youth, for it began with freedom for children, self-government in the schools. Then, according to Reich, the psychologists took charge and youth became sacrificed to political anti-life, so that today communism has no connection with individual freedom to grow naturally. Indeed I often wonder why the Americans are so scared of communism. Both systems believe in the terror of the bomb; both discipline and castrate children; both believe that education means subjects and exams and acquired knowledge. The only difference I can see is who takes the profit? The Russian Revolution proved that the sickness of the world cannot be cured by politics.

The only answer that I can think of is freedom for children, individual freedom, social freedom, sexual freedom as in a small way practiced in Summerhill.

I said that I thought Wilhelm Reich the greatest psychologist since Freud. His diagnosis of man's sickness is deep and wise. Man flees from natural sex by armoring himself against joy in life, stiffening his body, fearing any signs of genitality, changing good emotions into "emotional plague," in short, becoming anti-life, hence wars and many diseases and child-beating. Even if one accepts Reich's diagnosis the question arises: What can be done about it? How can we prevent folks from becoming anti-sex and anti-life? Analysis of any school is not the answer. What effect on humanity have all the case histories ever published? Do all the things Melanie Klein found in babies have any bearing on the education of children? So far psychology has been a matter of diagnosing without any salient suggestions for a cure. Ah, yes, some cases of cures of individual neurotics, but the cure for a sick world, none. A Scientologist has just told me that he could cure any problem child in my school in 10 days.

Are we all fakers? Self-deluders? Do the hundreds of books on psychology published every year have any effect at all? I am inclined to say none, but I am biased, for I cannot read a book on psychology now.

The psychologists have narrowed the science—or is it an art? The doctors have limited psychology to the consulting room and the rich and those with time to spare. How many psychoanalysts have opened schools? A few—Anna Freud, Susan Isaacs, e.g., but the main body of Freudians has done nothing in the way of prophylaxis. The Summerhill Society of New York issues a list of schools claiming to have self-regulation and self-government. Some may be excellent but, as I have not seen any of them, I cannot give an opinion pro or anti. I do not think that they belong to any special schools of psychology and I sincerely hope that they don't. I am sure that the list does not contain the name of the school that claimed to be Summerhillian and washed out a boy's mouth with soap and water when he swore.

The future of psychology should lie not in the consulting room or the hospital for neurosis but in the infant bedroom and the infant school. Mr. Brown's phobia of spiders may fascinate his analyst but his phobia is as nothing in a world of millions of half-alive children.

To return to Summerhill, it went through the stages of the Century—the faith in analysis, the futile attempt to find the original trauma in a young thief. I read them all—Freud, Jung, Adler, Rank, Stekel, Reich—and got more and more confused by their psychological jargon. I never learned the meaning of words like manic-depression, compulsive neurosis, hysteria, etc. Never knew how specialists could draw the line between one and another. Oh, so many were brilliant in their diagnosis and treatment, but in the end what did one learn? And today I feel as confused about the Interpersonal Relationship folks, for, if men like Stekel seemed to overemphasize sex, they seem to denigrate it altogether. So I left schools of thought and concentrated on Summerhill, forgetting theory and avoiding words like complex. "Everyone is right in some way," Reich used to say, the corollary being that everyone is wrong in some way.

Let us face the truth, that we are all little men, even the greatest among us. We do not know how and why the super Rolls Royce, the human body, ticks. We know nothing about life and how it began, nor can we account for the universe. We do not know why Brown dies of cancer and his brother of diabetes. In the psychological realm we cannot account for a Bach or a Milton or a Hitler. We know little about heredity or the origins of love and hate. A doctor does not know what causes a headache. So that we should be wary of panaceas of all kinds—Zen Buddhism, Scientology, Theosophy, psychoanalysis, Moral Rearmament, and a few score of other isms and ologies. We must go on enquiring, searching for the truth, but if we follow a creed, if we become disciples, if we label ourselves Freudian or Reichian or Hubbardian or any other ian we have stopped growing, stopped enquiring; we become "yes" men. It worries me to hear of schools in the U.S.A. that call themselves Summerhills. One should take from others what one feels is good. No one should accept any creed, religious or political or psychological. I got much from Homer Lane; later I got much from Reich. But in both men were views that I could not accept, and thus I escaped discipleship. If a teacher claims that Summerhill inspired him, good, I wish him luck, but if a school claims to be a new Summerhill I fear it will fail. There is a pioneer in each of us, an explorer, a visionary. As in sport we pay others to play the game for us, so in pioneering; we find it easy to look for a leader and be content to be a humble follower of Billy Graham, Sigmund Freud, Barry Goldwater, Karl Marx. Fans are arrested creators, arrested pioneers. And the big question is: in a world in which the vast majority are fans, how can a few independent people set about "curing" the Establishment?

We must remember that the Establishment has the ultimate power. A bureaucratic Ministry of Education could close my school on material grounds alone: not enough lavatories, not enough cubic feet per child in a bedroom. But, to be fair, the Ministry has not interfered with me in the 44 years Summerhill has been in England. But now that the National Union of Teachers and many Labor M.P.s demand the closing of all private schools, pioneering in education is going to have a bad time. Had there been no private schools there could not have been a Summerhill; the State, the Establishment will allow new methods of teaching history or maths but it is unlikely to tolerate new methods of living in a school. Really I should vote Tory, for the Tories will not lightly give up their Etons and Harrows, and as long as we have the public schools like Rugby the smaller private schools will be protected. Alas, the private school is I fear doomed by lack of finance alone. Summerhill would have died seven years ago had not the publication of *Summerhill* in the U.S.A. brought a flood of American pupils. Today people in England do not have the money to support private schools. Those who do, select the established schools, the public schools and the big co-ed schools with their well-equipped libraries, labs, etc. Parents, like teachers, still look on education as learning in all countries East and West. Educational journals seldom mention the child or freedom or creation. When I write a letter about the teaching of English I get quite a few replies, but when I write an article on the psychology of the child no teacher answers.

I want to claim that Summerhill has for 47 years demanded that character is of more moment than the ability to learn subjects. I have never denigrated learning; all I have done is to put it in its second or 10th place. But what effect the school has had on education I cannot judge. Some say that the permissiveness of some schools stems from Summerhill. Who can know? I like to think that it isn't Summerhill, that it is the *Zeitgeist*, the longing of youth for freedom. Maybe some *History of Education* in the year 2000 will have a footnote about a school called Summerfield run by a mad Scot called S. A. Neale. Sorry I won't be there to laugh at the footnote.

We recently had the opportunity to visit Summerhill and to talk with A. S. Neill. Neill is a relaxed man, and Summerhill is a relaxed and relaxing place because of the one outstanding factor that keeps Summerhill going! *Neill likes children!*

Another person who likes children is Mary Northway. And her ideas about children are similar to Neill's. Perhaps not as extreme in some aspects, they lean in the same direction. These ideas are based on her own years of experience with children at the University of Toronto Institute of Child Study. We wish that we could include the entire book, *Laughter in the Front Hall*, but this brief essay will convey its spirit, and perhaps you will wish to get the book (it's just a little one) and read it all.

13

FASTER! FASTER!

MARY L. NORTHWAY

'Now! Now!' cried the Queen. 'Faster! Faster!'

You may remember that after Alice had run as fast as she could, she found herself under the same tree she had started from. 'Well, in *our* country,' said Alice . . . , 'you'd generally get to somewhere else—if you ran very fast for a long time. . . .'

'A slow sort of country' said the Queen. 'Now, *here*, you see, it takes all the running *you* can do, to keep in the same place. If you want to get somewhere else, you must run at least twice as fast as that!'

Nowadays, everyone seems to be living in the 'Looking Glass' country. We not only go faster and faster, but we feel there is some moral virtue in so doing. We boast of having driven three thousand miles in six days, but say little of what

SOURCE: Reprinted from *Laughter in the Front Hall* by Mary L. Northway. Copyright 1966 by Longman Canada Limited.

we saw on the way. We are proud of having attended ten committee meetings in a week, but hate to admit we enjoyed any of them. We exult in the fact that we obtained our Ph.D. or became assistant manager at an earlier age than any other candidate. Conversely, we are reluctant to admit that we spent an evening sitting at home; if we do find time to stand and stare, we assume that it is a sin to waste time—we would never admit that it might be a sin to waste energy. Like the busy bee, we feel we must improve each shining hour, forgetting that the bee is as conscious of the sunshine and the nectar as of his efforts at self or social improvement. Our race to come first, to get ahead, usually takes us back to the same tree, having achieved only breathlessness, fatigue, ulcers or a neurosis, on the way; we have had no time to enjoy the view.

The faster-faster principle is deeply embedded in our cultural pattern, however, and if we adults choose to ride on a continuously accelerating merry-go-round, that is our business. We obtain the illusion of progress; if we are fast enough, we may even catch the 'ring,' in which case we can travel onward again, until finally we become at best bored, and at worst dizzy. But when we put our children on the merry-go-round, we all too often drive them to nothing but distraction. When we force them to run faster-faster, they become anxious, tired, and a little crabby. They would rather have stayed where they were, playing under the tree.

Parents hurry children and judge their worth according to a law of conservation of time and expenditure of energy. The child who can read at four years is deemed better than the child who reads at six, even though they both read only comics. The child who has made many friends is considered better than the child who has made few. The child who dawdles, and thus violates the folkways of 'getting on with the job,' is thought to present a problem so serious that it requires special consideration at the Institute's parent-education meetings. To help our children conform to the faster-faster principle, we arrange each hour of their day with worth-while activities: music lessons, dancing classes, sports, art classes, extra reading, and supervised play.

But parents are no more inculcated with the hurry-up approach than are psychologists. For years, these scientists have been conducting experiments on learning, with both children and animals. Through these experiments, they have unquestionably assumed that learning can be evaluated in terms of the speed with which it has been acquired. Rats who are slow to find the cheese, or children who take a long time in learning vulgar fractions, are said to be stupid. No one suspects that both the rats and the children may simply have been wise enough to know that both cheeses and fractions could wait, and that there were more interesting things to do and see en route to these laudable goals.

It is too much to suggest that we all stop running and sit under the tree where we are—such an incredible idea would disrupt our cultural pattern more drastically than an invasion. But without being considered a social revolutionist, could I hesitantly advocate a play-time, freedom-from-hurry plan? Could play become play again instead of 'organized recreation'? Could camps provide periods for dabbling and dawdling, instead of days filled with instructional periods and interest groups? Could we abolish badges for achievement and bestow them for enjoyment? Could we proclaim one day a year on which everyone did exactly as he liked—and even the clocks ceased to run? Could we give our children, if not ourselves, the privilege of believing that the process is more important than the product, that the journeying is as significant as the destination? Could we help them to discover that they learn to live, rather than live to learn? Can't the curriculum of living provide its real recesses?

Such thoughts .are not mere facetious wanderings of the imagination. I honestly feel that the pressures placed on the child of today to 'get on,' to 'make good,' to 'do well,' to 'maintain and surpass standards,' place heavy strains on his development. All too easily, the child learns to conform to our demand that he run faster-faster. In doing so, he often misses the beauty of the world around him, and in the end he may discover that the prizes of the race are only baubles; or the strain on his psychological muscles may be so great that he becomes a deformed or broken creature.

Perhaps it is too late to teach ourselves, but we might teach our children that it is never a waste of time to waste time, and that incessant running leaves you at the same tree, the only difference being that you are now tired, hot, and thirsty, and neither able to enjoy the beauty that is around you nor to explore at ease the surrounding country-side.

Mary Northway pleads that children be given the right to develop at a natural rate and to enjoy the process. In our next selection, the Russells speak of the "creative frankness" of children and make a plea that an attempt be made to retain that enthusiasm, that "fire," into the adult years. Oldsters have been told frequently that they are past redemption when they pass thirty. Now we find the writers of a psychology book saying that "all too little flicker remains in all too many of us by the age of thirty."

Actually, they lead us into a later chapter in which creativity is discussed at greater length.

14

FREEDOM AND ROUTINE
CLAIRE RUSSELL AND W. M. S. RUSSELL

The paintings produced by almost all young children have two things in common. They are technically inexpert, but they are vivid and imaginative. Sooner or later, a change takes place in the paintings of all children who are not destined to be Rembrandts or Picassos. Technically there may be some improvement: principles of perspective may have been inculcated, and the rules of colour mixing. But this is regularly accompanied by a loss of vigour and imaginative abandon. 'One can trace the gradual process of growing up, with its gain in realism and skill. Unfortunately this is often accompanied by a corresponding loss in spontaneity' (Nairn, 1957). One can watch this process at a glance in any good exhibition of children's art where the age-groups are shown in different rooms of a gallery. One simple criterion will serve to illustrate the change (Morris, personal communication): the paintings of the younger children fill the whole of the paper available, a sufficient sign of confident exuberance.

As people grow up, the great majority cease to paint at all. Of those who continue to do so, only a handful of individuals in any generation retain the imaginative freedom of the child while acquiring a new mastery of technique. Among the handful, of course, are the great painters of history. 'Now and then the creative frankness may with care be preserved, to become one of the greatest assets a painter can possess' (Nairn, 1957). For most of us, the situation is all too like that of Alice in Wonderland. When we are small, we cannot reach the key of technical assurance; when we are bigger we cannot squeeze through the door into the garden of creative imagination.

. . . An experienced adult actor who appears with a child may be acted off the stage or screen. We can watch the same trend in mime, in dancing, in musical performance. Children show an unrivalled gift for accurate observation and for com-

SOURCE: Abridged from *Human Behaviour*, London: Andre Deutsch, 1961. Pp. 11–15. Reprinted by permission of David Higham Associates, Ltd.

municating what they observe through all the media of human expression. It was the little boy in the Anderson story who both saw and said that the Emperor had no clothes on. One telling illustration comes from an unexpected source—the experience of the police. In his book *Crime and the Police* (1951), Martienssen discusses the differences between witnesses. 'Children,' he writes, 'are generally the best witnesses of all. They are unaffected by preconceived adult ideas and they usually describe exactly what they have seen.'

In other words, young human individuals are full of varied and versatile creative potential; few, when adult, realize more than a tithe of this potential in even one pursuit; vanishingly few, like Leonardo da Vinci, retain their versatility. The more one confronts these facts, the greater the impression that human attainment, wonderful as it is, falls far short of what it could be. Nor is this impression in any way contradicted by what we know and conjecture of the function of the human brain—even the bare numerical aspect. The number of nerve cells in the human nervous system is of the order of ten thousand million. 'All artificial automata made by man' [such as the giant computing machines] 'have numbers of parts which by any comparable schematic count are of the order of' a thousand to a million (Von Neumann, 1951). The conclusion seems inevitable that practically every adult is using only a fraction of his brain for constructive purposes.

This appears in other, at first sight less tangible, ways. Everyone must have tried to find words for the enthusiasms and ambitions of the young—one speaks of the 'fire' of youth, or uses some kindred metaphor. 'The Youth . . . by the vision splendid is on his way attended; at length the Man perceives it die away, and fade' into a monotonous routine of life. One still meets, of course, adults who seem to retain this fire—concentrated, perhaps, in some special furnace: artists, scientists, engineers, technicians, industrialists, statesmen (like Sir Winston Churchill), craftsmen (amateur or professional), workers in any field who enjoy what they are doing. But all too little flicker remains in all too many of us by the age of thirty.

It is a problem of central importance, whether this deterioration is *necessary*, whether all Miltons but one must remain mute and inglorious; whether, with Shelley, we must contemplate

> *many a Newton, to whose passive ken*
> *Those mighty spheres that gem infinity*
> *Were only specks of tinsel, fixed in Heaven,*
> *To light the midnights of his native town!*

The poets were thinking chiefly, perhaps, of economic obstacles, of poverty, of lack of opportunity. There is no doubt that, as opportunity spreads, much creative talent is being released; there is little doubt that economic pressures in the past have deprived us of many achievements. Perhaps, for one thing, they helped to rob us of half the incomparably fertile life of Mozart. But the vision fades for rich no less than for poor, and despite economic improvement it continues to fade as relentlessly as ever.

Perhaps we cannot all be Miltons or Newtons, still less Darwins or Shakespeares, but need the differential be so great, and cannot the whole fellowship of mankind move upwards on the scale of versatility and imagination? Perhaps, more to the point, we do not all want to be Darwins or Shakespeares. But what we have been saying applies to other things than science and the arts. It applies to everything that makes for anyone's happiness.

Move the starting-point a little later in life, and we see the same process at work in human relationships; most obviously, perhaps, in those between the sexes. 'Falling in love,' as we shall see later, is a term that covers a multitude of unhappy and destructive states of mind. Falling in love with Carmen is like falling in love with cocaine. But the term is also used of a quite different experience, the experience, in most intense form, of Romeo and Juliet. Many couples are in love in this vital and positive sense, for a longer or shorter period. While the mood lasts, they enjoy a heightened awareness not only of their own sexual wishes, but of all their sensations. The fiery imagination of childhood returns, enriched with new colours. Between the two partners there is a rapid and liberating interchange of thought and feeling, expressed not only in love-making itself but in all aspects of their relationship. In few couples does this second dawn persist for long in its full splendour. For too many, their relationship subsides into a routine, or gives place to others, equally short-lived. Nor is this trend confined to sexual relationships. The young respond eagerly to the great variety of social intercourse; the older are apt to settle into grooves of social interaction, in which nothing is really interchanged and each pursues his own routine, which merely meshes with those of his companions. The members of such a group may go to bed with each other in rotation; or they may play bridge; or they may exchange predictable arguments in the pub. . . .

We know very well that social relations need not be like this—if only from what we can observe in the special condition of emergency. Not long ago the news-reels showed a fire in Oxford Street. Before the Brigade had even arrived, a magnificent piece of rescue work was organized and executed, with lightning speed and perfect efficiency, by an ordinary London crowd. For those brief moments, these individuals, strangers to each other and to those in danger, responded with alert awareness to their fellows and the situation. Everyone who remembers the last war can remember also the exceptional atmosphere of friendliness and mutual interest, which broke all usual social distinctions and reticences. Here is another potential which normally 'fusts in us unused,' unless called into action by the otherwise undesirable stimulus of emergency.

These instances show that some, at least, of the capacities we have mentioned are, in most people, dormant rather than dead. . . .

But the question must be stated, and if possible answered, as generally and comprehensively as possible. A useful distinction has been made between 'ageing' as a mere increase of years and 'senescence' as that decline of vitality some of whose aspects we have been considering (Medawar, 1952). The question can now be fairly put: must senescence accompany ageing, and both, as Minot put it, start at birth? Must it, at all events, be so rapid and far-reaching in the province of human behaviour? There are two ways of approaching the problem, a problem vital for human happiness. One is to examine the whole nature of 'vitality,' 'fire,' 'imaginative freedom' and 'creative performance' in the context of behaviour, and in the light of what we may expect of something like the human brain. The other is to search for clear-cut factors which can be shown to cause or accelerate behavioural senescence, and to show that these factors can, in principle and even in practice, be controlled—and controlled by the individual.

REFERENCES

Martienssen, A. (1951). *Crime and the Police*. Secker and Warburg, London.

Medawar, P. B. (1952). *An Unsolved Problem of Biology*. Inaugural Lecture at University College London; Lewis, London.

Morris, D. personal communication.

Nairn, A. (1957). The Tenth National Exhibition of Children's Art. in: *Catalogue of National Exhibition Children's Art, 1957*, 4-5; publ. *Sunday Pictorial*.

Von Neumann, J. (1951). The General and Logical Theory of Automata, in: *Cerebral Mechanisms in Behavior*, ed. Jeffress, 1-31; John Wiley, New York; Chapman and Hall, London.

Artistic expression in its various forms is but one area in which humans change as they grow older. We need to ask several questions if we seek to come to an understanding of this area. Is deterioration necessary? If not, how can it be prevented? How much of the change that takes place is the result of inborn tendencies? How are these innate factors and environmental factors related? We have indicated that the child is most receptive to certain kinds of environmental stimuli at certain stages of development. What are the experiences that should be made available and at what ages or stages of development?

One phase of development is the emotional (and there will be more about this in a later chapter). Various experiences are meaningless to a child, until—until he is ready! If you doubt this, try to explain to a ten-year-old boy, in words only, the nature of a passionate kiss. If he truly understands a word you say, he is a most precocious child. Then, if you will, induce an attractive eighteen-year-old girl (woman) to kiss him passionately. If you wish to set up a controlled experimental situation, have her then try the same kiss on an eighteen-year-old boy (man). Will the reactions differ? We'll leave the answer to you.

The whole area of developmental psychology is extremely relevant to contemporary society. There is the much discussed issue of sex education. At what age should children be instructed in the facts of life? Or perhaps this question should be stated differently; at what age should formal sex instruction be begun if it is to keep ahead of what the child learns on the street and the playground?

How should schools be organized? Should all children be required to attend school? To what age? Or should all classroom instruction be optional for all children of all ages? Is the traditional age of six years the proper time to begin to teach a child to read? Or should we teach reading at five? Or four? Or even earlier? Or should we wait until the child is seven or eight?

Ask yourself: Was my early schooling fully satisfying to me? If I were to become a member of the Board of Education, what psychological principles would I invoke to justify what changes in the schools?

IN SEARCH OF NEW IDEAS

For an emphasis different from that which we have presented here, we suggest a recent article by Maya Pines, "A Child's Mind is Shaped Before Age 2," (*Life,* December 17, 1971). Also by Maya Pines, *Revolution in Learning: The Years from Birth to Six* (Harper and Row, 1967).

You will find varying points of view in a book edited by Morris and Natalie Haimowitz, *Human Development: Selected Readings*, 3rd edition (Thomas Y. Crowell Company, 1973).

To learn more about Summerhill, and if you have not already read it, try A. S. Neill, *Summerhill: A Radical Approach to Child Rearing* (Hart Publishing Company, 1960). For widely divergent opinions read *Summerhill: For and Against* (Hart Publishing Company, 1970). The very concept of Summerhill is controversial. If you become curious about what happens to Summerhill boys and girls when they become men and women, read Emanuel Bernstein, "What Does a Summerhill Old School Tie Look Like?" (*Psychology Today,* October, 1968). Genuine Summerhill fans, of whom there are many, will wish to read A. S. Neill's autobiography, *"Neill! Neill! Orange Peel!"* (Hart Publishing Company, 1972).

Our own students have told us that they have found John Holt's *How Children Fail* (Pitman Publishing Company, 1964) and *How Children Learn* (Pitman Publishing Company, 1967) both interesting and helpful. Students have also endorsed Haim Ginott's *Between Parent and Child* (Macmillan, 1965).

A recent article, "The Dangers of Early Schooling," by Raymond and Dennis Moore (*Harpers,* July, 1972) questions the policy of pushing children and states that there is "no conclusive proof that even the best known early-schooling plans are working, and there is considerable evidence that most are not." These writers go on to say that there is much research that indicates that late starters generally do better throughout school than do children who start early, and that early schooling may actually be damaging to the child.

Part Six

Perceiving: Guessing What's Out There

Each of us is constantly bombarded with stimuli from the world outside our bodies. First, of course, for us to *perceive* something, there must *be* something *out there.* But, just being there is not enough. It must be something that can be picked up by the body's receiving apparatus. It may be light waves; that is, provided they are within a restricted range. No matter how plentiful are ultraviolet or infrared waves, we cannot see them.

What's out there may be sound waves—again provided they are not too high in frequency, are not within the supersonic range. We are not able, directly and unaided, to pick up radio waves. In fact, we are insensitive to stimuli along most of the total energy spectrum. We are equipped to pick up certain portions of the visual spectrum, a wide range of sound waves, odors from certain volatile substances, chemical reactions from certain foods in the mouth. We receive the message when we are bumped, are turned upside down, are moved rapidly through space (until we adapt to it).

How do we know that a certain visual pattern means that there is a chair over there? Or that those particular sounds now invading the otherwise quiet of the living room mean that the fellow down the street has just revved up his motorcycle?

Perception, the process of perceiving, is something more than just the impinging of physical stimuli on certain sensitive membranes of the body. These stimuli, these patterns of light waves, of sound waves, of pressures and tastes and smells must be carried by the nerves to the central nervous system. They must become more than what William James called the "blooming, buzzing confusion" of the world of the newborn infant. They must, in some way, become meaningful. Only then are they of any value to us. We must make the best guess we can as to what *is* out there.

We tend to take all of this for granted. We cannot remember how or when we learned to interpret certain combinations of stimuli as meaning *apple pie,* or *airplane; mouse* or *mountain.* And, most of the time, we don't confuse them.

Let us, however, look at a bit of the world through the eyes of a person who is seeing something for the first time, who is being presented stimuli that have never before come to his senses.

15

SOME OBSERVATIONS REGARDING THE EXPERIENCES
AND BEHAVIOR OF THE BaMBUTI PYGMIES

COLIN M. TURNBULL

The identity of the BaMbuti Pygmies of the Ituri Forest in the Congo with the forest itself goes beyond their social life; they are also psychologically conditioned by their environment. This can best be illustrated by some observations that I made during a recent field trip in their country.

Distance- and size-perception

At the end of a particularly long and tiring period of trekking through the forest from one hunting group to another, I found myself on the eastern edge, on a high hill which had been cleared of trees by a missionary station. There was a distant view over the last few miles of forest to the Ruwenzori Mountains: in the middle of the Ituri Forest such views are seldom if ever encountered. With me was a Pygmy youth, named Kenge, who always accompanied me and served, amongst other capacities, as a valid introduction to BaMbuti groups where I was not known. Kenge was then about 22 yr. old, and had never before seen a view such as this. He asked me what the "things" before us were (referring to the mountains). "Were they hills? Were they clouds? Just what were they?" I said that they were hills bigger than any in his forest, and that if he liked we would leave the forest and go and see them and have a rest there. He was not too sure about this, but the BaMbuti are an incorrigibly curious people and he finally agreed. We drove by automobile in a violent thunderstorm which did not clear until we entered the Ishango National Park at the foot of the mountains and on the edge of Lake Edward. Up to that moment from the time we had left the edge of the forest, near Beni, visibility had been about 100 yd.

As we drove through the park the rain stopped and the sky cleared, and that rare moment came when the Ruwenzori Mountains were completely free of cloud and stood up in the late afternoon sky, their snow-capped peaks shining in the sun. I stopped the car and Kenge very unwillingly got out. His first remark was to reiterate, what he had been saying ever since the rain stopped and we could see around us, that this was a very bad country, there were no trees. Then he looked up at the mountains and was completely unable to express any ideas

SOURCE: Abridged from *American Journal of Psychology*, 1961, 74, 304–307.

—quite possibly because his language had no suitable terms, being limited to the experience of a strictly forest people. The snow fascinated him, he thought it must be some kind of rock. More important, however, was the next observation.

As we turned to get back in the car, Kenge looked over the plains and down to where a herd of about a hundred buffalo were grazing some miles away. He asked me what kind of insects they were, and I told him they were buffalo, twice as big as the forest buffalo known to him. He laughed loudly and told me not to tell such stupid stories, and asked me again what kind of insects they were. He then talked to himself, for want of more intelligent company, and tried to liken the buffalo to the various beetles and ants with which he was familiar.

He was still doing this when we got into the car and drove down to where the animals were grazing. He watched them getting larger and larger, and though he was as courageous as any Pygmy, he moved over and sat close to me and muttered that it was witchcraft. (Witchcraft, incidentally, is known to the BaMbuti only through association with the Bantu. They have no similar concept of the supernormal.) Finally when he realized that they were real buffalo he was no longer afraid, but what puzzled him still was why they had been so small, and whether they *really* had been small and had suddenly grown larger, or whether it had been some kind of trickery.

As we came over the crest of the last low hill, Lake Edward stretched out into the distance beyond, losing itself in a hazy horizon. Kenge had never seen any expanse of water wider than the Ituri river, a few hundred yards across. This was another new experience difficult for him to comprehend. He again had the same difficulty of believing that a fishing boat a couple of miles out contained several human beings. "But it's just a piece of wood," he protested. I reminded him of the buffalo, and he nodded unbelievingly.

Later we went all over the National Park with one of the African guides. He and Kenge conversed in KiNgwana, the *lingua franca* of the area, and Kenge was constantly looking out for animals and trying to guess at what they were. He was no longer afraid or unbelieving; he was trying to adapt himself, and succeeding, to a totally new environment and new experience.

The next day he asked to be taken back to the forest. He reverted to his original argument. "This is bad country, there are no trees."

The inability of the BaMbuti to correlate size-constancy and distance had never even struck me as a possibility. In the forest, vision is strictly limited to a matter of yards, the greatest distance one can see, when up a tree looking down onto a camp, being a hundred feet or more below. Kenge was, however, a sophisticated and well travelled Pygmy. He had been with me a long time, had travelled along roads where he could see for as much as a quarter of a mile, and had seen aircraft and knew that they contained people. Such instances, however, were rare, and on the whole his experience of visual distance was limited to the relatively slight diminution of size in seeing a person or people walking along a road a quarter of a mile away. He had seldom seen any animal from further away than a few yards, he had never seen any boat bigger than a dug-out canoe, and that no further away than a few hundred feet.

Number-perception
Size-perception is, however, only one of many phenomena of interest to the psychologist. The Pygmy, unless he is one who has constant dealings with the Bantu, is unable to count above four. He has, however, such an eye for patterns that, for example, if several arrows are taken from a bunch, he can detect the reduction and can usually replace the correct number withdrawn to bring the bunch to its original size. In a gambling game (*panda*) common in the region, up to 40 or so pebbles, seeds, or beans are thrown onto a mat. In a single glance the Pygmy can tell you if they form a multiple of four, or how many—one, two, or three—have to be added to make it into such a multiple. The game is a test of skill in number perception and manipulation. Spare beans are concealed between the fingers and toes, and as a player makes his throw, while the beans are still rolling on the mat, he has already made his calculation and added the requisite number from his concealed reserve to bring the total to the winning multiple.

Art:
(1) *Visual.* Another phenomenon worthy of study, and again associated with environmental influence, is the almost total lack of any form of physical art. The BaMbuti refer to white, black and red by color names, for other colors they make comparisons —"like leaves," "like leopards," instead of "green" or "yellow." They use red or blue-black dyes in the crude decoration of their bark cloths, smearing the dye on with their fingers. More complicated are the designs painted on the bodies of the girls and women, using the black stain obtained from the gardenia fruit. Except for these decorations, visual art is lacking. Wooden implements are never carved or decorated or even polished. Perhaps the world of the BaMbuti is too close around him, too confined and colorless, too much lacking in variety, to produce a visual art.

(2) *Auditory.* In contrast to this lack the Pygmy has the most complex music in the whole of Africa. It is complex not only in terms of rhythm, melody, and harmony (the latter surprising

enough in Africa), but also in terms of technique. The BaMbuti can improvise a 15 part liturgy or canon, with melodies frequently running in parallel seconds, and hold it without the slightest difficulty. When this gets too tame, they divide the melodic line up, note by note, among the performers, each of whom will hoot his note at the appropriate moment. The melody then travels counter-clockwise around the group who may be sitting about a central fire or even in the natural circle formed by their huts, each at his own hearth. There is obvious material here for anyone interested in esthetics, as well as for those who might be more interested in the relatively small part that vision plays in the life of these forest nomads. (Even when hunting, a great deal is done by hearing rather than seeing, and perhaps even smell is more important as a sense. Vision is used by the hunters in the examination of tracks, but the firing of an arrow is often done by sound rather than sight.) I should mention again that music permeates their whole life.

We see that the young Pygmy was unable to make the same guess, the same interpretation of his surroundings, as did his companion. Why did these interpretations differ? Why did the two men come up with different guesses? At least one of the reasons is that the previous experiences of the two observers were quite different.

Suppose we were to record all of our impressions from the time we were born. We could then have a record of the way in which new stimulus situations appeared to us as they came along. We could then discover how we learned to test our first interpretations of these stimuli against reality. We could, in this way, acquire a great amount of knowledge about the development of the perceptive process. But six-month-old infants don't write their memoirs. This valuable information is lost to us.

However, an accident many years ago, unfortunate though it was for the person sustaining it, proved to be a fortunate occurrence for learning something about the way in which perceptions develop. In this case the man involved, although an adult and with an adult's capacity to learn, had lost all memory. And, because he could no longer remember, even the commonest of sensations were largely without meaning to him. He virtually had to begin all over again to build his own perceptual world.

This case appears in an old book which was written about the rather rare phenomenon of *multiple personality*. This man, having lost all memory of who he was and what he was, had to build a new person of himself. Later, he regained the lost memories and for a time oscillated between being the new person he had become and the old person he had been before the accident.

Our reason for including the story is a different one. For our purposes portions of this case history tell us much about the way in which perceptions are developed.

16

THE HANNA CASE
BORIS SIDIS AND S. P. GOODHART

About seven o'clock in the evening of April 15, 1897, Rev. Thomas Carson Hanna, while returning home in his carriage from the town of M., attempted to alight in order to adjust the harness, lost his footing and fell to the ground head foremost. He was picked up in a state of unconsciousness by his brother, who, for some minutes, vainly endeavored to restore him. His eyelids were closed and his breathing faint. Not the slightest movement was noticeable, and, but for the feeble respiration, life seemed extinct.

Mr. Hanna was removed to the house of a friend and medical aid summoned. For a period of about two hours he lay in an unconsious state. Three attending physicians regarded life as almost extinct and heroic means of restoration were adopted.

. . . . .

Finally Mr. Hanna began to move, then opened his eyes, looked around, moved his arm, then sat upright in bed, arose, reached toward one of the physicians and attempted to push him. Thinking the patient in a state of delirium, and fearing an attack, they seized him and attempted to push him back upon the bed. Mr. Hanna resisted vigorously and a struggle ensued, in which the three physicians were considerably worsted. The Rev. Mr. Hanna is normally a strong man, but on this occasion his strength seemed herculean. He was finally overpowered, securely bound with straps and placed in bed. He lay perfectly quiet and made no attempts to release himself.

At the suggestion of a newcomer, Mr. C., the straps were

SOURCE: Abridged from *Multiple Personality*, New York: Appleton, 1904.

removed. The patient remained quiet and made no further attempt to rise.

Although Mr. Hanna's eyes were open and clear and he was looking about him in an apparently curious and inquisitive way, when spoken to he did not understand the meaning of the words. It was not only that he had lost the faculty of speech so that he could not answer the interrogations put to him, but he had also lost all power of recognition of objects, words and persons. He was in a state of complete mental blindness.

Although the functions of the sense-organs remained intact and the peripheral sensory processes remained normal, so that he experienced all the sensations awakened by external stimuli, yet there was a loss of all mental recognition and of interpretation of incoming sensations; all recognition of the external world was lost. Stimuli from without acted upon his sense-organs, gave rise to sensations, but perceptions and conceptions were entirely absent. The man was mentally blind. He could feel, but could not understand. He was as a newly born infant opening his eyes for the first time upon the world.

The world was to Mr. Hanna but a chaos of sensations, not as yet elaborated and differentiated into a system of distinct percepts and concepts; neither objects, nor space, nor time, in the form as they are presented to the developed adult mind, existed for him. So totally obliterated from memory were the experiences of his past life that even the requirements of the simplest mental processes by which the appreciation of distance, form, size, magnitude is acquired, were effaced from his mind.

Movement alone attracted his attention. He did not know the cause and meaning of movement, but a moving object fastened his involuntary attention and seemed to fascinate his gaze. He made as yet no discrimination between his own movements and those of other objects, and was as much interested in the movement of his own limbs as in that of external things. He did not know how to control his voluntary muscles, nor had he any idea of the possibility of such a control.

From the more or less involuntary, chance movements made by his arms and legs, he learned the possibility of controlling his limbs. The full voluntary power over his muscles he only learned from instructions by others. He could not co-ordinate the movements of his legs, hence he could not walk.

·   ·   ·   ·   ·

Although impressions were received by his sense-organs, still the only sensations prominent in his mind were darkness, light and color. Everything was close to his eyes,—objects near and far seemed equally distant.

. . . . .

When food was offered him he did not understand the purpose of it; nor when it was placed within his mouth did he know how to masticate and swallow it. In order to feed him, fluid nourishment had to be placed far back into the pharynx, thus provoking reflex swallowing movements.

. . . . .

It goes without saying that the very first objects for which he felt the most intense interest were those that had relations to the elementary and at the same time indispensable sensation for the maintenance of life, namely, hunger. Words denoting articles of food were the first he acquired for the purposes of intercommunication with his environment.

The first word he learned to know and to repeat was "apple." An apple was given to the patient when he was hungry and the attendant, pointing to the fruit, pronounced the word "apple" several times with great emphasis. The patient repeated "apple, apple," but did not grasp the import of the word as relating to this one particular object. To him "apple" was in a vague way associated with hunger and craving for food. When later he again became hungry, he called for "apple," but when the fruit was brought to him he rejected it in disgust. He wanted some of the other articles of food or dainties that had been given to him, but which were not "apple."

. . . . .

At first Mr. Hanna had no idea that there were terms for all classes of objects . . . . He had no idea of words having a universal significance, such as food, fruit, etc. He learned only the names of particular objects. He did not seem to learn words of universal import, words which would have been of far greater use to him. "When they had given me three or four things," he told us afterward, "I began to think there were other things to eat, too and *I wanted to learn the names of all those things*. If I had only known the word 'food' or 'eat' or any of those words."

Although Mr. Hanna was mentally blind and had lost all knowledge formerly possessed, both in relation to the external and internal world; although he was mentally reduced to a state of infancy, strange to say, his intelligence remained intact. His curiosity for acquiring knowledge was keener than ever, and the use of his acquisitions was truly astonishing. His faculty of judgment, his power of reasoning were as sound and vigorous as ever. The content of knowledge seemed to have been lost, but the form of knowledge remained as active as before the accident and was perhaps even more precise and definite.

·   ·   ·   ·   ·

It is highly instructive to follow Mr. Hanna's acquisition of knowledge of space. Immediately after the accident he was found to have no knowledge of space whatever. He possessed, however, sensations of color, of light, of shades, of darkness, but the concept of space was not present in his mind. He had no idea of distance and made efforts to grasp far-off objects, such, for instance, as ornaments and pictures that were beyond his reach.

To illustrate the total lack of appreciation of distance, we may mention his effort, one day while still confined to his bed, to grasp a distant tree perceived through the window. The tree was to him an object of interest, presented to his eye as a series of sensations attracting his attention, and he naturally endeavored by reaching out his hand, to get hold of it. Like an infant, he would not have hesitated to grasp the moon or take hold of a star.

Mr. Hanna, in the early stage of his secondary life, having as yet no perception of distance, had the sensation that everything was "close" to his eyes. The sense-elements, however, that go to make up the concept of space were present. Thus, he had some appreciation of room, volume. Shortly after recovering consciousness, with his eyes still closed, having none but internal sensations, and even of these no proper perception, he still had some idea of volume. He wondered how much room there could be, although he could not clearly formulate this idea. From constant efforts to reach objects, and from the many failures attending his early attempts, he gradually gained an idea of distance and learned the relation of objects to each other in space.

Mr. Hanna seemed to acquire the knowledge of space along with that of movement. At first he was not aware of the fact that he could control his muscles. He could not adapt and co-ordinate his movements to seize near and distant objects. He knew not how much force to put forth,—how much energy to exert to grasp objects of various size and weight. By daily effort, however, at first rather involuntary, by automatic movement and by constant exertion, the voluntary gradually emerging from the involuntary, Mr. Hanna learned to grasp objects—to feel and handle them—and thus the kinaesthetic sense was trained. The ideas of space and movement were so interlaced that their development seemed to go hand in hand.

. . . . .

He did not yet discriminate between his own movements and those outside himself. He gradually learned the difference between these two kinds of movement by the observation that he had control over his own movements, but not over those of others. This also was a basis originally of differentiation between himself and the external world.

. . . . .

He did not analyze a complicated object into its different qualitative components, simply because he lacked the knowledge of the individual constituents. This was well illustrated by the following amusing incident: He saw a man sitting in a carriage and driving a horse, and observing that all moved together, he regarded them as one object, one living being. Later on, learning that there were various kinds of beings, he thought a man mounted upon a bicycle was a kind of man different from those he was accustomed to see. When, however, he learned to know the objects separately, he gained the proper conception of each.

When he acquired knowledge of the existence of living beings, it was still hard for him to realize what persons really were in contradistinction to other living beings, and when he learned to differentiate the two, it was difficult for him to realize that he, too, was a person. Persons, he thought, moved about, while he was lying in bed; then, too, they were dressed, while he was not. The manner in which he learned that he, too, was a being like other people is interesting. Mr. Hanna, pointing to himself, asked an attendant, "people? people?" meaning to inquire whether he himself belonged to the same beings, and receiving an affirmative reply, he understood that he, too, was "people." Here again his imitative proclivity manifested itself in that he wished to be dressed and appear like other people. He was anxious to feel that he also was a person. To emphasize the fact to himself and others, and at the same time thinking this condition indispensable for personality, he was desirous of appearing dressed like those about him.

It was difficult for Mr. Hanna to realize that, although he was a person, still his personality differed from that of others. It was hard to convey to him the different shades of meaning of words that indicate consciousness of individuality. The ego or self-consciousness came rather late in his present mental development. He was certainly conscious and the activity of that consciousness was very intense. He was most eagerly taking in and elaborating impressions coming from the external world, impressions that were to him entirely new; still, the consciousness of self was for some time absent. It was only after prolonged efforts on the part of his teachers that he could grasp the meaning of words conveying the idea of personal relations.

We cannot discover directly from infants very much of anything about how they learn to interpret sensations. We have to turn to people like the BaMbuti Pygmy, Kenge, and Mr. Hanna for information. Informal observations such as these enable us, at least, to make some assumptions about the development of the process of perceiving.

It is also possible to explore the field of perception by using experimental methods. G. M. Stratton, back in the eighteen nineties and, more recently, Ivo Kohler, are among the many experimental psychologists who have studied the perceptual process. Some of the work of these two investigators is summarized in the next selection. The Stratton studies are genuine classics in psychology and the serious student may wish to go directly to them. Citations are given at the end of the selection.

17

IN TOPSY-TURVY LAND
GEORGE A. MILLER

The fact that the apparatus by which we learn about the world is itself in part a product of learning is demonstrated by our ability to relearn according to new rules. If the outcome of our perceptual transformations persists for a long enough time in looking strange and unusual, we may eventually come to terms with it. The remarkable extent of human plasticity was demonstrated by G. M. Stratton as early as 1896. Stratton constructed an optical headgear that rotated the visual field 180 degrees; not only was the world turned upside down, but left and right were reversed. It was a clumsy thing consisting of a tube eight inches long mounted in a plaster cast, but he wore it for eighty-seven

SOURCE: From pp. 117–119 in *Psychology: The Science of Mental Life* by George A. Miller. Copyright © 1962 by George A. Miller. By permission of Harper & Row, Publishers, Inc.

hours over a period of eight days, replacing it by a blindfold while he slept. His right eye could see through the tube, although the inverted field was greatly reduced in size; his left eye remained covered by the plaster cast. In spite of the inconveniences of this gadget, Stratton was able to make some instructive observations.

On his first day in topsy-turvy land he was thoroughly disoriented. His feet were above his head; he had to search for them when he wanted to see if he could walk without kicking things. His hands entered and left his field of view from above instead of from below. When he moved his head, his visual field swung rapidly in the same direction. He could not easily recognize familiar surroundings. He made inappropriate movements and could scarcely feed himself. In spite of nausea and depression he kept going and gradually he began to get accustomed to his rig. By the second day his movements had grown less laborious. By the third he was beginning to feel at home in his new environment. By the fifth day the world had stopped swinging when he moved his head; he was thinking about his body in terms of new images and was often able to avoid bumping into objects without thinking about them first. Most of his world was still upside down, but this didn't bother him much any more. Stratton commented that he did not modify his old conception of space; he simply suppressed it and learned a whole new set of visual-motor relations. His old, familiar conception of the world was no help to him. In fact, the conflict between the old and the new was the major obstacle he had to overcome. When the experiment was finished and he took the lenses out of the tube, he was again disoriented and bewildered for several hours before he became accustomed to the normal view of things.

Stratton's experiment has been repeated; there is no doubting the validity of his observations. The most extensive studies of this type have been reported by Ivo Kohler, who used either left-right or up-down reversals, but not both at the same time. The up-down reversal is easier to adapt to, but in both cases a person learns to make correct movements days or even weeks before he begins to perceive a scene as if it were normally oriented. Even then there are puzzling effects when one part of the scene looks normal but another part looks reversed; perceptual adaptation becomes complete only after many weeks of wearing the lenses.

These experiments demonstrate that a completely new relation between the visual world and the world of muscular movements can be learned in a relatively short period of time. The visual-motor relation we are accustomed to is not inviolate. It is simply something we have learned to live with.

REFERENCES

Kohler, I. Rehabituation in perspective. *Die Pyramide*, 1953, Nos. 5–7.

Stratton, G. M. Some preliminary experiments on vision without inversion of the retinal image. *Psychological Review*, 1896, *3*, 611–617.

Stratton, G. M. Vision without inversion of the retinal image. *Psychological Review*, 1897, 4, 341–360, 463–481.

The following is a humorous discussion of the problem of inverted vision. Even though written completely in humorous vein, this article considers the same basic concept that was discussed in the last selection. Hopefully, it will aid the reader in understanding that concept. Even if it does not, there should be no harm in taking space and time for a little levity.

18

A NOTE ON MAN-ANIMAL, ANIMAL-MAN, AND ANIMAL-ANIMAL PERCEPTION

JOHN H. SLATE

It was William James who pointed out that we do not see the bear, become frightened, and run away; but, rather, that we see the bear, run away, and become frightened.

Yet even today, seventy-five years after publication of James's monumental *Principles of Psychology*, little has been done to interpret (let alone ameliorate) this position. To be sure, much has been written about becoming frightened, and still more about running away. However, the mechanism enabling us to *see* the bear is still only imperfectly understood.

Nor are we alone in this regard. For the bear himself, while fully conversant with frightened running, would be ill prepared to say why we see him, he sees us, or even when he sees other bears.

The ultimate *why* of anything may well exceed our reach, if not our grasp (thus, *why* do we so often ask "why"?). Yet we

SOURCE: Abridged from *Atlantic*, April, 1965. Copyright © 1965 by The Atlantic Monthly Company, Boston, Mass. Reprinted with permission.

may at least essay the ostensibly more modest, but in a deeper sense more vainglorious, question *how* this, as well as other things, has come about.

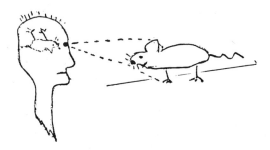

A. MAN-ANIMAL   Figure 1 shows, in schematic outline, how we see the bear. Actually, the animal is not necessarily a bear, but has been generalized so as to represent any animal of suitable size and shape.

Rays of light (consisting of photons and other lightlike items) leave the extremities of the bear and enter the human eye. Due to some mixup in the eye or the brain or both, an *inverted* image of the bear is then formed in our heads.

There is some reason to suppose that it is this inversion which is responsible for much of the fright to which James alluded. However, this aspect of the matter is, in reality, beyond the scope of the present discussion.

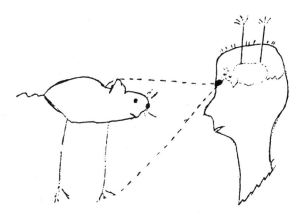

B. UNSUITABLE ANIMAL   Figure 2. Here the vital importance of not looking at large animals is illustrated. Thus a bear with unsuitably long legs would, as indicated in the plate, form an optical image with the legs (from, roughly, the knee down) protruding *upward* through the observer's skull. This could have the most serious consequences.

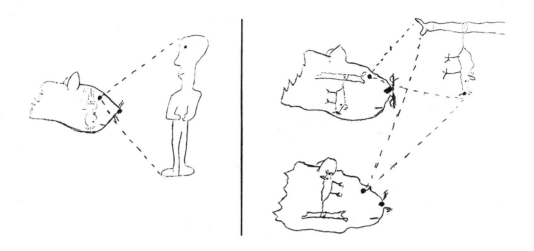

C. BEAR'S-VIEW   In Figure 3A, a bear is shown seeing a man. Here again inversion of the optical image has, unfortunately, occurred. However, Figure 3B suggests two possible expedients. The bears in the plate are both looking at a tree sloth, which, of course, normally resides upside down. The upper bear is wearing corrective lenses so that his image of the sloth is inverted once by the lenses and then reinverted in his head. As a result he "sees" the sloth as it usually appears in nature.

The lower bear is a wild one whom it was not feasible to fit out in this way. However, as shown by the plate, *he* sees the sloth right side up, which, in all probability, will prove more satisfactory in the long range.

The question of the sloth's-eye view of these two bears is far too complex to admit to definitive analysis here. Presumably, however, the problems neither of physical nor of optical inversion would, in this instance, be of overriding concern. For if the sloth is prepared to accept the inversion of everything else with equanimity, it is difficult to see why an exception should be made for bears.

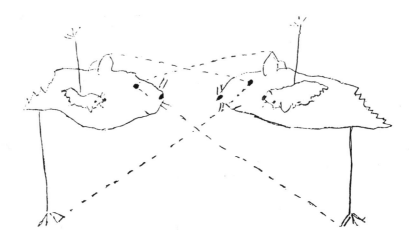

D. RECIPROCALLY
UNSUITABLE
BEARS

Figure 4 depicts two long-legged bears (actually, animals, as noted above) looking at each other.

As a practice exercise, the reader should list the three salient features of animal-animal perception which are illustrated by this drawing.

The advanced student may also wish to pursue this subject further, by applying the principles set out in this paper to cognate problems such as the worm's-eye view. (Hints: To a worm, which way is "up"? Do worms see *anything* worthy of the name?)

We now change our approach from humor to fantasy and ask the question: What is it that a perceiving being has that a lesser species lacks? Just what is there about an organism that can perceive that is different from one that cannot perceive?

19

THE MAGIC TREE
GEORGE A. MILLER

The importance of movement can be emphasized by a short detour into fantasy. Imagine a special tree that through some

SOURCE: From pp. 119–120 in *Psychology: The Science of Mental Life* by George A. Miller. Copyright © 1962 by George A. Miller. By permission of Harper & Row, Publishers, Inc.

kind of druidical magic is half animal and half plant. This wonderful tree has sense organs—receptors sensitive to light, sound, odor, taste, touch, static position—connected by sensory nerves to a large and elaborate brain. The tree has everything that an animal has, except that it lacks a motor output. There are no motor nerves, no muscles, no glands. In short, the tree cannot *do* anything about the information it picks up. It must stand rooted in one spot, as trees have always done, moving only with the wind.

Here is the question: Would this strange tree have any advantages over an ordinary tree?

Any knowledge the imaginary tree might acquire would, of course, be useless. What good would it do the tree to see lumberjacks coming? What advantage can it gain from knowing the forest is on fire if it can do no more than feel pain? Without muscles, the tree cannot speak; it has no way to communicate its knowledge to other trees or to share in their experiences.

But to discuss the tree in these terms seems to imply that a motionless tree can accumulate knowledge. The implication may go too far. A tree that cannot move can know almost nothing, even though it has all the marvelous equipment of receptors, nerves, and brain. A basic difficulty the magical tree can never overcome is that it cannot move its sense organs. Animals can move, not only to approach the things they want and to avoid the things they fear, but also to change the location of their eyes and ears. This simple fact has a tremendous influence on the way they must organize their experience.

A tree with eyes might see a house nearby, but the tree could never suspect that the house had another side concealed from view. To discover the thickness of reality it is necessary to move around in it. We must be able to walk around the house and then, somehow, to construct a single object that accounts for all the different views we had of it. A tree with eyes but unable to move would not need an explanation for such diversity as movement generates; it would never see deeper than the flat surface of appearances. The tree's world would have the same flatness a child sees when it looks at the stars as tiny holes in the great black dome of the night.

Moreover, our tree would not be able to distinguish size from distance. When things approached the tree they would be seen as expanding in size. The tree would have no way to learn that it takes a long time to move through a long distance. And without motions through distances, the tree would have no use for time, and hence no way to date its memories. In place of three dimensions of space and one of time, the motionless tree would have but two dimensions of space. In fact, if the tree's eyes were exactly like ours, it might see nothing but movements: when a visual image is completely stabilized on our retinas so that it continues to stimulate the same visual receptor cells in spite of our eye-movements, the image will disappear entirely in twenty or thirty seconds. It is another case of sensory adaptation. For our visual system to work at all, it must experience continuous change in the images that fall on it. This change comes automatically when we move about.

REFERENCES

Dichburn, R. W. & Ginsborg, B. L. Vision with a stabilized retinal image. *Nature, 1952, 170, 36–38.*

Riggs, L. A., Ratliff, F. R., Cornsweet, J. C., & Cornsweet, T. N. The disappearance of steadily fixated test-objects. *Journal of the Optical Society of America, 1953, 43, 495–501.*

Sometimes students have troubles understanding what the professors and other supposed experts have written. This is at least partly because the professors and the experts have, like people in all special fields, developed their own jargon. They use words students don't know—words they have had no reason to know. Then, too, much of the literary fare served students was not especially prepared for them. It was written by professionals who wished to communicate with other professionals.

There are various possible solutions to this as a problem. One that we have tried, and which sometimes works quite well, involves (1) selecting outstanding students who are also good writers, (2) providing a list of source materials, and (3) asking them each to write a paper on some topic of their own selection within a given area.

One such group of students, some years ago, were asked to select some topic within the broader area of perception. But one young lady chose to summarize the whole field of perception. She did such a good job of it that we asked her permission to keep a copy of the paper for future use. Here it is.

20

PERCEPTION
EVANGELINE BERG LEASH

You see a pair of laughing eyes,
And suddenly you're sighing sighs . . .

Whether he knows it or not, the enamoured young man contributing this bit of information in these lines from a popular song has just provided an example of the essential elements in the process we call perception: first, the absorption and selection of stimuli by the sensory apparatus of the body, the integration and interpretation of the stimuli into meaning, and finally the response of the organism to its perceptions.

Disturbances affect us. Energy impinges on the body. But of all the physical energies and disturbances in the world about us, our sensory mechanisms are adapted to picking up only a percentage. Certain sounds are too high or too low for the human ear. Colors above and below the red and violet of the spectrum have never been seen by humans. Such phenomena are said to be below the sensory threshold of the human organism. And even yet we are drenched in a mass of stimuli which, if we were conscious of it all at one moment, would vivify to us William James' "blooming, buzzing confusion" of a world. We would be overwhelmed, unable to respond to all the stimulation. And here the selective mechanism of attention comes into play. The mass of incoming stimuli is organized, some selected to be the object of the organism's conscious consideration, and the rest shoved into the unconscious background.

Let's illustrate this with our young man. At the particular moment that he is gazing into the young lady's eyes, he is being bombarded by a vast amount of information from his sense organs. His auditory mechanisms are probably picking up such diverse sounds as music from a phonograph, people chattering, glasses clinking, somebody laughing; his olfactory apparatus may be registering the smell of food, the scent of flowers, someone's perfume; nerve endings in his skin may report warmth or cold, the softness of his shirt or the scratchiness of his starched collar, perhaps pain from his too-tight shoes. But his attention is directed toward certain of the light rays flowing in through his corneas from all angles of his 180-degree field of vision, and by the image on his lenses being brought into focus, albeit upside-down, on the back of his retina.

Now the structural determinants of the object of his attention

SOURCE: Unpublished paper reprinted with permission of the author.

are in place on the retina. What he sees are certain odd shapes and forms in a variety of colors and degrees of brightness. What they are he doesn't know—yet. It remains for the second element of perception to clarify the image. As a result of some unexplained chemical change, nerve current is generated and rushes along to the brain. And here the mass of sensory stimuli under consideration is integrated and interpreted. Past experience, attitudes, needs, values, and emotions modify and mold the stimuli into something meaningful. The odd shapes and forms on the young gentleman's retina become the face and especially the eyes of a young lady; past experience tells him that this is the shape girls' faces usually come in; his attitudes tell him that he rather likes them; his pleasant emotions make her eyes seem to be laughing—if he were unhappy, perhaps they would seem mocking.

But the nerve impulse does not merely pass *to* the brain centers. It goes *through* them to produce a response in the organism that is in accord with its perceptions. The young man begins to sigh. This is the function of the perceptual process, to place the world in relation to the organism. That he may satisfy his needs and avoid dangers, the individual must know (1) that there is an object in the environment, (2) that it is in a specific direction, (3) that it is at a certain distance, and (4) that it possesses certain characteristics that are important to him. Thereon he can base his actions. Perception is essentially composed of sensation plus interpretation, and it is the whole of the process from stimulus to response.

ATTENTION   In a closer examination of some of these perceptual elements, let us turn first to the process of attention.

Continuously we are evaluating, comparing, judging. Some things are in the center or focus of our attention, others are on the fringe, and the slightest shift in attention will bring different stimuli into power—rather like a palace revolution; one regime is overthrown, another steps into its place.

Although a single act, attention is a complex with certain interrelated aspects. First, in attending to something, the body and its sensory apparatus adjust themselves to focusing on certain stimuli more than others. This postural response indicates attention. The doctor with his stethoscope is bending all his faculties toward the sounds in the patient's chest. He may even close his eyes to shut out distracting visual stimuli, subordinating all other sense data to that supplied by his auditory mechanism. Second, to attend is to be ready to respond, to be "set" toward action. A runner is literally "ready" and "set" to "go" when the command is given. His response indicates to what action he was set, and the ready runner will be away before the unready one.

But what are the factors that determine to what we give our attention? There are three general conditions of attention adjustment. The first is dominated by motivation. In order to accomplish or to experience something we may *voluntarily* orient ourselves toward certain stimuli. Voluntary attention persisting over a long period may become *habitual;* through practice certain stimuli may come to draw automatically attention in a manner similar to that involved in the third condition, *involuntary* attention. Loud, sudden noises, sharp tactual sensations—such stimulations are prepotent in compelling attention, even if the organism is oriented in a different direction. No previous experience, no practice, is involved here, as it is in habitual attention.

Besides these, certain specific factors are usually influential in attracting attention. Some of these characterize the stimulus object itself, for example:

1. change; movement in any direction, from one place to another or from one intensity to another.
2. size; large objects are usually noticed before small.
3. intensity; loud sounds, bright colors are usually prepotent over quietness and drabness.
4. novelty; that which is unusual in its surroundings is noticed quickly.

Others are intrinsic in the observer, are subjective factors, such as one's interests or organic condition—if he is hungry, that which reminds him of food will be most attractive to him.

But attention does not remain focused solely on one set of stimuli indefinitely. Eyes continually dart everywhere; ears pick up every sort of sound but seldom does one remain predominant for long. When attention shifts involuntarily, it is being *distracted.* It is almost impossible to ignore completely such prepotent stimuli as that described above. When the distraction involves the same sense organ presently in attention—as when noise interrupts someone listening to the radio–the weaker stimulus tends to be drowned, and unflagging attention cannot persist.

Sensory information is information about the world around us. Attention helps us to organize and concentrate upon this information so that we might efficiently deal with it. But yet we cannot tell what is actually "out there"; we must add interpretation to the sensory data before we can perceive. And even yet there is a difference between what actually exists, what our senses tell us exists, and what we perceive as existing. For example, a rectangular shape with four legs may exist in the visual field. The eyes probably report a trapezoidal surface with zero to four legs, depending on the angle of view. The gap between these two versions is filled as we summon up our past experiences, expectations, and desires to have nothing ambiguous, and we perceive this object as being rectangular and four-legged and a table. Since attention is limited in its scope and subjective factors have so great an influence on perception, it is plain that the perceptual field is not the same as the physical field. The perceptual field of a photographer intent on taking pictures of a herd of African giraffe may not contain a charging water buffalo, but it is there, nonetheless. Behavior is guided by the perceptual field, not the physical field, and therefore the subjective factors having so great an influence in perception, and thus making it liable to error, deserve consideration.

ROLE OF PAST EXPERIENCE A most influential role in perception is played by an individual's body of past experiences. When confronted by certain stimulations, perhaps a grayish moving shape of soft fur accompanied by a low murmuring sound, he searches his memory for past acquaintance with this complex of stimuli and recognizes it as a kitten. When a disparity occurs between an object as it exists and as it is reported by the sense organs, past experience and present expectations can step in and reconcile the two. For example, when we watch a person walking away from us, his image as projected on the retina shrinks. But we know that he cannot actually be shrinking; any reasonable expectation would be that he will have the same stature next time we see him. Past experience tells us what his true height is, and as he walks away we make an unconscious correction and perceive him as retaining his true height.

Invoking past experience can, however, lead to misinterpretation. Usually in our experience when two objects side by side begin to change, one growing larger or brighter and the other smaller and dimmer, one has begun to move toward us and the other away. So when a subject in a dark room looks with one eye at a brightening light and a dimming light, both stationary and equidistant from him, he will report that one is advancing and the other receding. Motion to us is a successive stimulation of sensory receptors. A moving image in the visual field stimulates progressively different cells on the retina, and something moving across the skin successively stimulates different nerve endings. Because of this perception we are subject to the illusionary *phi phenomenon*, a string of lights flashing successively on and off at a certain fixed interval gives the illusion of movement.

NEEDS, VALUES, ATTITUDES We see not only what we expect to see but also what we would like to see. That an individual's organic condition influences his perceptions is demonstrated in the following experiment. A group of college students were shown drawings of ambiguous objects at certain intervals after eating. The number of food-related interpretations of these pictures increased sharply as time went by and hunger increased.

A communist and a capitalist would not view a hammer and sickle emblem in the same way. One's needs, values, and attitudes are definitely important. Utterly incorrect perceptions can result from prejudice, when the reports from the sense organs are superseded or twisted in order to fit the situation to the preconceived ideas of the observer. Differences in mood can also cause differences in perception. In an experiment demonstrating this, a group of subjects were hypnotized and put into moods, first of happiness, then criticalness, and finally anxiety. While in each of these moods they were shown six photographs of college age people in a variety of situations: dancing, lounging, in battle, etc. After showing the six pictures once, the mood and the memory of the pictures was erased and the next mood suggested. The results showed that mood affects to quite an extent what one perceives, but even more how one interprets what he observes. For example, concerning a photograph of a wounded soldier being carried to a plane, the same subject reported that he was (happy) "well taken-care of," (critical) "wounded or killed," (apprehensive) "in bad shape and may not live." Describing another picture, of young people digging in a swampy area, one subject said, (happy) "looks like fun . . . that's what life is for, working out in the open, really living," (critical) "pretty horrible land . . . ought to be something more useful to do. It's filthy and dirty and good for nothing," (apprehensive) "They're going to get hurt or cut."

All of these—sensations, attention, interpretations—that compose perception have as their purpose the intent to contribute to the maintenance of the organism's homeostasis. There is no comfort in the partially known—only fear. That which cannot be definitely identified is identified anyway, even if incorrectly, because the organism cannot tolerate ambiguity. Perhaps the roots of this lie with our primitive ancestor, who had to be sure of everything around him in order merely to exist. Essential to the whole process of survival is perception.

REFERENCES

Ittelson, W. H. and F. P. Kilpatrick, "Experiments in Perception," *Scientific American*, August, 1951, *185* (2), 50–55.

Johns, Ralph L., *Psychology in Everyday Living*, New York: Harper and Brothers, 1950.

Leuba, Clarence and Charles Lucas, "The Effects of Attitudes on Descriptions of Pictures," *Journal of Experimental Psychology*, 1945, *35*, 517–524.

Ruch, Floyd, *Psychology and Life,* 5th ed., Chicago: Scott, Foresman and Co., 1958.

Stagner, Ross and T. F. Karwoski, *Psychology,* New York: McGraw-Hill Book Company, 1952.

Witkin, H. A., "The Perception of the Upright," *Scientific American,* February, 1959, *200* (2), 50–56.

Wittreich, Warren J., "Visual Perception and Personality," *Scientific American,* April, 1959, *200* (4), 56–60.

Perception—or the process of perceiving—is commonly defined as the awareness, or process of becoming aware, of the environment by means of the senses. There must first be sensation. When, and only when, the sensory input comes to have meaning, does one perceive. Sensation plus meaning equals perception.

The meaning component of perceiving will vary with different people. Each has had his own unique experiences. Who can be sure if you hear a continuing "clop, clop, clop" sound as the ticking of a clock, and I hear it as the sound of a horse on the pavement outside? Regardless of which of us is correct, each will develop his own perception based on his previous experiences and feelings and his present situation. If you are seated in a living room and you know the family has an old grandfather's clock in the hallway, it probably is a clock. But if I hear the same sound in a riding academy, wouldn't you bet on my perception?

The definition we have come to prefer is that perception is *one's best guess as to what's out there.*

Try to think of as many situations as you can when you have guessed wrong. Was that the slamming of a door, a car exhaust, or a gun shot? (Think of the hunter who was certain it was a deer. It just did not look like the farmer's cow!) When you have come up with two or three, try to figure out *why* you made the mistake. What were the factors in your experience that caused you to guess wrong about what was out there? Or if you guessed right, why?

INCREASING YOUR PERCEPTIONS

Why does it take the infant so long to develop perceptions? T. G. R. Bower, in an article "The Visual World of Infants" (*Scientific American,* December 1966), says that infants have a lower information processing capacity in dealing with sensory data than do adults. W. H. Ittelson and F. P. Kilpatrick describe experiments in perception in an article called just that, "Experiments in Perception" (*Scientific American,* August 1951).

We have already suggested the Stratton articles mentioned by Miller. A more recent study of visual adaptation is Charles S. Harris, "Adaptation to Displaced Vision: Visual, Motor or Proprioceptive Change?" (*Science,* 1963, *140,* 812–13).

Miller gives a reference to Kohler's studies, but a more readily available source is Ivo Kohler, "Experiments with Goggles" (*Scientific American,* May 1962).

For a human interest discussion of perception as it relates to us all, we suggest S. Howard Bartley, *Perception in Everyday Life* (Harper and Row, 1972).

There seems, ordinarily, to be more interest in visual perception than in perception arising from any other sense field. Two very readable books are by R. L. Gregory, *Eye and Brain* (McGraw-Hill, 1966) and *The Intelligent Eye* (McGraw-Hill, 1970).

The popular press abounds with amazing stories about people who can "see" with their fingers and other unusual perceptual phenomena. For a discussion and explanation of some of these "offbeat" stories, see Martin Gardner, "Dermo-optical Perception: A Peek Down the Nose" (*Science,* 1966, *151,* 654–57).

Part Seven

I'm one of only 4 rope walking Chickens in the World °°

Learning: More or Less Permanent Change

At this point in your life you are an avowed professional learner, and have been for some time. Did you ever stop to analyze the process? Psychologists have tried to, because it is a particularly intriguing part of human behavior. When you stop to consider how much learning you've engaged in so far, it is really monumental. As we mature we change from an infant, incapable of doing little more than crying, sleeping, sucking, swallowing, kicking and grasping, into someone who can walk, talk, read, add and subtract, drive a car, recite poetry; the list goes on and on. We continue to learn, all our lives, each time we encounter a new situation requiring some new response.

Sometimes we learn whole new skills, not much like anything we have ever done before. Do you remember learning to swim underwater? There were a host of new responses to be made: staying under and moving forward meant using arms, legs, hands and feet in ways very unlike their use back on shore. Inhibiting the urge to breathe was another important response, too; sometimes learning *not* to do something is as important as what we learn to do.

At times we add to an already acquired skill. After riding a bicycle for years, we find it reasonably easy to learn to ride a motorcycle. After learning to do one kind of dancing, we find it easier to learn another. After all, now we know how to respond to a beat, how to keep time, how to respond to a partner. These skills are common to many kinds of dancing.

Sometimes we learn not overt physical responses but ways of perceiving (remember Mr. Hanna) and ways of thinking about a new kind of problem. We learn to read phonetically, to recognize a pun, and to identify sports cars.

Of course, what we are able to learn is bounded by our individual capabilities. Some responses cannot be acquired until we reach a certain level of maturation; no amount of training can force a child to walk before his muscles and coordination are ready. Some responses are impossible, given our physical structure. We cannot learn to fly, to stay underwater for hours, no matter how long we practice. A dog cannot learn to speak, whatever the method we employ to teach him. We, in turn, find it difficult to track rabbits by their scent.

Besides differing from animals in the skills we acquire, we differ among ourselves when it comes to learning. Some skills are more easily acquired by some people than by others. We will be discussing these individual differences in greater depth in a later chapter.

Whether we focus on animals (surely useful in the learning laboratory!) or on humans, we can infer that learning has occurred only from the *performance* we can observe. As you yourself know, this has its disadvantages. Haven't we all taken exams which did not fairly assess all that we had learned? Nevertheless, these inferences are the best we can do. We cannot observe the minute chemical changes that go on as learning takes place. We are not even sure exactly what these changes are. For now, we must define learning on the basis of observations made in the laboratory coupled with scientific guesses.

Edwin R. Guthrie, a noted learning theorist, discusses in the next selection some of the problems we face in defining and studying learning.

21

DEFINING LEARNING
EDWIN R. GUTHRIE

Psychologists nowhere depart further from common sense than in their notion of the nature of minds. The man on the street acknowledges that minds are rather mysterious, but he is definitely sure that a mind is something that you either have or you haven't. Bricks haven't. He has, and knows that he has. Dogs also have minds. Angleworms? Here he becomes a little doubtful. Angleworms seem very definitely to resent indignities in a way that a brick does not. And their daily round of activity seems to have something of a plan and purpose behind it. A brick reacts to a kick by moving over, but there is a distinctly passive and helpless air about the brick's behavior. And the brick is so dependable; it regularly does the expected thing when it is disturbed. If it behaves differently on a second occasion we can find the occasion for the difference. It is a different brick. If it did not fall apart at one blow of the hammer, but now does fall apart when struck the second time with the same force, we take for granted that the first blow cracked it. If a bridge timber gives way after years of use under a load that it has held up to the present moment, we assume that it is a different timber; dry rot has invaded it or past stresses have cracked it.

But do angleworms have minds? Are growth and reproduction and defensive reaction enough to qualify the worm for that distinction? Plants also grow and multiply and defend themselves

Source: "Introduction" in *The Psychology of Learning*, Rev. Ed., by E. R. Guthrie. Copyright, 1935, 1952 by Harper & Row, Publishers, Inc. Reprinted by permission of the publishers.

not only by their structures but in many cases by movement. Common sense is inclined to deny that plants have minds, for this is an opinion shared only by a very few detached sentimentalists.

What is it then that plants lack that is to be found in creatures which common sense endows with minds? Strangely enough, common sense will be found to offer a very good answer to this question. Growth and reproduction and defense reactions are life, but they are not mind. Mind is these and something more; it is growth and reproduction and reactions serving these ends plus something that common sense might call profiting by experience. The answer to the question of the angleworm's status will be determined by the answer to the question: Does the worm always respond the same way to the same combination of circumstances, or does the worm alter its response as a result of its past experience?

Of course, a full worm and an empty worm respond differently to the world. This is not what is meant by profiting by experience. The altered behavior here is like the altered behavior of the bridge timber; it can be referred to differences in the present circumstances. The difference can be examined and the response understood on the basis of what is now the condition of the worm.

Now it happens that a psychologist has established that worms can profit by experience. Yerkes many years ago placed earthworms in a T-shaped maze and found that if a slight electric shock was always administered when the worm turned, say, to the left, ultimately the worm was in some fashion changed so that it more or less regularly turned to the right and avoided the shock.

The difference between a worm that has received this Harvard laboratory training and a worm that has not is a difference that can not be discovered by examining the worm. The training leaves no observable changes. All psychologists believe that differences accounting for the altered behavior exist in the worm's "brain," but it is doubtful whether we shall ever be able to examine these brain differences either during the lifetime of the organism or at a post-mortem. Such traits as an acquired liking for mince pie, or skill at chess, or an ambition to travel, which are all modifications of behavior like the right-turning habit of the earthworm, are not by any present technique possible of demonstration at an autopsy. We may speculate concerning the nature of the brain changes that lie behind these habits, but that speculation will throw no light on the nature of the habits.

These changes in behavior which follow behavior we shall call learning. The ability to learn, that is, to respond differently to a situation because of past response to the situation, is what distinguishes those living creatures which common sense endows with minds. This is the practical descriptive use of the term "mind." Another use, the theological or mythological notion of mind as a substance, as a mysterious hidden cause of action, we may dismiss at once. Our interest is scientific, and we are dealing only with observable features of the world about us. Mind must be for us a mode of behavior, namely, that behavior which changes with use or practice—behavior, in other words, that exhibits learning.

Learning, as so defined, does not include all changes in behavior tendencies. Fatigue, for instance, is a change in behavior, but it is referred not to action primarily as its occasion but to altered chemical states in muscle and in the blood stream. There are other changes in behavior tendencies which might be included in the term "learning" if we were so inclined. When continuous pressure is exerted on a touch receptor, Adrian has recorded instances in which the receptor responds only for a brief period. Impulses from the sense organ are demonstrable in the sensory nerve only for a few seconds, though the pressure on the sense organ is continued. This is a change in behavior tendency, since the organism will no longer respond, though the stimulus continues; but this is a very temporary change and from it there is a quick recovery.

The definition of learning used by a psychologist selects the facts which he observes and records. Using the common-sense definition of learning as improvement leads to the observation of such items as the number of errors made in achieving a goal, or the time required, or the effort used, or an increased percentage of success. Nearly all the thousands of studies of maze learning by rats have recorded only the facts of improvement, not the facts of changed behavior. These records are of little or no interest to the psychologist who thinks of learning in terms of changed response to a stimulus, because no record is made of specific alterations of behavior at choice points. Only total errors or total time from start to goal are noted. The fact that at the fifth choice point a given animal took the "correct" turn for the first time on the eleventh trial and persevered in this from that trial on is not in the record.

Common sense and many psychologists have used "learning" to refer only to those changes which contribute to the accomplishment of some end or purpose. In this sense learning always means learning to do something, learning to write, learning to skate—learning, in short, which results in an ability or a skill or a capacity for some achievement. This identification of learning with the attainment of a good result is all very well for common sense, but for a scientific understanding of human behavior it will not serve. And the reason that it will not serve is that in the same manner and in the same ways that human beings acquire skills and capacities they also acquire faults and awkwardnesses and even lose capacities which they once possessed. Since virtues and skills are acquired in the same way that faults and awkwardnesses are acquired, it seems unreasonable to limit the meaning of the word learning to achievement. It is true that the changes referred to as "learning" do generally turn out to be beneficial, that they are in the long run adaptive, and this must be looked into; but we have deserted the methods of empirical science if we assume that all learning is good, that every action has its goal. There are psychologists who believe this, not only of their own actions but of all the actions of all animals. The hen lays her egg, not because it has reached an embarrassing size, but because the species must be preserved. She is aiming at motherhood and carrying a torch for her species, not just laying an egg.

In this present account it will not be assumed that all learning is a progress toward betterment. Learning will be understood as change rather than as improvement. Our task is to understand the circumstances under which learning takes place and the nature of the changes that it involves. Our method should be to survey the experimental work on learning, to review what is common knowledge of learning, and to try to discover any generalizations that can be made from our survey. Can we find any rule or uniformity in the phenomena? Can we describe any circumstances which regularly have a certain kind of outcome? Does the animal which has had one kind of history tend afterward to do certain things? *Under what circumstances do the specific changes in behavior we call learning take place?*

If we find such rules, they will not only be an adequate theory of learning; they will also direct the practical advice we give to persons who are guiding learning. Our rules, to be good theory, must be based on observation and verified by observation. This is one requirement. Another is that they shall be as concise and clear as we can make them. Our antecedent circumstances must be so clearly described that from our description other persons can recognize instances of what we describe; and this must also be true of our alleged consequences. If our descriptions are vague or ambiguous our rules can not be verified; nor can they be used for the anticipation and control of behavior. These are the important requirements for psychological theory, and we may note that these would be the most important requirements for practical advice.

If we can find, on examining our common knowledge and the experimental work on learning, that certain describable, observable, and recognizable antecedent conditions enable us to predict certain describable, observable, and recognizable changes in behavior, we shall have discovered laws of learning. These laws will constitute our explanations of learning, for all scientific explanations are nothing more than generalized laws or rules which cover the event needing explanation.

The search for these laws has certain inherent difficulties. The first of these difficulties has to do with language. Putting events into words is never entirely satisfactory. Here are pupils in a classroom. The teacher gives them a spoken direction. How are we to describe this as a stimulus to the pupils? No two pupils see the teacher from the same angle or hear her voice from the same distance. No two pupils move their eyes alike, consequently no two have the same retinal activity. The optical properties of different eyes differ. What the pupils hear and what they see depends on the form of their present attention and on their previous experiences, which are various. We are forced to speak of the voice of the teacher as a stimulus, but we are forced to speak vaguely. We can never be sure that the stimulus of the voice does not affect different pupils in essentially different ways.

Reactions are just as hard to describe and name. Popular names for most acts are names for end results which may be accomplished in an indefinite variety of ways. Accepting an invitation, going to market, attending a dinner, playing a tune, catching a fish—all name acts, but the acts they name are left indefinite. It is only because the acts we name have a rough practical equivalence that we are able to undertake their prediction. Under these handicaps our forecasts of action are bound to be inaccurate and we must be resigned to finding exceptions to all our rules. We shall be dealing with tendencies and not with certainties.

A second difficulty in codifying the laws of learning has been introduced by psychologists themselves. Experimenters in the field of learning have failed to make clear to the public or to themselves that two fundamentally different kinds of research have been in progress. Some psychologists and physiologists have been interested in the prediction of movement or glandular secretion without any reference to the utility of the movement or to its consequences. Pavlov, for instance, was interested in discovering the circumstances under which a dog will secrete saliva in response to stimuli that were previously ineffective. The ability to secrete saliva at the sound of a bell or at a touch on the flank is of no use to the dog after the experiment, though similar conditioning in natural conditions may be useful. Pavlov was interested in the phenomenon of conditioning, not in its utility. Tolman, on the other hand, records the fact that the rat in the maze reaches food, its goal, and is not concerned about the movements by which the goal is reached. The psychologist whose interest is in the goal-reaching capacities of animals will make goal attainment the entry in the record, and not the means used, which may be varied. One experimenter like Pavlov is interested in the process; other experimenters are interested in the results. It is to be expected that the two types of workers will discover very different laws of learning. The conditions under which goals are reached are not at all the conditions under which habits are stereotyped. A day-old chick will peck at grains and capture a certain percentage of them. Its percentage of success increases rapidly with practice, but if the chick formed a stereotyped habit of pecking in one direction and with a fixed reach it would retrieve very few grains.

The differences in the results announced by different psychologists arise from differences in the modes of behavior that they are intent on predicting. Their findings are not contradictory. Empirical studies, if they are honest, can not be contradictory. Pavlov's question, under what circumstances can a stimulus not previously the occasion of a response become a substitute cue for that response, will have one answer; and the question, under what circumstances will a man or a dog acquire a certain skill or ability, will have another. It is, of course, this second question that has more practical interest. . . .

Two sources of difficulty in the formulation of laws of learning have been mentioned—the difficulty of fitting language to the description of the confused and intricate flow of behavior, and the failure of experimenters to record the same features of behavior. There is a third difficulty. We can not record or control all the conditions under which our experiments are made, or record all the details of any sample of behavior. The physicist is less embarrassed by this obstacle. He does not concern himself about the recent night life or the childhood experiences of the bit of metal whose density he is determining, whereas such items of history may lead to very bizarre results in the psychological laboratory. Even with this advantage we find that the physicist tends to flee from reality into a dream world of "ideal" gases and liquids, because these are the only ones that will obey the laws of physics. Boyle's law that in a gas with temperature held constant the product of pressure and volume is a constant is not true of any real gas. And when the physicist turns engineer and undertakes to predict the behavior of actual things in a real world, he protects himself with safety factors of 600 to 1000 percent to allow for any shortcomings in his predictions.

The psychologist must resign himself to the fact that no psychological event is ever really repeated. The second repetition of a stimulus is only roughly and for practical purposes equivalent to the first; his laboratory subject is only substantially or approximately the same person who sat in the chair the day before. Since that time he has slept, eaten a little, learned a little, and this will alter his response no matter what precautions have been taken to have conditions the same. No two responses are alike. Two trips through a maze, two conditioned salivary reflexes may be substantially the same, but they are always the same with a difference.

Learning, then, as psychologists define it, is *the more or less permanent change in behavior resulting from experience.* As Guthrie pointed out, there are different explanations for learning, and different approaches to studying it. In this chapter we shall be looking at some of the approaches.

One of the simplest examples of learning to be studied in a laboratory was the conditioned response. In 1904 a Russian physiologist, Ivan Pavlov, was investigating the salivating response in dogs. He found that, instead of salivating when food was placed in their mouths, the dogs in his laboratory salivated at the *sight* of food. In fact, they salivated at the sight of the food dish before it was filled, and at the sound of the lab assistants' footsteps when they brought the food! Intrigued by this behavior, Pavlov designed some experiments to study the matter further. This time he paired the sound of a bell with the presentation of food. After a number of such pairings, he discovered that the sound of the bell alone could elicit salivation, even when no food was in sight. In this instance Pavlov referred to the food as the *unconditioned stimulus* (UCS), which could elicit the *unconditioned response* (UCR) of salivating—in other words, the dog needed no learning (or conditioning) to salivate when food was placed in its mouth. The sound of the bell Pavlov termed the *conditioned stimulus* (CS); it came to elicit the *conditioned response* (CR) of salivating.

Pavlov, of course, was not the only person to notice the conditioned salivary response. You have probably experienced it yourself. Doesn't the sight of your favorite food, or even a picture of it, make *your* mouth water? And have you ever had the mumps? If anybody had been cruel enough to offer you a dill pickle or a slice of lemon, your conditioned response to the sight would have made you all the more painfully aware of your swollen salivary glands.

As you read on your own now, you may, if you look, find many examples of a conditioned response. The author of the next article did just that. Can you recognize the UCS, the UCR, the CS, and CR?

22

LOPE DE VEGA ON EARLY CONDITIONING

W. A. BOUSFIELD

Professor J. H. Arjona of the University of Connecticut, the leading authority on the Spanish playwright Lope de Vega, recently sent me a copy of his admittedly free translation of a story in Lope's play *El Capellán de la Virgen* (The Chaplain of the Virgin). This play was probably written in 1615. Accompanying the translation was the pointed observation, "This antedates your scientific experiments by about three centuries."

With Professor Arjona's permission, I am submitting his translation for the possible edification of the profession through *The American Psychologist*. It would appear that the highly prolific Lope was somewhat of an authority on classical conditioning.

Saint Ildefonso used to scold me and punish me lots of times. He would sit me on the bare floor and make me eat with the cats of the monastery. These cats were such rascals that they took advantage of my penitence. They drove me mad stealing my choicest morsels. It did no good to chase them away. But I found a way of coping with the beasts in order to enjoy my meals when I was being punished. I put them all in a sack, and on a pitch black night took them out under an arch. First I would cough and then immediately whale the daylights out of the cats. They whined and shrieked like an infernal pipe organ. I would pause for awhile and repeat the operation—first a cough, and then a thrashing. I finally noticed that even without beating them, the beasts moaned and yelped like the very devil whenever I coughed. I then let them loose. Thereafter, whenever I had to eat off the floor, I would cast a look around. If an animal approached my food, all I had to do was to cough, and how that cat did scat!

Did you guess that "whaling the daylights" out of the cats was the UCS—and that their UCR (while caught in the sack), "whining and shrieking"? The CS, of course, was de Vega's cough, and the CR, more whining and shrieking—and escape from the situation, when possible.

The next passage illustrates an example of the conditioning of human infants, from Aldous Huxley's political novel, *Brave New World*. Look out, again, for the UCS, UCR, CS and CR.

SOURCE: W. A. Bousfield, "Lope de Vega on Early Conditioning," *American Psychologist*, 10, 1955, 828. Copyright © 1968 by the American Psychological Association, and reproduced by permission.

23

NEO-PAVLOVIAN CONDITIONING
ALDOUS HUXLEY

Mr. Foster was left in the Decanting Room. The D.H.C. [Director of Hatcheries and Conditioning] and his students stepped into the nearest lift and were carried up to the fifth floor.

INFANT NURSERIES. NEO-PAVLOVIAN CONDITIONING ROOMS, announced the notice board.

The Director opened a door. They were in a large bare room, very bright and sunny; for the whole of the southern wall was a single window. Half a dozen nurses, trousered and jacketed in the regulation white viscose-linen uniform, their hair aseptically hidden under white caps, were engaged in setting out bowls of roses in a long row across the floor. Big bowls, packed tight with blossom. Thousands of petals, ripe-blown and silkily smooth, like the cheeks of innumerable little cherubs, but of cherubs, in that bright light, not exclusively pink and Aryan, but also luminously Chinese, also Mexican, also apoplectic with too much blowing of celestial trumpets, also pale as death, pale with the posthumous whiteness of marble.

The nurses stiffened to attention as the D.H.C. came in.

"Set out the books," he said curtly.

In silence the nurses obeyed his command. Between the rose bowls the books were duly set out—a row of nursery quartos opened invitingly each at some gaily coloured image of beast or fish or bird.

"Now bring in the children."

They hurried out of the room and returned in a minute or two, each pushing a kind of tall dumb-waiter laden, on all its four wire-netted shelves, with eight-month-old babies, all exactly alike (a Bokanovsky Group, it was evident) and all (since their caste was Delta) dressed in khaki.

"Put them down on the floor."

The infants were unloaded.

"Now turn them so that they can see the flowers and books."

Turned, the babies at once fell silent, then began to crawl towards those clusters of sleek colours, those shapes so gay and brilliant on the white pages. As they approached, the sun came out of a momentary eclipse behind a cloud. The roses flamed up

SOURCE: From pp. 20–24 in *Brave New World* by Aldous Huxley. Copyright 1932, 1960 by Aldous Huxley. By permission of Harper & Row, Publishers, Inc. Permission also granted by Mrs. Laura Huxley and Chatto and Windus Ltd., London.

as though with a sudden passion from within; a new and profound significance seemed to suffuse the shining pages of the books. From the ranks of the crawling babies came little squeals of excitement, gurgles and twitterings of pleasure.

The Director rubbed his hands. "Excellent!" he said. "It might almost have been done on purpose."

The swiftest crawlers were already at their goal. Small hands reached out uncertainly, touched, grasped, unpetaling the transfigured roses, crumpling the illuminated pages of the books. The Director waited until all were happily busy. Then, "Watch carefully," he said. And, lifting his hand, he gave the signal.

The Head Nurse, who was standing by a switchboard at the other end of the room, pressed down a little lever.

There was a violent explosion. Shriller and ever shriller, a siren shrieked. Alarm bells maddeningly sounded.

The children started, screamed; their faces were distorted with terror.

"And now," the Director shouted (for the noise was deafening), "now we proceed to rub in the lesson with a mild electric shock."

He waved his hand again, and the Head Nurse pressed a second lever. The screaming of the babies suddenly changed its tone. There was something desperate, almost insane, about the sharp spasmodic yelps to which they now gave utterance. Their little bodies twitched and stiffened; their limbs moved jerkily as if to the tug of unseen wires.

"We can electrify that whole strip of floor," bawled the Director in explanation. "But that's enough," he signalled to the nurse.

The explosions ceased, the bells stopped ringing, the shriek of the siren died down from tone to tone into silence. The stiffly twitching bodies relaxed, and what had become the sob and yelp of infant maniacs broadened out once more into a normal howl of ordinary terror.

"Offer them the flowers and the books again."

The nurses obeyed; but at the approach of the roses, at the mere sight of those gaily-coloured images of pussy and cock-a-doodle-doo and baa-baa black sheep, the infants shrank away in horror; the volume of their howling suddenly increased.

"Observe," said the Director triumphantly, "observe."

Books and loud noises, flowers and electric shocks—already in the infant mind these couples were compromisingly linked; and after two hundred repetitions of the same or a similar lesson would be wedded indissolubly. What man has joined, nature is powerless to put asunder.

"They'll grow up with what the psychologists used to call an 'instinctive' hatred of books and flowers. Reflexes unalterably conditioned. They'll be safe from books and botany all their lives." The Director turned to his nurses. "Take them away again."

Still yelling, the khaki babies were loaded on to their dumb-waiters and wheeled out, leaving behind them the smell of sour milk and a most welcome silence.

Pavlovian, or classical conditioning as it has come to be called, always starts with the presentation of a stimulus which is sure to evoke a particular response from a normal subject: food in the mouth elicits salivation, electric shock elicits a withdrawal response, a puff of air on the eyeball elicits a blink. But what if we wish to condition responses which are not reflex actions—responses for which we don't know the eliciting stimulus?

This brings us to consider a different kind of conditioning, one which depends on the principle of trial-and-error learning, coupled with the principle of reinforcement. The idea is not a new one. It was first investigated systematically by an American psychologist, Edward L. Thorndike, a contemporary of Pavlov.

Thorndike proposed that an animal would learn to perform a response which was rewarded by gradually abandoning those responses which were not rewarded. Thus, if a cat were unwillingly cooped up in a "puzzle box," he should eventually learn which action was necessary to obtain release from the box, whether it be pulling a loop or pressing a lever. On subsequent trials in the box, he would perform the successful motion which released him before, having abandoned those moves which got him nowhere. Thorndike designed experiments to test his hypotheses, and concluded that they were correct.

A contemporary version of this approach to studying learning is offered by B. F. Skinner, a psychologist at Harvard. It is called *instrumental conditioning* because the subject's response is "instrumental" in gaining a reward or avoiding punishment. (It has also been referred to as "operant behavior," that is, behavior which has an effect on the environment.) Skinner has investigated the effect different schedules of reinforcement (rewards and punishment) have on the performance of learned responses.

The next selection is our second example of a paper written by a student in a general psychology class. Students were asked to apply the principles of instrumental conditioning to a practical problem of teaching. Some students used brothers, sisters, and roommates, as subjects; some used dogs, and some used white rats. This young lady was the proud owner of a pet burro, who has now made a place for himself in the field of psychology.

24

AN EXPERIMENT IN OPERANT
CONDITIONING
LOUANNA CRAIN

Jack, my pet burro, has always been the spoiled one among the corral animals. Unlike the horses, he did not respond to the usual training (based on mild punishment as a reinforcement) used to break young horses into the world of subservience to riders. Instead, he seemed to realize that he didn't have to do what we wanted him to, that we couldn't actually force him to go when he would rather stop and eat the grass, to run when he would rather amble along, or to turn a corner when he would rather go the other way. We had given up on him and allowed him to become quite spoiled, letting him have a morsel of food if he could find it in our pockets and, indeed, even encouraging such behavior even though he had done nothing to deserve a reward.

Consequently, I decided to use Jack for my experiment in learning, just to see if I could teach him to obediently perform some action. Bowing seemed to be an ideal trick to teach him, since it is not a natural maneuver for donkeys, but, being relatively uncomplicated, would nevertheless not be too hard to learn.

Basing my procedure plan on suggestions in B. F. Skinner's "How to Teach Animals," I decided to first accustom Jack to a specific reinforcement. When this was established, I would begin to reward random movements which resembled standing with the head down. After this action was learned, I would go on to reinforce only positions of lowered head and extended right foreleg, and so on until he learned the complete bowing position—lowered head, weight balanced on the extended right foreleg, and the left leg bent and placed behind the head.

Since Jack was so used to being "friendly" and nudging us for food all the time, I anticipated difficulty in establishing a reinforcement that would not be centered directly on my movements. Therefore, I set up an elaborate scheme in a tree: my sister Sandi would sit up on a limb and, at my signal, strike a

SOURCE: Unpublished paper reprinted with permission of the author.

suspended cymbal and drop a carrot piece through a pipe down onto a tray fastened to the trunk of the tree about three feet above the ground. From experience, I knew that Jack's love for carrots would provide sufficient motivation; I only hoped he would understand that he must now work for what he had previously gotten free.

To teach him what the tray was for, I led him up to it and instructed Sandi to sound the cymbal and drop a carrot bit intermittently, about once a minute. At first, especially since he wasn't aware that Sandi was in the tree, the sound and the dropping carrot scared him. After about five tries, however, he caught on and immediately checked the tray for a carrot when he heard the cymbal. I then stepped away from the tree to see if he would stay there waiting for carrots or follow me and try my pockets. Just as I had expected, he came after me. Finding nothing, he looked away disappointedly, at which time Sandi immediately crashed the cymbal and dropped the reward. Jack ran over to the tray and ate the carrot, waited a while, then came back to me. After several such occurrences, he stopped begging me for the carrots; merely standing by and looking the other way seemed to be sufficient to get what he wanted. Thus, my first step was completed—Jack knew that he would get carrots only from the tray, and only after the cymbal sounded.

My next task was to get him to stand and lower his head. My outlined procedure proved very successful in this; after only four minutes Jack was standing in front of the carrot tray, lowering his head to the ground, lifting it to the tray at the sound of the cymbal, then lowering it again immediately.

From here, though, the task became more difficult; in his random movements Jack did not normally extend his right forefoot and lower his head at the same time. My plans called for withholding reinforcement until such a movement or tendency toward it occurred. However, in waiting, I noticed that since he was no longer being reinforced, extinction of the head-lowering action was beginning to take place. We therefore reverted back to the reinforcement of the head movement until it was completely relearned—it required a few trials—and then employed a stick as an aid in showing Jack what was now expected of him. By tapping him on the back of his leg, just above the hoof, I was able to induce him to extend it somewhat in front of the other. Then, when he chanced to lower his head, he was immediately rewarded. After a while, he extended his foot and lowered his head as soon as he felt the tapping signal, but he would not do it without feeling the stick first. Realizing he had become dependent on the stick signal and not knowing how to eliminate this dependence, I decided to substitute a verbal signal for the physical one. Each time before I tapped his foot I commanded him to "bow, Jack!" It took him a few minutes to catch on, but finally he was able to respond to the verbal signal alone, reaching out and lowering his head every time he was commanded to bow.

Getting him to bend his other leg at the same time was more difficult. I decided to return to my stick signals. At first I tried tapping him on the front of the left leg, but found that there was a transfer of learning—he remembered the tapping signal and promptly extended this foot as well as the other, and waited expectantly for the reward. Anxious to avoid such negative transfer, I changed my signal to a small sharp blow on the inside of the knee while commanding him to bow. Apparently this came as a surprise to him, for he kicked up his heels and ran off.

After coaxing him back to the carrot tree, I spent a couple of minutes re-reinforcing the head and right leg movements, and then turned again to the problem of getting him to lean on the extended leg while "kneeling" on the other. Since poking and tapping with the stick in various places on his leg proved unsuccessful, I finally tried lifting his leg for him and folding it back under him, repeating the command to bow while doing so. After almost five minutes, he finally completed the action satisfactorily at only a verbal command, sometimes on his own initiative and almost always at my command. I decided, for practical reasons, to reward only those bows responding to a verbal command since otherwise the practice might undergo extinction if he were to bow and expect immediate reinforcement when no one was present to award it to him.

In the end he was bowing superbly at every command. My only problem now was to get him to do it anywhere, not just under the tree in front of the tray. The cymbal-carrot-tray system was no longer necessary, since he had, at least for the time, forgotten his muzzling behavior. For this reason I started giving him positive reinforcement from my hand at the sound of the cymbal (but still only after a bow). Finally, I successfully replaced the cymbal sound with verbal praise, and Jack's lesson was completed.

Thus, using operant conditioning based on Skinner's helpful hints, I was able to teach Jack to perform a simple stunt, which he now does even without the carrot reward. The pocket muzzling behavior did not become completely extinct due to the variable-ratio reinforcement he was accustomed to, but he now also bows to gain attention, praise and, hopefully, something to eat.

REFERENCE

Skinner, B. F. How to teach animals. *Scientific American*, December 1951.

Learning can be more complex than the simple examples of conditioning described so far, as you have no doubt noticed in school. Do we always learn by a trial-and-error method? What about learning by insight—that "aha!" feeling? Is learning *always* improved when followed by a reward? These questions are discussed in the next article by Moyra Williams, a British psychologist who also happens to be an avid horse lover. Her description of experiences with her own horses helps to illustrate some important concepts in the study of learning.

LEARNING
MOYRA WILLIAMS

In the first place, it might be advisable to point out briefly the difference between learning and problem-solving, for although these are much alike they are not really identical.

When an individual solves a problem he is dealing with something here and now, of immediate practical importance; he is striving for a definite goal. When we speak of him learning we imply that he has added to his experience and his general store of knowledge and that he is better equipped to deal with future problems of the same sort than he was before.

All animals can and do modify their behaviour in the light of experience and thereby show some degree of what might be called learning; but such behaviour is not all in the same category as that of the monkey in the puzzle-box or Clever Hans with his mathematical tutor. Broadly speaking learning can be divided into several types—unconscious or unintelligent learning of the sort shown by many simple organisms; and conscious or intelligent learning of the sort shown by the higher animals and man.

But not all the higher animals learn equally quickly or in quite the same way. Let us go back again and consider once more an animal in the classical puzzle-box. All it has to do in order to escape is to press down the lever and swing open the door. . . . Human beings and monkeys will usually sit down quietly to examine the c .tch in order to find out how it works. Although they may make several tentative trials and different movements, they will analyse their failures as well as their suc-

SOURCE: From *Horse Psychology*. London: Methuen & Co., Ltd., 1956. Pp. 131–142. Reprinted by permission.

cess, with the object to discovering the basic principle of the mechanism. Once this has been found—even if it was not discovered spontaneously but had to be demonstrated by an outsider— the human being and intelligent animal will grasp the idea and at the same time get a pleasant flash of insight commonly known as the 'Aha'-feeling. If put in the puzzle-box a second time they will have no difficulty: the catch will be opened at once, and the animals will obtain their liberty without delay.

But cats and dogs are incapable, or almost so, of a reaction such as this. They bump about blindly inside the box until by chance they happen to push against the lever and the door swings open. They do not seem to be interested in principles. Their solution is usually quite fortuitous, and their only consideration is for the bait. Yet if such an animal is put back into the puzzle-box again it may be noticed that despite this attitude it will tend to hit against the lever and open the door more quickly than at the first attempt. The third time it will open the door more quickly still, and the fourth time quicker even than that. Finally there comes a moment when the animal is no sooner inside the box than it dashes to the lever and depresses it. Its escape during this final stage is just as quick and effective as that of the human or the monkey with insight.

Why and how trial-and-error learning leads to such efficient ends is still rather a mystery. It was suggested by Thorndike, who made a special study of this subject, that each time a movement leads to success, and therefore pleasure, there is a greater tendency to reproduce it in the future, whereas each time it leads to failure or displeasure the tendency to reproduce it is decreased. To put it shortly, 'Pleasure strengthens, and displeasure weakens.' However, rewards and punishments are not the only factors causing an act to be repeated. Once an act of any sort has been performed there is a tendency for it to be perpetuated, even though it may be utterly useless and unpleasant. The very fact of its having entered the individual's repertoire seems to lend it a momentum and it quickly becomes established as a habit. Wrong or useless habits often become as firmly established as useful ones, even though they are always punished and never rewarded, and these can be a serious obstacle to efficient learning. Because in trial-and-error learning the number of different acts tried out is usually much greater than in learning by insight, the number of bad habits which can be developed is higher in the former than in the latter. Hence learning by insight is a better and more successful way of learning than the trial-and-error method. But this is not the only advantage gained by insight. The animal which learns the principle of a puzzle-box can escape from it a second time almost as quickly as it will ever be able to do; one which learns only by trial and error may take

20, 30, or even 40 trials before it can manipulate the lever with any real efficiency. In addition, the animal which learns by insight can usually use its knowledge in a far greater variety of situations than one that is merely repeating a stereotyped habit. The ape or child who understands the principle of a puzzle-box latch will deal with any new but similar puzzle-box into which it is put without much difficulty. The animal which learns by trial and error, however, is in no such happy situation. In a new puzzle-box it will have to begin its bumping, jumping and rubbing all over again.

No one who has had the experience of schooling many different horses can have escaped being struck by the different speeds with which different individuals learn. Undoubtedly there are some who learn by insight and some only by trial and error. Some will pick up the meaning of an aid quickly and show an obvious change in their behaviour as they experience the 'Aha'-feeling; others have to have every movement and every new tactic drummed into them as with a sledge-hammer.

It is true that the intelligent horse may still make an occasional slip even after his initial flash of insight, but in this respect he is not alone. The schoolboy who is told how to solve a mathematical problem and who grasps the principle all right at the first demonstration may still forget it after a little while and have to have the method explained to him again. Insight does not, any more than trial and error, always lead to lasting and complete mastery of a situation. It can waver, be lost and regained, and lost again. All the same, in contrast to its complete absence, a flash of insight in a pupil now and then is a great consolation to a teacher.

Unus was always quick to learn, and in contrast to him Secunda, who had to have every movement dinned into her a hundred times, was the equivalent in the horse world of a 'dumb blonde.' Day after day, week in and week out, I tried to teach her not only the elements of balance, but also the rudiments of jumping. Day after day she would clout the 2-foot high pole and rap her shins, and even when the pole was fixed and the result a pair of temporarily disfigured knees she continued to hit it with alarming unconcern.

However, in her later history, Secunda exhibited one of those paradoxes of learning which make the whole process so confusing and difficult to understand. She was just beginning to develop balance of a sort and was starting for the first time to show some signs of jumping well when she became severely ill with a poisoned leg, which put her out of action for about 9 months. At the end of this period, which included 4 months at grass, I had expected her to have forgotten everything she ever knew and to be worse than ever. But this was not the case at all. Within a week of my beginning to ride her again she was not only back to where we had left off before her illness, but now without any trouble she was doing things which I had striven for months to teach her before and had despaired she would ever learn. The greatest surprise came over her jumping. Starting off again with the little poles which she had been fluffing previously, I was raising them to 3 ft. 6 ins. within a month, and within 2 months of riding her again she won two working-hunter classes and gave me one of the most enjoyable rides of my life in some Hunter Trials.

In this story of Secunda one sees what I should have been anticipating from the experience of other psychologists, but had overlooked—namely, the value of the latent period or a period of rest. One famous psychologist, William James, summed this up by suggesting that one learns to swim in winter and to skate in summer, meaning that the long rests between the seasons often help what has been learnt previously to consolidate and become truly assimilated. Those who have done a lot of horse-breaking may also have realized this principle when recommending, as is often done, that the elementary work, including a very brief backing, should be undertaken in the spring and the animal then turned out until the autumn. Whether they have recognized the value of the intermediate rest, or whether this is merely recommended from the point of view of convenience and because at these times, there being less distraction, more care can be devoted to the young horse, I do not know. However, it is certainly a recommendation which would have the support of scientific findings.

But the latent period during learning need not be as long as any of these stories suggest. Short latent periods can be of great assistance during all stages of learning, and rest periods, if carefully spaced, are seldom time wasted. It has been found during the course of innumerable experiments on animals and men that a thing which cannot be learned in under ten trials, if these are given immediately one after the other, can often be learned in half that number of trials if the lessons are spaced out. Moreover, the skills or knowledge acquired during these spaced trials are much more likely to be remembered over long periods than those that are acquired during a concentrated attack. During some work that I was doing on the study of memory I once carried out some experiments with human beings. My subjects had to remember long lists of word-pairs, such as dog-cat, house-castle, station-religion; the lists were read over and over again to them until they had learned the pairs by heart. Some of the lists were read over and over during the course of a single afternoon until the subjects had learned their quota, but others were read out once a week only during successive weeks until learned.

About a month or so after it was all over I met a number of these subjects again and asked them, out of interest, how many of the word-pairs they could still remember. The pairs which had been learned during the concentrated sessions had almost entirely been forgotten, but those which had been read out once each week were still clearly remembered by nearly everyone.

This principle seems to apply to all forms of learning and can be put to good use in the training of horses. Better and more lasting results will almost always be obtained if schooling is restricted to short-spaced sessions—if necessary two per day—than if an attempt is made to cram too much into a single ride.

But, returning to Secunda, the improvement she showed after her illness might also have been accounted for to some extent by the influence of another factor in learning besides that of the long rest. This factor is referred to usually as 'latent learning', implying that a lesson has really been assimilated although demonstration of it is still awaited. Thus, even though an animal shows no sign of having profited by an experience at the immediate time, his subsequent behaviour often indicates that something of it must have sunk in. It is as though learning were at work under the surface; as though some information were being stored, even though the animal might show no sign of this at the time.

That such learning frequently occurs in horses must be known to all who have tried to school them. The instructor struggles and sweats one day to teach his animal some simple manoeuvre—feeling that it is wrong to give in until the horse has made a response, however elementary, in the right direction—until in the end, exhausted and exasperated, he packs up, defeated, swearing to send the brute to the next sale or give it to the first passer-by. Perhaps the next day, perhaps a week later, he decides to make one last attempt. The incredible happens, and the horse responds at the first touch as if it had been doing that particular thing all its life. Despite its seeming obstinacy on the previous occasion, it had apparently been learning all the time, and it merely needed a short pause for the proof of this to become evident.

There is an important question here. Would the same results have been obtained equally well without the sweat and struggle of the previous session? Could the rider have spared both himself and his horse some anguish if he had buried his pride and given in earlier? The answer is almost certainly 'Yes.' Moreover, by packing up before tempers become too frayed the rider would not only have saved himself much pain, but would have avoided the risk of upsetting his horse too far. There is always a danger that an animal which loses confidence, instead of absorbing its lesson at however elementary a level, may resort instead to some unwanted action which serves to minimize the discomfort of the moment. These actions quickly tend to become perpetuated as stereotyped habits, and once such a habit is developed it is very difficult to eradicate later.

I had an unfortunate experience of this once with Tertia. The little mare was coming along quite nicely and had got to the stage of cantering round in circles, leading off on either leg as required, when one day, for some unknown reason, she refused to lead on the off-fore when given the office to do so. Perhaps her leg was painful, or perhaps she just did not feel in the mood —I do not know. At any rate, I am sure that had I been wise I would have abandoned riding her on that day and tried again quietly at some future date. Instead of doing this, I got obstinate and decided to go on until she obeyed. After a little while we were both extremely angry, and instead of giving way from the pressure of my leg Tertia started slewing her quarters round into it and kicking out at the side. The next day she did the same thing, and the more I punished her the more stubbornly she kicked. By the end of that week this action had become firmly established, and as soon as she was touched with either leg she threw her quarters into it, kicking out to the side, instead of bending away. It finally became necessary to go right back to the beginning of her schooling and spend several weeks walking, trotting, and cantering in a small confined ring again before she overcame the fault and returned to where we had been before. Even then the habit was only lying dormant, to reappear once more when opportunity arose. About a year after Tertia left us her new owner, having been unable to ride for some time, sent her back to me again to have her tuned up before she was re-sold. Tertia was in great fettle, very full of beans and clearly beside herself with the joys of life. The thought of concentrating on doing what she was told did not enter her head for some days, and at the slightest touch of a leg she would slew her quarters into it in exactly the same way as she had done on the previous occasion, kicking out violently to the side. Not till she had disposed of her rider several times and had spent a little of her energy breaking various bits of harness was she again in the mood to remember what she had learned and abandon this uncomfortable tendency.

It may be wondered, however, how Tertia was ever to know that by throwing her quarters into the leg instead of giving away from it she was not doing what was wanted of her. How does a horse that is being schooled ever know, in fact, when it is doing right and when wrong? Even granted that it has to learn by trial and error, where are the rewards for the correct trials in such a situation and where the punishments for the wrong ones?

There are of course no natural rewards or punishments for such actions as walking, trotting and cantering to command, for backing, turning and halting, or leading at a canter on one leg as opposed to another. Whatever rewards there are are dependent entirely on the rider and on his ability to give the aids consistently and promptly. We cannot tell the horse what to do except by saying 'yes' when it does right and 'no' when it does wrong. But it is not an easy matter for a horse to guess what is wanted of it with no more explanation than this. In order to find out just how difficult it is we decided at Stones Farm to try a little experiment of the same sort on ourselves, using a modified version of the parlour game 'Twenty Questions.' One of the party was sent out of the room, and those who remained decided between themselves what she should be made to do on her return. The only words which could be spoken after her readmission were 'yes' and 'no' (not even the back-chat of the question-master was allowed here). One person kept a tally of the number of prompts (yes's and no's) given for each job, and another a record of the time taken to guess it.

I should perhaps explain that besides wanting to see life from the horse's viewpoint we were interested in finding out whether there were any basic principles in this kind of learning which could help us in our training of horses. Was there one thing which we should teach before another, one kind of act that was easier to learn than another, one way of giving the prompts which assisted learning more readily than another? In order to answer these questions we chose several different kinds of job and gave our cues in several different ways.

As might be expected, we found that the ease with which the job was guessed depended very much on three things: (1) on the job itself and its relevance to the situation; (2) on the speed and consistency with which the prompts were given; (3) on the presence or absence of other cues. The job of washing eggs—a not very much beloved but routine evening performance—was guessed easily in 45 seconds and after only 10 prompts, although when the same person was faced with the job of tying a knot in the tea-towel—a thing which one would not normally do—this was only guessed after the most insightless struggle as pathetic as that of any cat in a puzzle-box. The interesting point in this case was that the girl picked up the tea-towel after 30 seconds and 12 prompts, but having done so she could think only of the things she would normally do with a tea-towel and had great difficulty in putting these out of her mind before she could imagine anything new.

This experience suggests that when schooling a young horse one should always start with the simplest and most obvious manoeuvres first, leading on from these to more difficult ones gradually. One should never start the day by trying to teach something completely new. Start with a familiar lesson as like the new as possible and lead on from this lesson slowly.

But to return to our own experiments, we found that the effect of the way in which the prompts were given was no less drastic than the nature of the job itself. If the prompts were given consistently and at the earliest possible moment—'yes' as soon as the person turned even her eyes in the right direction, 'no' as soon as she moved a foot away from the goal—the job was guessed with the minimum difficulty—by one person in 20 seconds with only 5 prompts. If no prompts were given at all and the person was merely allowed to wander around till she finally hit on what was required, the whole of her behaviour and attitude changed. She became hesitant, disgruntled, and lost interest. She saw no point in going on with the experiment. She would start one thing after another, never finishing a job or worrying about what it was. She would try to pick up cues in our looks and giggles, and the fact that one of our experimentees did hit on the right job after about 4½ minutes was rather more by good luck than anything else.

However, the most disturbing effect of all was caused by the inclusion of one or two false prompts—a 'yes' when the person moved in the wrong direction, or a 'no' when she moved in the right one. Even though on every other occasion the prompts had been given quickly and consistently and though the tasks were straightforward and simple, these occasional false moves threw the experimentees completely out of gear. One girl gave up after 3 minutes and 70 prompts, and another after 5½ minutes and 93 prompts. One realizes from this how much damage may be done to an animal from even one single act of inconsistency in the early stages of training, such as patting a horse if it refuses a fence or jabbing it in the mouth if it jumps well. However unpleasant for a horse the right response may be, the wrong one should be even more so. This need not necessarily be cruel, even though it may sound hard. An unhappy animal is one that is in a state of constant uncertainty and apprehension, one who never knows from which direction danger threatens and who never knows when the blow may fall. An animal that has been hurt in the past and who knows what actions to avoid in the future is not necessarily more unhappy than a child who has burnt his fingers in the fire. This is not meant to imply that the harder a horse is hit for its offences the better and the kinder, but only that there are times when even severe punishment may be justified as long as it is applied consistently and promptly.

At the same time, not all punishment need be severe or even painful. It is possible, in horses as in humans, to make the words 'yes' and 'no' develop a definite significance, so that they can be used as token rewards or token punishments and substituted for actual acts. Horses . . . quickly learn to associate sounds with pleasure or displeasure, and such associations persist with very little reinforcement later. It is well worth while to teach a young horse that 'yes' means 'good' and 'no' means 'bad' at a very early stage, so that the use of the stick can be minimized later on.

During our experiment in the kitchen we found, however, that the guessers were not only responding to the promptings intentionally given to them: they were deriving cues from all sorts of other sources as well, such as the looks on our faces, the appearance of the room, or our attitude when they entered. In one case, a rude giggle as the experimentee came into the kitchen gave her the right idea at once: she ran into the lavatory and pulled the plug!

That horses respond similarly to involuntary or extraneous cues I have no doubt. When we approach the stables on a Saturday morning in winter wearing our hunting clothes instead of the usual dirty 'macs and gum-boots, the horses know at once what is in the air and become restive. After they hear the horse-box being started in the summer, they behave quite differently when brought into the stables and groomed than if they are simply being prepared for a normal daily ride. Very often such cues can be used to great advantage in training, but it is possible for them also to be a considerable hindrance by distracting the horse's attention from the job in hand.

When I first started teaching Unus to show jump I believed very strongly in interfering as little as possible with the horse by telling it when to take off and how to balance itself. I believed that if it was merely rewarded every time it did well and punished every time it did badly it would become a better and safer jumper in the end than if all the decisions were taken by a fallible rider. This, I must hasten to add, was in the days when show jumping was untimed and when the majority of obstacles were simple uprights covered with slats. Unus was very quick to learn and was soon jumping consistently well in the field at home, so that within a few weeks we were ready to embark on our first public venture. But in my calculations and training I had forgotten to allow for the possible effect of outside cues. Unus had only learned the effects of reward and punishment in our field at home and apparently he did not associate such experiences with the new situation or the obstacles he suddenly saw before him. The horses outside the ring formed a far greater attraction than the empty inside of the ring itself, and my principle of giving him no help till after the event—i.e., till after he had either jumped or refused—very nearly ended in disaster. Receiving no special preliminary orders from me, he naturally refused the first fence, and after receiving the appropriate hiding even more naturally came to regard the show ring as a perfectly beastly place which it would be wise to leave as soon as possible. Our next attempt was little more successful than the first. Unus was by now firmly convinced that all the good he got out of entering the ring was a thrashing and decided he would have none of it. It was necessary to nurse him very carefully over several novice courses before his confidence was restored and the same rewards and punishments could be applied to his performance in the show ring as at home.

LEARNING MORE ABOUT THE SUBJECT

There is just not room, in a book of this nature, to give adequate attention to all the different theories of learning although there *are* many. There are some psychologists who do not believe that reinforcement is critical to the acquisition of a learned response, but to the *motivation to perform* that response after it has already been learned. Guthrie maintains, for example, that all learning proceeds as does simple classical conditioning, from a response being performed in the presence of some stimulus. A very readable discussion of this viewpoint is Guthrie's book, *The Psychology of Learning* (Harper & Row, 1935).

For other articles illustrating simple classical conditioning, you would probably find H. D. Ephron, "Re Early Conditioning" (*American Psychologist,* 1957, *12,* 158) enjoyable, along with an article by K. M. Dallenbach, "Twitmyer and the Conditioned Response" (*American Journal of Psychology,* 1959, *72,* 633–638).

Are you the kind of student who studies a subject in short, spaced periods—or do you prefer to sit down for one long session to really concentrate on it? Did you ever wonder which is the more efficient method? Try reading Irwin Rock, "Repetition in Learning" (*Scientific American,* August, 1958).

A more in-depth discussion of instrumental conditioning is Jozef Cohen's book, *Operant Behavior and Operant Conditioning* (Rand-McNally, 1969). For anyone interested in trying his own version of LouAnna Crain's experiment with her burro, B. F. Skinner's article "How to Teach Animals" (*Scientific American,* December, 1951) would be useful. If you'd rather use reinforcement principles on somebody other than a pet, Joel Greenspoon, "The Effect of Two Spoken Sounds on the Frequency of Two Responses" (*American Journal of Psychology,* 1955, *68,* 408–416) describes one method. A word of caution, here, however. Students who have tried out Greenspoon's approach have complained to us that their verbal approval was not always reinforcing for a younger brother or sister. You may not always want to recruit a sibling for a subject!

Part Eight

Applied Learning: Influencing the Process

Why, after all, do we study learning? One thing psychologists hope to do is to contribute to our understanding of ourselves. Man's capacity to learn is much greater than that of other animals or any computer. Understanding how the process works can help us better define ourselves as uniquely human.

We have used examples of animal learning to illustrate basic principles. But one of the ways we differ from animals is in our capacity to learn *about* a large number of things without having to experience them directly. This is why each successive generation can build on, not merely repeat, the experiences of those who went before—as long as it is known what those experiences have been! One of the ways this transfer of knowledge occurs is by means of formal education.

Besides achieving a better understanding of ourselves as humans, we ought to be able to apply principles of learning to our educational process and improve it—both as instructors and as students. As you read the articles in this part, try to look at them from both sides of the coin. How could you, as students (which you will always be, in one form or another), benefit from them? And how could you, as a teacher (as we all are, sometime, in one form or another) profit?

We are making the distinction here between formal, *intentional learning* (and teaching!) and *incidental learning.* Intentional learning is the only kind we can do much about, for one thing, and it is certainly the more efficient mode of learning. (Some years ago, G. C. Myers [1] demonstrated this by asking subjects to count the number of *O's* printed on a page containing a variety of letters of different colors. Later, he asked them questions about *other* letters on the page. He found that without the intent to learn, students had paid no attention to—and learned almost nothing about—the other letters.)

The article following is a concise summary of the conclusions one educator feels we can draw from the various studies of learning. Although his approach is that the teacher, try to translate, as you go along, what each of his propositions means to the student intent on improving his learning skills.

[1] Myers, G. C. A Study in Incidental Memory. *Archives of Psychology,* 1913, No. 26.

26

WHAT DO WE KNOW ABOUT LEARNING?
GOODWIN WATSON

What do we really know today about learning? Although no scientific "truths" are established beyond the possibility of revision, knowledgeable psychologists generally agree on a number of propositions about learning which are important for education. The educator who bases his program on the propositions presented below is entitled, therefore, to feel that he is on solid psychological ground and not on shifting sands.

Behaviors which are rewarded (reinforced) are more likely to recur.

This most fundamental law of learning has been demonstrated in literally thousands of experiments. It seems to hold for every sort of animal from earthworms to highly intelligent adults. The behavior most likely to emerge in any situation is that which the subject found successful or satisfying previously in a similar situation. No other variable affects learning so powerfully. The best-planned learning provides for a steady, cumulative sequence of successful behaviors.

Reward (reinforcement), to be most effective in learning, must follow almost immediately after the desired behavior and be clearly connected with that behavior in the mind of the learner.

The simple word, "Right," coming directly after a given response, will have more influence on learning than any big reward which comes much later or which is dimly connected with many responses so that it can't really reinforce any of them. Much of the effectiveness of programed self-instruction lies in the fact that information about success is fed back immediately for each learner response. A total mark on a test the day after it is administered has little or no reinforcement value for the specific answers.

Sheer repetition without indications of improvement or any kind of reinforcement (reward) is a poor way to attempt to learn.

Practice is not enough. The learner cannot improve by repeated efforts unless he is informed whether or not each effort has been successful.

Threat and punishment have variable and uncertain effects upon learning: They may make the punished response more likely or less likely to recur: they may set up avoidance tendencies which prevent further learning.

SOURCE: From *NEA Journal*, March, 1963, pp. 20–22. Reprinted by permission.

Punishment is not, psychologically, the reverse of reward. It disturbs the relationship of the learner to the situation and the teacher. It does not assist the learner in finding and fixing the correct response.

Readiness for any new learning is a complex product of interaction among such factors as (a) sufficient physiological and psychological maturity, (b) sense of the importance of the new learning for the learner in his world, (c) mastery of prerequisites providing a fair chance of success, and (d) freedom from discouragement (expectation of failure) or threat (sense of danger).

Conversely, the learner will not be ready to try new responses which are beyond his powers or are seen as valueless or too dangerous.

Opportunity for fresh, novel, stimulating experience is a kind of reward which is quite effective in conditioning and learning.

Experiments indicate that lower animals (rats, dogs, monkeys) will learn as effectively when they receive rewards of new experience or satisfied curiosity as they will when the rewards gratify physical desires. Similarly, stimulating new insights have been found to be effective as rewards for the learning efforts of human beings.

The sense of satisfaction which results from achievement is the type of reward (reinforcement) which has the greatest transfer value to other life situations.

Any extrinsic reward—candy, or stars on a chart, or commendation—depends on its dispenser. There is no need to strive if the reward-giver is out of the picture. Also, cheating can sometimes win the extrinsic reward. The internal reward system is always present for the learner, and he sees little gain in fooling himself.

Learners progress in an area of learning only as far as they need to in order to achieve their purposes. Often they do only well enough to "get by"; with increased motivation, they improve.

Studies of reading speed show that practice alone will not bring improvement; a person may have read books for years at his customary rate, but with new demands and opportunities he may be able to double that rate.

The most effective effort is put forth by children when they attempt tasks which are not too easy and not too hard—where success seems quite possible but not certain. It is not reasonable to expect a teacher to set an appropriate level of challenge for each pupil in a class; pupils can, however, be helped to set their own goals to bring maximum satisfaction and learning.

Children are more likely to throw themselves wholeheartedly into any learning project if they themselves have participated in the selection and planning of the project.

Genuine participation (not pretended sharing) increases motivation, adaptability, and speed of learning.

Excessive direction by the teacher is likely to result in apathetic conformity, defiance, scapegoating, or escape from the whole affair.

Autocratic leadership has been found to increase dependence of members on the leader and to generate resentment (conscious or unconscious) which finds expression in attacks on weaker figures or even in sabotage of the work.

Overstrict discipline is associated with more conformity, anxiety, shyness, and acquiescence in children; greater permissiveness is associated with more initiative and creativity.

In comparisons of children whose parents were most permissive in home discipline with those whose parents were most strict (both groups of parents loving and concerned), the youngsters from permissive homes showed more enterprise, self-confidence, curiosity, and originality.

Many pupils experience so much criticism, failure, and discouragement in school that their self-confidence, level of aspiration, and sense of worth are damaged.

The pupil who sees himself at his worst in school is likely to place little value on study and to seek his role of importance outside the classroom. He may carry through life a sense of being not good for much. He is likely also to feel resentment at schools, teachers, and books.

When children or adults experience too much frustration, their behavior ceases to be integrated, purposeful, and rational. The threshold of what is "too much" varies; it is lowered by previous failures.

Pupils who have had little success and almost continuous failure at school tasks are in no condition to think, to learn, or even to pay attention. They may turn their anger outward against respectable society or inward against themselves.

Pupils think whenever they encounter an obstacle, difficulty, puzzle, or intellectual challenge which interests them. The process of thinking involves designing and testing plausible solutions for the problem as understood by the thinker.

It is useless to command people to think; they must feel concerned to get somewhere and eager to remove an obstruction on the way.

The best way to help pupils form a general concept is to present the concept in numerous and varied specific situations—contrasting experiences with and without the desired concept—and then to encourage precise formulations of the general idea and its application in situations different from those in which the concept was learned.

For example, the concept of democracy might be illustrated not only in national government but also in familiar situations of home, school, church, jobs, clubs, and local affairs. It is best understood when it is contrasted with other power structures such as autocracy, oligarchy, or *laissez faire*.

The experience of learning by sudden insight into a previously confused or puzzling situation arises when (a) there has been a sufficient background and preparation, (b) attention is given to the relationships operative in the whole situation, (c) the perceptual structure "frees" the key elements to be shifted into new patterns, (d) the task is meaningful and within the range of ability of the subject.

The term "cognitive reorganization" is sometimes applied to this experience. Suddenly the scene changes into one that seems familiar and can be coped with.

Learning from reading is facilitated more by time spent recalling what has been read than by re-reading.

In one experiment (typical of many), students who spent eighty percent of their learning periods trying to remember what they had read surpassed those who spent only sixty percent of the time on recollection. The students who spent all the time reading and re-reading the assignment made the poorest record.

Forgetting proceeds rapidly at first—then more and more slowly. Recall shortly after learning reduces the amount forgotten.

Within twenty-four hours after learning something, a large part is forgotten unless efforts are made to prevent forgetting. A thing can be relearned more quickly than it was learned originally, however, and if it is reviewed several times at gradually increasing intervals, it can be retained for some time.

People remember new information which confirms their previous attitudes better than they remember new information which runs counter to their previous attitudes.

Studies consistently show that individuals who feel strongly on a controversial issue, and who are asked to read presentations of both sides, remember the facts and arguments which support their feelings better than they recall those on the opposite side.

What is learned is most likely to be available for use if it is learned in a situation much like that in which it is to be used and immediately preceding the time when it is needed. Learning in childhood, then forgetting, and later relearning when need arises is not an efficient procedure.

The best time to learn is when the learning can be useful. Motivation is then strongest and forgetting less of a problem. Much that is now taught children might be more effective if taught to responsible adults.

If there is a discrepancy between the real objectives and the tests used to measure achievement, the latter become the main influence upon choice of subject matter and method. Curriculum and teaching geared to standardized tests and programed learning are likely to concentrate only on learnings which can be easily checked and scored.

The most rapid mental growth comes during infancy and early childhood; the average child achieves about half of his total mental growth by age five.

In the first two years a normal child transforms the "big, buzzing, blooming confusion" of his first conscious experience to organized perception of familiar faces, spoken words, surroundings, toys, bed, clothing, and foods. He differentiates himself from others, high from low, many from few, approval from disapproval. He lays a foundation for lifelong tendencies toward trust or mistrust, self-acceptance or shame, initiative or passivity; and these vitally condition further growth.

Not until adolescence do most children develop the sense of time which is required for historical perspective. The so-called facts of history—1492, 1776, and all that—can be learned by children but without any real grasp of what life was like in another period or in a different country. Most instruction in ancient, medieval, and even modern history is no more real to children than are fairy tales.

Ability to learn increases with age up to adult years. The apparent decline is largely the result of lack of motivation. We can coerce children into school activities; adult education is mostly voluntary. Men and women *can*, if they wish, master new languages, new ideas, and new ways of acting or problem-solving even at sixty and seventy years of age.

Did Watson make any points which struck you as particularly relevant from the learner's viewpoint? What about his comments about threat and punishment? These usually act to impair learning. And yet, often enough students spur themselves on to learn something in school by threatening themselves. It might be useful to compare your feelings toward the subject you most dislike and the one you most enjoy, in light of Watson's article. Is there any difference in your motivation to study? In which subject are you the more successful learner? Does Watson have any suggestions that you could use to improve your learning of the despised subject?

The author of the next selection, like Watson, approaches his topic from the instructor's point of view. J. S. Bruner is interested in how best to teach a subject so that the student appreciates "the structure, the rightness and the beauty" of it. How could the student employ Bruner's methods in his own learning endeavors?

27

STRUCTURES IN LEARNING

JEROME S. BRUNER

Every subject has a structure, a rightness, a beauty. It is this structure that provides the underlying simplicity of things, and it is by learning its nature that we come to appreciate the intrinsic meaning of a subject.

Let me illustrate by reference to geography. Children in the fifth grade of a suburban school were about to study the geography of the Central states as part of a social studies unit. Previous units on the Southeastern states, taught by rote, had proved a bore. Could geography be taught as a rational discipline? Determined to find out, the teachers devised a unit in which students would have to figure out not only where things are located, but why they are there. This involves a sense of the structure of geography.

The children were given a map of the Central states in which only rivers, large bodies of water, agricultural products, and natural resources were shown. They were not allowed to consult their books. Their task was to find Chicago, "the largest city in the North Central states."

The argument got under way immediately. One child came up with the idea that Chicago must be on the junction of the three large lakes. No matter that at this point he did not know the names of the lakes—Huron, Superior, and Michigan—his theory was well-reasoned. A big city produced a lot of products, and the easiest and most logical way to ship these products is by water.

But a second child rose immediately to the opposition. A big city needed lots of food, and he placed Chicago where there are corn and hogs—right in the middle of Iowa.

A third child saw the issue more broadly—recognizing virtues in both previous arguments. He pointed out that large quantities of food can be grown in river valleys. Whether he had learned this from a previous social studies unit or from raising carrot seeds, we shall never know. If you had a river, he reasoned, you had not only food but transportation. He pointed to a spot on the map not far from St. Louis. "There is where Chicago *ought* to be." Would that graduate students would always do so well!

Not all the answers were so closely reasoned, though even the wild ones had about them a sense of the necessity involved in a city's location.

SOURCE: From *NEA Journal*, March, 1963, pp. 26–27. Reprinted by permission.

One argued, for example, that all American cities have sky-scrapers, which require steel, so he placed Chicago in the middle of the Mesabi Range. At least he was thinking on his own, with a sense of the constraints imposed on the location of cities.

After forty-five minutes, the children were told they could pull down the "real" wall map (the one with names) and see where Chicago really is. After the map was down, each of the contending parties pointed out how close they had come to being right. Chicago had not been located. But the location of cities was no longer a matter of unthinking chance for this group of children.

What had the children learned? A way of thinking about geography, a way of dealing with its raw data. They had learned that there is some relationship between the requirements of living and man's habitat. If that is all they got out of their geography lesson, that is plenty. Did they remember which is Lake Huron? Lake Superior? Lake Michigan? Do you?

Teachers have asked me about "the new curricula" as though they were some special magic potion. They are nothing of the sort. The new curricula, like our little exercise in geography, are based on the fact that knowledge has an internal connectedness, a meaningfulness, and that for facts to be appreciated and understood and remembered, they must be fitted into that internal meaningful context.

The set of prime numbers is not some arbitrary nonsense. What can be said about quantities that cannot be arranged into multiple columns and rows? Discussing that will get you on to the structure of primes and factorability.

It often takes the deepest minds to discern the simplest structure in knowledge. For this reason if for no other, the great scholar and the great scientist and the greatly compassionate man are needed in the building of new curricula.

There is one other point. Our geographical example made much of discovery. What difference does discovery make in the learning of the young? First, let it be clear what the act of discovery entails. It is only rarely on the frontier of knowledge that new facts are "discovered" in the sense of being encountered, as Newton suggested, as "islands of truth in an uncharted sea of ignorance." Discovery, whether by a schoolboy going it on his own or by a scientist, is most often a matter of rearranging or transforming evidence in such a way that one is now enabled to go beyond the evidence to new insights. Discovery involves the finding of the right structure, the meaningfulness.

Consider now what benefits the child might derive from the experience of learning through his own discoveries. These benefits can be discussed in terms of increased intellectual potency, intrinsic rewards, useful learning techniques, and better memory processes.

For the child to develop *intellectual potency*, he must be encouraged to search out and find regularities and relationships in his environment. To do this, he needs to be armed with the expectancy that there is something for him to find and, once aroused by this expectancy, he must devise his own ways of searching and finding.

Emphasis on discovery in learning has the effect upon the learner of leading him to be a constructionist—to organize what he encounters in such a manner that he not only discovers regularity and relatedness, but also avoids the kind of information drift that fails to keep account of how the information will be used.

In speaking of *intrinsic motives* for learning (as opposed to extrinsic motives), it must be recognized that much of the problem in leading a child in effective cognitive activity is to free him from the immediate control of environmental punishments and rewards.

For example, studies show that children who seem to be early overachievers in school are likely to be seekers after the "right way to do it" and that their capacity for transforming their learning into useful thought structures tends to be less than that of children merely achieving at levels predicted by intelligence tests.

The hypothesis drawn from these studies is that if a child is able to approach learning as a task of discovering something rather than "learning about it" he will tend to find a more personally meaningful reward in his own competency and self-achievement in the subject than he will find in the approval of others.

There are many ways of coming to the *techniques of inquiry* or the heuristics of discovery. One of them is by careful study of the formalization of these techniques in logic, statistics, mathematics, and the like. If a child is going to pursue inquiry as an eventual way of life, particularly in the sciences, formal study is essential. Yet, whoever has taught kindergarten and the early primary grades (periods of intense inquiry) knows that an understanding of the formal aspect of inquiry is not sufficient or always possible.

Children appear to have a series of attitudes and activities they associate with inquiry. Rather than a formal approach to the relevance of variables in their search, they depend on their sense of what things among an ensemble of things "smell right" as being of the proper order of magnitude or scope of severity.

It is evident then that if children are to learn the working techniques of discovery, they must be afforded the opportunities of problem solving. The more they practice problem solving, the more likely they are to generalize what they learn into a style of inquiry that serves for any kind of task they may encounter. It is doubtful that anyone ever improves in the art and technique of inquiry by any other means than engaging in inquiry, or problem solving.

The first premise in a theory concerning the *improvement of memory processes* is that the principal problem of human memory is not storage, but retrieval. The premise may be inferred from the fact that recognition (i.e., recall with the aid of maximum prompts) is extraordinarily good in human beings—particularly in comparison to spontaneous recall when information must be recalled without external aids or prompts. The key to retrieval is organization.

There are myriad findings to indicate that any organization of information that reduces the collective complexity of material by imbedding it into a mental structure the child has constructed will make that material more accessible for retrieval. In sum, the child's very attitudes and activities that characterize "figuring out" or "discovering" things for himself also seem to have the effect of making material easier to remember.

If man's intellectual excellence is the most important among his perfections (as Maimonides, the great Hispanic-Judaic philosopher once said), then it is also the case that the most uniquely personal of all that man knows is that which he discovers for himself. What difference does it make when we encourage discovery in the young? It creates, as Maimonides would put it, a special and unique relation between knowledge possessed and the possessor.

Besides understanding better how to educate ourselves, we may also apply the principles of learning to animal training. Keller Breland studied at Harvard with B. F. Skinner and became intrigued, as did Skinner, with the possibilities offered by instrumental conditioning techniques. Instead of pursuing the matter on an academic front, he elected to start applying the principles immediately—and went into the business of teaching pigs to clean house!

28

A FIELD OF APPLIED ANIMAL PSYCHOLOGY
KELLER BRELAND AND MARIAN BRELAND

Recent developments in behavior theory have made possible a new field of applied psychology. This new field has yet to be finally christened. It might be called the field of applied animal psychology or the field of behavioral engineering. We consider it an excellent example of how the findings of "pure" research can be put to practical use.

The core of the field is the work of the neobehaviorists, which has so ordered the facts of behavior that many of their experimental data and those of earlier workers have become immediately applicable to the engineering of animal behavior. We have found most useful the systematic formulation presented by B. F. Skinner in *The Behavior of Organisms*. This body of theory has made it possible for us since the spring of 1947 to develop a flourishing and expanding business concerned with the mass production of conditioned operant behavior in animals.

Applied animal psychology brings together the two formerly unrelated fields of professional animal training and modern behavioral science. The field is new in that it represents, we believe, the first application of systematic behavior theory to the control of animal behavior. We are now in a position to outstrip old-time professional animal trainers in speed and economy of training. In many instances we can use automatic training methods. We can apply to our training the data of comparative psychology, utilizing new tricks, new animals. We can turn out multiple units—200 "Clever Hanses" instead of one. Furthermore, the systematic nature of the theory puts us in a position to advance to new and more elaborate behavior patterns, to predict results and forestall difficulties.

So far, all our applications have been made for the purpose of advertising exhibits for General Mills, Inc. We developed first a series of trained chicken acts, which were used for county fair booth exhibits in the Midwest, for the purpose of advertising farm feeds. These acts were performed by a group of two-year-old hens which had been culled from a neighbor's flock and were destined for the stew pot. We used a hen-sized stage, some specially constructed props, and a solenoid-driven automatic feed hopper for dispensing reinforcements in the form of scratch grain.

SOURCE: From *American Psychologist*, 1951, *6*, 202–204. Copyright © 1951 by the American Psychological Association and reproduced by permission.

One hen played a 5-note tune on a small piano, another performed a "tap dance" in costume and shoes, while a third "laid" wooden eggs from a nest box; the eggs rolled down a trough into a basket–the audience could call out any number of eggs desired, up to eight, and the hen would lay that number, nonstop.

The basic operation in all these acts was reinforcement at the proper moment in the behavior sequence, by presenting the chicken with a small amount of scratch grain from the solenoid-operated hopper. During the training period, successive approximations to the desired behavior, and component parts of the final pattern, were reinforced. During performances, longer ratios or more elaborate completed patterns were reinforced to keep the behavior at a high level of strength.

During the ensuing year, three sets of these acts were prepared and shipped all over the United States in the hands of men who had had only one or two days' training. The birds played thousands of performances without a single failure, except for an occasional sluggish performance due to ill health or overfeeding. The acts proved to be unprecedented crowd-stoppers at the fairs and feed-store "Openhouse" events where they played, showing to as many as 5,000 people in a day.

The success of these acts led to the development of a trained pig show, "Priscilla the Fastidious Pig," whose routine included turning on the radio, eating breakfast at a table, picking up the dirty clothes and putting them in a hamper, running the vacuum cleaner around, picking out her favorite feed from those of her competitors, and taking part in a quiz program, answering "Yes" or "No" to questions put by the audience, by lighting up the appropriate signs.

Priscilla was likewise shown at fairs and special feed-store events and conventions throughout the country. She also appeared on television. She was even more successful than the chicken acts at jamming fair booths and feed-stores with spectators. The pig act was in use almost steadily from the fall of 1948 to the summer of 1950. It was necessary to train a replacement about every 3 to 5 months, since the pigs rapidly became too large for easy shipping. After training, the pigs were turned over to their handler, usually a General Mills' feed salesman, who had had one or two days' instruction at our farm, or in the field under our supervision.

In addition to teaching handlers to manage the animals on the road, we have twice taught instructors to do the basic training of the animals and assist with the instruction of the handlers. Both experiences in training instructors were successful and demonstrated clearly that people with no special psychological background can learn the methods and theory behind our animal training procedures. One instructor was a woman college graduate who had taken her degree in statistics and sociology. The other was an average male high school graduate, whose only specialty had been radio repair work. Both acquired in a few weeks most of the techniques of training the existing acts, and enough of the theory and nature of the process to train acts on their own.

Our next development was a baby chick act. Sixty to 100 chicks are trained for one show. Beginning at about one week of age, they are trained for about 10 days. The show is run with about 10 or 12 chicks on stage. Each runs up a ramp or inclined plane to a platform from which he can reach a feed hopper. He "roots" the top chick off, grabs a bite of feed, then in turn gets pushed off by the next in line. As he goes, he falls onto a tilting pan and is deposited onto the stage floor, accompanied by the sounding of a chime and flashing of a trade name sign. This sequence of behavior results in an endless chain of baby chicks running up the ramp and sliding off. When the group becomes sleepy, they are replaced by a fresh batch, and the show can thus go on indefinitely; it has actually been used about 12 hours a day in most cases.

This act is our first "packaged act." It is designed to run virtually automatically. It requires only the attendant to keep the feed hopper full and change the group of chicks on stage when they become sleepy. No special training is required for the attendant; mimeographed directions are shipped out with the chicks and provide the only necessary instruction. This act has been a perennial favorite and we have trained more than 2,500 chicks to fill orders for this display.

We have developed two variations on the baby chick act. One uses a projector to present advertising copy, with an endless chain of baby chicks in motion around it. The other variation substitutes for the ramp a series of steps onto which the chicks must jump.

A calf was trained for the General Mills' booth at the International Dairy Exposition at Indianapolis. "Larro Larry" took part in a quiz program by lighting up "Yes" and "No" signs, as did Priscilla the Pig, and played "Bull in the China Shop" by systematically upsetting an elaborate display of dishes, to the great alarm of the passing crowd.

A turkey act has been developed in which members of the audience play a game with the turkey. The bird is placed in a display case and has access through an opening to part of the miniature playing field. The turkey is trained to rake a steel ball off this field into his goal. The audience player is given a long pole with a magnet on one end and tries to guide the ball along the playing field into his goal before the turkey wins. Various barriers are placed along the playing field to make the game more difficult for both players.

Additional acts using grown chickens have been designed and used, two involving discrimination problems: the Card Sharp, who picks out a better poker hand than a member of the audience, and the Old Shell Game, in which the chicken picks out the shell with the bean under it; and two contests between two birds, a High Jump contest, and a Strength of Pull test. Another automatic act was created by training a hen, on a very high fixed ratio, to beat a toy drum for hours at a time. We also trained a hen in some bizarre contortions; the hen twisted her neck to one side and over her back so that she appeared to be looking frantically in all directions at once. This was billed as "The Civilian Aircraft Spotter" or "The Atom Bomb Neurosis." We have done a few experiments and some developmental work on rats, hamsters, guinea pigs, ducks, pigeons, rabbits, cats, dogs, and crows.

There are, obviously, innumerable other possibilities in the field of advertising exhibits. One is the perfection of the "packaged act," the fully automatic unit which can be shipped anywhere, set up in a store window or convention booth, and operated day in and day out with no more instructions than are necessary for the operation of any machine designed for such use. One adaptation of the automatic act is the animated display —show window advertising in which live animals take the place of puppets and robots.

However, probably the biggest applications exist in the entertainment world. Here we can take over the formal animal training involved in the standard animal act for stage, circus, and movies, and do it faster, cheaper, better, and in multiple units. It is possible to create new acts, whole new circuses, in fact, using unusual animals and unusual acts, and again do it cheaply, quickly, and in numbers limited only by time and production facilities. Television offers unusual opportunities. We can invade the field of night-club entertainment with novel small animals. We can sell or rent trained animal units to hospitals, doctors' offices, waiting rooms of various sorts, or even to private individuals, supplying instructions on care and maintenance.

Another important application of animal psychology is the training of farm animals. Farm dogs and horses could be rendered much more useful to the average farmer if they were given appropriate training. Farmers could themselves be instructed in training and handling their own animals.

The training of dogs for the blind could probably be done on a larger scale, more rapidly and efficiently. One of the big problems of the "Seeing Eye" institution was obtaining instructors. The difficulty was, apparently, that the first masters of the art did not have a sufficiently precise theoretical formulation in training the dogs and hence could not pass the information on to new instructors. They then encountered another problem in instructing the blind to handle the dogs and met numerous failures here in adapting client to dog. Many of these failures could now doubtless be avoided.

Dogs, of course, can be trained more readily with the new methods in all the traditional fields of canine service to mankind: hunting, guarding children and property, and detective work. Military use of dogs in such tasks as guard duty and carrying messages can also be made more effective.

This, then, seems to be the general outline of a promising new field which we have only begun to explore. It is so vast, we feel, that we cannot begin to develop one-tenth of the projects we have thought of. More psychologists, grounded in the theory, are needed to advance the technology and explore the undeveloped portions of this program. Furthermore, once the technology gets under way and the business develops, there will be active need for academic psychologists to do the background research necessary for full development of the program. And, of course, as psychologists continue to do basic research using animals as subjects, one by-product will be new and better methods of applied animal psychology.

Two types of problems have cropped up repeatedly in our efforts. (1) Apparatus problems have consumeed much more time than problems connected with the behavior. The apparatus must be suited to the physique of the particular animal, must be durable enough to stand up under cross-country shipment, and must be foolproof enough to be operated by relatively untrained personnel. (2) We need to know the answers to various "academic" problems, such as "What sort of fixed ratio will an animal sustain on a response made to a disappearing manipulandum, a key available, for example, only every three minutes?" "What would constitute an adequate reinforcement for a hamster, to sustain performances over several hours without satiation?" "What are the emotional characteristics of rabbits and guinea pigs—to what sort and magnitude of stimuli will they adapt, and what is the nature of the curve of recovery from such an adaptation?"

The study of these and related questions—in short, the reexamination of the whole field of comparative psychology in this new light—by psychologists who have available the facilities of an animal laboratory, would greatly speed up the development of the applied field.

In conclusion, we feel that here is a genuine field of applied psychology, old as "group living" and "parenthood" in its subject matter, but new in method and approach, which psychologists can enter with promise of financial reward and a sense of accomplishment and ultimate benefit to the science. For we all know that there is nothing as convincing to the layman of the worth of a discipline as achievement, and the present field offers the psychologist a fine opportunity to demonstrate control of his subject matter.

LEARNING MORE

The principles of instrumental conditioning employed by the Brelands to train their show animals have been adapted for human learning "machines" also. In the past few years, there has been increased use of teaching machines and programmed learning materials, both for supplementary use in the schools and for self-tutoring purposes. Basically, programmed learning proceeds on the assumption that immediate feedback of his progress improves the learner's performance. The teaching machine and programmed text allow the student to proceed at his own pace. They present the subject matter in small progressive units (frames) and require the student's mastery of each unit before proceeding to the next. Any mistakes are corrected immediately, by the student himself, privately, without implied value judgment.

If you should be interested in seeing how a programmed text in psychology is organized, you might read J. G. Holland and B. F. Skinner, *The Analyses of Behavior: A Program for Self-Instruction* (McGraw-Hill, 1961).

The use of teaching machines and programmed texts, however, is not without its critics. Sidney L. Pressey, in an article entitled "Teaching Machine (and Learning Theory) Crisis," (*Journal of Applied Psychology*, 1963, *47,* 1–6) charges that material cannot be meaningfully presented to human beings by a machine perfected on animal learning behaviors. The overall structure and meaning of a subject cannot, he maintains, survive the transformation into teaching machine frames.

If you are interested in the debate, you might pick up a copy of the Holland and Skinner text, see how it helps you in your study of psychology—and then read Pressey's article (or vice versa: we wouldn't want to prejudice you). Which one do you agree with?

Part Nine

Motivation:
The Measure
of Desire

We easily differentiate between inanimate objects and living beings. It is obvious that the brick of which Guthrie speaks (in the part on learning) can really *do* nothing. It can only be *done to.* All activity originates with and is controlled by forces outside the object. In a person, a beast of the jungle, an insect; in any of these, activity can be induced by factors within the organism. The living being contains, within its makeup, a mechanism for choice, a means of expressing desire.

In the novel *The Professor's House,* Willa Cather had the professor say, "If there were an instrument by which to measure desire, one could foretell achievement."

It may be that some desires are preprogrammed either by the genes or by previous environmental controls, or by a combination of these. Some people would claim that *all* choices, all desires, are preprogrammed. But this is not the place to get into an argument about free will. The important fact for present purposes is that choices are made by the individual. And the question we need to examine has to do with determining just what are the factors in the present or past of the individual that influence the various choices he makes.

When we do something, why do we do that particular something? Actually, why don't we living beings just sit like the brick, waiting for something to be done to us? Why do we do anything?

These questions can be approached in various ways. We could examine various theories of motivation. We could have a look at experimental studies involving animals or experiments with humans. We could look at empirical studies of people in day-to-day real-life situations. We prefer the real live people approach. We can follow that with a little theorizing.

One experience that almost all of us have had in common is the experience of being children in school. We know, too, that the problem of motivation is critical to any school program. We have already considered this problem in the selections concerned with psychological development.

John Holt deals directly with children in situations in which they sometimes are motivated to do and sometimes not motivated to do what, at least other people think, they should do. If the title of Holt's book, *How Children Fail,* seems a bit negative, recall that he has also written a book entitled *How Children Learn.*

29

FEAR AND FAILURE

JOHN C. HOLT

March 27, 1958

We agree that all children need to succeed; but do we mean the same thing? My own feeling is that success should not be quick or easy, and should not come all the time. Success implies overcoming an obstacle, including, perhaps, the thought in our minds that we might not succeed. It is turning "I can't" into "I can, and I did."

We ought also to learn, beginning early, that we don't always succeed. A good batting average in baseball is .300; a good batting average in life is a great deal lower than that. Life holds many more defeats than victories for all of us. Shouldn't we get used to this early? We should learn, too, to aim higher than we think we can hit. "A man's reach should exceed his grasp, or what's a Heaven for?" What we fail to do today, we, or someone, may do tomorrow. Our failure may pave the way for someone else's success.

Of course we should protect a child, if we can, from a diet of unbroken failure. More to the point, perhaps, we should see that failure is honorable and constructive, rather than humiliating. Perhaps we need a semantic distinction here, between nonsuccess and failure.

It is tempting to think that we can arrange the work of unsuccessful students so that they think they are succeeding most of the time. But how can we keep secret from a child what other children of his own age, in his own or other schools, are doing? What some of these kids need is the experience of doing something really well—so well that they know themselves, without having to be told, that they have done it well. Maybe this means that someone must supply them, from outside, with the concentration and resolution they lack.

December 3, 1958

The other day I decided to talk to the other section about what happens when you don't understand what is going on. We had been chatting about something or other, and everyone seemed in a relaxed frame of mind, so I said, "You know, there's something I'm curious about, and I wonder if you'd help me."

SOURCE: From the book *How Children Fail* by John Holt. Copyright © 1964 by Pitman Publishing Corp. Reprinted by permission of Pitman Publishing Corp. Pp. 37–42 and 47–49.

They said, "What?" I said, "What do you think, what goes through your mind, when the teacher asks you a question and you don't know the answer?"

It was a bombshell. Instantly a paralyzed silence fell on the room. Everyone stared at me with what I have learned to recognize as a tense expression. For a long time there wasn't a sound. Finally Ben, who is bolder than most, broke the tension, and also answered my question, by saying in a loud voice, "Gulp!"

He spoke for everyone. They all began to clamor, and all said the same thing, that when the teacher asked them a question and they didn't know the answer they were scared half to death. I was flabbergasted—to find this in a school which people think of as progressive; which does its best not to put pressure on little children; which does not give marks in the lower grades; which tries to keep children from feeling that they're in some kind of race.

I asked them why they felt gulpish. They said they were afraid of failing, afraid of being kept back, afraid of being called stupid, afraid of feeling themselves stupid. Stupid. Why is it such a deadly insult to these children, almost the worst thing they can think of to call each other? Where do they learn this?

Even in the kindest and gentlest of schools, children are afraid, many of them a great deal of the time, some of them almost all the time. This is a hard fact of life to deal with. What can we do about it?

December 30, 1958

All fall long, I wondered why Jack fell down so much playing soccer. He is an agile, well-coordinated boy. His balance is good. People don't knock him over. Why was he on the ground so often? Suddenly, the other day, I had the answer.

I discovered it while trying to learn to control the tension that builds up in me when I practice the flute. Music is a good thing for teachers to study, because it creates in us the kind of tension that children live under all the time in the classroom, and that most adults have long forgotten. Incidentally, it is most interesting, when Gattegno explains the Cuisenaire rods to teachers, to see them under this very tension. They react to it very much like children, by getting sore at Gattegno, or fighting his ideas, by saying in elaborate language what fifth graders say when they are startled by a new idea—"This is crazy, nutty, cuckoo."

I have observed many times that children who can do one or two problems of a certain kind, with no trouble, collapse when given a big sheet of them. Something like this is true of exercises in music. When I am trying to play an exercise at (for me) high speed, I am under tension. If the exercise is short, I feel that I can get through it before tension gets the better of me. But if it is long, I am less confident from the start that I can get through without a mistake, and as I play, the inner voice that comments on what I am doing says: "All right so far; watch that G sharp; oops! narrow escape, you almost played F sharp instead of F natural, etc., etc." The voice gets louder and louder, until finally the communication channels are clogged up, coordination breaks down, and I make the mistake I have been fearing to make.

I haven't forgotten Jack and his falling down. One thing I have discovered is that there is a peculiar kind of relief, a lessening of tension, when you make a mistake. For when you make one, you no longer have to worry about whether you are going to make one. Walking a tightrope, you worry about falling off; once fallen off, you don't have to worry. Children, to whom making mistakes is acutely painful, are therefore under great tension when doing something correctly. Worrying about the mistakes they might make is as bad—no, worse—than worrying about the mistakes they have made. Thus, when you tell a child that he has done a problem wrong, you often hear a sigh of relief. He says, "I *knew* it would be wrong." He would rather *be* wrong, and know it, than not know whether he was wrong or not.

Well, the reason Jack falls down is that this relieves him, for a few seconds, of the great tension he is under when he plays soccer. Being small, he is afraid of crashing into bigger boys, but he is also afraid of showing his fear, and resolutely tries to play the game as he feels he should. This puts his nervous system under a strain that is too much for it. Being a boy, he can't pull out of the game, as a girl might do, or just get out of the way of bigger boys when they come at him. So, every now and then, he falls down, and thus gets an honorable rest period for a second or two.

This makes me think about written work. Some say that children get security from large amounts of written work. Maybe. But suppose every teacher in the school were told that he had to do ten pages of addition problems, within a given time limit and with no mistakes, or lose his job. Even if the time given were ample enough to do all problems carefully with time over for checking, the chances are that no teacher would get a perfect paper. Their anxiety would build up, as it does in me when I play the flute, until it impaired or wholly broke down their coordination and confidence. Have you ever found yourself, while doing a simple arithmetic problem, checking the answer over and over, as if you could not believe that you had done it right? I have. If we were under the gun as much as the kids in our classes are, we would do this more often.

Perhaps children need a lot of written work, particularly in math; but they should not get much of it at one time. Ask children to spend a whole period on one paper, and anxiety or boredom is sure to drive them into foolish errors. It used to puzzle me that the students who made the most mistakes and got the worst marks were so often the first ones to hand in their papers. I used to say, "If you finish early, take time to check your work, do some problems again." Typical teacher's advice; I might as well have told them to flap their arms and fly. When the paper was in, the tension was ended. Their fate was in the lap of the gods. They might still worry about flunking the paper, but it was a fatalistic kind of worry, it didn't contain the agonizing element of choice, there was nothing more they could do about it. Worrying about whether you did the right thing, while painful enough, is less painful than worrying about the right thing to do.

One way to keep down tension is to be aware of it. I told the math class that to let something go by in class without knowing what it means, and without saying anything, is like leaving something in Howard Johnson's on a long car trip. You are going to have to go back for it eventually, so the sooner the better. This foolish metaphor has helped the kids, or so they say. They have learned to recognize, if only a little, the feeling of panicky confusion that slowly gets hold of them. To be able to say, "I'm getting left at Howard Johnson's" helps them to control this feeling, and if it gets too much for them they can always tell me that they have been left behind; then I can do something about picking them up.

We must set a limit to the tension that we put children under. If we don't, they will set their own limits by not paying attention, by fooling around, by saying unnecessarily, "I don't get it." We should let them know in advance that they will not have to be under tension for an entire period, and that, if need be, they have the means to bring it to a stop.

Perhaps this is a reason why people like Gattegno, who go around teaching demonstration math classes, get such spectacular results. The kids know that this is not real school, that this strange man is not their teacher, that if they make mistakes nothing serious will happen, and that, in any case, it will be over soon. Thus freed from worrying, they are ready to use their brains. But how can we run a class from day to day and keep that spirit? Can it be done at all?

February 5, 1959

. . . The poor thinker dashes madly after an answer; the good thinker takes his time and looks at the problem. Is the difference merely a matter of a skill in thought, a technique which, with ingenuity and luck, we might teach and train into children? I'm afraid not. The good thinker can take his time because he can tolerate uncertainty, he can stand not knowing. The poor thinker can't stand not knowing; it drives him crazy.

This cannot be completely explained by the fear of being wrong. No doubt this fear puts, say, Monica under heavy pressure; but Hal is under the same pressure, and maybe I am as well. Monica is not alone in wanting to be right and fearing to be wrong. What is involved here is another insecurity, the insecuritiy of not having *any* answer to a problem. Monica wants the right answer, yes; but what she wants, first of all, is an answer, any old answer, and she will do almost anything to get some kind of answer. Once she gets it, a large part of the pressure is off. Rachel was like this; so was Gerald, and many others. They can't stand a problem without a solution, even if they know that their solution will probably be wrong. This panicky search for certainty, this inability to tolerate unanswered questions and unsolved problems seems to lie at the heart of many problems of intelligence. But what causes it?

Some might say here that this is all a matter for the psychiatrists. I am not so sure. A person might well be distrustful in personal relationships and still have a kind of intellectual confidence in the universe. Or is this possible? And if so, can it be taught in school?

June 16, 1959

A year ago I was wondering how a child's fears might influence his strategies. This year's work has told me. The strategies of most of these kids have been consistently self-centered, self-protective, aimed above all else at avoiding trouble, embarrassment, punishment, disapproval, or loss of status. This is particularly true of the ones who have had a tough time in school. When they get a problem, I can read their thoughts on their faces, I can almost hear them, "Am I going to get this right? Probably not; what'll happen to me when I get it wrong? Will the teacher get mad? Will the other kids laugh at me? Will my mother and father hear about it? Will they keep me back this year? Why am I so dumb?" And so on.

Even in the room periods, where I did all I could to make the work non-threatening, I was continually amazed and appalled to see the children hedging their bets, covering their losses in advance, trying to fix things so that whatever happened they could feel they had been right, or if wrong, no more wrong than anyone else. "I think it will sort of balance." They are fence-straddlers, afraid ever to commit themselves—and at the age of ten. Playing games like Twenty Questions, which one might have expected them to play for fun, many of them were concerned only to put up a good front, to look as if they knew what they were doing, whether they did or not.

These self-limiting and self-defeating strategies are dictated, above all else, by fear. For many years I have been asking myself why intelligent children act unintelligently at school. The simple answer is, "Because they're scared." I used to suspect that children's defeatism had something to do with their bad work in school, but I thought I could clear it away with hearty cries of "Onward! You can do it!" What I now see for the first time is the mechanism by which fear destroys intelligence, the way it affects a child's whole way of looking at, thinking about, and dealing with life. So we have two problems, not one: to stop children from being afraid, and then to break them of the bad thinking habits into which their fears have driven them.

What is most surprising of all is how much fear there is in school. Why is so little said about it? Perhaps most people do not recognize fear in children when they see it. They can read the grossest signs of fear; they know what the trouble is when a child clings howling to his mother; but the subtler signs of fear escape them. It is these signs, in children's faces, voices, and gestures, in their movements and ways of working, that tell me plainly that most children in school are scared most of the time, many of them very scared. Like good soldiers, they control their fears, live with them, and adjust themselves to them. But the trouble is, and here is a vital difference between school and war, that the adjustments children make to their fears are almost wholly bad, destructive of their intelligence and capacity. The scared fighter may be the best fighter, but the scared learner is always a poor learner.

In the part on psychological development we questioned William James' assumption of fear as a necessary motivating factor in the schoolroom. Holt has demonstrated the negative results of too much fear.

To state that fear is a motivating factor is to say that the individual does what he does to escape punishment of some kind. To fear is to have learned that the consequence of some behavior is punishment. Fear as a motivator involves the use of a powerful negative reinforcer. Yet we know enough about learning to know that reward is usually much more effective than is punishment. The results of using punishment (negative reinforcement) are highly unpredictable.

Fear may cause a running away from the situation, an escape reaction. As Holt related, fear caused intelligent children to act unintelligently.

The opposite of fear is security. When a person feels that

he is an accepted and important part of a group, he is secure in that group. He is then more highly motivated to play an active role in the affairs of the group. Quite some years ago Gordon Allport took a look at the effects of participation as a factor in motivation. Allport, in this selection from a longer article, begins with an empirical situation and moves from there to a bit of theorizing.

30

ACTIVITY *VERSUS* PARTICIPATION
GORDON W. ALLPORT

. . . people have to be active in order to learn, in order to store up efficient memories, to build voluntary control, to be cured when they are ill, restored when they are faint.

But implied in much American work is the proposition that one activity is as good as any other activity. It is *random* movement, according to much of our learning theory, that brings the organism to an eventual solution. And according to one experimentalist, "If the body muscles are tense, the brain reacts much more quickly and intensely, if they are relaxed, it may react weakly or not at all" (2, p. 23).The implication seems to be that tenseness of any kind makes for mental alertness. Activity as such is approved.

Random movement theories of learning, muscular tension theories of efficiency, speed theories of intelligence, and motor theories of consciousness do not make a distinction that seems to me vital, namely, the distinction between mere *activity* as such and true, personal *participation*.

Before we examine this distinction as it affects psychological theory and practice, I should like to point out that the self-same distinction occurs in the economic and social life of the common man.

Take, for example, Citizen Sam who moves and has his being in the great activity wheel of New York City. Let us say that he spends his hours of unconsciousness somewhere in the badlands of the Bronx. He wakens to grab the morning's milk left at the door by an agent of a vast Dairy and Distributing system whose corporate manœuvres, so vital to his health, never consciously concern him. After paying hasty respects to his landlady, he

SOURCE: Abridged from Gordon W. Allport, "The Psychology of Participation," *Psychological Review*, 1945, 52, 117–132. Copyright 1945 by the American Psychological Association, and reproduced by permission.

dashes into the transportation system whose mechanical and civic mysteries he does not comprehend. At the factory he becomes a cog for the day in a set of systems far beyond his ken. To him (as to everybody else) the company he works for is an abstraction; he plays an unwitting part in the 'creation of surpluses' (whatever they are), and though he doesn't know it his furious activity at his machine is regulated by the 'law of supply and demand,' and by 'the availability of raw materials' and by 'prevailing interest rates.' Unknown to himself he is headed next week for the 'surplus labor market.' A union official collects his dues; just why he doesn't know. At noontime that corporate monstrosity, Horn and Hardart, swallows him up, much as he swallows one of its automatic pies. After more activity in the afternoon, he seeks out a standardized day-dream produced in Hollywood, to rest his tense, but *not* efficient mind. At the end of his day he sinks into a tavern, and unknowingly victimized by the advertising cycle, orders in rapid succession Four Roses, Three Feathers, Golden Wedding and Seagram's which "men who plan beyond tomorrow" like to drink.

Sam has been active all day, immensely active, playing a part in dozens of impersonal cycles of behavior. He has brushed scores of 'corporate personalities,' but has entered into intimate relations with no single human being. The people he has met are idler-gears like himself meshed into systems of transmission, far too distracted to examine any one of the cycles in which they are engaged. Throughout the day Sam is on the go, implicated in this task and that,—but does he, in a psychological sense, *participate* in what he is doing? Although constantly *task-involved*, is he ever really *ego-involved?*

Now this problem is familiar to all of us, and one of the most significant developments of the past decade is its entrance into both industrial and social psychology. The way the problem has been formulated by industrial psychologists is roughly this:

The individual's desire for personal status is apparently insatiable. Whether we say that he longs for *prestige*, for *self-respect*, *autonomy*, or *self-regard*, a dynamic factor of this order is apparently the strongest of his drives. Perhaps it is an elementary organismic principle as Angyal (1) and Goldstein (3) would have it; perhaps it is rather a distillation of more primitive biological drives with social competitiveness somehow added to the brew. For our purposes it does not matter.

What the industrial psychologist has discovered is that when the work-situation in which the individual finds himself realistically engages the status-seeking motive, when the individual is busily engaged in using his talents, understanding his work, and having pleasant social relations with foreman and fellow-worker, then he is, as the saying goes, 'identified' with his job. He likes his work; he is absorbed in it; he is productive. In short, in McGregor's term he is industrially *active;* that is to say, he is participant (6).

When, on the other hand, the situation is such that the status-motive has no chance of gearing itself into the external cycles of events, when the individual goes through motions that he does not find meaningful, when he does not really participate, then come rebellion against authority, complaints, griping, gossip, rumor, scape-goating, disaffection of all sorts. The job-satisfaction is low. In McGregor's terms under such circumstances the individual is not active; he is industrially *reactive.*

In the armed forces, in federal employment, in school systems, the same principle holds. Ordinarily those at the top find that they have sufficient comprehension, sufficient responsibility, and sufficient personal status. *They* are not the ones who gripe and gossip. It is the lower-downs who indulge in tendency-wit against the brass hats, who complain, who go AWOL, become inert, or gang up against a scapegoat. When in actual combat, all the energies and training, all the personal responsibility of which a soldier is capable, are called upon, then egos are engaged for all they are worth. Men are active; they have no time to be reactive; nor have they reason to be.

Accepting this analysis as correct the problem before us is whether the immense amount of reactivity shown in business offices and factories, in federal bureaus, in schools, can be reduced, as it is when men at the front are using all their talents and are participating to the full in life-and-death combat.

We are learning some of the conditions in which reactivity does decline. Friendly, unaffected social relations are the most indispensable condition. Patronizing hand-outs and wage-incentive systems alone do not succeed. Opportunities for consultation on personal problems are, somewhat surprisingly, found to be important. And as members of this Society have shown, group decision, open discussion, and the retraining of leaders in accordance with democratic standards yield remarkable results. One of Lewin's discoveries in this connection is especially revealing. People who dislike a certain food are resistant to pressure put upon them in the form of persuasion and request; but when the individual himself as member of a group votes, after discussion, to alter his food-habits, his eagerness to reach this goal is independent of his personal like or dislike (4). In other words, a person ceases to be reactive and contrary in respect to a desirable course of conduct only when he himself has had a hand in declaring that course of conduct to be desirable.

Such findings add up to the simple proposition that people must have a hand in saving themselves; they cannot and will not be saved from the outside.

In insisting that participation depends upon ego-involvement, it would be a mistake if we were to assume that we are dealing with a wholly self-centered and parasitic ego that demands unlimited status, and power for the individual himself (7). Often, indeed, the ego is clamorous, jealous, possessive and cantankerous. But this is true chiefly when it is forced to be *reactive* against constant threats and deprivations. We all know of 'power-people' who cannot, as we say, 'submerge their egos.' The trouble comes, I suspect, not because their egos are unsubmerged, but because they are still reactive toward some outer or inner features of the situation which are causing conflicts and insecurity. Reactive egos tend to perceive their neighbors and associates as threats rather than as collaborators.

But for the most part people who are participant in coöperative activity are just as much satisfied when a teammate solves a common problem as when they themselves solve it (5). Your tensions can be relieved by my work, and my tensions by your work, provided we are co-participants. Whatever our egos were like originally, they are now for the most part socially regenerate. Selfish gratifications give way to coöperative satisfaction when the ego-boundaries are enlarged.

REFERENCES

1. Angyal, A. *Foundations for a science of personality.* New York: Commonwealth Fund, 1941.
2. Bills, A. G. *The psychology of efficiency.* New York: Harper & Bros., 1943.
3. Goldstein, K. *Human nature in the light of psychopathology.* Cambridge: Harvard University Press, 1940.
4. Lewin, K. The dynamics of group action. *Educational Leadership,* 1944, *1*, 195-200.
5. Lewis, H. B. An experimental study of the role of the ego in work. I. The role of the ego in coöperative work. *Journal of Experimental Psychology,* 1944, *34*, 113–126.
6. McGregor, D. Conditions of effective leadership in the industrial organization. *Journal of Consulting Psychology,* 1944, *8*, 55-63.
7. Spoerl, H. D. Toward a knowledge of the soul. *The New Philosophy,* 1944, *47*, 71-81.

More and more people seem to be coming to see that, as Allport states, "people must have a hand in saving themselves." As we write this, there is much in the news about a high school teacher and scoutmaster who lavished special attention on black and chicano students, only to have them turn against him. They brought charges of racism against the very man who thought he had done so much for them. This apparent inconsistency is explained by the statement reportedly contained in a resolution adopted by the local NAACP: "Paternalism touched with condescension is one of the worst by-products of racial injustice."

Have you encountered this kind of experience? Do you know people who are trying to do *too much* for other people? How often do we fail to realize that every person must participate in his own salvation?

Just how far can participation go? Increasingly, students are asking for, sometimes demanding, participation in making many of the decisions that affect their lives in school and college. Workers are becoming militant in their demands for participation. Recently we read, in a report published by the Center for the Study of Democratic Institutions, of a movement for self-management in industry which "is now spreading in many countries." [1]

A few years ago the late Abraham Maslow was engaged by an electronics manufacturing firm, Non-Linear Systems, Inc., of Del Mar, California, and apparently was given complete freedom to investigate whatever he wished and to comment on what he found. Maslow had developed a theory of motivation [2] and presumably the company was interested in applying the principles he had developed to problems of industrial production. But there was nothing formal about his assignment at Non-Linear Systems. Nor was there anything formal about his published report. It was simply a transcription of his day-by-day notes which had been dictated on a tape recorder, published with little editing. Rather than present any of Maslow's more formal theorizing, we have selected a section of this report. We think that this informal approach will give a good idea of Maslow's theory of motivation.

We have said that each person must participate in his own salvation. According to Maslow, the road to personal salvation is an indirect road.

[1] Self-Management: Has Its Time Come? *Center Report,* December, 1971.
[2] See his *Motivation and Personality* (Harper and Row, 1954) and *Toward a Psychology of Being* (Van Nostrand, 1962).

31

ADDITIONAL NOTES ON SELF-ACTUALIZATION, WORK, DUTY, MISSION, ETC.

ABRAHAM H. MASLOW

After talking recently with various students and professors who "wanted to work with me" on self-actualization, I discovered that I was very suspicious of most of them and rather discouraging, tending to expect little from them. This is a consequence of long experience with multitudes of starry-eyed dilettantes—big talkers, great planners, tremendously enthusiastic—who come to nothing as soon as a little hard work is required. So I have been speaking to these individuals in a pretty blunt and tough and nonencouraging way. I have spoken about dilettantes, for instance (as contrasted with workers and doers), and indicated my contempt for them. I have mentioned how often I have tested people with these fancy aspirations simply by giving them a rather dull but important and worthwhile job to do. Nineteen out of twenty fail the test. I have learned not only to give this test but to brush them aside completely if they don't pass it. I have preached to them about joining the "League of Responsible Citizens" and down with the free-loaders, hangers-on, mere talkers, the permanent passive students who study forever with no results. The test for any person is—that is you want to find out whether he's an apple tree or not—Does He Bear Apples? Does He Bear Fruit? That's the way you tell the difference between fruitfulness and sterility, between talkers and doers, between the people who change the world and the people who are helpless in it.

Another point that has been coming up is the talk about personal salvation. For instance, at the Santa Rosa existential meetings there was much of this kind of talk, and I remember exploding in a kind of irritation and indicating my disrespect for such salvation seekers. This was on the grounds that they were selfish and did nothing for others and for the world. Besides, they were psychologically stupid and psychologically incorrect because seeking for personal salvation is *anyway* the wrong road to personal salvation The only real path, one that I talked about in my public lecture there, was the path set forth in the Japanese movie "Ikiru," i.e., salvation via hard work and total commitment to doing well the job that fate or personal destiny calls you to do, or any important job that "calls for" doing.

SOURCE: Reprinted with permission from Maslow, *Eupsychian Management* (Homewood, Ill.: Richard D. Irwin, Inc.) 1965 c., pp. 5–13.

I remember citing various "heroes," people who had attained not only personal salvation but the complete respect and love of everybody who knew them; all of them were good workers and responsible people, and furthermore all of them were as happy as was possible for them to be in their circumstances. This business of self-actualization via a commitment to an important job and to worthwhile work could also be said, then, to be the path to human happiness (by contrast with the direct attack or the direct search for happiness—happiness is an epiphenomenon, a by-product, something not to be sought directly but an indirect reward for virtue). The other way—of seeking for personal salvation—just doesn't work for anybody I have *ever* seen —that is the introspection, the full-time-in-a-cave all by one's self some place. This may work for people in India and Japan— I won't deny that—but I have never seen it work for anybody in all my experience in the United States. The only happy people I know are the ones who are working well at something they consider important. Also, I have pointed out in my lecture and in my previous writings that this was universal truth for all my self-actualizing subjects. They were metamotivated by metaneeds (B-values) (3) expressed in their devotion to, dedication to, and identification with some great and important job. This was true for every single case.

Or I can put this very bluntly: *Salvation Is a By-Product of Self-Actualizing Work and Self-Actualizing Duty.* (The trouble with most of these youngsters who have been after me is that it seems they have in the back of their heads some notion of self-actualization as a kind of lightning stroke which will hit them on the head suddenly without their doing anything about it. They all seem to want to wait passively for it to happen without any effort on their part. Furthermore, I think that practically all of them have tended unconsciously to define self-actualization in terms of the getting rid of all inhibitions and controls in favor of complete spontaneity and impulsivity. My impatience has been largely because of this, I guess, that they had no stubbornness, no persistence, no frustration tolerance, etc.,—apparently just these qualities they consider as the opposite of self-actualization. Maybe this is what I should talk about more specifically.)

One thing about this whole business is that S-A work transcends the self without trying to, and achieves the kind of loss of self-awareness and of self-consciousness that the easterners, the Japanese and Chinese and so on, keep on trying to attain. S-A work is simultaneously a seeking and fulfilling of the self *and* also an achieving of the selflessness which is the ultimate expression of *real* self. It resolves the dichotomy between selfish and unselfish. Also between inner and outer—because the cause for which one works in S-A work is introjected and becomes part of the self so that the world and the self are no longer different. The inner and the outer world fuse and become one and the same. The same is true for the subject-object dichotomy.

A talk that we had with an artist at Big Sur Hot Springs—a real artist, a real worker, a real achiever—was very illuminating on this point. He kept on pressing Bertha (my wife) to get to work on her sculpture, and he kept on waving aside all her defenses and her explanations and excuses, all of which were flossy and high-toned. "The only way to be an artist is to work, work, and work." He stressed discipline, labor, sweat. One phrase that he repeated again and again was "Make a pile of chips." "Do something with your wood or your stone or your clay and then if it's lousy throw it away. This is better than doing nothing." He said that he would not take on any apprentice in his ceramics work who wasn't willing to work for years at the craft itself, at the details, the materials. His good-by to Bertha was, "Make a pile of chips." He urged her to get to work right after breakfast like a plumber who has to do a day's work and who has a foreman who will fire him if he doesn't turn out a good day's work. "Act as if you have to earn a living thereby." The guy was clearly an eccentric and talked a lot of wild words —and yet he *had* to be taken seriously because there were his products—the proofs that his words were not merely words.

(Bertha had a very good research idea when we talked about this conversation: The hypothesis is that the creative person loves his tools and his materials, and this can be tested.)

(A good question: Why do people *not* create or work? Rather than, Why *do* they create? Everyone has the motivation to create and to work, every child, every adult. This can be assumed. What has to be explained are the inhibitions, the blocks, etc. What stops these motivations which are there in everyone?)

(Side idea: About D-motivated creators [2], I have always attributed this to special talent alone, i.e., to special genius of some sort which has nothing to do with the health of the personality. Now I think I must add just plain hard work, for one thing, and for another, just plain nerve, e.g., like someone who arbitrarily defines himself as an artist in a nervy and arrogant way and therefore *is* an artist. Because he treats himself like an artist, everybody tends to also.)

If you take into yourself something important from the world, then you yourself become important thereby. You have made yourself important thereby, as important as that which you have introjected and assimilated to yourself. At once, it matters if you die, or if you are sick, or if you can't work, etc. Then you must take care of yourself, you must respect yourself, you have to get plenty of rest, not smoke or drink too much, etc. You can no longer commit suicide—that would be too selfish. It would be a loss for the world. You are needed, useful. This is the easiest way to feel needed. Mothers with babies do not commit suicide as easily as nonmothers. People in the concentration camps who had some important mission in life, some duty to live for or some other people to live for tended to stay alive. It was the other ones who gave up and sank into apathy and died without resistance.

This is an easy medicine for self-esteem: Become a part of something important. Be able to say, "We of the United Nations. . . ." or "We physicians. . . ." When you can say, "We psychologists have proven that. . . ." you thereby participate in the glory, the pleasure, and the pride of all psychologists any place.

This identification with important causes, or important jobs, this identifying with them and taking them into the self, thereby enlarging the self and making it important, this is a way of overcoming also actual existential human shortcomings, e.g., shortcomings in I.Q., in talent, in skill, etc. For instance, science is a social institution, with division of labor and colleaguehood *and* exploitation of characterological differences—this is a technique for making uncreative people creative, for enabling unintelligent men to be intelligent, for enabling small men to be big, for permitting limited men to be eternal and cosmic. *Any* scientist must be treated with a certain respect, no matter how minor a contributor he may be—because he is a member of a huge enterprise and he demands respect by participation in this enterprise. He represents it, so to speak. He is an ambassador. (This makes a good example also: The ambassador from a great country is treated differently from the ambassador from some dopey or inefficient or ineffective or corrupt country—even though they are both individual human beings with individual human shortcomings.)

The same is true for a single soldier who is a member of a huge victorious army by contrast with a single soldier who is a member of a defeated army. So all the scientists and intellectuals and philosophers, etc., even though they are limited figures taken singly, taken collectively they are very important. They represent a victorious army, they are revolutionizing society; they are preparing the new world; they are constructing Eupsychia. So they become heroes by participation in heroic enterprises. They have found a way for small men to make themselves big. And since there exists in the world only small men (in various degrees) perhaps some form of participation in, or identification with, a worthwhile cause may be essential for any human being to feel a healthy and strong self-esteem. (That's why working in a "good" company [prestige, good product, etc.] is good for the self-esteem.)

This is all related to my thinking on "Responsibility as a Response to the Objective Requirements of the Situation." "Requirements" equals that which "calls for" an appropriate response, that which has "demand-character," which rests so heavily on the self-perceived constitution or temperament or destiny of the perceiver. That is, it is that which *he* feels impelled to make right, to correct; it is the burden that fits *his* shoulders, the crooked picture on the wall that *he* of all people in the world has to straighten. To some extent this is like a recognition of one's self out there in the world. Under ideal conditions there *would* be isomorphism, a mutual selection between the person and his S-A work (his cause, responsibility, call, vocation, task, etc.) That is, each task would "call for" just that one person in the world most uniquely suited to deal with it, like a key and a lock, and that one person would then feel the call most strongly and would reverberate to it, be tuned to its wave length, and so be responsive to its call. There is an interaction, a mutual suitability, like a good marriage or like a good friendship, like being designed for each other.

What happens then to the one who denies this unique responsibility? who doesn't listen to his call-note? or who can't hear at all any more? Here we can certainly talk about intrinsic guilt, or intrinsic unsuitability, like a dog trying to walk on his hind legs, or a poet trying to be a good businessman, or a businessman trying to be a poet. It just doesn't fit; it doesn't suit; it doesn't belong. One must respond to one's fate or one's destiny or pay a heavy price. One must yield to it; one must surrender to it. One must permit one's self to be chosen.

This is all very Taoistic. It's good to stress this because responsibility and work are seen unconsciously under the terms of McGregor's Theory X, as duty, as picking up a burden reluctantly because forced to do so by some external morality, some "should" or "ought" which is seen as different from natural inclination, different from free choice through delight or through tasting good. Under ideal conditions—that is, of healthy selfishness, of deepest, most primitive animal spontaneity and free choice, of listening to one's own impulsive voices—one embraces one's fate as eagerly and happily, as one picks one's wife. The yielding (surrender, trusting response receptivity) is here the same as in the embrace of the two people who belong together. The polarity between activity and passivity is here transcended and resolved just as it is in the love embrace or in the sexual act when this is ideal. So also is the will-trust dichotomy resolved. So also the difference between the Western and the Eastern. So also the dichotomy between free will and being determined. (One can embrace one's determinants—but even that statement is too dichotomous. Better said—one can recognize that what *appear* to be one's determinants out there in the world are really one's self which seems to be out there, which appear to be different from the self because of imperfect perception and imperfect fusion. It's a kind of self-love, or a kind of embracing one's own nature. Those things that belong together melt into each other and enjoy that melting, preferring it to being separated.)

(So, Letting-Go [rather than self-control] equals Spontaneity and is a *kind* of activity, which is not other than, which is not separated from, which is not different from passivity.)

So—to recognize one's responsibility or one's work out there is like a love relationship, a recognition of a belongingness, a *Zusammenhang;* it has many of the paradoxical or dichotomy-transcending qualities of sexual intercourse and love embracing, of two becoming one perfectly. This also reminds me of C. Daly King [1] and his notion of "paradic design" which equals a recognition of suitability and belongingness and normality and rightness through the recognition of the intention or fate implied by the design.

(When I spoke of all of this with Evelyn Hooker in relationship to her data on homosexuals and her feeling that they could be normal, that they weren't necessarily sick or neurotic, I disagreed with her, partly on the grounds of this idea of paradic design. I felt that the homosexual male could be considered to be simply wrong to choose the poorer rather than the better, because the mouth or the rectum or the armpit or the hand or whatever else in his male homosexual partner, were simply none of them as well designed for the penis as the vagina is designed. The vagina and the penis fit together very well in a biological way by inherent paradic design. They evolved isomorphically. I cited other biological examples of this sort which we consider abnormal. The man who prefers an uncomfortable shoe for his foot is biologically wrong as well as psychologically. There are biological suitabilities and this is what paradic design means. Applying this whole notion to the relationship between a person and his work destiny is difficult and subtle, but not much more so than applying this principle to the relationships between the two people who should get married as compared to two people who obviously should not get married. One personality can be seen to fit with another personality in this same paradic design. Hooker objected to, or at least felt uneasy about, all of this and warned about the philosophical dangers of using the word "natural." I'm willing to acknowledge these dangers but I also wish to stick to my guns on the essential point of normality and paradic design even if it is hard to express in words.)

[1] C. D. King, "The Meaning of Normal," *Yale Journal of Biology and Medicine,* 1945, *17,* 493–501.

In Likert's book [2] in the section on integrating principle, pages 102 ff., all of this is really talk about self-esteem. If work is introjected into the self (I guess it always is, more or less, even when one tries to prevent it), then the relationship between self-esteem and work is closer than I had thought. Especially healthy and stable self-esteem (the feeling of worth, pride, influence, importance, etc.) rests on good, worthy work to be introjected, thereby becoming part of the self. Maybe more of our contemporary malaise is due to introjection of nonprideful, robotized, broken-down-into-easy-bits kind of work than I had thought. The more I think about it, the more difficult I find it to *conceive* of feeling proud of myself, self-loving and self-respecting, if I were working, for example, in some chewing gum factory, or a phony advertising agency, or in some factory that turned out shoddy furniture. I've written so far of "real achievement" as a basis for solid self-esteem, but I guess that is too general and needs more spelling out. Real achievement means inevitably a worthy and virtuous task. To do some idiotic job very well is certainly *not* real achievement. I like my phrasing, "What is not worth doing is not worth doing well." (1)

BIBLIOGRAPHY

A complete bibliography of the published writings of A. H. Maslow up to 1964 is contained in the book from which this chapter is taken. Items below are those mentioned in the chapter.
1. Problem-centering vs. means-centering in science. *Philosophy of Science*, 1946, 13: 326–31.
2. Deficiency motivation and growth motivation in M. R. Jones (Ed.), *Nebraska Symposium on Motivation: 1955* (Lincoln: University of Nebraska Press, 1955). Reprinted in *General Semantics Bulletin*, 1956, Nos. 18 and 19, 33–42. Reprinted in J. Coleman, *Personality Dynamics & Effective Behavior* (Chicago: Scott, Foresman & Co., 1960). Reprinted in J. A. Dyal (Ed.), *Readings in Psychology: Understanding Human Behavior* (New York: McGraw-Hill Book Co., Inc., 1962). Reprinted in R. C. Teevan and R. C. Birney (Eds.), *Theories of Motivation in Personality and Social Psychology* (New York: D. Van Nostrand, 1964).
3. Notes on Being-Psychology. *Journal of Humanistic Psychology*, 1962, 2, 47–71. Reprinted in *WBSI Report* No. 7, 1961. Reprinted in H. Ruitenbeek (Ed.), *Varieties of Personality Theory* (New York: E. P. Dutton, 1964).

[2] R. Likert, *New Patterns in Management* (New York: McGraw-Hill Book Co., Inc., 1961).

Let's look, for just a moment, at Maslow's more formal theorizing. There are, he says, five general types of needs. They are arranged in a hierarchy, from low to high. First, there are the physiological needs. Then, in order, come the safety needs, the belonging needs, and the status needs. These are all *deficit* needs. At the top is the need for self-actualization, which is a *growth* need. The deficit needs are urgent and necessary. Their satisfaction makes living possible. But personal satisfactions, morale in any organization, industrial production, all of these and more, result from self-actualization.

Look at the various organizations of which you are or have been a member. This could include the family, the school class, a club, an informal gang, a work group—any kind of organization, formal or informal. Which of these organizations are, in your judgment, really effective? Which are ineffective?

Next, make a checklist of which of the five classes of needs are met by each group. Can you come to any conclusion from this?

IF YOU ARE REALLY MOTIVATED

You may wish to read all of the Allport article. We have given you only a part of it. And, if you should get seriously interested in motivation, particularly if you have had work experience, you will probably wish to read all of Maslow's *Eupsychian Management.*

Incidentally, in case you've wondered about that word— in the preface to the book Maslow says, "I've coined the word Eupsychia and defined it as the culture that would be generated by 1,000 self-actualizing people on some sheltered island where they would not be interfered with."

We might suggest a shortcut to an understanding of Maslow's theory of motivation, a section entitled "A Theory of Human Needs" on pages 24–31 in H. C. Smith, *Psychology of Industrial Behavior,* Second edition (McGraw-Hill, 1964). This particular section is included in the chapter "Why Men Work," which discusses other approaches to industrial motivation, as well.

For another readable source of information on motivation, try William N. Dember, "The New Look in Motivation" (*American Scientist,* 1965, *53,* 409–427).

Part Ten

Pablo Picasso, *Study of Weeping Head,* May 24, 1937

Emotion:
Filter of
Our Universe

"We all live in two universes, one outer, the other inner. The inner universe contains our attitudes, emotions, beliefs, hangups, self-image. It is the window through which the outer universe gets filtered."[1]

Certainly how we *feel* about something is just as important as what we know about that something. In fact, what we *think* we know about almost anything is affected by how we feel about it.

We use the words "feelings" and "emotion" somewhat interchangeably. We do tend to reserve "emotion" for the "deeper feelings." As things around us happen, as the outside world communicates to us, we filter most all that comes in. To some we react pleasantly. Other things are unpleasant to us. Seldom are we completely neutral.

Not only are we sometimes pleased and sometimes displeased. We sometimes experience states of inner excitement. At the same time we may laugh or we may cry. We may tremble, scream, blush. We may breathe rapidly. The heart rate increases, perspiration increases, pupils dilate, muscles tense. The digestive process slows down. We may even vomit or defecate. The body, internally and externally, is in a state of readiness for action.

This is complex behavior. But almost every person seems to be able to perform, and without taking lessons—or at least without much awareness of having taken lessons. Apparently, certain *basic* emotional responses are inborn. Then, through a process of learning, various of these unlearned emotional responses can be attached to new stimuli.

We want to take you back more than half a century to one of the earliest published studies of human emotional behavior. "Baby Albert" may or may not have grown up to be a famous man. But he did become a famous infant.

Psychologists today are much more sophisticated about experimental procedures than they were in 1920. No one now would consider making broad generalizations on the basis of experience with one subject. This was very much a pioneer study.

[1] From Max Lerner's syndicated column. "True Political Man Knows Power," *The Daily Californian,* El Cajon, California, January 24, 1972.

32

CONDITIONED EMOTIONAL REACTIONS

JOHN B. WATSON AND ROSALIE RAYNER

In recent literature various speculations have been entered into concerning the possibility of conditioning various types of emotional response, but direct experimental evidence in support of such a view has been lacking. If the theory advanced by Watson and Morgan (1) to the effect that in infancy the original emotional reaction patterns are few, consisting so far as observed of fear, rage and love, then there must be some simple method by means of which the range of stimuli which can call out these emotions and their compounds is greatly increased. Otherwise, complexity in adult response could not be accounted for. These authors without adequate experimental evidence advanced the view that this range was increased by means of conditioned reflex factors. It was suggested there that the early home life of the child furnishes a laboratory situation for establishing conditioned emotional responses. The present authors have recently put the whole matter to an experimental test.

Experimental work has been done so far on only one child, Albert B. This infant was reared almost from birth in a hospital environment; his mother was a wet nurse in the Harriet Lane Home for Invalid Children. Albert's life was normal: he was healthy from birth and one of the best developed youngsters ever brought to the hospital, weighing twenty-one pounds at nine months of age. He was on the whole stolid and unemotional. His stability was one of the principal reasons for using him as a subject in this test. We felt that we could do him relatively little harm by carrying out such experiments as those outlined below.

At approximately nine months of age we ran him through the emotional tests that have become a part of our regular routine in determining whether fear reactions can be called out by other stimuli than sharp noises and the sudden removal of support. Tests of this type have been described by the senior author in another place (2). In brief, the infant was confronted suddenly and for the first time successively with a white rat, a rabbit, a dog, a monkey, with masks with and without hair, cotton wool, burning newspapers, etc. A permanent record of Albert's reactions to these objects and situations has been preserved in a motion picture study. Manipulation was the most usual reaction called out. *At no time did this infant ever show fear in any situ-*

SOURCE: From *Journal of Experimental Psychology*, 1920, *3*, 1–14.

ation. These experimental records were confirmed by the casual observations of the mother and hospital attendants. No one had ever seen him in a state of fear and rage. The infant practically never cried.

Up to approximately nine months of age we had not tested him with loud sounds. The test to determine whether a fear reaction could be called out by a loud sound was made when he was eight months, twenty-six days of age. The sound was that made by striking a hammer upon a suspended steel bar four feet in length and three-fourths of an inch in diameter. The laboratory notes are as follows:

One of the two experimenters caused the child to turn its head and fixate her moving hand; the other, stationed back of the child, struck the steel bar a sharp blow. The child started violently, his breathing was checked and the arms were raised in a characteristic manner. On the second stimulation the same thing occurred, and in addition the lips began to pucker and tremble. On the third stimulation the child broke into a sudden crying fit. This is the first time an emotional situation in the laboratory has produced any fear or even crying in Albert.

We had expected just these results on account of our work with other infants brought up under similar conditions. It is worth while to call attention to the fact that removal of support (dropping and jerking the blanket upon which the infant was lying) was tried exhaustively upon this infant on the same occasion. It was not effective in producing the fear response. This stimulus is effective in younger children. At what age such stimuli lose their potency in producing fear is not known. Nor is it known whether less placid children ever lose their fear of them. This probably depends upon the training the child gets. It is well known that children eagerly run to be tossed into the air and caught. On the other hand it is equally well known that in the adult fear responses are called out quite clearly by the sudden removal of support, if the individual is walking across a bridge, walking out upon a beam, etc. There is a wide field of study here which is aside from our present point.

The sound stimulus, thus, at nine months of age, gives us the means of testing several important factors. I. Can we condition fear of an animal, e.g., a white rat, by visually presenting it and simultaneously striking a steel bar? II. If such a conditioned emotional response can be established, will there be a transfer to other animals or other objects? III. What is the effect of time upon such conditioned emotional responses? IV. If after a reasonable period such emotional responses have not died out, what laboratory methods can be devised for their removal?

I. The establishment of conditioned emotional responses. At first there was considerable hesitation upon our part in making the attempt to set up fear reactions experimentally. A certain responsibility attaches to such a procedure. We decided finally to make the attempt, comforting ourselves by the reflection that such attachments would arise anyway as soon as the child left the sheltered environment of the nursery for the rough and tumble of the home. We did not begin this work until Albert was eleven months, three days of age. Before attempting to set up a conditioned response we, as before, put him through all of the regular emotional tests. *Not the slightest sign of a fear response was obtained in any situation.*

The steps taken to condition emotional responses are shown in our laboratory notes.

11 Months 3 Days

1.   White rat suddenly taken from the basket and presented to Albert. He began to reach for rat with left hand. Just as his hand touched the animal the bar was struck immediately behind his head. The infant jumped violently and fell forward, burying his face in the mattress. He did not cry, however.
2.   Just as the right hand touched the rat the bar was again struck. Again the infant jumped violently, fell forward and began to whimper.

In order not to disturb the child too seriously no further tests were given for one week.

11 Months 10 Days

1.   Rat presented suddenly without sound. There was steady fixation but no tendency at first to reach for it. The rat was then placed nearer, whereupon tentative reaching movements began with the right hand. When the rat nosed the infant's left hand, the hand was immediately withdrawn. He started to reach for the head of the animal with the forefinger of the left hand, but withdrew it suddenly before contact. It is thus seen that the two joint stimulations given the previous week were not without effect. He was tested with his blocks immediately afterwards to see if they shared in the process of conditioning. He began immediately to pick them up, dropping them, pounding them, etc. In the remainder of the tests the blocks were given frequently to quiet him and to test his general emotional state. They were always removed from sight when the process of conditioning was under way.

2. Joint stimulation with rat and sound. Started, then fell over immediately to right side. No crying.
3. Joint stimulation. Fell to right side and rested upon hands, with head turned away from rat. No crying.
4. Joint stimulation. Same reaction.
5. Rat suddenly presented alone. Puckered face, whimpered and withdrew body sharply to the left.
6. Joint stimulation. Fell over immediately to right side and began to whimper.
7. Joint stimulation. Started violently and cried, but did not fall over.
8. Rat alone. *The instant the rat was shown the baby began to cry. Almost instantly he turned sharply to the left, fell over on left side, raised himself on all fours and began to crawl away so rapidly that he was caught with difficulty before reaching the edge of the table.*

This was as convincing a case of a completely conditioned fear response as could have been theoretically pictured. In all seven joint stimulations were given to bring about the complete reaction. It is not unlikely had the sound been of greater intensity or of a more complex clang character that the number of joint stimulations might have been materially reduced. Experiments designed to define the nature of the sounds that will serve best as emotional stimuli are under way.

II. When a conditioned emotional response has been established for one object, is there a transfer? Five days later Albert was again brought back into the laboratory and tested as follows:

11 Months 15 Days

1. Tested first with blocks. He reached readily for them, playing with them as usual. This shows that there has been no general transfer to the room, table, blocks, etc.
2. Rat alone. Whimpered immediately, withdrew right hand and turned head and trunk away.
3. Blocks again offered. Played readily with them, smiling and gurgling.
4. Rat alone. Leaned over to the left side as far away from the rat as possible, then fell over, getting up on all fours and scurrying away as rapidly as possible.
5. Blocks again offered. Reached immediately for them, smiling and laughing as before.

The above preliminary test shows that the conditioned response to the rat had carried over completely for the five days in which no tests were given. The question as to whether or not there is a transfer was next taken up.

6. Rabbit alone. The rabbit was suddenly placed on the mattress in front of him. The reaction was pronounced. Negative responses began at once. He leaned as far away from the animal as possible, whimpered, then burst into tears. When the rabbit was placed in contact with him, he buried his face in the mattress, then got up on all fours and crawled away, crying as he went. This was a most convincing test.

7. The blocks were next given him, after an interval. He played with them as before. It was observed by four people that he played far more energetically with them than ever before. The blocks were raised high over his head and slammed down with a great deal of force.

8. Dog alone. The dog did not produce as violent a reaction as the rabbit. The moment fixation occurred the child shrank back and as the animal came nearer he attempted to get on all fours but did not cry at first. As soon as the dog passed out of his range of vision he became quiet. The dog was then made to approach the infant's head (he was lying down at the moment). Albert straightened up immediately, fell over to the opposite side and turned his head away. He then began to cry.

9. The blocks were again presented. He began immediately to play with them.

10. Fur coat (seal). Withdrew immediately to the left side and began to fret. Coat put close to him on the left side, he turned immediately, began to cry and tried to crawl away on all fours.

11. Cotton wool. The wool was presented in a paper package. At the end the cotton was not covered by the paper. It was placed first on his feet. He kicked it away but did not touch it with his hands. When his hand was laid on the wool, he immediately withdrew it but did not show the shock that the animals or fur coat produced in him. He then began to play with the paper, avoiding contact with the wool itself. He finally, under the impulse of the manipulative instinct, lost some of his negativism to the wool.

12. Just in play W. put his head down to see if Albert would play with his hair. Albert was completely negative. Two other observers did the same thing. He began immediately to play with their hair. W. then brought the Santa Claus mask and presented it to Albert. He was again pronouncedly negative.

11 Months 20 Days

1. Blocks alone. Played with them as usual.
2. Rat alone. Withdrawal of the whole body, bending over to left side, no crying. Fixation and following with eyes. The response was much less marked than on first presentation the previous week. It was thought best to freshen up the reaction by another joint stimulation.
3. Just as the rat was placed on his hand the rod was struck. Reaction violent.
4. Rat alone. Fell over at once to left side. Reaction practically as strong as on former occasion but no crying.
5. Rat alone. Fell over to left side, got up on all fours and started to crawl away. On this occasion there was no crying, but strange to say, as he started away he began to gurgle and coo, even while leaning far over to the left side to avoid the rat.
6. Rabbit alone. Leaned over to left side as far as possible. Did not fall over. Began to whimper but reaction not so violent as on former occasions.
7. Blocks again offered. He reached for them immediately and began to play.

All of the tests so far discussed were carried out upon a table supplied with a mattress, located in a small, well-lighted darkroom. We wished to test next whether conditioned fear responses so set up would appear if the situation were markedly altered. We thought it best before making this test to freshen the reaction both to the rabbit and to the dog by showing them at the moment the steel bar was struck. It will be recalled that this was the first time any effort had been made to directly condition response to the dog and rabbit. The experimental notes are as follows:

8. The rabbit at first was given alone. The reaction was exactly as given in test (6) above. When the rabbit was left on Albert's knees for a long time, he began tentatively to reach out and manipulate its fur with forefingers. While doing this the steel rod was struck. A violent fear reaction resulted.
9. Rabbit alone. Reaction wholly similar to that on trial (6) above.
10. Rabbit alone. Started immediately to whimper, holding hands far up, but did not cry. Conflicting tendency to manipulate very evident.
11. Dog alone. Began to whimper, shaking his head from side to side, holding hands as far away from the animal as possible.

12. Dog and sound. The rod was struck just as the animal touched him. A violent negative reaction appeared. He began to whimper, turned to one side, fell over and started to get up on all fours.
13. Blocks. Played with them immediately and readily.

On this same day and immediately after the above experiment Albert was taken into the large well-lighted lecture room belonging to the laboratory. He was placed on a table in the center of the room immediately under the skylight. Four people were present. The situation was thus very different from that which was obtained in the small darkroom.

1. Rat alone. No sudden fear reaction appeared at first. The hands, however, were held up and away from the animal. No positive manipulatory reactions appeared.
2. Rabbit alone. Fear reaction slight. Turned to left and kept face away from the animal but the reaction was never pronounced.
3. Dog alone. Turned away but did not fall over. Cried. Hands moved as far away from the animal as possible. Whimpered as long as the dog was present.
4. Rat alone. Slight negative reaction.
5. Rat and sound. It was thought best to freshen the reaction to the rat. The sound was given just as the rat was presented. Albert jumped violently but did not cry.
6. Rat alone. At first he did not show any negative reaction. When rat was placed nearer he began to show negative reaction by drawing back his body, raising his hands, whimpering, etc.
7. Blocks. Played with them immediately.
8. Rat alone. Pronounced withdrawal of body and whimpering.
9. Blocks. Played with them as before.
10. Rabbit alone. Pronounced reaction. Whimpered with arms held high, fell over backward and had to be caught.
11. Dog alone. At first the dog did not produce the pronounced reaction. The hands were held high over the head, breathing was checked, but there was no crying. Just at this moment the dog, which had not barked before, barked three times loudly when only about six inches from the baby's face. Albert immediately fell over and broke into a wail that continued until the dog was removed. The sudden barking of the hitherto quiet dog produced a marked fear response in the adult observers!

From the above results it would seem that emotional transfers do take place. Furthermore, it would seem that the number of transfers resulting from an experimentally produced conditioned emotional reaction may be very large. In our observations we had no means of testing the complete number of transfers which may have resulted.

III. The effect of time upon conditioned emotional responses. We have already shown that the conditioned emotional response will continue for a period of one week. It was desired to make the time test longer. In view of the imminence of Albert's departure from the hospital we could not make the interval longer than one month. Accordingly no further emotional experimentation was entered into for thirty-one days after the above test. During the month, however, Albert was brought weekly to the laboratory for tests upon right and left-handedness, imitation, general development, etc. No emotional tests whatever were given and during the whole month his regular nursery routine was maintained in the Harriet Lane Home. The notes on the test given at the end of this period are as follows:

1 Year 21 Days

1. Santa Claus mask. Withdrawal, gurgling, then slapped at it without touching. When his hand was forced to touch it, he whimpered and cried. His hand was forced to touch it two more times. He whimpered and cried on both tests. He finally cried at the mere visual stimulus of the mask.
2. Fur coat. Wrinkled his nose and withdrew both hands, drew back his whole body and began to whimper as the coat was put nearer. Again there was the strife between withdrawal and the tendency to manipulate. Reached tentatively with left hand but drew back before contact had been made. In moving his body to one side his hand accidentally touched the coat. He began to cry at once, nodding his head in a very peculiar manner (this reaction was an entirely new one). Both hands were withdrawn as far as possible from the coat. The coat was then laid on his lap and he continued nodding his head and whimpering, withdrawing his body as far as possible, pushing the while at the coat with his feet but never touching it with his hands.
3. Fur coat. The coat was taken out of his sight and presented again at the end of a minute. He began immediately to fret, withdrawing his body and nodding his head as before.
4. Blocks. He began to play with them as usual.
5. The rat. He allowed the rat to crawl towards him without withdrawing. He sat very still and fixated it intently. Rat then touched his hand. Albert withdrew it immediately, then leaned back as far as possible but did not cry. When the rat was placed on his arm he withdrew his body and began to

fret, nodding his head. The rat was then allowed to crawl against his chest. He first began to fret and then covered his eyes with both hands.

6. Blocks. Reaction normal.

7. The rabbit. The animal was placed directly in front of him. It was very quiet. Albert showed no avoiding reactions at first. After a few seconds he puckered up his face, began to nod his head and to look intently at the experimenter. He next began to push the rabbit away with his feet, withdrawing his body at the same time. Then as the rabbit came nearer he began pulling his feet away, nodding his head, and wailing "da da." After about a minute he reached out tentatively and slowly and touched the rabbit's ear with his right hand, finally manipulating it. The rabbit was again placed in his lap. Again he began to fret and withdrew his hands. He reached out tentatively with his left hand and touched the animal, shuddered and withdrew the whole body. The experimenter then took hold of his left hand and laid it on the rabbit's back. Albert immediately withdrew his hand and began to suck his thumb. Again the rabbit was laid in his lap. He began to cry, covering his face with both hands.

8. Dog. The dog was very active. Albert fixated it intensely for a few seconds, sitting very still. He began to cry but did not fall over backwards as on his last contact with the dog. When the dog was pushed closer to him he at first sat motionless, then began to cry, putting both hands over his face.

These experiments would seem to show conclusively that directly conditioned emotional responses as well as those conditioned by transfer persist, although with a certain loss in the intensity of the reaction, for a longer period than one month. Our view is that they persist and modify personality throughout life. It should be recalled again that Albert was of an extremely phlegmatic type. Had he been emotionally unstable, probably both the directly conditioned response and those transferred would have persisted throughout the month unchanged in form.

IV. "Detachment" or removal of conditioned emotional responses. Unfortunately Albert was taken from the hospital the day the above tests were made. Hence the opportunity of building up an experimental technique by means of which we could remove the conditioned emotional responses was denied us. Our own view, expressed above, which is possibly not very well grounded, is that these responses in the home environment are likely to persist indefinitely, unless an accidental method for removing them is hit upon. The importance of establishing some method must be apparent to all. Had the opportunity been at hand we should have tried out several methods, some of which we may mention. (1) Constantly confronting the child with those stimuli which called out the responses in the hopes that habituation would come in corresponding to "fatigue" of reflex when differential reactions are to be set up. (2) By trying to "recondition" by showing objects calling out fear responses (visual) and simultaneously stimulating the erogenous zones (tactual). We should try first the lips, then the nipples and as a final resort the sex organs. (3) By trying to "recondition" by feeding the subject candy or other food just as the animal is shown. This method calls for the food control of the subject. (4) By building up "constructive" activities around the object by imitation and by putting the hand through the motions of manipulation. At this age imitation of overt motor activity is strong, as our present but unpublished experimentation has shown.

INCIDENTAL OBSERVATIONS (a) Thumb sucking as a compensatory device for blocking fear and noxious stimuli. During the course of these experiments, especially in the final test, it was noticed that whenever Albert was on the verge of tears or emotionally upset generally he would continually thrust his thumb into his mouth. The moment the hand reached the mouth he became impervious to the stimuli producing fear. Again and again while the motion pictures were being made at the end of the thirty-day rest period, we had to remove the thumb from his mouth before the conditioned response could be obtained. This method of blocking noxious and emotional stimuli (fear and rage) through erogenous stimulation seems to persist from birth onward. Very often in our experiments upon the work adders with infants under ten days of age the same reaction appeared. When at work upon the adders both of the infants' arms are under slight restraint. Often rage appears. They begin to cry, thrashing their arms and legs about. If the finger gets into the mouth crying ceases at once. The organism thus apparently from birth, when under the influence of love stimuli is blocked to all others (3). This resort to sex stimulation when under the influence of noxious and emotional situations, or when the individual is restless and idle, persists throughout adolescent and adult life. Albert, at any rate, did not resort to thumb sucking except in the presence of such stimuli. Thumb sucking could immediately be checked by offering him his blocks. These invariably called out active manipulation instincts. It is worth while here to call attention to the fact that Freud's conception of the stimulation of erogenous zones as being the expression of an original "pleasure" seeking principle may be turned about and possibly better described as a compensatory (and often conditioned) device for the blockage of noxious and fear and rage producing stimuli.

(b) Equal primacy of fear, love and possibly rage. While in general the results of our experiment offer no particular points of conflict with Freudian concepts, one fact out of harmony with them should be emphasized. According to proper Freudians sex (or in our terminology, love) is the principal emotion in which conditioned responses arise which later limit and distort personality. We wish to take sharp issue with this view on the basis of the experimental evidence we have gathered. Fear is as primal a factor as love in influencing personality. Fear does not gather its potency in any derived manner from love. It belongs to the original and inherited nature of man. Probably the same may be true of rage although at present we are not so sure of this.

The Freudians twenty years from now, unless their hypotheses change, when they come to analyze Albert's fear of a seal skin coat—assuming that he comes to analysis at that age—will probably tease from him the recital of a dream which upon their analysis will show that Albert at three years of age attempted to play with the pubic hair of the mother and was scolded violently for it. (We are by no means denying that this might in some other case condition it.) If the analyst has sufficiently prepared Albert to accept such a dream when found as an explanation of his avoiding tendencies, and if the analyst has the authority and personality to put it over, Albert may be fully convinced that the dream was a true revealer of the factors which brought about the fear.

It is probable that many of the phobias in psychopathology are true conditioned emotional reactions either of the direct or the transferred type. One may possibly have to believe that such persistence of early conditioned responses will be found only in persons who are constitutionally inferior. Our argument is meant to be constructive. Emotional disturbances in adults cannot be traced back to sex alone. They must be retraced along at least three collateral lines—to conditioned and transferred responses set up in infancy and early youth in all three of the fundamental human emotions.

REFERENCES AND NOTE

1. 'Emotional Reactions and Psychological Experimentation,' *American Journal of Psychology*, April 1917, Vol. 28, pp. 163–174.
2. 'Psychology from the Standpoint of a Behaviorist,' p. 202.
3. The stimulus to love in infants according to our view is

stroking of the skin, lips, nipples and sex organs, patting and rocking, picking up, etc. Patting and rocking (when not conditioned) are probably equivalent to actual stimulation of the sex organs. In adults, of course, as every lover knows, vision, audition and olfaction soon become conditioned by joint stimulation with contact and kinaesthetic stimuli.

You may, by now, be comparing this study with Huxley's *Brave New World.* The fact that the experimenters *felt* that they could do Albert *relatively* little harm does not placate us.

But the study was done. And it did demonstrate that emotional reactions could be learned by a simple conditioning process. It suggests that, not only *could* we learn to react emotionally in various situations, we probably do just that in our daily living from infancy on. Conditioning has created emotional filters through which all outside information comes to us. The emotions we express now have been conditioned in us by past events.

This study is far from complete in itself. We can find much about it to criticize. But it was a basic study and laid the groundwork for much that has been learned about emotion in the last half century. Many emotional responses which had, prior to this study, been considered instinctive, were now seen to be the result of conditioning.

We have said that emotional behavior is complex behavior. It includes both internal bodily changes and external motions. Many of these emotional gestures seem to be the common behavior of all people when they experience a given emotion. All of us "telegraph" our emotional states to those around us. We all seem to understand the signals.

The writer, particularly the novelist or short story writer, is able to take advantage of this. He need not tell us that his hero was frightened. He describes the sudden pallor of the cheek, the cold sweat, the prickly scalp.

But are these emotion-indicating behaviors truly universal? It seems quite probable that some of them are inborn reactions, but others may have been learned and may be universal only within a given culture.

If we examine the literature of a culture quite different from ours, do we find the same behaviors described to indicate certain emotions as we do in the literature of our own culture? Is it possible that, in doing this, we can get some tentative clues as to which behaviors are inborn and which are learned?

33

EMOTIONAL EXPRESSION IN CHINESE LITERATURE

OTTO KLINEBERG

The fact that the expression of the emotions is at least to some extent patterned by social factors is probably known to all psychologists. Even in our own society there is considerable evidence that this is so. When we turn to the descriptions of other cultures, instances of this patterning occur frequently. One of the most striking examples is the copious shedding of tears by the Andaman Islanders and the Maori of New Zealand when friends meet after an absence, or when two warring parties make peace. Another is the smile with which the Japanese responds to the scolding of his superior, or which accompanies his announcement of the death of his favorite son.

This paper presents part of a more extensive study of emotional expression among the Chinese, an investigation made possible by a Guggenheim Fellowship and a supplementary grant from the Social Science Research Council. Among the various techniques employed, it seemed valuable in the case of a civilization as articulate as the Chinese to examine at least a portion of the Chinese literature for the light it might throw on this problem. There is not much precedent for the reading of novels as a technique of psychological investigation, but in this case it seemed warranted at least as an introduction to more objective methods.

Before turning to the question of the kind of expression involved, a word should be said as to the related question of the amount of expression which the culture permits. There are, for example, many admonitions—especially to the young girl—not to show emotion too readily. In *Required Studies for Women* we find such warnings as the following: "Do not show your unhappiness easily and do not smile easily"; also, "Do not let your teeth be seen when you smile," that is, your smile must be so circumspect that the teeth do not show. On the other hand, there are many occasions on which the emotion of grief has to be displayed. One piece of advice from the same volume reads, "If your father or mother is sick, do not be far from his or her bed. Do not even take off your girdle. Taste all the medicine yourself. Pray your god for his or her health. If anything unfortunate happens cry bitterly."

The alleged inscrutability of the Chinese, which as a matter

SOURCE: From *Journal of Abnormal and Social Psychology*, 1938, *33*, 517–520.

of fact has been greatly exaggerated, completely breaks down in the case of grief. Not only is grief expressed, but there is an elaborate set of rules and regulations which insure that it shall be properly expressed. One of the Chinese classics is *The Book of Rites,* a considerable portion of which is devoted to the technique of the mourning ceremonial, with elaborate instructions as to just what procedure should be followed in order that the expression of the grief may be socially acceptable.

The most extreme degree of patterning of emotional expression is found on the Chinese stage, and is illustrated by the following examples from a Chinese *Treatise on Acting.* There is an occasional pattern which does conform closely to our own; for example, "taking the left sleeve with the right hand and raising it to the eyes as if to wipe the tears" is clearly an expression of sorrow. There are others, however, that are not so clear. To "draw one leg up and stand on one foot" means surprise. To "raise one hand as high as the face and fan the face with the sleeve" means anger, as does also to "blow the beard to make it fly up." Joy or satisfaction is represented by stretching "the left arm flatly to the left and the right arm to the right." To "move one hand around in front of the middle of the beard and touch your head with the fingers of the other hand" means sorrow, while to "put the middle part of the beard into the mouth with both hands and bite firmly" indicates that one has come to a decision. To "raise both hands above the head with the palms turned outwards and the fingers pointing up, let the sleeves hang down behind the hands, then walk towards the other person, shake the sleeves over, and let the hands fall" means love.

There were two long novels which were read for this study; one, *The Dream of the Red Chamber,* was read in Chinese, with considerable help from Miss Wu T'ien Min, a graduate student at Yenching University, and the other, *All Men are Brothers,* in Pearl Buck's English translation. These represent two of the three most famous Chinese novels, the third being *The Romance of the Three Kingdoms. The Dream of the Red Chamber* is a love story; *All Men are Brothers* is a tale of swashbuckling adventure dealing with the so-called "bandits" who are among the most picturesque figures of Chinese legend and history. Besides these, several modern stories were also consulted.

In some cases the descriptions of emotional expression correspond closely to our own. When we read (D.R.C.), for example, that "everyone trembled with a face the color of clay," there can be little doubt that fear is meant. The same holds for the statement that "every one of his hairs stood on end, and the pimples came out on the skin all over his body" (from "Married Life Awakening the World"). Other descriptions of fear (A.M.B.) are the following: "A cold sweat broke forth on his whole body, and he trembled without ceasing"; "it was as though her two feet were nailed to the ground and she would fain have shrieked but her mouth was like a mute's"; "they stood like death with mouths ajar"; "they were so frightened that their waters and wastes burst out of them." In general, it may be said that fear is expressed in very much the same way in the Chinese literature as in our own. As far as other emotions are concerned, in the sentence, "He gnashed his teeth until they were all but ground to dust," we recognize anger; "He was listless and silent" suggests sorrow; "His face was red and he went creeping alone outside the village" clearly indicates shame. There is no doubt of the frequent similarity between Chinese and Western forms of expression.

There are also differences, however. When we read, "They stretched out their tongues" (D.R.C.), most of us would not recognize this description as meaning surprise, except for the context. This phrase as an expression of surprise occurs with great frequency, and it would be easy to give many examples. The sentence "Her eyes grew round and opened wide," would probably suggest to most of us surprise or fear; to the Chinese it usually means anger. This expression, with slight variations, also occurs very often. In the form "He made his two eyes round and stared at him" (A.M.B.), it can mean nothing but anger. "He would fain have swallowed him at a gulp" (A.M.B.) implies hatred; our own "I could eat you up!" has a somewhat different significance. "He scratched his ears and cheeks" would probably suggest embarrassment to us, but in the *Dream of the Red Chamber* it means happiness. "He clapped his hands" (D.R.C.) is likely to mean worry or disappointment.

The case of anger appears to be particularly interesting. We have already noted the expressions connected with "round eyes," "eyes wide open," "staring," etc. We find in addition descriptions like these: "He laughed a great ho-ho," and "He smiled a chill smile," and "He looked at them and he smiled and cursed them" (A.M.B.). Both the laugh and the smile of anger or contempt occur in our own culture, but apparently not nearly so frequently as in China and the Chinese literature. More curious still is the phrase "He was so angry that several times he fainted from his anger" (A.M.B.). This expression occurs frequently. When I showed wonder as to why this should be, Chinese friends said that they in turn could never understand why European women fainted so frequently in the mid-Victorian literature with which they were acquainted. Certainly the delicately nurtured young women of not so long ago did faint with astonishing ease and regularity; there were even etiquette books which taught them how to faint elegantly. Such a custom is certainly no less surprising than that the Chinese should faint in anger. The conclusion seems clear that fainting, like tears, may be conditioned by social custom to appear on widely varying occasions.

Most striking of all perhaps, is the indication in the literature that people may die of anger. "His anger has risen so that he is ill of it and lies upon his bed, and his life cannot be long assured." " 'Today am I killed by anger' . . . and when he had finished speaking he let his soul go free" (A.M.B.). This phenomenon, incidentally, mysterious though it may sound, is reported as still occurring, and I saw one patient in a hospital in Peiping whose father was said to have died of anger after losing a lawsuit. It is important to note that a death of this kind cannot be explained as due to anything like an apoplectic stroke; it does not occur suddenly as a stroke would. When someone is very angry but is forced to suppress his anger because there is nothing he can do about it, he may become ill, faint many times and take to his bed; death may follow after the lapse of some days or weeks. The only explanation is in terms of suggestion; the belief that people die of anger when they can do nothing about it, may succeed in actually bringing on the death of an impressionable person. There is the parallel case of the Polynesian native who inadvertently eats the tabooed food of the chief, remains perfectly well as long as he does not know it, but may die when he learns what he has done.

These examples indicate that, although there are many similarities between the literary descriptions of the emotions in China and in the West, there are also important differences which must be recognized if Chinese literature is to be read intelligently. When the literary pattern is such that the expression alone is described but not labeled, real misunderstandings may arise. When I first read, for instance, "They stretched out their tongues," I did not know that surprise was meant. Our own literature is of course also rich in these unlabeled expressions. We read, "His jaw dropped"; "He gnashed his teeth"; "His lip curled"; "His eyes almost popped out of his head"; "He clenched his fists," etc., and in each case we know at once what emotion is indicated. These expressions are a part of language and must be learned in order to be understood.

The question arises as to the degree to which these Chinese literary expressions are related to expression in real life. Caution must certainly be exercised in inferring from one to the other. A Chinese reader of our literature, for instance, might conclude that laughter was dangerous to Westerners, in view of the frequency with which he read the expression "I nearly died laughing." I think I may say, however, on the basis of information obtained by methods other than the reading of novels, that the Chinese patterns which I have described do appear not only in the literature but also in real life. I may add that photographs illustrating these literary expressions are judged more easily by Chinese than by American subjects.

It seems to me to be worth while to extend this literary approach to other cultures. In the writings of India, Japan, and other peoples of the Near and Far East, material must certainly be available which would further illustrate the extent and the nature of the cultural patterning of emotional expression.

Why not try a little investigation of your own? Perhaps you are taking a literature course in which you read short stories or novels, or maybe you are reading fiction just for your own pleasure. Make a list of the various ways in which a writer lets you, the reader, know something about the emotional states of his characters.

We live in a culture that tends to require us to inhibit emotional display. Each of us is to keep his "cool." "Big boys don't cry!" This may have effects on the development of personality.

Emotional behavior is such an important aspect of all behavior that it cannot be dealt with adequately in isolation. Later, when we discuss the topic of personality, we shall return to a consideration of emotions. And, of course, when we discuss disturbances of personality we shall be discussing maladaptive emotional behavior.

Just to emphasize the importance of emotion in our lives, consider this question: How would you like being a person with absolutely no feelings, no emotion? The question cannot, of course, be answered.

FOR THOSE WHO WOULD *LIKE* MORE ABOUT EMOTION

An early study of emotional development in young children by K. M. B. Bridges, "Emotional Development in Early Infancy" (*Child Development,* 1932, *3,* 324–341), concluded that the first emotion expressed was general excitement. Within a few weeks, however, the infant can indicate distress and some time later, delight. Bridges goes on from there to indicate the sequence in which various emotional patterns emerge during infancy. A later study, K. M. Banham, "Senescence and the Emotions: A Genetic Theory" (*Journal of Genetic Psychology,* 1951, *78,* 175–183), outlines a rather comprehensive theory of emotional change. This involves the differentiation of emotional responses from infancy to maturity, then the gradual consolidation and eventual restriction of responses as the individual goes from full maturity into old age.

Support for a genetic theory of emotional development is contained in a study by David Gutman, "The Hunger of Old Men" (*Transaction,* November–December, 1971). Gutman states that "Young men in Kansas City are more like young Navajo men than they are like old men in Kansas City. Old Druze tribesmen from the hills of Galilee are very like old Maya Indians from Mexico; the resemblances between the two are stronger than any similarities between young and old Maya or young and old Druze men." You may find this study worth looking into.

Emotional development can be explored farther in Jerome Kagan and H. A. Moss, *Birthday to Maturity: A Study of Psychological Development* (John Wiley and Sons, 1962) and in Stella Chase, Alexander Thomas and Herbert G. Birch, *Temperament and Behavior Disorders in Children* (Viking Press, 1965). These three authors have an article, "The Origin of Personality" (*Scientific American,* August 1970), in which they conclude "that the debate over the relative importance of nature and nurture only confuses the issue. What is important is the interaction between the two—between the child's own characteristics and his environment."

Someone has said that "the eyes are the windows of the soul." One way in which the eyes reveal the feelings inside is discussed by E. H. Hess, "Attitude and Pupil Size" (*Scientific American,* April 1965).

Part Eleven

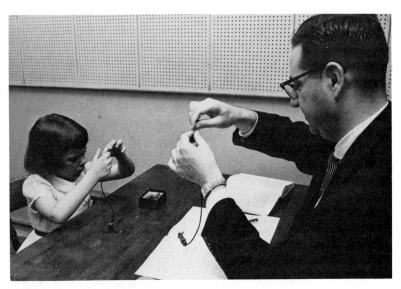

Measuring
Individual
Differences:
"I Will
Test Them!"

There is nothing more obvious than that all people are not alike. Of course there is the very obvious division of the human race, like all mammals, into two sexes. But, apart from this, they come in different sizes and varying temperaments. Some are very musical, others less so in degrees, and then there are some who cannot carry a tune or distinguish one note from another.

We could go on for several pages, cataloging the dimensions that could be measured. Many such measurements are useful. For example, certain measures of musical talent enable music schools to select applicants who have the qualities required to become musicians. The same goes for medical schools. The Air Force selects pilot trainees. Many employers select the few most likely candidates from a large number of applicants.

Two writers in the field of industrial psychology have said that "the idea of predicting occupational success in advance of actual trial on the job is a very old one."[1] They give as one example Plato's proposal, in his *Republic*, that candidates for the military be pre-selected by means of tests of "toil and pain." Then they point to Gideon's selection of a small battle force as another.

[1] T. A. Ryan and Patricia C. Smith, *Principles of Industrial Psychology.* Ronald Press, 1954. p. 170.

34

GIDEON'S ARMY
JUDGES 7: 4-8

And the Lord said to Gideon, "The people are still too many; take them down to the water and I will test them for you there; and he of whom I say to you, 'This man shall go with you,' shall go with you; and any of whom I say to you, 'This man shall not go with you,' shall not go."

So he brought the people down to the water; and the Lord said to Gideon, "Every one that laps the water with his tongue, as a dog laps, you shall set by himself; likewise every one that kneels down to drink." And the number of those that lapped, putting their hands to their mouths, was three hundred men; but all the rest of the people knelt down to drink water. And the Lord said to Gideon, "With the three hundred men that lapped I will deliver you, and give the Midianites into your hand; and let all the others go every man to his home." So he took the jars of the people from their hands, and their trumpets; and he sent all the rest of Israel every man to his tent, but retained the three hundred men; and the camp of Midian was below him in the valley.

If you know the Bible story, you will recall that the next morning, with much blowing of trumpets and smashing of pitchers, this selected group of soldiers conquered the enemy. Just what factor, what dimension of human ability, was measured by the aptitude test in this account, we do not know. Perhaps it was alertness. Perhaps it was general intelligence.

When the United States became involved in the 1917–18 World War, the military leaders may have been reading their Bibles. At least they, like Gideon, sought help in "placing each enlisted man where he has the opportunity to make the most of his talent and skill." Gideon had called on God for assistance. The United States Army called on a group of psychologists.

We shall not comment as to the relative merits of the two choices. We will, however, present a rather old selection, an article that discusses the problem of testing individual differences in what we might call "early modern" times.

Edward L. Thorndike was one of the pioneers of American psychology. His interests within psychology were varied, but both psychological measurement and the nature of intelligence received a considerable share of his attention.

Most psychologists concerned with measuring human differences have operated on the basis of certain assumptions. Only very recently are some of these assumptions being questioned.

Thorndike's thinking about the measurement of intelligence largely dominated the development of mental tests in America for half a century. Actually, his theorizing has, in some aspects, remained in advance of practice. He saw the necessity of measuring various aspects of intelligence, rather than assuming that all of the abilities which matter could be summarized in a single score. He pointed out that there were many dimensions of intelligence, particularly mechanical and social, and that tests of these variables were only then being developed. Here, developments have not kept up with his expectations. We still do not have adequate measures of these aspects of the abilities of mankind.

Thorndike placed emphasis on measuring *abstract* intelligence as having value for many purposes. But he proceeded on the assumption that "a well-chosen series of tests" was adequate for measuring the abstract intelligence of, at least, all school children. He seems to have been unaware of the very wide variations in the environment that concern us today.

More than half a century has passed since Thorndike wrote this article. But, functionally, in the schools—where most intelligence testing is done—Thorndikian concepts seem still to be in command. Is it not possible that this is one of the factors at the heart of the class (race) struggle? Is it not possible that the establishment has created its own intelligentsia who still, emotionally if not always intellectually, accept the idea of a group of people who are better in *every* way than the blacks, the browns, the poor, the "laboring classes," etc.? And may it not be that they then attempt to prove this superiority by giving intelligence tests? May it not be that what Thorndike describes is still happening in America today? We would rather not admit that it is so. We cover it up by much theoretical rhetoric. But we treat people as though what Thorndike said is true.

35

INTELLIGENCE AND ITS USES
EDWARD L. THORNDIKE

In the last hundred years the civilized world has learned to trust science to teach it how to make the powers of wind and water, the energy of chemicals, and the vibrations of the ether do man's will and serve his comfort. Physical forces are being conquered by science for man. We may hope that man's own powers of intellect, character, and skill are no less amenable to understanding, control, and direction; and that in the next hundred years the world may improve its use of man-power as it has improved its use of earth-power.

Not only philanthropists and philosophers, but hard-headed, practical men of affairs in business, education, and government, are now looking to psychology, the science of human behavior, to provide principles for human engineering—for the efficient private and public management of man-power or "personnel." For example, the Secretary of War and Adjutant-General McCain, in seeking specialists to help "(1) secure a contented and efficient army by placing each enlisted man where he has the

SOURCE: Copyright © 1919, by Minneapolis Star and Tribune Co., Inc. Reprinted from the January 1920 issue of *Harper's Magazine* by permission of the author's heirs. Slightly abridged.

opportunity to make the most of his talent and skill, (2) to commission, assign and promote officers on merit, and (3) to simplify the procedure of discovering talent and assigning it where most needed," intrusted the task to psychologists. The co-operation between psychologists and business men in the organization that resulted (the Committee on Classification of Personnel in the Army) made clear to each group how much it had to learn from the others. And, in general, to-day, science is eager to make use of the practical experience of men and women who succeed in managing human nature; and men of affairs are realizing that the experiments and measurements and formulae of the scientific man may turn out to be the most "practical" things in the world.

As a sample to illustrate both what the scientific study of personnel has done and what it has to do, we may take the problem of intelligence and its uses.

Men talk freely about intelligence, and rank their acquaintances as having very little, little, much, or very much of it. If, however, they try to state just what it is, and how it is to be measured, there is difficulty. One says, "It is thought-power; and it is measured by the person's ability in school and in life." Another retorts, "What is thought-power?" and calls attention to the fact that ability in school and ability in life are different things. Smith declares that "Intelligence is ability to learn," and when asked, "To learn what?" adds, "To learn anything." A teacher present then observes that one of the slowest boys at learning Latin whom he ever knew made record progress in learning to swim, skate, and play ball. Jones, who has turned to the dictionary, says: "This suits me, '*Readiness of comprehension*'! I call a man intelligent who can understand questions— see the point. Give me fifteen minutes' interview with a man and I can give you a measure of his intelligence." Some one at once objects that a man may be slow and incorrect in responding to questions, but quick and sure in locating the trouble with an automobile, or in seeing a bargain, or in sizing up the temper of a mob of strikers.

The facts of every-day life, when inspected critically, indicate that a man has not some one amount of one kind of intelligence, but varying amounts of different intelligences. His ability to think with numbers may be great; his ability to think with words small. He may be a successful student of history and a failure at learning physics. Compare Grant's intelligence in using an army with his intelligence as a business trader. In our ratings of men we unconsciously strike a sort of average of his abilities in learning, thinking, and acting. The source or cause of this average ability is what we really have in mind when we speak of his intelligence.

Numerous scientific investigations of human intellectual abilities confirm and extend this view. No man is equally intelligent for all sorts of problems. Intelligence varies according to the life situations on which it works. A man so feeble-minded in most matters that he is confined in an asylum is found to play a first-rate game of chess. A man who in his day was famous the country over as editor, speaker, and executive never was able to pass freshman mathematics in college. Such extreme cases are, of course, found rarely. There is a general rough correspondence or correlation, such that a man notably intelligent in one respect will usually be above the average in others also. But the correlation is far from perfect. Shakespeare was successful as a business man, and doubtless would have made a good record as a lawyer, farmer, statesman, navigator, or grammarian; but no competent person believes that his intelligence was equally adapted to all these.

. . . . .

A perfect description and measurement of intelligence would involve testing the man's ability to think in all possible lines, just as a perfect description and measurement of the mineral wealth of a state would involve adequate testing for iron, copper, gold, silver, lead, tin, zinc, antimony, petroleum, tungsten, iridium, and the long list of rarer metals.

For ordinary practical purposes, however, it suffices to examine for three "intelligences," which we may call mechanical intelligence, social intelligence and abstract intelligence. By mechanical intelligence is meant the ability to learn to understand and manage things and mechanisms such as a knife, gun, mowing-machine, automobile, boat, lathe, piece of land, river, or storm. By social intelligence is meant the ability to understand and manage men and women, boys and girls—to act wisely in human relations. By abstract intelligence is meant the ability to understand and manage ideas and symbols, such as words, numbers, chemical or physical formulae, legal decisions, scientific laws and principles, and the like. Mechanical intelligence and social intelligence refer to thought and action directly concerned with actual things and persons in one's hands and before one's eyes. When the mind works with general facts *about* things and people, as in the study of physics and chemistry, or history and sociology, its action is referred to abstract intelligence.

Within any of these intelligences a man displays relatively great consistency. The man who learns carpentering quickly and well could commonly have done nearly as well as a mason, sailor, plumber, millwright, or auto-repair man. The man who succeeds as a politician would commonly have done well as a salesman, hotel clerk, confidence man, or, if provided with certain accessory traits, as a parish priest or school principal. The boy who cannot learn algebra, history, and sciences will probably be unable to learn law, engineering, philosophy, and theology.

Between one and another of the three there is relatively great disparity. The best mechanic in a factory may fail as a foreman for lack of social intelligence. The whole world may revere the abstract intelligence of a philosopher whose mechanical intelligence it would not employ at three dollars a day!

In recent years much progress has been made in devising means to measure intelligence, with the result that we can discover how individuals and races and the sexes differ in the amount of it which characterizes each; how this and that form of training influences it; how much of it is required for success in any given occupation, and how it is related to other desirable qualities, such as mental health, cheerfulness of disposition, leadership, industry, honesty, determination, public spirit, loyalty, and co-operativeness.

The greatest progress has been made in the case of abstract intelligence. . . . If John has devoted his mind chiefly to thinking with words, while James has devoted himself chiefly to thinking with chemical and electrical symbols, John will be overrated and James underrated. . . . Also, if Mary has devoted her mind almost exclusively to one subject, say music, while Jane has devoted hers about equally to a thousand subjects, any dozen short tests are likely to give Jane a better chance than Mary. If the test were, "Choose the thing you know most about and tell what you know about it," Mary would have an unfair advantage. Also, if an individual possesses a very high degree of intelligence, the tests may be too easy and the score may represent the speed with which he can think rather than the total efficiency of his thinking.

Other limitations will occur to the critical reader. The fact remains, however, that, life being as it is, all the limitations do not prevent a well-chosen series of tests, if used with ordinary discretion and interpreted with ordinary common sense, from giving an approximate measure of an individual's abstract intelligence, at least during childhood and youth. Schools find them useful as a means of grading pupils; employment managers find them useful in hiring and placing employees; the army found it profitable so to test nearly two million of its recruits.

When an individual is measured by any of the standard tests, he is given a score in such terms as make it convenient to compare him with other individuals and with various requirements. For example, John Smith, aged 15 years, 0 months, may be reported as: "Mental age 12 yr., 0 mo.," or as, "Intelligence quotient (or IQ) 80," or as "A 7-percentile intelligence," or as, "Int. $= -1.5$ S. D." Mental age, 12 yr., 0 mo., means that John did as well in the tests as the average child of 12 years, 0 months. IQ $= 80$ means that John's mental age as shown by the tests was 80 per cent. of his chronological age. A 7-percentile intelligence means that 7 per cent. of the population (white) of age 15 years, 0 months, will do worse than John in the series of tests in question, and 93 per cent. will do better. Int. $= -1.5$ S. D. means that John is below the average for his age to an extent of $1\frac{1}{2}$ times a certain standard amount. Thus, the adult inmates of asylums for the feeble-minded are mostly under 9 years, 0 months, in mental age. Children with IQ's of 60 or below later fill such asylums. An IQ of 100 means average intelligence. Unless he has extraordinary energy and devotion, a boy whose IQ is under 100 will be unable to graduate from a reputable American college. Children selected by competent observers as extremely intelligent will be found to have IQ's from 120 to 160.

Measurements of mechanical intelligence have received much less attention from psychologists and are not yet standardized, but they are under way. Two samples from a set of such tests may be briefly illustrated. The first is a series of dismembered objects to be put together. It begins with something the average child of four can do, such as to put a nut on its bolt, and progresses by graded steps to something which only the 90-percentile adult can do without special training, such as to put together the pieces of an electric pull-socket, or of a very intricate lock. The second consists of a set of materials out of which the individual tested is told to make something, or to make as many things as he can in an hour, or to make as good a cart, derrick, and boat as he can, or to use the material in some other prescribed way. The merit of the product which he produces is estimated in comparison with certain average performances of 6-year-, 8-year-, and 10-year-olds, and so on, under similar conditions.

Convenient tests of social intelligence are hard to devise. A child's wit in reading facial expression might perhaps be measured by his success in selecting from . . . photographs . . . when asked, "Which lady would you ask to help you?" "Which lady is thinking?" "Which lady is worried?" "Which lady is saying 'I will *not*'?" and the like. It is doubtful, however, whether pictures can be safely used in place of realities. And for most of the activities of intelligence in response to the behavior of human beings, a genuine situation with real persons is essential. Social intelligence shows itself abundantly in the nursery, on the playground, in barracks and factories and salesroom, but it eludes the formal standardized conditions of the testing laboratory. It requires human beings to respond to, time to adapt its responses, and face, voice, gesture, and mien as tools.

Whether we consider one of these intelligences or the composite of the three, it appears that each human being is equipped by nature with a certain degree of intelligence, much as he is equipped by nature with a certain strength of body or form of finger-prints. Individuals differ by original nature in intelligence as in stature or eye color or countenance. It is true that good training improves and bad training injures the mind, as it does the body; that nature's gift may be lost by accident or decreased by disease, neglect, and misuse. As things are in America to-day, however, the net effect of these disturbing factors does not greatly disarrange the order or decrease the differences of individuals in respect to intellect. A boy who is the brightest of a thousand at the age of five will usually be in the top fifty of the thousand at the age of ten. The child who is at the lowest of a thousand at ten will almost never rise above the bottom hundred at fifteen. Kelley and others have traced the records of the same children year after year in school and found that in general a child keeps about the same position relative to other children in late as in early years. Terman's measurement of the abstract intelligence of the same children (over a hundred of them) at two periods five years or more apart shows very great constancy. Intelligence grows with general growth from early childhood to adult years, but its growth is in proportion to what it already is. A child holds his place in comparison with other children nearly as closely after five years as after five days.

Because of the recency of the science of mental measurements, we lack tests of the same individual at 16 years of age, 18 years of age, 20, 22, 24, and so on. It may be that certain of the children who seemed essentially dull were only growing slowly; and these may catch up in adult years, and some of the children with high IQ's at 10 or 15 may have merely "got their intelligence" early, as some children get their teeth early; these may sink back relatively. It may also be that the new trends of mind due to sex and adult ambitions will act differently on different individuals, stimulating intelligence in different degrees and even subtracting from it in some cases. As a rule, however, those who progress most rapidly go farthest; and those who have the most intelligence are least likely to have it lessened by the distracting force of sex or display or rivalry. Intelligence probably does not fluctuate very much more from fifteen to fifty than from five to fifteen. An individual's intelligence compared with that of other individuals of his age is, within limits, a stable, permanent characteristic of him. It can be at least roughly measured and the measurement used to prophesy and direct his career.

If we take a group of individuals and measure their success in life, as students in school, or as money-makers, or as lawyers, or as carpenters, or as teachers of children, and then measure their intellect by some suitable series of tests and observations, we can determine how closely success in any line goes with the degree of intelligence shown by the test-score.

For example, consider the significance of abstract intelligence for success in schoolwork. If we take a thousand children twelve years old we may measure the success of each in schoolwork by the grade he has reached and by the quality of work he is doing in that grade. If we measure these same children with an adequate series of tests made up of giving the opposites of words, supplying missing words in sentences, solving practical problems, following directions, and putting facts in their proper relations, we have as a result a diagram which shows the *resemblance* or *correlation* between intelligence score and success in school in the individuals in question. The amount of the resemblance—the closeness of the correlation—is measured with great exactitude by a *coefficient of correlation*, called *r*, a number derived by suitable calculation from the thousand pairs of scores. This number varies from +1.00, or perfect correlation, to −1.00, perfect antagonism. Such coefficients of correlation are the shorthand in which science sums up the extent to which two things go together. The significance of intelligence for success in a given activity of life is measured by the coefficient of correlation between them.

Scientific investigations of these matters is just beginning: and it is a matter of great difficulty and expense to measure the intelligence of, say, a thousand clergymen, and then secure sufficient evidence to rate them accurately for their success as ministers of the Gospel. Consequently, one can report no final, perfectly authoritative results in this field. One can only organize reasonable estimates from the various partial investigations that have been made. Doing this, I find the following:

Intelligence and success in the elementary schools, r = +.80.
Intelligence and success in high school and colleges in the case of those who go, r = +.60; but if all were forced to try to do this advanced work, the correlation would be +.80 or more.
Intelligence and salary, r = +.35.
Intelligence and success in athletic sports, r = +.25.
Intelligence and character, r = +.40 or more.
Intelligence and popularity, r = +.20.

Whatever be the eventual exact findings, two sound principles are illustrated by our provisional list. First, there is always some resemblance; intellect always counts. Second, the resemblance varies greatly; intellect counts much more in some lines than in others.

The first fact is in part a consequence of a still broader fact or principle—namely, that in human nature good traits go together. To him that hath a superior intellect is given also on the average a superior character; the quick boy is also in the long run more accurate; the able boy is also more industrious. There is no principle of compensation whereby a weak intellect is offset by a strong will, a poor memory by good judgment, or a lack of ambition by an attractive personality. Every pair of such supposed compensating equalities that have been investigated has been found really to show correspondence. Popular opinion has been misled by attending to striking individual cases which attracted attention partly because they were really exceptions to the rule. The rule is that desirable qualities are positively correlated. Intellect is good in and of itself, and also for what it implies about other traits.

The second fact—that intellect varies in utility according to the work to be done—has permitted a very wide diversity in opinions about its utility. Ordinary observation of life is beset by such variety and complexity that persons of generally good judgment can be found who will rate the importance of intellect for success in, say, business, or art, or politics, almost all the way from 0 to 100 per cent. Only the painstaking investigation of each such problem can give the correct answer.

The correct answers will put an end to numerous superstitions and fancies about human achievement. About a generation ago America was obsessed by the superstition that money-making had a correlation of from $+.80$ to $+1.00$ with general intelligence and good-will, so that to get a representative of the people in Congress, or a trustee for a university, or a vestryman of a church, or a member of a commission on public health or charity or schools or playgrounds, you should look about for a man who had made a great deal of money. To-day the world is being assailed by the much more foolish superstition that money-making is correlated 0 with general intelligence and about $-.80$ to -1.00 with good-will, the maker of great profits being no more fit intellectually to run his business than his barber is, and being diabolically eager to amass dollars at the cost of misery to anybody who gets in his way and to all innocent bystanders.

Exact and complete knowledge about the correlations of mental traits will be of enormous importance for the utilization of man-power by schools, churches, employers, and the state. When we have such exact knowledge, we shall be able to make up a bill of specifications of the sort of intellect and character required for a certain job, select men efficiently instead of haphazard, and train them according to their individual needs instead of indiscriminately.

The present waste is great, both in efficiency and in happiness. W. P., whose IQ is 83, is being forced through high-school to college by his father. W. P. gets nothing but confusion and misery from his high-school work and is growing a little more inactive, sullen, and idle each year. He wants and has wanted to be a gardener, and could probably succeed and be useful to the world as such. There is not one chance in a hundred that he will graduate from college or get any good from college studies. L. C. was promoted to be foreman of the shop merely because he was the most skillful workman. He possessed very little social intelligence and was unhappy and inefficient in the new job. The management, realizing that it was to blame, continued him at a foreman's salary, but gave him a special mechanical job. P. S., a field salesman of extraordinary success by virtue of his great popularity, energy, and personal tact in face-to-face conferences, was promoted to be in charge of planning sales campaigns and selecting and directing the staff of salesmen. He failed, being only mediocre in general intelligence, and unable to understand the plans of the manufacturing department or teach his subordinates. In selecting these, also, he sometimes mistook "sportiness" for popularity and pleasant manners for real tact.

Knowledge of the correlations of mental traits will also be a protection against many unsound, impracticable theories of business and government. Consider, for example, the correlation between intellect and character. Dickson and Terman found, in the case of little children, that the IQ of abstract intelligence had correlations with the teachers' ratings for persistence, conscientiousness, co-operativeness, industry, courage, dependability, and unselfishness of from $+.30$ to $+.50$, with an average of $+.41$. Chassell has found, in the case of college students, correlations between intelligence and unselfishness, loyalty, justice, courage, self-control, reliability, and activity for social welfare, averaging $+.40$. Woods, rating some six hundred members of European royal families for intellect and for character, finds a correlation of about $+.40$. No impartial study of the matter has found any contrary result. The abler persons in the world in the long run are the more clean, decent, just and kind.

To this feature of human nature which has tied good-will toward men to ability, a large proportion of the blessings which the common man enjoys to-day are due. The brains and ability of the world have been, and still are, working for the profit of others. If Pasteur had been of mean and brutal nature, he could have kept his first discoveries as a trade secret, extorted a fortune in fees, and lived in sensuous idleness, leaving the world without his still more important later work. Flexner or Carrel could poison their enemies and rivals except for the tradition of justice and generosity which the positive correlation between intellect and morality has made a part of scientific work, and which their own natures gladly maintain.

The correlation between intellect and character has in fact within a few hundred years produced so strong a body of customs that the world rather expects a gifted man of science to be a public benefactor. It would have been greatly shocked if William James had given up psychology to establish a lucrative organization of spiritualistic mediums over the country, or if the Mayo brothers had retired from medicine to direct a chain of Mayo drug-stores!

The peasants of France did not themselves extort democracy from Louis's autocracy. They were led by intelligent aristocrats. The Russian serfs did not secure their own freedom. Africans did not abolish the slave-trade. In at least three out of four social reforms the reform is initiated and put through largely by leaders from above, men of high intelligence who act, often against their own selfish interests, for the common good. Many men of great intelligence will, of course, be unjust and cruel tyrants; the correlation is .40 or .50, not 1.00; the direction of the world's affairs by men who were guaranteed to be both of great ability and of fine impersonal devotion to the world's welfare, would be best of all. But, in the long run, it has paid the "masses" to be ruled by intelligence. Furthermore, the natural processes which give power to men of ability to gain it and keep it are not, in their results, unmoral. Such men are, by and large, of superior intelligence, and consequently of somewhat superior justice and good-will. They act, in the long run, not against the interest of the world, but for it. What is true in science and government seems to hold good in general for manufacturing, trade, art, law, education, and religion. It seems entirely safe to predict that the world will get better treatment by trusting its fortunes to its 95- or 99-percentile intelligences than it would get by itself. The argument for democracy is not that it gives power to all men without distinction, but that it gives greater freedom for ability and character to attain power.

This is perhaps a good place for a word of caution. Do not be misled by the correlations between intelligence and other factors which Thorndike gives. Take, for example, the correlation of $r = .25$ between intelligence and success in athletic sports. This does not indicate that Thorndike, or anyone else, believes that the brightest people are the best athletes or that world champion athletes are outstandingly intelligent. Not at all! It does mean that, according to studies available to Thorndike at the time he wrote, there was a *slight* relationship between intelligence and athletic prowess. *Other things being equal,* the more intelligent were *likely* to be better athletes. Of course, other things are not equal.

Some of the other correlations cited by Thorndike are small. They indicate that there seems to be some relationship between the two factors, though not much. It might be well to think of these relationships in this way: the percent in common between two measures is usually considered to be equal to the square of the correlation found between the two. Thus a correlation of $r = .40$ would indicate an estimated overlap of 16 percent. This hardly accounts for either being the principal determinant of the other. But it does indicate that the two have a small amount of something in common.

Psychologists have been constructing intelligence tests for more than fifty years. They have administered them to millions of subjects, both the willing and the unwilling. They have often been naming as "intelligence" the results they secure from all this testgiving.

One psychologist thinks that we should divide our concept of intelligence into two parts. *Intelligence A* should refer to "an innate potential for the development of intellectual capacities." [1] *Intelligence B* should refer to "the level of that development at a later time, when the subject's intellectual functioning can be observed." [2] Since we cannot measure Intelligence A, all we have are measures of development, Intelligence B. Little wonder, then, that Thorndike found a high correlation between intelligence and school success!

Thorndike was far too optimistic about the progress that had been made in measuring racial differences in intelligence. And he was too hopeful about what had been learned concerning the influence of training on intelligence. Nor do we yet have the answers regarding the relation of mental health to personality factors.

There will be other things in this selection with which there will be disagreement. We suggest that you now read the Kagan selection which follows. Compare these two selections. Perhaps you will wish to make a list of differences in what they say.

The questions that are being asked about the adequacy of intelligence testing are challenging basic assumptions.

[1] Donald O. Hebb, *A Textbook of Psychology,* Second edition. W. B. Saunders, 1966, p. 196.
[2] *Ibid.,* pp. 196–197.

Among these are the assumptions stated by Thorndike, assumptions too long accepted without question by too many
people. But only when we understand what these assumptions are can we understand the nature of the controversy.

Jerome Kagan has taken a good, hard look at intelligence
tests and at some of the assumptions, the "magical aura"
that has grown up around them.

36

THE MAGICAL AURA OF THE IQ
JEROME KAGAN

Every society, or large cohesive group within a society, recognizes that in order to maintain stability a small group must possess some power over the much larger citizenry. The power is
sometimes inherited, sometimes awarded, sometimes attained,
and sometimes seized. In actual practice, this lean and rather
raw description is usually disguised by a clever strategy—much
like a magician's wrist movement—that makes select psychological traits symbolic of highly valued, status-conferring attributes
—hence, they become the vessels from which power is inevitably drawn.

Tenth-century Europe awarded power to those who were assumed to be more religious than their brothers. The presumption
of a capacity for more intense religiosity provided a rationale
that allowed the larger society to accept the fact that a privileged
few were permitted entry into marble halls. Pericles' Athens and
Lee's Virginia both rationalized the subjugation of their slaves
on psychological grounds: "They were less than human and,
therefore, unfit for power." At other times and in other places
sexual abstinence, sexual potency, hunting skill, a capacity for
silent meditation, good soldiering, or efficient farming have been
dimensions along which men were ordered and, as a consequence
of that ranking, divided into unequal groups.

Contemporary American society uses intelligence as one of the
bases for ranking its members, and it makes the same arguments
that educated Athenians uttered 2,500 years ago. Major loci of
power in the United States reside in state and federal governments, major businesses, and the universities. All three of those
institutions require their members to be regarded by the citizenry
as intelligent, and many meet this requirement, in part, by com-

SOURCE: From *Saturday Review*, December 4, 1971. Copyright 1971 Saturday Review, Inc. Reprinted by permission of author and publisher.

pleting a minimal amount of formal education. Education is one of the best reflections of intelligence, the argument goes, for one could not master the school's task without intelligence.

Thus far the ritual and ideology are not very different from the Islamic Moroccan who celebrates the warrior-saint and invents ways to select him. It is more threatening, however, to note that the analogy with the Islamic Moroccan extends to our explanations of the unequal distribution of intelligence in our society. The majority of Americans believe that children are born with a differential intellectual capacity and that, as a result, some children are destined to assume positions of status and responsibility. "Nature intended it that way." A much smaller group believes that this psychological capacity has to be attained through early experience and will.

These opposing hypotheses are identical in substance to the two interpretations of differential "capacity for religiosity" held by Islamites in Morocco and Indonesia. The Moroccans believe that some are born with a greater capacity for strong and intense religious experience. The Javanese believe the greater capacity is attained following long periods of meditation. And they, like us, discover the small proportion of their population that fits the description of the pure, and allows them ascent. The Moroccans explain this phenomenon by arguing that those who possess power do so because they inherited some special capacity that, in our society, is intelligence.

I do not contest the obvious fact that there are real differences among individuals' psychological traits—such as intelligence—that our society values. But I do suggest that, given the insufficient and controversial quality of the information relevant to the causes of these differences, it is likely that deep personal attitudes rather than logic or sound empirical data dictate one's interpretations of the documented variability in IQ.

Let me try to support this rather strong statement with a fragmentary analysis of what an intelligence test is made of. For the widely publicized announcement that 80 per cent of intelligence is inherited and 20 per cent environmentally determined is based on information from two similarly constructed standardized IQ tests invented by Caucasian middle-class Western men to rank-order everyone.

The most important set of test questions (important because scores on this set have the highest correlation with the total IQ) asks the person being tested to define words of increasing rarity. Rarity is a relative quality, depending always on the language community one selects as referent. "Shilling" is a rare word in the language space of the American child, but so is "fuzz." The test constructors decided that rarity would be defined with respect to the middle-class Caucasian experience. And a child reared in a middle-class home is more likely to learn the meaning of shilling than the meaning of fuzz. If contemporary black psychologists had accepted the assignment of constructing the first intelligence test, they probably would have made a different choice.

A second set of IQ test questions poses the child some everyday problem and asks him to state what he would do in that situation. For example, one question asks a seven-year-old, "What should you do if you were sent to buy a loaf of bread and the grocer said he didn't have any more?" Clearly, this question assumes a middle-class urban or suburban environment with more than one grocery store within safe walking distance of the home. For the only answer for which maximal credit is given is, "I would go to another store." It is not surprising that rural and ghetto children are less likely to offer that answer. Recently I examined a set of protocols gathered on poor black children living in a large Eastern city and found that many of them answered the question by saying they would "go home"—a perfectly reasonable, even intelligent, answer for which they were not given credit.

A third class of IQ test questions, called analogies, has the same dubious validity that the vocabulary test does, for the concepts the child must reason about are of differential familiarity to various ethnic groups. The child is asked how a piano and a violin are alike, not how tortilla and frijole are similar.

The fourth class of questions asks the child to solve some arithmetic problems. Of course, if the child has not learned how to add, subtract, or multiply, he will not be able to solve them. If intelligence is presumed to be 80 per cent inherited, it seems inappropriate that this quality should be measured, in part, by whether one has learned to add.

Another class of IQ test items includes a line drawing of an object that has an element missing and requires the child to discover the missing feature. As one might suspect, the pictures are selected to favor middle-class children, for they depict a thermometer without mercury in the bulb and a hand without fingernail polish, rather than a door without a double lock.

One task that does not favor middle-class white children asks the testee to remember a list of four or five numbers read at the rate of one per second. It is relevant to add that this test usually yields minimal differences between class and ethnic groups in the United States.

Biases in the selection of questions comprise only part of the IQ test problem. There is also a serious source of error in the administration of the test. White middle-class examiners usually administer the tests to children of different linguistic backgrounds. The test protocols of the black children mentioned above, gathered by well-intentioned, well-trained examiners, indicated that the children often misunderstood the examiner's pronunciation. When asked to define the word "fur" some said, "That's what happens when you light a match." Clearly, the children who gave this reply had misinterpreted the word to be *fire* and received no credit. Similarly, when requested to define "hat," some children said, "When you get burned," indicating they perceived the word as *hot*, and again received no credit.

These few examples, which comprise only a small proportion of all the sources of error that could be documented, are persuasive of the view that the IQ test is a seriously biased instrument that almost guarantees middle-class white children higher IQ scores than any other group of children.

However, most citizens are unaware either of the fundamental faults with the IQ test or of the multiple bases for differences in tested intelligence. And, like the Greeks, Islamic Moroccans, and medieval Christians, we, too, need a trait whose content can form a rational basis for the awarding of power and prizes. Intelligence is an excellent candidate, for it implies alertness, language sophistication, and ease of learning new skills and ideas. Moreover, it is a characteristic of a single individual and, like his fingerprints, is not, in theory, linked with his religion, region, or eating habits. It is our modern interpretation of saintliness, religiosity, courage, or moral intensity, and, of course, it works. It works so well that when we construct an intervention project, be it a major effort like Headstart or a small study run by a university scientist, we usually evaluate the effects of the intervention by administering a standard intelligence test or one very similar to it.

Our practice reflects the unconscious bias that a child's IQ must be the essential dimension we wish to change. If an intervention does not alter this quintessential quality, the effort is probably not worthwhile. Hence, we create conditions in which poor four-year-olds leave their homes for a few hours a day to play with other children of their own and other ethnic groups and to interact with new adults. Then we evaluate the growth-enhancing quality of this experience by administering an IQ test, rather than by determining if the child has become friendlier or less suspicious of children and adults who don't come from his family or neighborhood.

What implications are to be drawn from this acerbic analysis of the IQ? The first may seem paradoxical, considering my apparently hostile critique of the IQ test. Despite the injustice inherent in awarding privilege, status, and self-esteem to those who possess more of some attribute the society happens to value, this dynamic seems to be universal, perhaps because it is necessary. Power—and I mean here benevolent power—probably has to be held unequally. Therefore the community must invent a complex yet reasonable rationale that will both permit and explain the limited distribution of this prized resource.

Knowledge of Western language, history, and customs is not altogether unreasonable as one of the bases on which to found the award. But let us be honest about the footing of this arbitrary decision and rid ourselves of the delusion that those who temporarily possess power are biologically more fit for this role because their brains are better organized. Sir Robert Filmer made this argument in 1680 to rationalize the right of kings to govern, and John Locke's political philosophy was shaped on a brilliant critique of Filmer's thesis. Moreover, the conclusion that those in power are biologically more intelligent does not fit either the mood of objectivity hammered out during the last 300 years of modern scientific work or the historical fact that the use of power for benevolent or malevolent ends has usually been independent of size of vocabulary, arithmetic skill, or analogical reasoning.

I do not deny the existence of biological differences, many of which are inherited between and within ethnic and racial groups. But we do not regard inherited characteristics such as eye color or tendency to perspire as entitling anyone to special favor. Similarly, we should reflect on the wisdom of using fifteen-point differences on a culturally biased test—regardless of the magnitude of the genetic contribution to the IQ—as a weapon to sort some children into stereotyped categories that impair their ability to become mayors, teachers, or lawyers.

It is possible to defend the heretical suggestion that for many contemporary occupations (note that I did not say all) IQ should not be the primary attribute upon which a candidate is screened. Of course, biological factors determine a person's muscle mass, brain size, and adrenaline secretion in response to stress. But let us not unfairly exploit these hard-won facts to rationalize the distribution of secular power, which is a political and sociological dimension. To do that would be to use fair science for dark deeds.

The built-in bias in almost all intelligence tests favors the WASP. If members of that favored group wish to understand the nature of the bias, they should try taking a test with a different bias. There are probably not many tests with a built-in bias toward any other culture, but we can offer you one example.

37

TAKING THE CHITLING TEST
NEWSWEEK

It doesn't take a high IQ to recognize that intelligence tests have a built-in cultural bias that discriminates against black children. Tests designed to measure how logically a child can reason often use concepts foreign to the ghetto: a Harlem child who has never handled money or seen a farm animal, for example, might be asked a question that assumes knowledge of quarters and cows.

Adrian Dove, a sociologist and a Negro, for one, knows that black children have their own culture and language that "white" tests don't take into account. He saw this clearly when he worked with white civic and business leaders after the Watts riots. "I was talking Watts language by day," he says, "and then translating it so the guys in the corporations could understand it at night." Dove then designed his own exam, the Dove Counterbalance General Intelligence Test (the "Chitling Test") with 30 multiple-choice questions, "as a half-serious idea to show that we're just not talking the same language." The test has appeared in the Negro weekly Jet as well as in white newspapers, but mostly, says the 32-year-old Dove, "it has been floating around underground." Some samples (see end of story for the correct answers):

1. A "handkerchief head" is: (a) a cool cat, (b) a porter, (c) an Uncle Tom, (d) a hoddi, (e) a preacher.
2. Which word is most out of place here? (a) splib, (b) blood, (c) gray, (d) spook, (e) black.
3. A "gas head" is a person who has a: (a) fast-moving car, (b) stable of "lace," (c) "process," (d) habit of stealing cars, (e) long jail record for arson.
4. "Down-home" (the South) today, for the average "soul brother" who is picking cotton from sunup until sundown, what is the average earning (take home) for one full day? (a) $.75, (b) $1.65, (c) $3.50, (d) $5, (e) $12.
5. "Bo Diddley" is a: (a) game for children, (b) down-home cheap wine, (c) down-home singer, (d) new dance, (e) Moe-joe call.
6. If a pimp is up tight with a woman who gets the state aid, what does he mean when he talks about "Mother's Day?"

SOURCE: Reprinted from *Newsweek*, July 15, 1968, by permission of the publisher. Copyright Newsweek, Inc., 1968.

(a) second Sunday in May, (b) third Sunday in June, (c) first of every month, (d) none of these, (e) first and fifteenth of every month.

7. "Hully Gully" came from: (a) East Oakland, (b) Fillmore, (c) Watts, (d) Harlem, (e) Motor City.

8. If a man is called a "blood," then he is a (a) fighter, (b) Mexican-American, (c) Negro, (d) hungry hemophile, (e) Redman or Indian.

9. Cheap chitlings (not the kind you purchase at a frozen-food counter) will taste rubbery unless they are cooked long enough. How soon can you quit cooking them to eat and enjoy them? (a) 45 minutes, (b) two hours, (c) 24 hours, (d) one week (on a low flame), (e) one hour.

10. What are the "Dixie Hummingbirds?" (a) part of the KKK, (b) a swamp disease, (c) a modern gospel group, (d) a Mississippi Negro paramilitary group, (e) Deacons.

11. If you throw the dice and seven is showing on the top, what is facing down? (a) seven, (b) snake eyes, (c) boxcars, (d) little Joes, (e) 11.

12. "Jet" is: (a) an East Oakland motorcycle club, (b) one of the gangs in "West Side Story," (c) a news and gossip magazine, (d) a way of life for the very rich.

13. T-Bone Walker got famous for playing what? (a) trombone, (b) piano, (c) "T-flute," (d) guitar, (e) "Hambone."*

Dove, now a human-resources analyst with the Federal Bureau of the Budget in Washington, is not sure what to do next with his Chitling Test. Topical questions have to be revised and, says Dove, "working in the government I have to hustle to keep in touch with the language of the ghetto. This is an unreal world."

* Those who are not "culturally deprived" will recognize the correct answers are 1. (c), 2. (c), 3. (c), 4. (d), 5. (c), 6. (e), 7. (c), 8. (c), 9. (c), 10. (c), 11. (a), 12. (c), 13. (d).

Try that on your friends! Estimate their intelligence levels from the results. Who among them seem to be the more intelligent? And who seem to be low in intelligence? Or perhaps they would prefer being classed as "culturally deprived."

Another person who has made some remarkable studies of intelligence as related to culture is Stanley Porteus. Dr. Porteus is a native of Australia and a long-time resident of Hawaii. He developed, and has administered to various culture groups, the Porteus Maze Test. This is a set of paper and pencil mazes. The subject is required to trace the correct path, proceeding from easy to ever more difficult maze patterns. It requires no ability to read or write. No verbal instructions are necessary. It is designed to measure foresight and planning capacity. There are probably very few tests that come as near being free of cultural bias as this test.

Many people consider the Australian aborigines to be among the least intelligent peoples in the world today. Read the next selection and see if you agree.

38

ON THE INTELLIGENCE OF AUSTRALIAN ABORIGINES
STANLEY D. PORTEUS

We can now return to the original purpose of my work undertaken in Australia in 1929—to obtain an answer to the question as to the influence of a harsh physical environment on the comparative intelligence of primitive groups, specifically aborigines living in the northwest of the continent, where food was plentiful, as against those living in Central Australia, where the struggle merely to survive was unceasing.

Contrary to all previous expectations, the natives in the Centre scored relatively higher in the Porteus Maze Tests. In the northwest, 65 males scored 10.48 years, while those in the Centre averaged 12.08 years, a quite significant superiority.

As to the relation of the Maze to intelligence, especially of a practical nature, there was at the time of the study by no means as much evidence of the sensitivity of the test as at present. Not until 15 years later was there a clear demonstration of the fact that Maze test performance was closely related to damage to the frontal lobes of the brain. Still later, other proof of its reliability as a "brain test" became available. Though these conclusions could only be demonstrated in civilized patients, there is no reason to doubt that they would also apply to primitive peoples.

Not only was Maze performance in the Centre superior to that of natives in the northwest, but in practically all the other measures used (Form and Assembling, Form Board, Digit Memory, Xylophone Memory, and Goodenough Drawing) the Arunta held a constant if lesser advantage.

SOURCE: From *A Psychologist of Sorts: The Autobiography and Publications of the Inventor of the Porteus Maze Tests*, Palo Alto, Calif.: Pacific Books, 1969. Copyright © by Stanley D. Porteus. Reprinted by permission of the author and publisher. Pp. 131–133.

Apparently, the keener struggle for existence brought about a greater demand for mental alertness and planning capacity. However, it was eventually shown that the Arunta constituted a superior sample of aborigines. Their success in the tests was probably not by any means wholly due to closer acculturation with whites. It is true that at the Finke River Mission the natives had been under somewhat longer and closer mission supervision, but at Beagle Bay, Lombadina, Moola Boola, Violet Valley, and Wyndham contact with whites had been almost as intimate. But the Arunta at Hermannsburg represented a concentration of males of superior practical abilities.

From all of my experiences with the aborigines, I came away with the highest opinion of their ability to adjust to their own environment, but I steadfastly refused to make comparisons between aboriginal and white intelligence. To my mind such comparisons take us back to an outmoded psychological viewpoint, namely, that intelligence is "a unit character." Surely the simplest survey of man's achievements, in our own way or any other culture, would show the futility of that conception. We have a hundred instances to prove that intelligence is "a many-splendored thing." It is like national currency, of full value in one set of financial circumstances, but useless in another. In other words, intelligence has no gold standard with which its value can be equated.

Elsewhere I have pointed out that intelligence is a complex of abilities with perhaps a strong tendency to cluster together in constellations. Apparently *verbal* facility is one of the most interchangeable of many such constellations, one that the poet, the novelist, the playwright, the teacher must each possess to a high degree. But a genius like Shakespeare needed much more than verbal facility; he possessed superlative empathy, the ability to enter into the minds of men to think as they think, to speak as they speak in many imagined situations involving many emotions. He was the social psychologist par excellence.

There is another constellation of abilities that involves the sound of music, and this requires quite another type of insight and expression. It would be utterly foolish to compare a Beethoven and a Shakespeare, or even an Einstein with a Michelangelo.

Similarly, at a very simple level, it seems purposeless to compare aboriginal with white intelligence. This is a mistake made, I think, by some of the best friends of the native. A review of a book quoted by the ethnologist Mountford (Walkabout, May 1966), stated that the reasonableness of the aboriginal way of life "is evidence enough of well-trained intelligence of such calibre as white man's." The conclusion would have been unassailable if the quotation had stopped at the word "intelligence." We have no single measure of intelligence calibre that is applicable. The fact that these primitive people are our living contemporaries is proof of intelligent behavior in their own environment. It proves nothing as to their ability to compete with whites in an environment largely of the latter's making.

All that my studies showed was that man's adjustment to a repressive environment depends largely on what strength he could draw from within. If using his own resources for survival were the sole criterion, then the aboriginal is greatly superior.

We are now in an area of great controversy. People take sides, stubbornly! The issues are not just academic. They involve the daily lives of millions of people. They involve our basic assumptions about racial and ethnic groups.

The student needs, first of all, to attempt to clarify the issues. The perpetual nature-nurture, heredity-environment question enters in strongly. Is *intelligence* the result of genetic factors? Is it entirely culturally determined? Is it a mix of the two? And if so, in what proportions?

It is asking too much to expect you to come up with firm answers to all of these questions. There *are* people, however, who are sure that they have all of the answers. We sometimes call them *bigots.* So, be careful! As an old professor used to say to us, "Wear your theories lightly."

ARMING YOURSELF FOR ARGUMENT,
OR SEARCHING FOR THE TRUTH

If either debate or research is your aim, you will want to read a comprehensive discussion of the nature-nurture controversy, particularly as it applies to race, in *Environment, Heredity, and Intelligence* (Reprint Series No. 2, Harvard Educational Review, 1969). This includes the basic article by Arthur R. Jensen, "How Can We Boost IQ and Scholastic Achievement?" which originally appeared in the *Harvard Educational Review,* Winter, 1969. Then there are discussions of this controversial article by several psychologists and a geneticist, all of which originally appeared in the *Harvard Educational Review,* Spring, 1969. There are lengthy bibliographies, should you wish to get deeply involved (or have a term paper to write).

A general article covering much of the same ground, but with a different slant, is by Richard Herrnstein, "IQ" (*Atlantic,* September, 1971). Sandra Scarr-Salapatek, "Unknowns in the IQ Equation" (*Science,* 1971, *174,* 1223–1228) is a critical review of some of the recent material, including Herrnstein's article. She concludes that "to assert, despite the absence of evidence, and in the present social climate, that a particular race is genetically disfavored in intelligence is to scream 'FIRE! . . . I think' in a crowded theater." [1]

There are some older studies of environmentally deprived, genetically stable groups. These might prove of interest. There is a small book by Mandel Sherman and T. R. Henry, *The Hollow Folk* (Thomas Y. Crowell, 1933), and there is a related article by Mandel Sherman and Cora B. Key, "The Intelligence of Isolated Mountain Children" (*Child Development,* 1932, *3,* 54–56). Another article, by L. R. Wheeler, is "A Comparative Study of the Intelligence of East Tennessee Mountain Children" (*Journal of Educational Psychology,* 1942, *33,* 321–334).

We have given you a very small sample from *A Psychologist of Sorts,* by Stanley Porteus. You will find much more in this book about his adventures as a mental tester among the aborigines of Australia and among remote tribes in Africa.

We may as well admit that we hope that you will come out with at least one of the conclusions that we have reached. That is, that there is still a long, long way to go in the development of truly adequate tests of intelligence. A British writer has expressed it beautifully: "The trouble, at present, is not that psychologists use tests, but that those which we do use are in an exceedingly primitive condition." [2] You may wish to read more of what he has to say, too.

Your class may take sides on these issues. Classes usually do. We suggest that you look ahead in this book to "The Test of Listening," by Thomas Gordon, in the chapter on Communication. Use this technique, carefully, and we'll almost guarantee that the result will be closer to an approach to the truth than it will be toward bolstering the preconceived ideas of the participants.

[1] Sandra Scarr-Salapatek, "Unknowns in the IQ Equation," *Science,* 1971, *174,* p. 1228.

[2] Liam Hudson, *Contrary Imaginations: A Psychological Study of the English Schoolboy,* London: Penguin, 1968, p. 3.

Part Twelve

Personality: Mask or Substance?

When we were born we did not have a sense of self. We did not know where we began and the rest of the world left off. We could not distinguish that our foot was a part of us and our sock was not. Even after we came to respond to our own name being called out, we did not know just who "we" were. We did not say "I" or "me" when we saw ourselves in a mirror or a picture. It was "Jane" or "John" or even just "baby." That special sense of being "me" was an extraordinary concept, after all, and it took a certain muscular, perceptual, and intellectual maturity before it could readily be understood.

After the sense of physical self had been established, an even more subtle distinction lay ahead. We had yet to develop the realization that we differed from other individuals. We were not just physically separate from others; we were unique in the way our thoughts, emotions, habits and traits fit together. We each had a distinct *personality.* When we perceived our uniqueness, we were on our way to a number of kinds of independence. Besides being acted upon by others, we were ready to start asserting ourselves— and we have been doing so ever since. "*I* am John." "*I* want." "*I* don't want." "*I* think." "*I* am the kind of person who likes . . . ."

From where did this sense of self come? Did we learn it? What about our other habits, traits, characteristics? Did we learn those, or were they inherited? If they were inherited, were they modified by experience?

We just do not know the exact answers to these questions. None of us can recollect clearly what went on in our heads when we were infants. We can only, from watching children develop, infer what is influencing them. There are a number of theories useful in describing personality development. For example, Freud helped focus our attention on unconscious motivation. He was one of the first to suggest that early childhood experiences can continue to influence our behavior as adults, even when we have no recollection of them. (Think of the Watson and Rayner experiment with little Albert.)

As in other heredity-environment debates, we may conclude that our personality develops from an interaction of inherited characteristics with physical and social forces in the environment. We know that "personality" described as it is by social judgments is culture bound. That is, what may be considered a "good," or "healthy," or "well-adjusted" personality in one society is not necessarily so in another.

As we grow, our experiences influence the way we feel about ourselves. Have we been allowed to assert ourselves? Did the people and the environment around us give way, a little—a lot—in acknowledging our presence? Did we feel successful—or otherwise? Do we, now, have a strong, secure sense of just who "we" are?

The selection following illustrates one step further in the quest for self-definition. Sara Davidson is a writer who comments on American life-styles, one aspect of which, in the past few years, has been a search for identity, for a philosophy which can help answer the question, "Who am *I*?" Do you think the search for self can be facilitated by others? Could we all profit from such a quest?

THE RUSH FOR INSTANT SALVATION
SARA DAVIDSON

It is the third day of our quest for enlightenment. We are wandering through leaves, in a birch grove, solitary figures, asking silently, intoning repeatedly until we are dizzy and numb: "Who am I?" We have suffered through intense desire and despair, weakness and exhilaration, doubt and calm disinterest. And now we are waiting.

What has kept us here is the wish, the hope for and the need to seek inner peace. We are sweating, and the men have three-day growths of stubble. We have eaten millet and swallowed great handfuls of vitamins, and slept on the floor, head to toe. We have screamed and cried and hugged and stared into space. What has carried us is the power of what we are promised: a sudden crack in the consciousness, a splitting open of the soul, when we are flooded with joyous certainty. A direct experience of who, exactly, we are. Salvation!

There is a movement easing across the land, a movement in which individuals are trying to work out personal salvation—a way to proceed through life with harmony and peace, a minimum of tension, and a maximum of fulfillment. What we are witnessing is the flowering of a generation of seekers, a generation whose world boundaries were shattered by drugs, politics, street-fighting, encounters, communes, or rapid social change, and who came to believe in the possibility of an answer, a key that would make life better immediately.

The keys now being taught, traded, and sold do not require withdrawal from the world or total rejection of straight society. One will not have to spend thousands of dollars, or five years in psychoanalysis, or twenty years of meditation in a cave. The methods are practical: exercise, chants, ritual, diet, relating systems, learning to control brain waves. They promise to bring a natural high, ecstasy while living the life of your choice. Each person cultivating his garden, seeking inner peace, will lead, it is felt, to world peace. Swami Kriyananda, an American who was initiated as a swami in the Self-Realization Fellowship, tells his disciples: "People must be saved and peaceful, before they can save the world and make it peaceful." Scott Wren, a thoughtful, twenty-year-old student in California, who has been practicing yoga for two years, says, "It's not a cop-out. I don't want to withdraw from the world, I want to change it. But how can we have a peaceful society if there's no peace within us?"

Because of doomsday warnings, which seekers take literally, there is an urgency to reach satori now. Crash programs are appealing. Many groups have accelerated enlightenment devices, and the Silva Mind Control Institute guarantees that after a four-day course, each person will be able to exercise psychic powers, to tap into the universal consciousness—or get his money back ($150). Charles Berner, who founded a religion called Abilitism and developed an "enlightenment intensive" which produces dramatic results in three to five days, says, "The emphasis everywhere is on technique. Kids are coming by the droves out of the drug experience into the spiritual movement, and they won't tolerate nonsense. They say, your ideas are wonderful but show me what to do. The sharper and more exact the technique, the more the kids respond. If the kids try your technique and it doesn't do what you say, they drop you. Those teachings which are doing well now are the ones that deliver the goods."

Success has not been limited, though, to groups which teach effective techniques. Virtually any spiritual organization that has outlined a path outside the establishment churches and synagogues has been flooded with seekers over the past several years. The 3H (Happy, Healthy, Holy) Organization, founded by Yogi Bhajan, who teaches kundalini yoga, opened more than fifty ashrams in three years. All schools of yoga have had wild bursts of growth, as have groups dedicated to Zen, transcendental meditation, Krishna consciousness, Jewish mysticism, Scientology, Abilitism, Gurdjieff, eductivism, light radiation, channeling, macrobiotics, Jesus Freaks, Fundamentalist Christianity, Sufism, mountain Buddhism, Taoism, Naturalism, psycho-cybernetics, and astral projection. The trend has also been reflected in rock music. *Jesus Christ Superstar* stayed at the top of the album charts for nine months, and record companies are investing heavily in "soft rock" that carries a spiritual message.

In none of the spiritual practices, except Zen, are there any formal qualifications or public certification for leaders. Anyone may call himself a swami, a guru, or a reverend, place an ad in the local underground paper and wait for the phone to ring. An Indian student in New York did so as a practical joke. "Guru recently arrived from India now accepting students," read the ad in the *East Village Other*. For three days, wearing a ratty silk bathrobe and a turban made of towels, he received applicants in his apartment. He giggled and told riddles while a friend snapped Polaroid pictures, but to his shock, only one out of thirty who visited him gave any indication of suspecting fraud.

While the Eastern and occult religions flourish, Christian churches last year showed the lowest gain in membership in this century. It is no coincidence that, in a period when young people are increasingly suspicious of and hostile to all authority, those religions which see God as the supreme authority to whom man must bow have failed to inspire interest. The notion of God being experienced and sought now is that of a force within us all, not outside sitting in judgment. The experience is found by taking Christ's word literally: "the kingdom of God is within you." Each person comes to his own experience of the truth, and all experiences are valid. It is an anarchic, egalitarian, self-determinist strain. Each man is seen as a continuous spirit, with the power to understand everything if he can just bring that power into consciousness!

It is 10:00 a.m., the first Sunday of spring. On the luxuriant grass mall of the Davis campus of the University of California, 1,000 people sit cross-legged, palms turned upward and resting on their knees, with the thumb and first finger meeting in little o's. Two women in saris, their hair pulled into topknots, bring flowers and burning incense to a makeshift stage. A bell tolls, and Yogi Bhajan strides out. He is a towering, heavyset man with the air of a potentate—jet-black eyes and beard, a turban, coral rings, and a costume all of white, with cloth wrapped like adhesive tape around his legs. "Children," he says, in a surprisingly shrill voice, "you are searching all the time for a teacher. Well, you are to become teacher for your own self. Who is teacher and who is student? Same one." He laughs. "Don't start on spiritual path unless you want to end up as a teacher."

The audience sits perfectly still, while dogs race pell-mell around the bodies. Bhajan says, "Let us meditate. Close your worldly eyes and see the sky within you. Breathe deep, and vibrate loud: 'Sat Nam.'" The crowd drones the syllables. Bhajan: "Inhale in you the kundalini, mother of creation—more, more! Pull the kundalini higher, towards the neck. Breathe deeper! That is vibration!" Sweat is pouring down his face. "Now chant: OM. Meditate on the sound current. Keep going—time is now! Three minutes only will give you an experience. Vibrate more powerfully!" He mops his brow, reaches out his arms and shouts: "Continuous! Infinity! Keep on, pull it up. Get over your hang-up, man! Strike when iron is hot! Add more power!" They om furiously, spines rigid, faces straining in the sun. "Inhale—meditate on the third eye. Now exhale, powerfully!" There is a loud, collective whoosh. Bhajan smiles. "Relax. This experience is your own. *You* got it, *you* did it. It is you alone who can raise the consciousness within you. Feel free, learn from everybody. Whatever can help you to reach the truth is the most beautiful thing. God bless you."

He walks away with slow steps, trailed by his retinue, and sits down on a blanket under a fir tree. Behind him, members of the 3HO ashram in San Rafael are selling candles, natural perfumes, organic fruit-nut balls, and T-shirts that have Bhajan's picture—a giant grinning head—silk-screened across the chest. A plump girl with auburn braids approaches one of Bhajan's aides. The girl says she is a teacher in Oakland. "I'm into kundalini, but I have a lot of hesitations, and I'd like to find out what those hesitations are. She rattles on for fifteen minutes, while the yogi listens, no hint of reaction on his face. At length, he asks what she is looking for. The girl puts a finger to her lips. "Well, I was seeking integration, psychologically. Realization of myself. I'd never thought about enlightenment. That's just recently come into the picture."

The yogi smiles.

Ten years ago, according to George Peters, who, as the founder of Naturalism, has been playing "salvation games" for almost that long, "no one in this country had ever heard of enlightenment. Now it's being offered in mail-order courses." As the notion of enlightenment is popularized, its meaning, predictably, becomes diluted. Many seekers anticipate it as a "blinding flash of white light" which will set them apart from their fellow-men. Others see it as a continual, steady growth toward realization of the truth, when the ego falls away, one transcends the mind and body, and merges with absolute being. The definition on which most spiritual teachers would agree is that enlightenment is a direct, personal experience of the truth. It is a truth which comes to one intuitively, which cannot be proved rationally but is felt so strongly as to be beyond doubt. Enlightenment has led to many different perceptions of truth, but consistent in all enlightenment experiences has been a sense of unity and continuity, of oneness with infinity.

When most people first come into the spiritual movement, though, they are not looking for much more than relaxation, or help in solving problems. Yoga institutes are constantly being referred people with back trouble, who have been advised by doctors that the exercise will be beneficial. These people may be confirmed atheists, but after a period of exposure to spiritual seekers, some begin to question the certainty of their atheism. In addition, they see teachers who, unlike psychiatrists, put themselves forward as models of tranquillity. A forty-nine-year-old dress manufacturer in Los Angeles, who has been in yoga classes a year, says, "You see people like Swami Satchidananda and Indra Devi, who have eyes that shine, who radiate so much love that you feel great just being around them, and you start to think, well, maybe they know something, maybe they're right. I've even started to consider enlightenment. The more I think about it, the more irresistible it becomes."

"We are here for you," reads a brochure taped outside the Los Angeles ashram of the Institute of Ability. Dozens of shoes lie in rows on the porch. Inside the stucco bungalow, fifteen people sit hushed on the floor, in front of Charles Berner, founder of the Institute. He is a soft-voiced man of forty-one, with blue eyes, a blondish-brown beard, and a round, open face that, if clean-shaven, would recall that all-American freshness projected in the Fifties by members of the Kingston Trio.

Before meeting Charles, I had read his booklet, "Abilitism, a New Religion." The theory he outlined seemed preposterous: each human being is a God, which is defined as "infinite ability." Before time, all of the Gods floated freely, unconscious of one another. Then, billions of Gods agreed to create time, space, energy, and mass, in order to be able to understand and experience each other. The purpose of life, Berner says, is for the Gods to open up and relate completely with each other. "Life is the courtship of the Gods."

Now, sitting in a corner of the bungalow, he talks about his background. "I had a happy childhood in Colton, near Los Angeles," he says. "When I was eight, I had the experience of waking up to life." He began asking himself who he was, and what life was about. He "searched fervently" through 134 religions from the orthodox to the esoteric cults, read philosophy and studied physics and engineering. "I was very disappointed to find that science didn't have all the answers." For nine years, he worked as a counselor in the Church of Scientology, then threw out everything he had learned to start over from scratch. Enlightenment came in the year 1964, on a day like any other. Charles was standing at the orange and white pick-up counter of an A and W Root Beer stand, "when this direct, conscious experience occurred. I realized that I am a God of infinite ability, and that the purpose of life is for us all to become conscious of each other as the individual Gods we are. I experienced this as the truth—beyond the realm of doubt. It's pure experience."

Soon afterward, Berner founded the Institute of Ability, and he and his wife Ava worked out a technique for enlightenment in which people would sit opposite each other, trying to experience who they are, and then present that experience to a partner. The stress is on communicating, unlike most other disciplines, where meditation is a solitary affair and enlightenment lies beyond words. Charles and Ava found that after a three-day "enlightenment intensive," about half the participants would become enlightened "wham—like that. The others make good gains, become more open and increase their awareness," Charles says. "If they just follow the technique, they can't help but have experiences. Their enlightenment may not match the Buddha's, but if they work, it will grow deeper and deeper." I ask if the intensive would benefit someone who couldn't conceive of himself as a God. Berner says, "We don't ask you to accept our ideas. Most people who go on intensives don't know a thing about Abilitism. Our masters never say one word about what you are or are not. But it's funny. Everyone always comes up with the same thing, in different words. No one has ever come up with, 'I'm a sack of mud,' or the Communist Manifesto. They could, but they never have."

And so I find myself on a Thursday midnight lugging a sleeping bag around the cavernous waiting room of the Philadelphia railroad station. A ragtag group gathers by the main door. We have come from all over the East Coast to pay $75 for a three-day intensive with Ava and Charles Berner. Charles, we learn, is sick with hepatitis, so Ava will preside with Leila Zimmermann, another Abilitist master. On the ride to Drexel Lodge, the driver, Arnie (I am changing the names of all participants), passes out incense sticks. Although he has the face of an undergraduate—sandy hair and freckles—he is thirty-seven, an engineer. "After my last meditation, it took me an hour to get up off the ground. Meditation is a better high than pot, you know? It's cheaper, no bum trips, and no hassles with the law." A girl asks why he is taking the intensive. "I want to become more aware. I'm sort of at loose ends."

"Watch out!" Arnie slams on the brakes; the car swerves around a bus. He mentions, later, that he took up yoga after wrenching his back in a car accident. Two more near-collisions and we pull up to the lodge: a quaint, pink saltbox with a green roof and rows of white windows. Inside is a single sparsely furnished room, logs sputtering in the fireplace, dark forms in sleeping bags sprawled on the floor, and a funny little stage with a dusty piano. Two of the men calmly remove their clothes and lie down on their backs. Two others are sitting in front of the fire, staring into each other's eyes. Judy, a travel agent from Washington, lingers nervously in the upstairs bathroom. "I've never been to anything like this. Some of these people have been on two or three intensives, I heard." Shrugging, she adds, "They seem to keep coming back."

"Start waking up. Start waking up." It is 5:45 a.m. A girl circles the room, speaking in a detached monotone. All the forms move at once—shuffling, sneezing, surveying each other in the gray, gloomy light. There are twenty-two of us, thirteen men and nine women, ranging from nineteen to forty-five, although most are in their twenties. In addition, there are the masters, Ava and Leila, four monitors, and a cook. While waiting to register, people assume twisted postures, some bowing to the trees, others doing violent kundalini breathing while jumping in place. No behavior is regarded with any surprise. Ava gives us our instructions. For the next three days, we are to do only what we are told, "don't eat or sleep unless we say so," no smoking, no sex, no drugs or medication, "except the natural vitamins we'll be giving you to keep your body in a balanced state," and no talking or thinking about anything but enlightenment. Ava says, "If you do the exercise perfectly for the next three days, you can't help but get enlightened. But the exercise is so simple, a lot of people don't do it."

We are to hold the question, "Who am I?" for the entire time. Those who have been on previous intensives work on other questions: what am I, what is life, or what is another? We will choose a different partner every hour, and alternate talking and listening for five-minute periods. The partner will say, "Tell me who you are" and we are to sit, open to whatever arises. "Anything that occurs to you as to who you are, tell your partner. Then go back to the question. Who? Who? You should have no expectations, you shouldn't want to experience this or that, you shouldn't even want to become enlightened. As a consequence, something will happen," Ava says.

When our partner is talking, we are to listen without judging. "To be open to your partner, don't analyze what he's saying or try to respond. Keep your mouth shut and just experience him. This is your chance to change your life-style, to be an open, flowing person. The complete end result of this is happiness."

We pair up and sit on the floor in two rows. My partner, Ruth, a social worker in her forties, says, "I'm here because I need inner peace, and I have to be less hard on my kids." Next to me, a girl is talking about her parents. Farther down, Fred, a young man with a frizzy beard and hawk nose, is shouting: "I am infinite ability! I am you. I am us." A timer goes off, and the monitor says, "Change over." The first five-minute session is unsufferably long; the hour seems unendurable. When the final bell rings, it is only 7:00 a.m.

We break to have tea and vitamin pills, which are arranged in bowls with signs, "Take one," or, "Take three." Ava says, "Keep holding your question. Who am I, drinking tea?" My next partner, Tim, a thirty-year-old computer programmer, laughs self-consciously. "It's hard to hold a one-way conversation. Who cares anyway? This is absurd. I know the answer to who I am—me. I'll probably go away with the same thing I started with. I guess the question is just a way of focusing your attention for three days so other things can happen. Like hallucinations, mind trips. I once drove to Mexico nonstop, and at the end, I had road hypnosis. I saw myself from the back seat."

Breakfast is a bowl of hot millet with honey, and more vitamins. Ava says, "If you get a red heat in your body, that's the vitamin. If you get nauseous, let me know about it." In midmorning, we bundle up for walking meditation. Spreading out from the lodge, we cross streams and weave over a hillside of silver birches. Some stand frozen, staring nowhere, bug-eyed. Others crunch rapidly through the leaves, sweating it: who is walking? what is walking?

The next period, Miles, a slender, wry biologist from Australia, says, "I'm just a mind and a body." We hear Fred shout: "I am the sun!" Miles says, "Seems like a lot of nonsense going on around me. I think some are faking it." He shakes his head. "I wonder if in three days I'll get through this blankness. I've got no thoughts."

The sessions change drastically with each partner. Some speak in highly personal, human terms and are always influenced by what their partner has just said. Others talk only in abstractions, straight past their partner on a separate beam. Some who insist, "I am you," or, "I am us," do not really communicate or feel their partner at all. And one man, Simon, is totally beyond reach. He sits in a rigid, catatonic lotus pose, and when not sitting, moves dreamily in a perpetual yoga exercise, eyes half-closed. He cannot look at anyone's face and is skittish about sitting close to others. In the exercises, he speaks with a lisp, feathery and baby-like. "I find it very distracting to be near people. I feel as if I am in the presence of a snake." His mouth twitches to one side. "I need someone to make me feel the presence of the God. There is no one here to do that."

After lunch—cottage cheese with bananas and sunflower seeds, plus eight pills—Ava gives a lecture about enlightenment. "Don't worry about whether you're going to get enlightenment or not. Somehow it will just come to you. Then you should spend a few more hours working until you can articulate it extremely well. That's the only kind of experience we're looking for, because that's the kind that will stay with you in life."

Ava is twenty-nine, with a childlike laugh and the radiance of a young girl. Her parents were both atheists, she says, "but when I was eight, I got enlightened and joined the Catholic Church. I saw a movie about Joan of Arc, which reminded me of an enlightenment from a previous lifetime, when I had spent all my time meditating from the age of thirteen until I died." In the present incarnation, she says, she became disenchanted with the Church at sixteen, and turned to occult religious ceremonies and flying-saucer meetings. She married Charles when she was nineteen, and worked with him in Scientology. "I've been like this since my last lifetime—just a religious nut!"

Ava stresses that we should have no preconceived ideas about how we'll experience ourselves, but there is subtle pressure as to what would be acceptable. At one point, she makes a derisive reference to the "mud theory—we are mud, we come from mud," and everyone laughs. I tell my next partner, a young nurse, that the mud theory makes more sense to me than any theology I've been exposed to. She screws up her face and says, laboriously, "I try very hard not to feel like a speck of dust. Sometimes when viewed in the infinite river of time, I seem very insignificant. But today, in this room, I feel much closer to that flow—it's as if it's coursing right through me, through you as well, through everything." She looks transfixed as the timer goes off.

The hours wear on, and exhaustion sets in. Legs are stiff from sitting, and muscles ache. We massage each other between each exercise. Any break in the schedule is a relief, even the period of "karma yoga"—work. We chop vegetables, mop floors, wash windows. One of the monitors says, "Try to be one with the task you're doing. Who am I, cleaning toilets?"

During dinner (brown rice, beets, and carrots) the monitors patrol to check that no one is "gossiping." There is a walking meditation in the dark, and many more exercises, more pairs of eyes, more of what sounds like sophomoric prattling. "I am what is! It just came to me," from a boy who, an hour later, keels over and is diagnosed as having the flu. Fred's shouts punctuate each session: "I am shock. Boo! I am God. Dammit!" Lee, a Japanese boy who glows with joy, says he has the urge to leave. "I don't care about enlightenment. I don't believe there should be a separation between the enlightened and those who aren't. Just love everybody." Lee is always the first partner to be chosen. People rush for him and make dibs for the next session. Simon is the last; he asks no one, and waits on the side, eyes averted.

Finally, midnight: time for "sleep meditation," after we swallow thirteen bioplasma pills. "Let your body go now," the monitor says, "but *you* hold the question."

I sit up during the night. A girl is walking by the windows, giving instructions: "Let your body rise and fall. The mind never sleeps . . ." Angrily, I pull a blanket over my head. Won't they even let us sleep in peace? Twice more, I wake up and the girl is still talking. In the morning, I ask the monitors who was patrolling all night. Leila stares at me. "It wasn't any of us." The others concur. "It was probably someone walking around in her astral body. These phenomena happen all the time."

Before the first exercise, Ava says, "I want to give you a standard for being open. If, when it's your turn to speak, you feel the need to respond in all sorts of ways to your partner, and don't get right back to your question, you're not being open."

Judy, the travel agent, says, "In life, don't people like you to respond to them? If you just sat there with a blank look . . ." Ava: "If everybody could do that for just one month—be open and listen, without trying to rescue each other—we'd have the most beautiful world you'd ever want to live in."

I have the sensation of floating, peacefully, not caring and not resisting. Around me, others are booming their questions like the caterpillar in *Alice in Wonderland.* "Whhhhhooo . . . are . . . YOU!" Ruth pounds her fists on the floor. Fred, who has been quiet for a time, yells: "I don't give a shit about this intensive! I don't give a shit about yoga. I don't give a shit about anything in my life!" Almost everyone giggles uncontrollably. Miles, the frail-looking biologist, laughs convulsively until he cries, flushing red. "It's the first time I've felt anything in these two days."

During our walk, the grounds take on the air of a loony farm. It is snowing, and Fred and two others run in circles, oinking and cackling. A man lies down in the river with all his clothes on. From afar comes a feminine shriek: "Fuuuck!" During the meals, hardly anyone talks. The monitors are content. Melvin, a young man with a haunted look, approaches a girl who is a monitor. "I feel rejected by you. I feel lonely," he says. The monitor, with a lack of emotion that is chilling, says, "Is that all?" Melvin: "I guess I want to make love to you. Do you love me?" The monitor takes regular bites of her cottage cheese. "Umm hmmm." Melvin: "I feel weak now. I feel like everything I do is just a release of steam, to avoid an explosion." She waits several minutes. "Well, I appreciate your telling me all that stuff. I understand it. You shouldn't let it keep you off the track from holding your question."

Late in the day, Leila, the co-master, says, "Okay, you should all be standing on the edge of the cliff, ready to jump off into enlightenment. We're going to narrow the field now. Don't say anything you're not experiencing directly as you. If you're not sure, if it can be argued, if you wouldn't stake your life on it, it's not an experience. Don't intellectualize or speculate. You're not looking for an answer, you're looking for yourself." She suggests we try asking, "Who's asking who am I?" and then, "Who's asking who's asking who am I?" and so on, "until you back yourself into a corner."

I try it, and my body starts to tingle. I review, palpably, everything that contributes to who I am: eyes, nerves, voice, skin, senses, mind, feelings, needs, opinions, humor, particular way of looking at the world, a way I have always had. On the night walk, seeing the stars, smelling the trees, and moving through space make me feel acutely, dizzyingly alive until I am drunk with it. When we return to the lodge, Ava announces, "Someone had an enlightenment this afternoon, and it was Ruth." The veterans of previous intensives clap their hands; the rest of us, slightly stunned, join in. One man gives a low whistle. "Today is really different from yesterday." Arnie says, "I'm beginning to feel something, a feeling of happiness and contentment all through me. But I can't verbalize it yet." Tim is getting his road hallucination. "When I stare at one spot," he tells his partner, "your whole face disappears." After each session, the pairs linger together, whispering and hugging.

A twenty-year-old pre-med student, Jimmy, delivers each word with his whole body shaking. "I am ev-ery-thing. The fire, the tree, the dog, the wind. I am any-thing. I feel to-tally enlightened." How can one doubt that his eyes, dilated and red, are perceiving a blinding white flash? He requests an interview, and later, Ava announces the enlightenment of Jimmy, and of Melvin, who has been repeating for thirty-six hours, "I am infinite ability!" Roger, who is a Zen student, shakes his head with disgust. "All I've heard from them is bullshit. If that's what it takes to get certification of enlightenment here, I don't know about the whole thing."

In the night, I have more hallucinations—no body this time, just a voice coming from all sides. I wake up feeling colossally down, with paralyzing aches in the back and neck. I'm fed up with people's bad breath and tired of being ordered around. It doesn't help to work with Fred, who belches at me and then proclaims, "I am burp!" Everyone except Fred is subdued today. We are all talking straight past each other, hearing what the other says but not responding, not taking his trip. We are into our own heads, on a depersonalized, metaphysical plane.

I ask Ava how she judges an enlightenment. "I acknowledge it if I see it coming directly from the person. But it's not important if I'm right or wrong. What's important is that the person lives a better life, and the way to a better life is to open up to others."

By midday, I feel so drained and dejected that I'm overcome with terror that I won't live through this. Leila tells us: "You're coming up against the last barrier now—the fear that you'll die, that what you've identified yourself with is gonna die and you'll die." In the next exercise, I work with Dan, one of the monitors, who has an Indianlike face with soft green eyes. I look at him through tears, trembling, and everything in the room—sounds, images—dissolves. It is as if we are spinning in a circle together, our eyes in the center, still. The room alternately lights up and grays over. We can barely talk, moving our lips but producing little sound. Somehow, his gentleness and intense warmth flow into me. At the end of the hour, I feel purged and calm.

Later, giddiness takes over. People say anything that pops into their head. Tim says, "Remember I started this thing saying I was me? Well, now I'm at this: who am I? Not me. I'm the illusion of me." Fred is into announcing himself as objects: Coca-Cola, a shoe, a razor blade. When a potato is dropped on his dinner plate, he says, "I am a baked potato!"

We wait our turn for interviews with Ava, like subjects filing up to see the Queen. She sits by herself "so her aura can be clear," wearing a black gown of cut velvet, her dark hair curling down her shoulders. After dinner, she announces two more enlightenments: Tim and Lee. Lee shakes his head. With his clipped Japanese accent, he says, "No, there is no enlightenment. It's her trip to say I'm enlightened." I ask Lee what he said in his interview. "I just told her I feel I have more courage to be who I am. And when I open up to another, it makes my life richer."

Lee is my partner during the next session, and I feel great power and love shooting between us like electricity. Everyone, it seems, is flashing on the energy within them. You can't spend three days looking at your soul and come up with mud. Instead, you get high on your power and strength, your love, warmth, and elemental goodness. Lee, his eyes glistening, says, "I never knew contacts between people could be so joyful. It blows my mind that you open yourself so totally to me. You don't tell me anything about your job, your family, your home—you just show me your power. I can hold it in my hands. If I never see you again, you will always be close to me."

And then Fred shouts: "I am the great pumpkin!" The whole room cracks up. Five minutes later, Ava announces Fred's enlightenment. As we applaud in disbelief, Fred claps his hands and punches them jubilantly over his head, like a boxing champ. "I just had a deepening enlightenment—I'm Chicken Little!"

The intensive ends promptly at 9:00 p.m. Ava says, "Okay. That's it. Everyone has showed a great increase in his ability to become conscious of who he is. Those of you catching the train must leave now." There is a euphoric flurry of hugging and dancing in circles. For the first time in three days, we learn each other's last names, what we do in life, where we live. Only six of the twenty-two have been acknowledged as enlightened, and all but one of these had been on previous intensives.

Roger drives seven of us in his Volkswagen to the station. "I'm disappointed," he says. "I thought everyone there would already know there is a God, and we're all part of God. The place was full of atheists!" He laughs. "If I'd known that I wouldn't have come. I'm going back to Buddha."

I did not enjoy most of the enlightenment intensive and would not want to go through it again. Once home, though, I notice surprising effects. I am far more interested in listening to people; when I do so, they seem to unfold, with great pleasure and trust. Most of us, apparently, are not used to being truly listened to, or to listening in a totally open state. I find, also, that I can be freed from unconscious dependency on the moods and emotions of the other person. I can absorb and understand someone's anger, or pain, or depression, without getting embroiled—feeling anger or depression in return. I keep in touch with some of the people who took the intensive; they are all trying to stay open and serene. One young man writes: "For the first time in my life, peace is mine to give."

In every major city, there are ashrams and institutes where those who wish to make a life in the spiritual movement live and work communally. The groups form a supportive national network. Members receive no salary, but their needs are taken care of while they study and teach. They can go anywhere in the country and be assured of a place to stay and a welcoming, loving "family." They have a culture all their own: food (vegetarian), language (they refer to the world, for example, as "this planet"), dress (Oriental fabrics, designs inspired from India, many choosing all white), and music (flutes, drums, and, for chants, the harmonium). In many of the disciplines, people tend to withdraw from sensual pleasures. The most serious are expected to be celibate. They give up smoking, liquor, and drugs. Convinced of the possibility of healing their own bodies, they avoid straight doctors, and would rather see a chiropractor, whose methods are felt to be more natural.

The intolerance of drugs is ironic, because the spiritual movement has reaped tremendous benefit from the drug culture. Acid and mescaline gave many people their first intimations of infinity and oneness with the universe. Since the acid experience could not be controlled, though, many began turning to techniques such as meditation by which people through the centuries have, by their own will, altered their states of consciousness. The success of spiritual groups in leading people away from drugs is one of their main sources of income. Almost every group has an anti-drug rehabilitation program, funded by charitable agencies and, in some cases, the government.

One of the dangers of immersion in the spiritual movement, especially for young dropouts, is that it is possible to lose perspective, to suspend critical judgment, as one loses touch with the larger society. Quite rapidly, anything seems plausible. Nothing is too bizarre or outrageous. A nineteen-year-old boy in Berkeley, whose current trip is kundalini, says "I don't know what common sense is anymore. I can't tell what's valid and what isn't." He fails to discern hype, or techniques that smack of quackery. He does not consider the evidence when a spiritual teacher is charged in court with fraud or financial mismanagement. When a yogi who has a large following in this country was sued in New Delhi for allegedly taking money to procure American wives for Indian men, his disciples dismissed it as a frame-up by jealous rivals.

Despite claims throughout the movement that each person is to be his own guru, many teachers, in fact, expect unquestioning devotion. Ronwen Proust, when she was eighteen, joined the staff of the Integral Yoga Institute. She was given the Sanskrit name Vathsala by the Institute's founder, Swami Satchidananda, the most charismatic and beloved spiritual figure in the counterculture. Vathsala says, "I got into this spacy kind of peace, but it was a false peace that was easily disrupted if I went somewhere else. Nobody at the Institute was asking any questions, like: why do you meditate? who are you? what is this peace? what's happening to you? The peace didn't come from my own consciousness. It was like I was stepping into someone else's aura and absorbing his peace."

There is a tendency, also, to lose sight of how closely related many spiritual techniques are to self-hypnosis, how they depend on the power of suggestion. Katherine Da Silva, a twenty-seven-year-old yoga teacher, met with hostility when she pointed this out to a crowd at a spiritual festival. Katherine lived for six years as a renunciate in the ashrams of Paramahansa Yogananda. Toward the end, because she was having what she calls "healthy, honest doubts," she felt it would be better to continue her spiritual work outside the cloister. "I'm so convinced of the power of suggestion," she says. "Things like breathing through your skin, and channeling light through your body—if you hear and believe these things, you actually start to feel yourself doing them."

Katherine is a dark beauty, with almond-shaped eyes, a graceful manner, and a voice whose cadences are highly pleasing. Despite her persistent questioning, men in the spiritual movement are magnetized by her; many declare love at first sight, and tell her they recall being her lover in previous incarnations. She suspects that being an ex-nun contributes to her attraction. Katherine has a school in New Jersey, and also teaches yoga to psychiatric patients at St. Joseph's Hospital in Paterson. One schizophrenic, she says, described experiences similar to those yogis talk of—traveling outside the body, and being flooded with light. She asked the doctors how they would distinguish between the experience of a yogi and a psychotic. "They told me they would look at the person's total behavior."

Katherine is aware that in yoga she uses techniques similar to hypnosis: the soft voice, the methodical way of speaking, and the concentration on parts of the body. Staring at a candle or chanting with eyes closed are used in meditation to induce a trance. "One of my problems now is that most mystics say their experiences come from an outside force—the hand of God. But when I see that, with self-hypnosis, people can induce similar states in themselves, I'm not convinced it's an outside force."

I know a person who's used an Alpha Wave headset for nine months, and he's almost enlightened.

—Peter Max

The ads show Buddha with electrodes pasted to his skull. "Now you can be taught to control your brain waves. Enhanced states of consciousness easily attained!!" For $250, you can buy a headset made by one of the companies that have rushed into business to capitalize on biological-feedback training (BFT). In the past few years, bio-feedback training has excited the scientific community, become an underground cult and the darling of the popular media. With BFT, people learn, through conditioning, to control functions of the mind and body that have long been considered involuntary: heart rate, blood pressure, muscle control, body temperature, brain waves, and thereby, states of mind. Example: a subject sits in a darkened cubicle; an electro-encephalograph traces the electrical impulses of his brain, and each time he produces alpha waves—one of four identified brain waves—a color flashes on a screen. After a number of sessions, the subject can learn to keep the color onscreen indefinitely, or prevent it from appearing. At this point he has learned to create, at will, a state of consciousness in which there is almost no anxiety, a state generally described as "calm, relaxed wakefulness."

In early experiments, it was found that the alpha state is similar to a state achieved during meditation by yogis and Zen masters. But conditioning is easier to learn than meditation, and you know immediately if you are "doing it right." As the alpha cult grew, droves rushed to volunteer as subjects in BFT experiments. Dr. Barbara Brown, a brilliant, salty, utterly captivating philosopher-scientist, has to fend off applicants from her office at the

Veterans Hospital in Sepulveda, California, where she has assembled one of the country's most sophisticated BFT laboratories. Dr. Brown says alpha conditioning is not a miracle-agent. "I'd put it in the category of aspirin, which is a useful drug for general annoyances but doesn't do anything specific that we know of." She says alpha conditioning could raise the threshold of our overall mental and physical state. "It's fairly well known that in a state of emotional well-being, people are highly resistant to infections and colds. Through mind control, there's great hope that people could chug along for long periods without having extreme anxiety attacks or developing any illness."

Dr. Brown has worked for thirty years in pharmacology, biology, psychiatry, and electronics. She has invented a number of mind-altering drugs, and administered one of the first doses of LSD to Aldous Huxley. Although she has read mystic and religious philosophy all her life, she says, "I never believed a bit of it. When you ask enough questions, you've shot it—there's nothing left to believe in. I don't believe in scientific facts. I suppose if I believe anything, it's that man's mind can do whatever it wants to do if it tries." She says our culture has never attempted to nourish the mind, "to see if it has any abilities beyond those we know of. We've stuffed it with facts, but we've been bloody repressive about all kinds of mental phenomena like ESP, and astral projection, which I prefer to call depersonalization. We're such a materialistic, exterior-oriented culture that we've squashed the mind and the brain under."

Sitting in her office, with walls of green blackboard, she utters a dreamy-eyed "whew," as she describes her future projects, in which people will paint canvases with their brain waves and create symphonies of "mind music." In five years, she predicts, there will be bio-feedback centers across the country, where people can learn, under supervision, to control all types of mind and body functions. "But that's just the beginning. We don't know where it will all lead. Individuals will be reproducing states of consciousness that are not well known to us at the moment. We're just approaching the foothills of the next evolutionary step —the evolution of the mind."

Dr. Brown has a sense of ironic resignation about "fringe groups" feeding on the interest in BFT. "Those headsets are utterly stupid and misleading, because it would be impossible, for $250, to construct an instrument that could accurately isolate brain waves. The components alone would cost $600." As to courses run by laymen, which advertise alpha conditioning as "the key to the promised land," Dr. Brown says: "It's true. Conditioning could be the key. Any of these techniques around now could help some people. LSD would have been a beautiful key to a better life, if it hadn't been misused. But people shouldn't accept anything as *the* final answer, or they will be disappointed.

It might be a key for you, but make sure, by comparing and asking: what does it do for me? does it last? is it real? is it valid?"

How, indeed, is one to judge the legitimacy of or find a sane path through the exotic array of salvation techniques? We all have urges and at some point have given in to the impulse to try a device that promised miracles: lose ten pounds in three days; free yourself from worry with this mental routine; experience bliss and Godhead by repeating a mantra. When it failed, some of us found it difficult to trust or try any similar techniques. The spiritual movement, however, is filled with people who search endlessly from one teacher or system to the next. When I began looking into it, I thought this insatiable seeking was a sign of desperation and delusion. Now I'm not sure. There are, of course, people who flit about in confusion, but I have met others who manage to glean the best and ignore the nonsense in whatever technique they try, and who say that with each experience, they learn more and gain more love, quietude, and detachment from fear and conflict. Vathsala, who has been a seeker all her life, says, "There's no end, that's the beautiful thing. There's no end to life, no end to seeking consciousness, no end to the peace and joy you can realize." The search becomes, in itself, the salvation.

The time has come for America to help the whole world with spirituality.

—Swami Satchidananda

Around the backyard swimming pool of the Integral Yoga Institute in Los Angeles, on a Sunday in March, sixteen spiritual teachers and their followers are gathered for a meeting of the World Congress for Enlightenment. The teachers take chairs in a circle, the followers sit on the grass, straining to hear, as Charles Berner explains what has happened to date: "Last fall, Swami Satchidananda, Yogi Bhajan, and I met by chance in Santa Cruz, and we talked about the need for better understanding between the spiritual teachers of this planet. We came up with the idea of holding a World Enlightenment Festival this August, where a large number of people could be with the teachers for a week, camping on the land, eating vegetarian food, with no drugs or alcohol, living in love and peace and thus demonstrating to the world the Aquarian way of life." Berner says he and his staff sent out hundreds of invitations to religious leaders in all countries. "We have over 200 acceptances. No one has turned us down. The idea is irresistible, because of the rising tide of spiritual awareness, because of the Aquarian Age."*

* Astrologers are in disagreement as to what and when the Aquarian Age is. One school says it started in the nineteenth century and is dominated by science. Other authorities say it won't begin until 2150, and will bring renewed spirituality. This seems certain: the Age lasts 2,000 years, and at the rate pop culture is exploiting it, we'll be sick of it before it even gets rolling.

Swami Vishnu-Devananda, head of the Sivananda Yoga Centers and Camps, who flies about in a private airplane, asks where they'll get the money for the festival. Berner suggests selling tickets for $5. Another teacher protests. "This site will be a temple, holy ground. I won't go near it if there's any money changing hands." Muriel Tepper-Dorner, who teaches light radiation, says, "Money is not good or bad, it's just energy. It can work to spread the light."

There is discussion later of how all the gurus at the festival can interact and "experience each other." Berner proposes meeting in groups of five. Laura Huxley, wife of Aldous Huxley, says, "Why don't we all fast for twenty-four hours?" Swami Vishnu shakes his head and giggles. "You can't tell all the teachers to fast, because if they don't agree they won't do it. Silence is the best thing—fifteen minutes' silence, everyone praying his own way." "No no," says another swami. "The emphasis should be on communicating, not silence." A Hawaiian "kahuna" (high priest) says the answer is to chant—a Polynesian chant. Berner disagrees. "Everyone here can come up with something like that, and I can show you 600 more. Everybody chants, everybody prays, everybody's into something. If we make any one technique mandatory, we're finished."

One month later, many of the same teachers assemble in Davis, 500 miles to the north, for a three-day Earth Rebirth Festival at the University of California. It is a test run, in many ways, of the great festival to come. About a thousand young people are camping in a field, wearing Indian print clothes and farm coveralls. They wander about carrying incense, wood flutes, and finger cymbals. Almost every hour, there is a speech, class, or spiritual entertainment being given in the quad. Only a small portion of the crowd are Davis students. Most have come from surrounding areas for the "holy man jam." Remarkably, there are no drugs being hawked, no beer cans or wine bottles to be seen. On the mall, girls are selling organic apple cider, pumpkin bread, vegetables and cara-coa cookies.

Katherine Da Silva gives a yoga class to several hundred people on the grass. Many hold infants in their laps during the exercises. A two-year-old towhead, who is named Siddhartha Greenblatt, wiggles between his parents, aping their movements. When the group does the dead man's posture, lying on their backs, it is an eerie sight: yards and yards of bodies, motionless in the sun, with only the dogs and babies crawling about. Later, people dance and gyrate to bongo drums, the men barechested, their stomachs sunken from fasting.

As the weekend progresses, the vibrations grow increasingly bizarre and increasingly ecstatic. There is a speaker who claims to be a messenger from Venus. The Rev. Kirby Hensley, an ex-Baptist who lives in Modesto, and who has a pink complexion and fly-away ears, offers to ordain everyone as ministers in his Universal Life Church. With one hand on his hip, the other sawing the air, he describes how the ministers will be able to perform marriages and divorces, get draft exemptions, fly at reduced rates on Ozark Airlines, and attend a new school Hensley is starting "where boys and girls can come to *practice* sex. You don't know how many homes get busted up because boys and girls didn't have no experience." "Far out, Reverend!" a boy yells. "Hallelujah." There is a scramble to get minister's credentials, and 116 are ordained, including one collie dog.

At sundown, Muriel Tepper-Dorner, who says she is a channel for the White Brotherhood, gives a demonstration of light radiation. "Breathe in the golden light, and see yourself as a sun. Radiate the light out to each other until we see this whole room filled with light. Now radiate more light, and see it flowing all over this campus, and now all over the planet." A freshman in a neat shirtdress whispers to her date, "I swear I can feel it coming out of my skin." The boy nods. "I have to be careful, or I'll get drained."

Next comes George Peters, the Abbie Hoffman of the spiritual movement, founder of Naturalism. George is thirty-two, a fast-talking New Yorker who sometimes says he is a psychiatrist. Wearing lavender suede pants, with black hair to his waist, he tells the crowd he gets people enlightened by locking them in black sensory-deprivation boxes for forty days, or by giving them knockout drops, stripping them, and letting them wake up in a deserted field.

Indra Devi, a seventy-two-year-old woman yogi who lives in Tecate, Mexico, shows films of Satya Sai Baba, who is believed by millions in India to be an avatar (an incarnation of God), and is said to have the power to materialize anything from thin air. Afterward, she plays tapes of Baba chanting, and everyone sings along. They walk off reeling, euphoric, having given up long ago any attempt to fit things into some rational framework.

The next day, Yogi Bhajan gives a mass meditation, followed by Swami Satchidananda, who is mobbed like·a rock star. His disciples float about him in clumps, singing softly in adoration: "Sri Ram, Jai Ram." Wherever the Swami walks, he is surrounded by this celestial singing, while crowds push and scramble to get near him, touch his orange gown, kiss his hand, or snap his picture.

After lunch, the teachers meet in the student union to discuss the World Enlightenment Festival. As at previous meetings, only teachers can sit in the inner circle and speak. A few staff members are disgruntled. "It's cronyism, like the smoke-filled room. Only this is the incense-filled room." Charles Berner suggests they break up into groups of five, as they hope to do for three days during the August festival. Yogi Bhajan says, "Good. I want five negative people, because I'm in a very fine mood." Berner, Bhajan, and Swami Satchidananda each start a separate circle. Ava Berner says, "The one rule is that you talk only about yourself, not about theology or your ashrams or disciples. Talk about what makes you unique, so the others can become conscious of you."

George Peters turns to Swami Satchidananda: "I once tried wearing an orange robe and getting people to hum, and I felt ridiculous. How do you manage?" The Swami says, "The robe is only an outward symbol of a person who dedicates his life to serving others. Because I feel this dedication, I have no hesitation to wear it." Jack Horner, a tall, gaunt man who created a technique called eductivism, tells the swami, "You're one of the most beautiful human beings I've ever seen. How did you get there?" Swami laughs. "It just happened, as a natural growth. I never even decided to renounce the world. I didn't plan to come to this country and start yoga centers. Things just happen. I believe in that. I feel that I'm always at ease, no worry, no disturbance."

After an hour, Ava says, "All right, we're through. At the festival, hopefully we could continue longer and have a chance to go deeper." Charles says, "We had a good time here." Yogi Bhajan announces: "We had very fine time." Swami Satchidananda fairly rises into the air with glee. "We had a *wonderful* time." Charles says, "After three days, I think you're gonna get onto each other and will have the greatest high on this planet!"

The schedule calls for the teachers to conduct closing ceremonies on the Davis quad at nightfall. They learn, though, that in their absence all afternoon, the field has been taken over by rowdy students and teen-agers from nearby high schools. While the holy men are experiencing each other, the scene outside looks like the last days of Rome. Much marijuana, liquor, people shedding clothes, dancing and making love on blankets. A high-decibel rock band blares across the campus.

Secluded in the pea-green conference room, the gurus are standing in concentric circles, eyes closed, arms entwined as they chant: "OM Shanti, OM Shanti, OM Shanti, OOOOOMMMMM."

SPECIAL GLOSSARY FOR
THE RUSH FOR INSTANT SALVATION

OM: Sacred word, felt to be pure sound, containing all sounds and being present in everything.

Astral Projection: Traveling outside the body in another dimension, apart from the physical world.

Kundalini: Mystic life-force which lies coiled, dormant, at the base of the spine. Kundalini yoga works to rouse this energy and send it rushing up the spine to the head, triggering enlightenment.

Meditation: Attempt to quiet the mind and body in order to realize the absolute. One concentrates on an image, repeats a sound, counts one's breathing, or tries to gently push away all thoughts until the mind is as still as possible. One comes out of meditation as from a refreshing sleep, and sees with fresh clarity.

Swami: Religious teacher who has taken vows of celibacy, usually from another swami or Hindu order.

Yogi: Person who dedicates his life to yoga; may or may not be celibate.

Yoga: System of exercises and teachings more than 3,000 years old, aimed at preparing man to attain unity, self-realization, and bliss. Various branches stress body exercise, breathing, meditation, chanting, study, and selfless service.

Of course, each person's unique essence, his personality, is at the same time the way he sees himself *and* the way other people see him. The characteristics he may think most prominent may or may not be the ones other people would readily identify with him. Psychologists interested in the study of personality have been plagued by the problem of which frame of reference to adopt, that of the individual or that of society around him?

In ancient theater, actors taking different roles held masks before their faces. These masks, representing the characters portrayed, were called *personas*. It is from this Latin word that the word "personality" is derived. It is this perspective that some psychologists prefer to adopt when they define personality as one's particular *social stimulus value*. That is, they would prefer to study the impact we make on others.

Other psychologists object to this perspective. As Gordon Allport has put it, "Robinson Crusoe in solitude had 'as much' personality before as after the advent of his man Friday." [1] The personality is a unique set of interrelated characteristics. Allport protests that we lose sight of the uniqueness and relatedness of personality when we confuse the person with the reputation.

This problem of perspective is not peculiar to psychologists. We confront it in some form or another every day. When we make judgments about other people, we can only

[1] Gordon W. Allport. *Personality and Social Encounter.* Boston: Beacon Press, 1960, p. 21.

judge on the basis of their impact on us. That impact will depend as much on us as it will on the other person.

Living in a society such as ours, we continually evaluate the people with whom we come in contact in relation to the nature of our interactions with them. We have to make decisions based on whatever information, sketchy or otherwise, is available to us. Should we trust this salesman? Should we give that student hitchhiker a ride? For which candidate shall we vote? If we make the wrong decision because we have incorrectly assessed individuals, we may suffer. Or we may cause others to suffer: the deserving hitchhiker we didn't pick up, the "better man" who lost the election, the honest salesman who didn't make the sale.

There are other implications of having to deal with the masklike aspects of personality. What happens when an individual appears *too* different to others, when he is unique in ways that make those around him uncomfortable? Groups generally have the means to hinder behaviors which they will not condone. We may say that individuals who are out of step are criminal, immoral or sick. Under our laws we suspend their rights to function freely within the society.

In the following selection, Robert Coles, a psychiatrist, discusses some of the ethical considerations that arise when the group is confronted by individuals who are "different."

40

A FASHIONABLE KIND OF SLANDER

ROBERT COLES

It may seem strange now, six or eight years later, but in respected and moderate circles of the South, and the rest of the nation, the Southern Freedom Riders and the Mississippi Project volunteers of 1964 were thought to be (were declared) wild, impetuous, thoughtless, self-destructive, and masochistic; and the plan to challenge the state of Mississippi was considered a crazy and romantic scheme, doomed from the start and potentially dangerous, or even ruinous, because of the response that powerful men like James Eastland and John Stennis and their allies would no doubt make.

I would like to single out three of the expressions I just used:

SOURCE: From *The Atlantic Monthly*, November, 1970. Copyright © 1970 by The Atlantic Monthly Company, Boston, Mass. Reprinted with permission.

masochistic, crazy, and *self-destructive.* For years in the South I heard those words directed at civil rights workers, and when I went to Appalachia to work with the Appalachian Volunteers, a similar group of dedicated, youthful political activists, I again heard the same thing. The line goes as follows: What's the matter with them? What kind of people do things like that? Why do they do such things? Do they really think anything will come of antics like theirs, rash and impulsive assaults? They are mistaken if they believe a small minority like them can prevail against the powers-that-be. Maybe they want to lose, though. Maybe they are stubbornly, uncompromisingly bent on the kind of confrontation that can lead only to violence, disorder—and a kind of retaliation that will not only put an end to their protest but set things even further back, create an even worse climate of fear and repression. In short, maybe those youths are irrational, deluded by a host of absurd and dangerous fantasies, violence-prone, and in some serious way, antisocial.

"SICK"   In 1963 I discovered how that kind of approach to activist, dissenting youths works. I heard a decidedly sensitive and well-educated Southern judge send a youthful black civil rights worker to a state hospital, where he was to be "observed," where his "mental status" was to be evaluated, where possible "delinquent" and "sociopathic" trends would be ascertained and studied—and where, perhaps, the young man would begin to get some "treatment." If he received no treatment the youth did have a chance to think, and what I heard from him was for me a professional confrontation of sorts, something I have never been able to forget, especially because I had worked with delinquent youth in the course of my training in child psychiatry: "It's quite a setup they've got. We protest our inability to vote, to go into a movie or restaurant everyone else uses, and they call us crazy, and send us away to be looked over by psychiatrists and psychologists and social workers and all the rest of them. The questions I've had put at me since I've been here! Were you a *loner* when you were a boy? Did people consider you *rebellious?* Were you *popular* or *unpopular* as a child? When you were younger did you have trouble *taking orders* from your parents or your teachers? Did your mother *discipline* you firmly, or did she more or less let you do as you please? And on and on they go, one question after another, and none of them very subtle.

"The guy doing the questioning told me he is a doctor, a psychiatrist, and I asked him why he wasn't interested in *what* I've done, and the *objective reasons* I've acted as I have. But he said he knew 'all that.' He told me his job is to examine my mind and find out what my 'motivations' are. He kept on asking me whether I feel angry at this person and that one, and if I have a temper, and how do I 'handle tension,' and he wanted to know whether people in 'authority' make me anxious, and whether I have trouble in 'controlling' myself, and whether I 'rush out and act' when I come upon an unpleasant situation, or instead do I stop and think and try to figure out the best possible 'attitude' to have. I wrote them down, as many of his words and questions as I could, because the way he put those questions was to me more abusive than anything I've ever heard from the poor, ignorant red-necks. At least they have the decency to insult you right to your face; so you know exactly where they stand and no one's fooling anyone, least of all himself. That doctor (I can tell from talking with him over a week) considers himself way above the red-neck; in his mind he is a careful, thoughtful, temperate man. He used that word 'temperate' two or three times with me. He kept on contrasting 'temperate behavior' with 'impulsive behavior,' and after we got talking more casually he told me that some people have a 'need'—that's right, a *need*—to disrupt the lives of others, and hurt them, and get hurt themselves. Did I think I was that kind of person?

"Soon you just slip into the whole scene. I mean, you stop noticing all the assumptions a guy like that constantly makes, and you simply try to answer him as best you can. And anyway, if you protest and tell him off, tell him what you think is implicit in his questions and his whole way of thinking, he's not going to take your argument seriously; he's going to go after *you*—and call you 'hostile' and 'defensive' and full of 'problems' and all the rest. He as much as told me so, that doctor did. He said a lot was going on inside my mind, and until I found out what 'really' was prompting some of my 'behavior,' I'd probably continue what I've been doing. He told me he was going to recommend to the court that I not be sent to jail. He said I needed treatment— but he was worried that I would be 'resistant' to it, and that would be 'too bad' for me, and later I would be sorry."

The youth then pointed out to me what I hope is obvious: the smug, self-righteous arrogance he had met up with, the pejorative use of psychiatric terminology, the limitless display of self-satisfaction and condescension, the essentially illogical and totalitarian nature of a mode of thought that claims to have the authority to decide who has a right even to discuss certain matters, and who (whatever he *thinks* he is saying or doing or trying to say or trying to do) is *really* "sick" or "resistant" or seriously in need of "help," and therefore thoroughly, hopelessly suspect. I was prepared to accept much of that from him—I had heard patients endlessly labeled in ways that robbed them of their dignity, and I had seen in myself as a psychiatric resident the awful tendency to dismiss a patient's disagreement or criticism as evidence of just about anything but his or her good judgment. But I was not so prepared to see how convenient it could be for that judge, and many like him, to have people around who would summon all the authority of medicine and science to the task of defending the status quo—which meant putting firmly in their place (a hospital or a clinic) those who choose to wage a struggle against that status quo.

"Paranoid"   Only over time did I begin to realize, often because I was brought up short by some very bright and clearheaded youths, that all sorts of phrases and concepts bandied about rather freely by me and my kind reveal as much about us as about those we describe. What indeed is "mental health"? Who indeed is "normal"? Were slave-holders "normal"? Did Nat Turner have a "problem with authority"? If a man tells me he is going to kill himself, I call him "suicidal" and want to hospitalize him. If a man in Vietnam runs into a burst of machine-gun fire, urging his comrades to do likewise, I call him a hero. If a man wants to kill someone, he is homicidal and needs confinement. If a man drops a bomb on people he doesn't even see or know, he is doing his duty. And if a man is *afraid* he might want to kill someone, he, of course, needs help or guidance or treatment to prevent a fear from becoming a deed; whereas if a pilot should become horrified at the thought of what *he* might do, the bombs he might cause to fall on fellow human beings, he would need that same "treatment"—presumably so that he will get over his hesitations and "do his duty." Certainly if he starts making a lot of noise about the fears and his misgivings he will be sent for "evaluation." And, of course, if the pilot never once has such hesitations and qualms, he is "normal" or "patriotic" or a "good soldier" or whatever.

Such ironies and vexing discrepancies ought to make us all at the very least aware that psychiatric judgments about what is or is not "appropriate" are not rendered in some scientific vacuum, but are made at a particular moment of history and in a given society by men who are distinctly part of that society—namely, its upper middle class.

The Southern youth who was just quoted knew in his bones what it takes some of us longer to realize, if indeed we ever do, no matter how thoroughly we analyze ourselves—that the assumptions we make about a person's social and political behavior have to do with the kinds of lives we ourselves live, and that the doctor in that mental hospital was nothing less than a willing and indeed eager representative of a particular kind of entrenched power, which wanted those protesting its authority discredited and knocked out of commission, one way or another. In the distant past, but also in recent times, dissenters have been banished to prison or sent to their death (or sent to America!) for their noisy, unorthodox, unsettling, and provocative words and acts. Many of us no doubt find such out-and-out repression distasteful, but we are not beyond our own ablty to call a person we oppose only thinly disguised names, to insult him and at the same time ignore the thrust of his declared purposes, his stated intentions, his deeds—which surely ought to be open for discussion on their own merits, rather than the merits of one or another person's psychiatric status. We dismiss, belittle, and run down those we disagree with *substantively* by doing them in *personally.*

For example, in response to a questionnaire put out by a magazine, a substantial number of American psychiatrists were willing just a few years ago to signify that yes, Barry Goldwater is not "psychologically fit" to be President of the United States. Later, we heard that George Wallace might also be "neurotic" and "unstable." I happen to feel, as a citizen, that I would prefer to have as my friend Barry Goldwater rather than Lyndon Johnson, that in fact Mr. Goldwater is more open as a person, less self-centered, and less given to pettiness or meanness—but I voted for Mr. Johnson because in 1964 his position on all sorts of issues seemed far wiser to me than Mr. Goldwater's. In 1964, to a supporter of Lyndon Johnson, his moodiness, his arrogance, his secretiveness were the foibles of a great, warmhearted humanitarian, just as to Richard Nixon's supporters today, his aloofness, his outbursts of anger when things have not gone as he likes are the way he chooses to deal with a difficult job, or the way he responds to outrageous provocations. Put differently, psychological evaluations inevitably are influenced by our disposition to like or dislike a person or his views; and that holds for psychiatrists, too—who can misuse their own professional language and applaud or condemn deeds or individuals with words like "ego-syntonic" (which means "good") and "pre-oedipal" (which means "bad").

Then there are today's students and demonstrators. What we don't hear about them! They are "products of permissive child-rearing practices." They are sons of self-made men who abhor the materialism of their fathers, and more than that, are struggling with some version of an "oedipal conflict." They are "immature." They have "poor ego controls." They are not in touch with "reality." They are "passive-aggressive." They are "exhibitionistic" or plagued by "omnipotent fantasies." They are "acting out" one or another "problem." Their words and thoughts and actions show them "paranoid," even in some cases "psychotic." Nor are those whose serious and carefully thought out ideas happen to capture the interest of the young immune from that kind of comment. The distinguished British psychoanalyst R. D. Laing, whose many books and papers require patient study, whose ideas are bold and challenging and singularly free of the banal and the pompous, is called a host of psychiatric names and ignored in all too many centers of psychiatric and psychoanalytic training. The well-known American psychiatrist Thomas Szasz, whose books constantly demand from his colleagues a willingness to look at the way unconventional people are commonly enough labeled "mentally ill" and locked up permanently, is himself called "paranoid" or possessed of a "one-track mind" or an "obsession"—as if men like Pasteur or Freud were not grandly preoccupied and maybe even "obsessed."

Needless to say, there are no limits to the abuses that can be perpetrated in the name of any ideological system. In the Soviet Union social critics and writers and scientists are regularly carted off to psychiatric hospitals, where they are called various high-sounding names and kept locked up. Here things are by no means as blatant and absurd, but with shrill rhetoric becoming almost our daily fare, it is hard to imagine any line of argument as off-limits today. And if young people or political activists are to be condemned for their "personality problems" rather than listened to (and thoroughly applauded or severely criticized) for the substance of what they propose or advocate, then surely we ought to turn the tables and ask some questions about other people—in order to end once and for all a silly and insulting way of dealing with issues.

"PROBLEMS"   What are we to say, for instance, about the "early childhood" or "mental state" of political leaders or business leaders or labor leaders who lie or cheat or order thousands to go off to fight and kill? What kind of "psychological conflict" enables a man to be an agent of the Central Intelligence Agency, or a pilot who drops napalm bombs, or a congressman who wants to use atomic and hydrogen bombs so that a nation will be "turned into a parking lot"? What kind of "oedipal conflict" enables so many people to demonstrate their obvious lack of real concern for millions of poor Americans—out of work, ailing, hungry? Do we ask about the psychological "factors" that enable a man to be hard-driving, competitive, on the rise, always on the rise, often over the backs of everyone else around? Do we question the "unconscious reasons" so many of us "adjust" to the injustice around us, become indifferent, become caught up in what is called a "rat race" or a "grind" even by those utterly uninterested in social change or protest? Moreover, if students are out to kill their "parent surrogates," what indeed about our desire as grown-ups to squelch the young, subtly and not so subtly degrade them, be rid of them—because they inspire envy in us; because they confront us with all the chances we forsook, all the opportunities we have lost, all the tricks and evasions and compromises and duplicities we have long since *rationalized* or *repressed* or *projected?*

So it goes, and so do we all suffer, I believe. Step by step we become the victims of various kinds of slander and invective, some obvious, some indirect and clothed in pietistic, sanctimonious language or in the jargon of the social sciences or psychiatry. Words like "fascist" and "elitist" are hurled indiscriminately and viciously at anyone and everyone, and of course "Communists" crop up everywhere in the minds of some. And if those more political modes of assault don't work, the rest of us, more "moderate" and maybe just as desperate and confused, can always dispense with a bothersome individual or political question by raising our eyebrows and calling into question a person's "psychodynamics" or damning an entire group with some psychological or sociological generalization. Why bother, after all, to remind ourselves that every single human being has "problems," struggles with love and hate and envy and fear and all the rest? Why bother to ask *whose* "law" and *whose* "order" are being assaulted, and for what *purpose?* Why bother asking ourselves what *in fact* so many youths, from so many different backgrounds and regions, are actually saying and asking of us? And finally, why trouble ourselves by asking how it has come about that we have lost faith in our ethical convictions, and so have to attack or defend people and entire political movements by resorting to words and concepts originally meant only to help doctors clarify for themselves the sorrow and pain felt by particular patients?

Cole's article leads us directly into the discussion of our next part, the topic of defining mental health and mental illness.

IN SEARCH OF MORE ABOUT PERSONALITY

The "Psychological Thrillers" article in the last part in this book mentions several books that would provide the interested student with more information about personality—about the whole person operating within a social context. Perhaps particularly pertinent are Virginia Voeks, *On Becoming an Educated Person*, 3rd ed. (Saunders, 1970); William E. Blatz, *Human Security: Some Reflections* (University of Toronto Press, 1966); and Hadley Cantril and Charles H.

Bumstead, *Reflections on the Human Venture* (New York University Press, 1960).

Ken Kesey's book, *One Flew Over the Cuckoo Nest* (Viking Press, 1962), may well be mentioned here in the context of Cole's article. While hardly yielding a realistic portrayal of a mental institution, it does illuminate Cole's points about the potential for the political abuse of psychology.

Students who prefer Gordon Allport's perspective in studying personality can turn to *Becoming* (Yale University Press, 1955) for a fuller development of the topic.

Part Thirteen

Personality Disorders: Individual or Society?

In the preceding chapter we discussed two major problems we face when we study personality. First, how to define personality, whether to focus on the individual's feelings about himself or on his impact on those around him. Second, there is much that is not yet known about how the personality develops. We also hinted about yet a third problem, determining what is the "normal" personality and what is to be done about personalities that are not normal.

All of these are interrelated problems. If we focus on personality from society's perspective, "abnormal" is likely to mean "what will not be tolerated." If the individual seeks treatment, the goal of psychotherapy might be the substitution of acceptable for socially unacceptable behaviors. There could well be the attempt to teach the individual that he may not infringe on the rights of others, that he has responsibilities to fulfill to his family, his friends, and the society in which he lives.

On the other hand, if we focus on the individual and his feelings about himself, "abnormal" may mean something quite different. We may be talking about someone who hates himself, or who hears voices when he is alone, or who is inordinately fearful all the time, or who cannot love. Although there may be problems with the way this person functions in society, psychotherapy would proceed with the primary goal of improving the individual's perceptions of himself. Often the assumption is made that once we can see ourselves realistically, and be accepting of ourselves, we cannot help but improve in our relations with others.

Naturally, these two perspectives often fuse. We see the individual who is acutely miserable and who, at the same time, is unable to function satisfactorily in society. Often, psychotherapy proceeds with two goals: aiding the individual to achieve personal adjustment, while guiding him to adopt more successful modes of behavior in his relations with those around him.

In the next selection, we look at the woman who is miserably aware that something is awry, and that she, and her family, are suffering as a result. Elton McNeil, the psychologist from whom she sought help, describes her case.

41

NEATNESS COUNTS!—GEORGIA M.

ELTON B. MCNEIL

PROLOGUE *Life* is a continual tug-of-war between love and hate, right and wrong, order and disorder, cleanliness and dirt. Yet, most of us manage to maintain a precarious balance between these extremes, and only a few of us become caricatures of normality in which a single aspect of life almost becomes one's sole reason for being.

In a psychoneurotic disorder marked by an obsessive-compulsive reaction, for example, we find human life frozen into a rigid pattern of inescapable thoughts and absolutely necessary actions if anxiety is to be avoided and sanity preserved. The unwilling victim knows his or her pattern of life is irrational, silly, stupid, futile, irritating to others, and hopeless, but absolutely indispensable to continued psychic comfort.

Each of us has suffered obsessive thoughts and been the prey of compulsive actions but these have usually been confined to haunting melodies we could not shake from consciousness or persistent concern with situations that lack any simple, elegant solution—worrying. We have all felt better after a ritual crossing of fingers or knocking on wood, but few of us have been terrorized by the thought that we might, for example, rise in some public gathering, surrounded by friends, and shout some obscenity that would shock and repel all those who know us. The specter of a socially unacceptable impulse bursting the cage that confines it and running amuck in society is not a part of the constant worry patterns of most of us.

Suppose you were to find yourself obsessed all day with thoughts of murdering those you thought you loved best? At first these vagrant mental images might easily be dismissed from mind and lost in a flurry of work or play. Then, these murderous thoughts would begin to appear when unsummoned, persist throughout one's waking hours, inhabit one's dreams, and dictate the performance of certain of your actions and behavior. At that moment, you would be experiencing a full-blown obsessive-compulsive neurosis. It is not unlikely that you would be plagued with thoughts that you are going insane and that you must be a disgustingly abnormal and horrifying person to think such evil, wicked, sinful thoughts.

SOURCE: From Elton B. McNeil, *The Quiet Furies*, © 1967. Reprinted by permission of Prentice-Hall, Inc., Englewood Cliffs, New Jersey. Pp. 23–33.

As you fight to quell these unsettling thoughts, you are likely to engage in a series of actions designed to neutralize or eliminate these breakthroughs of impulse and to defend yourself against the full awareness of the truth of the unconscious and unacceptable urge that fills your life. Survival comes first, and the pattern of behavior you devise to meet the threat you feel is about to engulf you may be painful to those who are closest to you, but you have no choice in the matter. You do what you feel you must to escape the anxiety ravenously gnawing at you.

The obsessive-compulsive person is driven to organize the world in a fashion designed to reassure, to assuage anxiety, and to make tolerable just living from one moment to the next. The obsessive person is often a socially submissive individual bound hand and foot by convention, conscientiousness in the extreme. A rigid person who seems regularly to be inadequate in meeting the challenges of life. He may already have organized his daily existence along methodical, predictable lines only to discover that this degree of systematization is insufficient to ward off the threat life poses. Suddenly, despite his attempts to build a stout fort to protect himself from attack, he discovers that the enemy is swarming over his defenses and he must rebuild the walls to an even greater height.

The last-ditch dictum becomes "a place for everything and everything in its place." The logic is that if the outside world is chaotic, messy, disorganized, and untrustworthy, at least one's personal life can be ritualized, timed, ordered, organized and made free of surprises via ritual, regularity, and rigidity. Life constrained in this fashion is absolutely predictable, avoids excessive exposure to temptation, and eliminates contact with those particular temptations that might prove to be irresistible. Little wonder that sudden or violent disruptions of this robot-like programming of events in one's life are viewed as threatening and dangerous. Spontaneous invitations to "cut loose" and "leave the dishes in the sink" are greeted only with horror and misgivings by the truly obsessed person. For them, order spells safety.

At the base of obsession-compulsion is a sense of worthlessness and culpability as a human being. Guilt, self-condemnation, and fear of punishment become the unconscious springs of motivation yet the seemingly senseless actions of the affected individual make a psychological sense to the astute observer. What is safe gets substituted for what is unsafe, the thinkable replaces the unthinkable, clean thoughts are substituted for their reprehensible other selves and anxiety is temporarily held at bay. The fear that one is not perfect (as everyone knows one ought to be) gets translated into actions that are calculated to correct this deficiency in a socially admirable fashion. When one feels unclean, exaggerated cleanliness is the only answer. Obsessive love can compensate for deep-reaching hate and, if it is effective, no one, including the self, need be the wiser.

Obsessive-compulsive patterns of behavior are self-defeating, primarily because of the difficulties they create in relationships with others. If one has never suffered anxiety attacks relievable only by compulsive behavior, the actions of the victim may seem bizarre, uncalled for, and worthy of criticism. The hostility and resentment of others that such encounters occasion drives the victim deeper into the distress of costly measures that are bound to fail in the long run. The compulsive act designed to satisfy the obsessive thought fails because it serves to remind its victim of the fundamental anxiety that is being eluded in the first place. Checking the gas jets to make sure they are turned off merely stimulates, again, the unconscious impulse to turn each of them full on.

Georgia M. acted out her fundamental problem as she sat nervously in my office. On this particular day, my office happened to be neater than usual, but Georgia M. apparently did not share my view of neatness. She was able in a speedy, all-encompassing glance to catalogue every detail of what had been neglected and what was unclean. She lowered herself into the proffered seat with some tentativeness—gingerly, as if it were crawling with filth.

As she talked she touched the objects on my desk in turn, shifting their positions slightly. She idly but disapprovingly ran her finger along a book case shelf, discovered some dust, and made a great show of dusting off her hands. She hand-brushed her clothes continuously as she talked and was one of the busiest and most efficient lint-removers I had ever seen.

I had several reactions as I watched her fuss away furiously at the condition of my office. It occurred to me that I would one day be able to observe improvement simply by watching the ratio of comfort-discomfort she would show on future visits. Like many people, I have never felt very comfortable in homes where everything is spick-and-span, exactly ordered, spotless, and fragile-looking. According to every American housewife, the usual condition of her house is "a mess." A mess, then, is the normal condition, but for some people what is normal is painful and intolerable. Such was the case with Georgia M.

Most "messy" houses I have entered have been staggeringly well kept, and it always seemed apparent that this frequent self-accusation on the part of housewives is a ritualized, conventional disavowal of responsibility—enter at your own risk. It is also a solemn and fashionable declaration that they would never have presented such a sloppy scene to offend your eyes had you given decent and proper advance notice of your coming. The regularity with which American women voluntarily declare their homes a disaster area does, however, tell us about the cultural ideal held out as a model for American womanhood. Cleanliness is next to godliness and neatness counts in our society. So much so, that European cultures have deridingly depicted us as an excessively scrubbed, well-plumbed, deodorized, sterile, and only slightly human version of a civilization.

Cleanliness is probably better than dirtiness. Tidiness is no doubt better than untidiness. But, according to Georgia M.'s husband, if neatness was an olympic sport Georgia would easily have been captain of the team. As he said,

> You remember that old joke about getting up in the middle of the night to go to the john and coming back to the bedroom to find your wife has made the bed? It's no joke. Sometimes I think she never sleeps. I got up one night at 4 a.m. and there she was doing the laundry downstairs. Look at your ash tray! I haven't seen one that dirty in years! I'll tell you what it makes me feel like. If I forget to leave my dirty shoes outside the back door she gives me a look like I had just crapped in the middle of an operating room. I stay out of the house a lot and I'm about half-stoned when I do have to be home. She even made us get rid of the dog because she said he was always filthy. When we used to have people over for supper she would jitterbug around everybody till they couldn't digest their food. I hated to call them up and ask them over because I could always hear them hem and haw and make up excuses not to come over. Even the kids are walking down the street nervous about getting dirt on them. I'm going out of my mind but you can't talk to her. She just blows up and spends twice as much time cleaning things. We have guys in to wash the walls so often I think the house is going to fall down from being scrubbed all the time. About a week ago I had it up to here and told her I couldn't take it any more. I think the only reason she came to see you was because I told her I was going to take off and live in a pig pen just for laughs.

Georgia's obsessive concern with cleanliness forced her to take as many as three showers a day, one in the morning, one before supper, and one before going to bed, and, on hot days, the number of showers would rise in direct proportion to the temperature. Her husband could not understand how she got dirty overnight, but Georgia always dismissed his objections by observing that "it isn't any skin off his nose if I take good care of myself" and that "he would be the first to holler if I turned sloppy."

The trouble in this family ran deeper than just neatness, of course. Georgia was aware, in part, of the effect she was having on her family and friends, but she also knew that when she tried to alter her behavior she got so nervous that she felt she was losing her mind. She was frightened by the possibility that "I'm headed for the funny-farm." As she said,

I can't get to sleep unless I am sure everything in the house is in its proper place so that when I get up in the morning the house is organized. I work like mad to set everything straight before I go to bed, but, when I get up in the morning, I can think of a thousand things that I ought to do. I know some of the things are ridiculous, but I feel better if I get them done, and I can't stand to know something needs doing and I haven't done it. I never told anybody but once I found just one dirty shirt and washed, dried, and ironed it that day. I felt stupid running a whole wash for one shirt but I couldn't bear to leave it undone. It would have bothered me all day just thinking about that one dirty shirt in the laundry basket.

What really bothers me is this whole business of sex. My husband acts like he wants it all the time and he always brings it up at times when it's impossible because I have so much to do. By nighttime I am tired and we live on different sleep schedules. I always have a million things to do and he's ready to go to bed. I like to make preparations, too. I think we both ought to take a shower and the bed should have clean sheets on it. But, he gets mad and says "the hell with it" and sulks. He's just like a big overgrown kid. In the last month he hasn't said anything about sex and I am beginning to think he is fooling around with some other woman. I got so suspicious that I thought about following him once or twice, but, with the kids and the house to take care of, I couldn't get free. Now he says he's going to leave me and that's the only reason I came to see you.

Adding it all up, I wasn't very encouraged by the prospect of making progress with this family. Georgia certainly had a problem. The children were suffering, and the marriage was about to come apart at the seams. I wished they had come to me before the marital issue had gotten quite as knock-down-and-drag-out as it seemed to be at the moment but it is often that way.

I asked both Georgia and her husband to see me regularly, but separately. My clinical goals with the husband were: 1) to explore in full the nature and extent of the symptoms Georgia was displaying, 2) to assess what resources the husband had that might be useful in establishing some new patterns of interpersonal relations with his wife, and 3) to examine the structure of complicity in the game they were playing. I reasoned that it took two to dance this complicated tango of life and that, somehow, he must contribute to the maintenance of so severe a set of symptoms. Did he marry her with this obsessive prospect lurking in his unconscious? Did he reward or encourage the first appearance of extraordinary neatness in her? Was she acting out a part of himself that would never otherwise reach the surface of his consciousness? There were a million such unanswered questions. Why did he insist, only now, that she enter therapy?

Why had he tolerated this condition so long? Why his evident glee in relating in fine detail the excruciating agony caused by her behavior? Why did his relationship with his children seem distant and cold (he never mentioned their names; he always designated them by relative age—the oldest kid, the middle kid, and the youngest kid)? Why did he always compare his wife to his own mother?

The first stages of therapy with Georgia and her husband Bill were remarkably alike, a fact which impressed itself on me because, at times, I would confuse who said what. At first there was resistance. It was not that they lied; it was rather that I never got more than part of the truth at any one time from either of them. It was as frustrating as being handed pieces to a picture puzzle one at a time. You needed a good memory to keep any kind of perspective because the same event would be described several times before, suddenly, I realized they were both talking about the same thing. It is an unsettling experience to become aware all at once that the argument being described is the same one you had discussed previously but failed to recognize when retold by the other combatant. More than once I was tempted to bring them together to discuss their two views of the same argument in the vain hope that with me acting as a judge the reality of the battle might finally emerge and be recognized by all. It was, as I said, a vain hope born of frustration since I knew full well that reality was clearly in the eye of the angry beholder. For some weeks it was like wading through a swamp of glue with both of them until we could have an hour free of resistance —an hour in which I would not silently say "en garde" as the conversation began.

Bill opened up first. He was describing something Georgia had recently done when he jumped from his chair and shouted, "Hey, that's just what my mother always used to do!" Then, as suddenly as he had jumped, he broke down and started to cry. I could only suspect what was taking place (this was his fourteenth hour with me), so I began to probe to find some solid ground for a firmer therapeutic footing. What poured out that hour changed our relationship dramatically. It was as if we had finally gotten the engine of insight started.

Bill had been raised in a small town in Illinois in which he had lived out the classic stereotype of the small-town boy. Barefoot and a little too fat for popularity, he hunted, fished, and spent his time at the local courthouse and lumber yard where the other kids gathered.

Bill's problem was, as I suspected, his mother. His father was a farmer and worked long hours in the fields and barn. He never said much and Bill learned to work silently beside him when he got old enough. When he did comment, Bill observed, it was usually pungent and crisply to the point. Bill recalled his father once saying, "the angels ain't as careful about Heaven as your mother is about that house. She should never have married a farmer 'cause farmers are in love with dirt. That's what makes things grow, and if it don't grow we don't have nothin'."

Bill could recall no other paternal comment directed at his mother's fastidiousness but item after item bounced into consciousness once he began to look closely at his early life. The parlor that was locked except on Sundays or special occasions and draped with dust shields during the week, the ritual of "washing outside" before going to supper, the classification of clothing as "work" or "Sunday-go-to-meetin'," and the ritual of having one's hands inspected for cleanliness before meals all came alive again in memory after the long unconscious sleep of repression. As the forgotten events washed across his consciousness he reacted much as one viewing color television for the first time. He was as much amazed at the clarity of his recollections as he was impressed by the events he thought long dead and forgotten.

Bill M., it appeared, had married a magnified version of his mother, and his oppressive guilt and sense of conscience, coupled with basic resentment of his mothers demands on him, had paved the way for trouble. He had decided unconsciously to be again the victim of an obsessively clean, demanding female. It was painful at the same time that it brought security and comfort. Georgia would never change until Bill solved some of his own problems. She sensed, somehow, that he applauded what he most strenuously objected to. She could not become someone else until he was capable of change.

Georgia M. was raised in a quite different setting. Different, in that it was a small town in Northern Michigan. Her parents were, in many ways, the opposite of Bill's. The prickling, violent, mutual resentment between her parents had always been open and frequently loud. Her early life had been disorderly in the extreme with nothing ever making sense twice in a row. There was nothing she could depend on as an anchoring point for her personal development. School offered her a way out because there, and only there, two and two always made four.

Georgia was somewhat ashamed of her parents and objected strenuously but fruitlessly to a number of their habits. Her father worked hard all day and wanted to relax when he got home. Since supper was always served in the kitchen, her father Charlie always came to the table in dirty work pants and no shirt. He had the "terrible" habit of buttering a whole piece of bread and then folding it over when he ate it. At other times he would use his bread like a mop to soak up the remaining gravy on his plate. Her father and mother said "ain't" where "isn't" was grammatically proper, and they were "coarse" and "vulgar" in conversation.

Georgia left home when she was 16 and attended high school in a larger neighboring town. On her own for the first time, she organized her life to suit herself and constructed a succession of myths to describe her origins and the character of her parents. After graduation from high school she moved 300 miles further south to a large metropolitan area in which she could totally reject her humble beginnings. She cultivated exotic and "arty" interests and seemed to spend the bulk of her time looking down her nose at the common people and all others who had "bad taste." She learned to speak a little restaurant French and consciously rejected the meat and potatoes school of eating to live rather than living to eat.

None of this was enough, however. Georgia equated freedom from parents with freedom from her past self, but she soon discovered that no matter how fast she ran she could never lose her former self. Freedom made her nervous because she could no longer make her parents scapegoats and blame them for all the anxious feelings she had. Georgia had been neat beyond reasonable expectations from the time she was a very young girl. She was fastidious in the care of her clothes, her room, and her personal possessions and had an immature tantrum whenever her things were rearranged as her mother cleaned. A number of hours of discussion with Georgia eventually revealed that this neatness served a number of purposes for her. It produced order where previously there had been disorder, of course, but this didn't explain her unusual need for a perfectly safe world. Not everyone is so frightened by the condition of the world. Her concern with dirt was intimately connected to the idea of disorder in her mind. Disorder and dirt meant two things to her. First, these twin evils meant that someone was being lazy, irresponsible, and expressing hostility to others. Whenever her mother's house was messy, it always made Georgia feel that her mother didn't care about her father and was immune to his anger about living in a "pig-pen." Georgia knew her mother deliberately neglected the housework to express irritation with her father, and Georgia feared that one day he would really walk out on them as he often threatened. These fears of marital discord resulting in separation were one basis for her excessive concern with spick-and-span housecleaning. Dusting furniture became, for her, a magic way of warding off husbandly (fatherly) discontent and possible divorce. The difficulty was that her husband was not her father and this unconscious confusion of the two was wreaking havoc with her marriage. Georgia was doing exactly what she unconsciously thought her mother ought to have done in life. Georgia's problem was that her actions were inappropriate because they had more to do with things in her anxious childhood than they did with her present adult life.

In addition, Georgia had long been obsessed with inescapable thoughts of sin, hellfires, and damnation. When she was very young, she was dismayed to discover that she was prone to thinking about sex. She recalled that once she was totally engrossed in a fantasy of what it must be like when her parents had intercourse when her mother happened to discover her and tongue-lashed her angrily for being slothful and lazy. This sudden confrontation with a mother she had been imagining in awkward and exotic sexual positions while doing "that dirty thing" so startled her that for a moment she felt her mother could read her mind and know what she had been thinking. Georgia was sure no other decent child ever wondered about or imagined such evil things and she was convinced something was wrong with her mind.

This combination of guilt over sinful thoughts and the need to quell her rising anxiety about losing one or both of her parents proved to be her psychological undoing. Undoing was exactly the proper word in her case. By her avoidance of sexual contact with her husband, her obsessive concern with neatness, and her anxious involvement in making the world a safe and orderly place in which to exist, Georgia was attempting to undo that part of her previous life she was most upset about and had least learned to live with and adjust to. As an adult she was still a captive of childish problems she had never been able to manage with any substantial success. The trouble was that the more Georgia relived the past and tried to undo its anxious hours, the more she was reminded of her ancient anxieties, and the more these provoked her into a new frenzy of redoubled effort to wipe out the past by sheer brute force. It was a losing game that was expensive to play.

As Georgia relived emotionally some of her early experiences and began to re-evaluate them in light of her adult responsibilities and status, she was willing to make an attempt to control the expression of her symptoms and to tolerate the anxiety this always produced. The beginning was a quite limited one. She decided to do her laundry every other day—rather than daily—and to discuss with me the feelings this act of gross neglect provoked in her. She was startled to discover this was a manageable experience and that the heavens didn't crash in on her as a consequence of her dereliction of duty. From these small beginnings we progressed to even more daring steps when she felt she could manage them, such as hiring a cleaning lady and showering only once a day.

This attempt to live life in a different fashion produced an unusual anxiety in Bill. He began to worry and get depressed despite the fact she was altering those habit patterns to which he most objected. From then on, it became a therapeutic game of tennis. She served, he returned, and once in a while they both called foul or argued that there was no point in continuing the game. The rapidly bouncing ball of increasing marital disharmony was difficult to deal with, but in somewhat less than a year it was apparent that the tide of discontent was being swept back a bit at a time.

Georgia and her husband remain in therapy with me at the present time but I see them only once a week and I see them together rather than separately. They have learned how to argue openly with one another without being afraid that harsh words will destroy their marriage and they have learned something of the value of honest expression of one's feelings in times of acute psychological distress. A reasonably solid foundation is developing for their marriage and while it may never become a model for others, it will survive and, perhaps, prosper.

There is one drawback to this case. Georgia has become almost as calculatedly messy as she was neat. I have started to discuss this with her and to examine its reasons. It will take time, of course, but at least she has stopped criticizing the usual condition of my office. The most startling change is the one that has been brought about indirectly in the children. Both Georgia and her husband report that the kids seem much happier and better behaved than before. The youngest girl has taken to approaching either or both parents at odd times, hugging them, and telling them how much she loves them. Children are resilient and can bounce high once the pressure is removed from them. Children are also trustworthy weather vanes that record almost instantly shifts in life's winds.

There is no therapeutic magic in the case of Georgia M. She came to treatment an unusual combination of the obsessed and the rational, and the changes she effected were more in the nature of self-help than therapeutic wisdom and guidance. The substitution of love for hate in her life and her attempt to reduce the anxiety of just being alive clearly occurred as a reaction against things she found repulsive in her early life. This defense was an expensive choice in the currency of human relations and Georgia continues to pay the price in personal unhappiness. The future is a treacherous one for Georgia M.

As we read the case of Georgia M., we could see how one therapist's assumptions about the nature of personality influenced the progress of treatment. McNeil points out to us the part Georgia's husband played in subtly encouraging his wife's behavior. We can glimpse the impact of Georgia's problem on her children.

We have used a number of terms here rather freely. We refer to Georgia's "problem," her "treatment," her "therapy." But have we decided exactly what was wrong with Georgia? We do have a label. Georgia was *obsessive-compulsive.* But was Georgia sick? In discussing abnormal behavior we often hear phrases like "mentally ill" and "mentally disturbed." What, exactly, do these imply?

In the article following, psychiatrist Thomas Szasz disputes the use of these terms.

THE MYTH OF MENTAL ILLNESS
THOMAS S. SZASZ

My aim in this essay is to raise the question "Is there such a thing as mental illness?" and to argue that there is not. Since the notion of mental illness is extremely widely used nowadays, inquiry into the ways in which this term is employed would seem to be especially indicated. Mental illness, of course, is not literally a "thing"—or physical object—and hence it can "exist" only in the same sort of way in which other theoretical concepts exist. Yet, familiar theories are in the habit of posing, sooner or later—at least to those who come to believe in them—as "objective truths" (or "facts"). During certain historical periods, explanatory conceptions such as deities, witches, and microorganisms appeared not only as theories but as self-evident *causes* of a vast number of events. I submit that today mental illness is widely regarded in a somewhat similar fashion, that is, as the cause of innumerable diverse happenings. As an antidote to the complacent use of the notion of mental illness—whether as a self-evident phenomenon, theory, or cause—let us ask this question: "What is meant when it is asserted that someone is mentally ill?"

In what follows I shall describe briefly the main uses to which the concept of mental illness has been put. I shall argue that this notion has outlived whatever usefulness it might have had and that it now functions merely as a convenient myth.

SOURCE: From *American Psychologist*, 1960, *15*, 113–118. Copyright ©
1960 by the American Psychological Association, Inc. Reproduced by permission.

MENTAL ILLNESS
AS A SIGN OF
BRAIN DISEASE

The notion of mental illness derives its main support from such phenomena as syphilis of the brain or delirious conditions—intoxications, for instance—in which persons are known to manifest various peculiarities or disorders of thinking and behavior. Correctly speaking, however, these are diseases of the brain, not of the mind. According to one school of thought, *all* so-called mental illness is of this type. The assumption is made that some neurological defect, perhaps a very subtle one, will ultimately be found for all the disorders of thinking and behavior. Many contemporary psychiatrists, physicians, and other scientists hold this view. This position implies that people *cannot* have troubles —expressed in what are *now called* "mental illnesses"—because of differences in personal needs, opinions, social aspirations, values, and so on. *All problems in living* are attributed to physicochemical processes which in due time will be discovered by medical research.

"Mental illnesses" are thus regarded as basically no different from all other diseases (that is, of the body). The only difference, in this view, between mental and bodily diseases is that the former, affecting the brain, manifest themselves by means of mental symptoms; whereas the latter, affecting other organ systems (for example, the skin, liver, etc.), manifest themselves by means of symptoms referable to those parts of the body. This view rests on and expresses what are, in my opinion, two fundamental errors.

In the first place, what central nervous system symptoms would correspond to a skin eruption or a fracture? It would *not* be some emotion or complex bit of behavior. Rather, it would be blindness or a paralysis of some part of the body. The crux of the matter is that a disease of the brain, analogous to a disease of the skin or bone, is a neurological defect, and not a problem in living. For example, a *defect* in a person's visual field may be satisfactorily explained by correlating it with certain definite lesions in the nervous system. On the other hand, a person's *belief*—whether this be a belief in Christianity, in Communism, or in the idea that his internal organs are "rotting" and that his body is, in fact, already "dead"—cannot be explained by a defect or disease of the nervous system. Explanations of this sort of occurrence—assuming that one is interested in the belief itself and does not regard it simply as a "symptom" or expression of something else that is *more interesting*—must be sought along different lines.

The second error in regarding complex psychosocial behavior, consisting of communications about ourselves and the world about us, as mere symptoms of neurological functioning is *epistemological*. In other words, it is an error pertaining not to any mistakes in observation or reasoning, as such, but rather to the way in which we organize and express our knowledge. In the present case, the error lies in making a symmetrical dualism between mental and physical (or bodily) symptoms, a dualism which is merely a habit of speech and to which no known observations can be found to correspond. Let us see if this is so. In medical practice, when we speak of physical disturbances, we mean either signs (for example, a fever) or symptoms (for example, pain). We speak of mental symptoms, on the other hand, when we refer to a patient's *communications about himself, others, and the world about him.* He might state that he is Napoleon or that he is being persecuted by the Communists. These would be considered mental symptoms *only* if the observer believed that the patient was *not* Napoleon or that he was *not* being persecuted by the Communists. This makes it apparent that the statement that "X is a mental symptom" involves rendering a judgment. The judgment entails, moreover, a covert comparison or matching of the patient's ideas, concepts, or beliefs with those of the observer and the society in which they live. The notion of mental symptom is therefore inextricably tied to the *social* (including *ethical) context* in which it is made in much the same way as the notion of bodily symptom is tied to an *anatomical* and *genetic context* (Szasz, 1957a, 1957b).

To sum up what has been said thus far: I have tried to show that for those who regard mental symptoms as signs of brain disease, the concept of mental illness is unnecessary and misleading. For what they mean is that people so labeled suffer from diseases of the brain; and, if that is what they mean, it would seem better for the sake of clarity to say that and not something else.

MENTAL ILLNESS AS A NAME FOR PROBLEMS IN LIVING
The term "mental illness" is widely used to describe something which is very different from a disease of the brain. Many people today take it for granted that living is an arduous process. Its hardship for modern man, moreover, derives not so much from a struggle for biological survival as from the stresses and strains inherent in the social intercourse of complex human personalities. In this context, the notion of mental illness is used to identify or describe some feature of an individual's so-called personality. Mental illness—as a deformity of the personality, so to speak—is then regarded as the *cause* of the human disharmony. It is implicit in this view that social intercourse between people is regarded as something *inherently harmonious*, its disturbance being due solely to the presence of "mental illness" in many people. This is obviously fallacious reasoning, for it makes the abstraction "mental illness" into a *cause*, even though this abstraction was created in the first place to serve only as a short-

hand expression for certain types of human behavior. It now becomes necessary to ask: "What kinds of behavior are regarded as indicative of mental illness, and by whom?"

The concept of illness, whether bodily or mental, implies *deviation from some clearly defined norm*. In the case of physical illness, the norm is the structural and functional integrity of the human body. Thus, although the desirability of physical health, as such, is an ethical value, what health *is* can be stated in anatomical and physiological terms. What is the norm deviation from which is regarded as mental illness? This question cannot be easily answered. But whatever this norm might be, we can be certain of only one thing: namely, that it is a norm that must be stated in terms of *psychosocial, ethical,* and *legal* concepts. For example, notions such as "excessive repression" or "acting out an unconscious impulse" illustrate the use of psychological concepts for judging (so-called) mental health and illness. The idea that chronic hostility, vengefulness, or divorce are indicative of mental illness would be illustrations of the use of ethical norms (that is, the desirability of love, kindness, and a stable marriage relationship). Finally, the widespread psychiatric opinion that only a mentally ill person would commit homicide illustrates the use of a legal concept as a norm of mental health. The norm from which deviation is measured whenever one speaks of a mental illness is a *psychosocial and ethical one*. Yet, the remedy is sought in terms of *medical* measures which—it is hoped and assumed—are free from wide differences of ethical value. The definition of the disorder and the terms in which its remedy are sought are therefore at serious odds with one another. The practical significance of this covert conflict between the alleged nature of the defect and the remedy can hardly be exaggerated.

Having identified the norms used to measure deviations in cases of mental illness, we will now turn to the question: "Who defines the norms and hence the deviation?" Two basic answers may be offered: (*a*) It may be the person himself (that is, the patient) who decides that he deviates from a norm. For example, an artist may believe that he suffers from a work inhibition; and he may implement this conclusion by seeking help *for* himself from a psychotherapist. (*b*) It may be someone other than the patient who decides that the latter is deviant (for example, relatives, physicians, legal authorities, society generally, etc.). In such a case a psychiatrist may be hired by others to do something *to* the patient in order to correct the deviation.

These considerations underscore the importance of asking the question "Whose agent is the psychiatrist?" and of giving a candid answer to it (Szasz, 1956, 1958). The psychiatrist (psychologist or nonmedical psychotherapist), it now develops, may be the agent of the patient, of the relatives, of the school, of the military services, of a business organization, of a court of law, and so forth. In speaking of the psychiatrist as the agent of these persons or organizations, it is not implied that his values concerning norms, or his ideas and aims concerning the proper nature of remedial action, need to coincide exactly with those of his employer. For example, a patient in individual psychotherapy may believe that his salvation lies in a new marriage; his psychotherapist need not share this hypothesis. As the patient's agent, however, he must abstain from bringing social or legal force to bear on the patient which would prevent him from putting his beliefs into action. If his *contract* is with the patient, the psychiatrist (psychotherapist) may disagree with him or stop his treatment; but he cannot engage others to obstruct the patient's aspirations. Similarly, if a psychiatrist is engaged by a court to determine the sanity of a criminal, he need not fully share the legal authorities' values and intentions in regard to the criminal and the means available for dealing with him. But the psychiatrist is expressly barred from stating, for example, that it is not the criminal who is "insane" but the men who wrote the law on the basis of which the very actions that are being judged are regarded as "criminal." Such an opinion could be voiced, of course, but not in a courtroom, and not by a psychiatrist who makes it his practice to assist the court in performing its daily work.

To recapitulate: In actual contemporary social usage, the finding of a mental illness is made by establishing a deviance in behavior from certain psychosocial, ethical, or legal norms. The judgment may be made, as in medicine, by the patient, the physician (psychiatrist), or others. Remedial action, finally, tends to be sought in a therapeutic—or covertly medical—framework, thus creating a situation in which *psychosocial, ethical,* and/or *legal deviations* are claimed to be correctible by (so-called) *medical action.* Since medical action is designed to correct only medical deviations, it seems logically absurd to expect that it will help solve problems whose very existence had been defined and established on nonmedical grounds. I think that these considerations may be fruitfully applied to the present use of tranquilizers and, more generally, to what might be expected of drugs of whatever type in regard to the amelioration or solution of problems in human living.

THE ROLE OF ETHICS IN PSYCHIATRY Anything that people *do*—in contrast to things that *happen* to them (Peters, 1958)—takes place in a context of value. In this broad sense, no human activity is devoid of ethical implications.

When the values underlying certain activities are widely shared, those who participate in their pursuit may lose sight of them altogether. The discipline of medicine, both as a pure science (for example, research) and as a technology (for example, therapy), contains many ethical considerations and judgments. Unfortunately, these are often denied, minimized, or merely kept out of focus; for the ideal of the medical profession as well as of the people whom it serves seems to be having a system of medicine (allegedly) free of ethical value. This sentimental notion is expressed by such things as the doctor's willingness to treat and help patients irrespective of their religious or political beliefs, whether they are rich or poor, etc. While there may be some grounds for this belief—albeit it is a view that is not impressively true even in these regards—the fact remains that ethical considerations encompass a vast range of human affairs. By making the practice of medicine neutral in regard to some specific issues of value need not, and cannot, mean that it can be kept free from all such values. The practice of medicine is intimately tied to ethics; and the first thing that we must do, it seems to me, is to try to make this clear and explicit. I shall let this matter rest here, for it does not concern us specifically in this essay. Lest there be any vagueness, however, about how or where ethics and medicine meet, let me remind the reader of such issues as birth control, abortion, suicide, and euthanasia as only a few of the major areas of current ethicomedical controversy.

Psychiatry, I submit, is very much more intimately tied to problems of ethics than is medicine. I use the word "psychiatry" here to refer to that contemporary discipline which is concerned with *problems in living* (and not with diseases of the brain, which are problems for neurology). Problems in human relations can be analyzed, interpreted, and given meaning only within given social and ethical contexts. Accordingly, it *does* make a difference—arguments to the contrary notwithstanding—what the psychiatrist's socioethical orientations happen to be; for these will influence his ideas on what is wrong with the patient, what deserves comment or interpretation, in what possible directions change might be desirable, and so forth. Even in medicine proper, these factors play a role, as for instance, in the divergent orientations which physicians, depending on their religious affiliations, have toward such things as birth control and therapeutic abortion. Can anyone really believe that a psychotherapist's ideas concerning religious belief, slavery, or other similar issues play no role in his practical work? If they do make a difference, what are we to infer from it? Does it not seem reasonable that we ought to have different psychiatric therapies—each expressly recognized for the ethical positions which they embody—for, say, Catholics and Jews, religious persons and agnostics, democrats and communists, white supremacists and Negroes, and so on? Indeed, if we look at how psychiatry is actually practiced today (especially in the United States), we find that people do seek psychiatric help in accordance with their social status and ethical beliefs (Hollingshead & Redlich, 1958). This should really not surprise us more than being told that practicing Catholics rarely frequent birth control clinics.

The foregoing position which holds that contemporary psychotherapists deal with problems in living, rather than with mental illnesses and their cures, stands in opposition to a currently prevalent claim, according to which mental illness is just as "real" and "objective" as bodily illness. This is a confusing claim since it is never known exactly what is meant by such words as "real" and "objective." I suspect, however, that what is intended by the proponents of this view is to create the idea in the popular mind that mental illness is some sort of disease entity, like an infection or a malignancy. If this were true, one could *catch* or *get* a "mental illness," one might *have* or *harbor* it, one might *transmit* it to others, and finally one could get *rid* of it. In my opinion, there is not a shred of evidence to support this idea. To the contrary, all the evidence is the other way and supports the view that what people now call mental illnesses are for the most part *communications* expressing unacceptable ideas, often framed, moreover, in an unusual idiom. The scope of this essay allows me to do no more than mention this alternative theoretical approach to this problem (Szasz, 1957c).

This is not the place to consider in detail the similarities and differences between bodily and mental illnesses. It shall suffice for us here to emphasize only one important difference between them: namely, that whereas bodily disease refers to public, physicochemical occurrences, the notion of mental illness is used to codify relatively more private, sociopsychological happenings of which the observer (diagnostician) forms a part. In other words, the psychiatrist does not stand *apart* from what he observes, but is, in Harry Stack Sullivan's apt words, a "participant observer." This means that he is *committed* to some picture of what he considers reality—and to what he thinks society considers reality—and he observes and judges the patient's behavior in the light of these considerations. This touches on our earlier observation that the notion of mental symptom itself implies a comparison between observer and observed, psychiatrist and patient. This is so obvious that I may be charged with belaboring trivialities. Let me therefore say once more that my aim in presenting this argument was expressly to criticize and counter a prevailing contemporary tendency to deny the moral aspects of psychiatry (and psychotherapy) and to substitute for them allegedly value-free medical considerations. Psychotherapy, for example, is being widely practiced as though it entailed nothing other than restoring the patient from a state of mental sickness to one of mental health. While it is generally accepted that mental illness has something to do with man's social (or interpersonal) relations, it is paradoxically maintained that problems of values (that is, of ethics) do not arise in this process.[1] Yet, in one sense, much of psychotherapy may revolve around nothing other than the elucidation and weighing of goals and values—many of which may be mutually contradictory—and the means whereby they might best be harmonized, realized, or relinquished.

The diversity of human values and the methods by means of which they may be realized is so vast, and many of them remain so unacknowledged, that they cannot fail but lead to conflicts in human relations. Indeed, to say that human relations at all levels —from mother to child, through husband and wife, to nation and nation—are fraught with stress, strain, and disharmony is, once again, making the obvious explicit. Yet, what may be obvious may be also poorly understood. This I think is the case here. For it seems to me that—at least in our scientific theories of behavior—we have failed to *accept* the simple fact that human relations are inherently fraught with difficulties and that to make them even relatively harmonious requires much patience and hard work. I submit that the idea of mental illness is now being put to work to obscure certain difficulties which at present may be inherent—not that they need be unmodifiable—in the social intercourse of persons. If this is true, the concept functions as a disguise; for instead of calling attention to conflicting human needs, aspirations, and values, the notion of mental illness provides an amoral and impersonal "thing" (an "illness") as an explanation for *problems in living* (Szasz, 1959). We may recall in this connection that not so long ago it was devils and witches who were held responsible for men's problems in social living. The belief in mental illness, as something other than man's trouble in getting along with his fellow man, is the proper heir to the belief in demonology and witchcraft. Mental illness exists or is "real" in exactly the same sense in which witches existed or were "real."

[1] Freud went so far as to say that: "I consider ethics to be taken for granted. Actually I have never done a mean thing" (Jones, 1957, p. 247). This surely is a strange thing to say for someone who has studied man as a social being as closely as did Freud. I mention it here to show how the notion of "illness" (in the case of psychoanalysis, "psychopathology," or "mental illness") was used by Freud—and by most of his followers—as a means for classifying certain forms of human behavior as falling within the scope of medicine, and hence (by *fiat*) outside that of ethics!

CHOICE,
RESPONSIBILITY,
AND PSYCHIATRY

While I have argued that mental illnesses do not exist, I obviously did not imply that the social and psychological occurrences to which this label is currently being attached also do not exist. Like the personal and social troubles which people had in the Middle Ages, they are real enough. It is the labels we give them that concerns us and, having labelled them, what we do about them. While I cannot go into the ramified implications of this problem here, it is worth noting that a demonologic conception of problems in living gave rise to therapy along theological lines. Today, a belief in mental illness implies—nay, requires—therapy along medical or psychotherapeutic lines.

What is implied in the line of thought set forth here is something quite different. I do not intend to offer a new conception of "psychiatric illness" nor a new form of "therapy." My aim is more modest and yet also more ambitious. It is to suggest that the phenomena now called mental illnesses be looked at afresh and more simply, that they be removed from the category of illnesses, and that they be regarded as the expressions of man's struggle with the problem of *how* he should live. The last mentioned problem is obviously a vast one, its enormity reflecting not only man's inability to cope with his environment, but even more his increasing self-reflectiveness.

By problems in living, then, I refer to that truly explosive chain reaction which began with man's fall from divine grace by partaking of the fruit of the tree of knowledge. Man's awareness of himself and of the world about him seems to be a steadily expanding one, bringing in its wake an ever larger *burden of understanding* (an expression borrowed from Susanne Langer, 1953). *This burden, then, is to be expected and must not be misinterpreted.* Our only *rational* means for lightening it is *more understanding,* and appropriate *action* based on such understanding. The main alternative lies in acting as though the burden were not what in fact we perceive it to be and taking refuge in an outmoded theological view of man. In the latter view, man does not fashion his life and much of his world about him, but merely lives out his fate in a world created by superior beings. This may logically lead to pleading nonresponsibility in the face of seemingly unfathomable problems and difficulties. Yet, if man fails to take increasing responsibility for his actions, individually as well as collectively, it seems unlikely that some higher power or being would assume this task and carry this burden for him. Moreover, this seems hardly the proper time in human history for obscuring the issue of man's responsibility for his actions by hiding it behind the skirt of an all-explaining conception of mental illness.

CONCLUSIONS   I have tried to show that the notion of mental illness has out-lived whatever usefulness it might have had and that it now functions merely as a convenient myth. As such, it is a true heir to religious myths in general, and to the belief in witchcraft in particular; the role of all these belief-systems was to act as *social tranquilizers*, thus encouraging the hope that mastery of certain specific problems may be achieved by means of substitutive (symbolic-magical) operations. The notion of mental illness thus serves mainly to obscure the everyday fact that life for most people is a continuous struggle, not for biological survival, but for a "place in the sun," "peace of mind," or some other human value. For man aware of himself and of the world about him, once the needs for preserving the body (and perhaps the race) are more or less satisfied, the problem arises as to what he should do with himself. Sustained adherence to the myth of mental illness allows people to avoid facing this problem, believing that mental health, conceived as the absence of mental illness, automatically insures the making of right and safe choices in one's conduct of life. But the facts are all the other way. It is the making of good choices in life that others regard, retrospectively, as good mental health!

The myth of mental illness encourages us, moreover, to believe in its logical corollary: that social intercourse would be harmonious, satisfying, and the secure basis of a "good life" were it not for the disrupting influences of mental illness or "psychopathology." The potentiality for universal human happiness, in this form at least, seems to me but another example of the I-wish-it-were-true type of fantasy. I do believe that human happiness or well-being on a hitherto unimaginably large scale, and not just for a select few, is possible. This goal could be achieved, however, only at the cost of many men, and not just a few being willing and able to tackle their personal, social, and ethical conflicts. This means having the courage and integrity to forego waging battles on false fronts, finding solutions for substitute problems—for instance, fighting the battle of stomach acid and chronic fatigue instead of facing up to a marital conflict.

Our adversaries are not demons, witches, fate, or mental illness. We have no enemy whom we can fight, exorcise, or dispel by "cure." What we do have are *problems in living*—whether these be biologic, economic, political, or sociopsychological. In this essay I was concerned only with problems belonging in the last mentioned category, and within this group mainly with those pertaining to moral values. The field to which modern psychiatry addresses itself is vast, and I made no effort to encompass it all. My argument was limited to the proposition that mental illness is a myth, whose function it is to disguise and thus render more palatable the bitter pill of moral conflicts in human relations.

REFERENCES

Hollingshead, A. B., & Redlich, F. C. *Social class and mental illness.* New York: Wiley, 1958.

Jones, E. *The life and work of Sigmund Freud.* Vol. III. New York: Basic Books, 1957.

Langer, S. K. *Philosophy in a new key.* New York: Mentor Books, 1953.

Peters, R. S. *The concept of motivation.* London: Routledge & Kegan Paul, 1958.

Szasz, T. S. Malingering: "Diagnosis" or social condemnation? *AMA Arch Neurol. Psychiat.*, 1956, *76,* 432-443.

Szasz, T. S. *Pain and pleasure: A study of bodily feelings.* New York: Basic Books, 1957.   (a)

Szasz, T. S. The problem of psychiatric nosology: A contribution to a situational analysis of psychiatric operations. *American Journal of Psychiatry,* 1957, *114,* 405-413.   (b)

Szasz, T. S. On the theory of psychoanalytic treatment. *International Journal of Psycho-Analysis,* 1957, *38,* 166-182.   (c)

Szasz, T. S. Psychiatry, ethics and the criminal law. *Columbia Law Review,* 1958, *58,* 183-198.

Szasz, T. S. Moral conflict and psychiatry, *Yale Review,* 1960, *49,* 555–566.

Szasz talks of "sociopsychological problems in living." It would be misleading to imply that there are always nice solutions to problems arising when the needs of the individual collide head-on with those of society. We do not know that the individual *should* always "fit in." The authors of the next selection are two black psychiatrists who are acutely aware of this issue.

43

A WORD ON THE NATURE OF MENTAL ILLNESS AND TREATMENT

WILLIAM H. GRIER AND PRICE M. COBBS

Mental illness arises from a conflict between the inner drives pushing for individual gratification and the group demands of the external environment. The method of expressing inner needs has developed in contact with and in response to the environment provided by the parents and that segment of the broader society which impinges on the child. It is as if the child takes into himself a part of the world he experiences while quite young and makes that an integral part of his inner self. It is the synthesis of his own personal drives and his early, now incorporated, environment that he subsequently elaborates into his inner self and it is this which is in conflict with the external world.

Something must change—his inner world, the outer world, or both. Too much psychotherapy involves striving only for a change in the inner world and a consequent adaptation to the world outside. Black people cannot abide this and thoughtful therapists know it. A black man's soul can live only if it is oriented toward a change of the social order. A good therapist helps a man change his inner life so that he can more effectively change his outer world.

Finally, psychotherapy itself is an indifferent instrument, profoundly effective in the hands of an artist, and worse than a waste of time in the hands of an incompetent. The interpretations and constructions are important, but a lot of patients have been made well with inexact interpretations. The essential ingredient is the capacity of the therapist to love his patient—to say to him that here is a second chance to organize his inner life, to say that you have a listener and companion who wants you to make it. If you must weep, I'll wipe your tears. If you must hit someone, hit me, I can take it. I will, in fact, do *anything* to help you be what you can be—my love for you is of such an order.

How many people, black or white, can so open their arms to a suffering black man?

Contempt and hatred of black people is so thoroughly a part of the American personality that a profound convulsion of society may be required to help a dark child over his fear of the dark.

SOURCE: Excerpted from *Black Rage* by William H. Grier and Price M. Cobbs; Basic Books, Inc., Publishers, New York, 1968. Pp. 150–151.

We have said before that the "healthy personality" must be defined in the context of the society in which the individual lives. What is considered maladjusted today in this society may be perfectly acceptable behavior in another culture or another time. The same act may alternately be described as heroic in wartime and demented in peace. Walking about unclothed may be unremarkable for an Australian aborigine, yet be seen as sexual perversion on the streets of New York.

Recently a psychiatrist from India, now working in Great Britain, gave us an example of this discrepancy. If someone in Britain were to indicate to his psychiatrist that he had been talking with God, the psychiatrist would consider this a significant symptom of some kind of disturbance. In India, were a patient to state that he had been talking with God, the psychiatrist would consider it a strength on which to build.

Suicide is another example. In Japan and in India the taking of one's own life has been considered acceptable behavior. Under some circumstances it was considered the *only* honorable course of action. The humiliated Samurai in Japan who did not commit *hara-kiri* or the bereft widow in India who did not commit *suttee* was usually put to death by the aggrieved contemporaries.

Today, in our Western society, we tend to see suicide as maladjusted behavior. We actively deny the individual the right to take his own life. If he tries to do so, and fails, he is strongly encouraged to seek psychotherapy. The following selection was written by a man who *did* try to end his own life, and who very nearly succeeded. As you read, ask yourself: Was this man sick? Did he have the right to kill himself? Could anyone have helped him? How?

ATTEMPT

A. ALVAREZ

> This is the Hour of Lead—
> Remembered, if outlived,
> As Freezing persons, recollect the Snow—
> First—Chill—then Stupor—then the letting go.
> —Emily Dickinson

I have to admit that I am a failed suicide. It is a dismal confession to make, since nothing, really, would seem to be easier than to take your own life. Seneca, the classical authority on the subject, pointed out disdainfully that the exits are everywhere: each precipice and river, each branch of each tree, every vein in your body will set you free. But in the event, this isn't so. No one is promiscuous in his way of dying. A man who has decided to hang himself will never jump in front of a train; and the more sophisticated and painless the method, the greater the chance of failure. I can vouch, at least, for that. I built up to the act carefully and for a long time, with a kind of blank pertinacity. It was the one constant focus of my life, making everything else irrelevant, a diversion. Each sporadic burst of work, each minor success and disappointment, each moment of calm and relaxation, seemed merely a temporary halt on my steady descent through layer after layer of depression, like a lift stopping for a moment on the way down to the basement. At no point was there any question of getting off or of changing the direction of the journey. Yet, despite all that, I never quite made it.

I see now that I had been incubating this death far longer than I recognized at the time. When I was a child, both my parents had halfheartedly put their heads in the gas oven. Or so they claimed. It seemed to me then a rather splendid gesture, though shrouded in mystery, a little area of veiled intensity, revealed only by hints and unexplained, swiftly suppressed outbursts. It was something hidden, attractive, and not for the children, like sex. But it was also something that undoubtedly did happen to grown-ups. However hysterical or comic the behavior involved—and to a child it seemed more ludicrous than tragic to lay your head in the greasy gas oven, like the Sunday joint—suicide was a fact, a subject that couldn't be denied; it was something, however awful, that people did. When my own time came, I did not have to discover it for myself.

Maybe that is why, when I grew up and things went particularly badly, I used to say to myself, over and over, like some latter-day Mariana in the Moated Grange, "I wish I were dead." It was an echo from the past, joining me to my tempestuous childhood. I muttered it unthinkingly, as automatically as a Catholic priest tells his rosary. It was my special magic ritual for warding off devils, a verbal nervous tic. Dwight Macdonald once said that when you don't know what to do with your hands, you light a cigarette, and when you don't know what to do with your mind, you read *Time* magazine. My equivalent was this one sentence repeated until it seemingly lost all meaning: "Iwishiweredead. Iwishiweredead. Iwishiweredead . . ." Then one day I understood what I was saying. I was walking along the edge of Hampstead Heath, after some standard domestic squabble, and suddenly I heard the phrase as though for the first time. I stood still to attend to the words. I repeated them slowly, listening. And realized that I meant it. It seemed so ob-

vious, an answer I had known for years and never allowed myself to acknowledge. I couldn't understand how I could have
been so obtuse for so long.

After that, there was only one way out, although it took a
long time—many months, in fact—to get there. We moved to
America—wife, child, *au pair* girl, myself, and trunk-load upon
trunk-load of luggage. I had a term's appointment at a New
England university and had rented a great professorial mansion
in a respectably dead suburb, ten miles from the campus, two
from the nearest shop. It was Germanic, gloomy, and far too
expensive. For my wife, who didn't drive, it was also as lonely
as Siberia. The neighbors were mostly twice her age, the university mostly ignored us, the action was nil. There wasn't even a
television set in the house. So I rented one, and she sat disconso-
lately in front of it for two months. Then she gave up, packed
her bags, and took the child back to England. I didn't even blame
her. But I stayed on in a daze of misery. The last slide down the
ice slope had begun, and there was no way of stopping it.

My wife was not to blame. The hostility and despair that poor
girl provoked in me—and I in her—came from some pure, infantile source, as any disinterested outsider could have told me.
I even recognized this for myself in my clear moments. I was
using her as an excuse for troubles that had their roots deep in
the past. But mere intellectual recognition did no good, and
anyway, my clear moments were few. My life felt so cluttered
and obstructed that I could hardly breathe. I inhabited a closed,
concentrated world, airless and without exits. I doubt if any of
this was noticeable socially: I was simply tenser, more nervous
than usual, and I drank more. But underneath I was going a bit
mad; my life was being lived for me by forces I couldn't control.

When the Christmas break came at the university, I decided
to spend the fortnight in London. Maybe, I told myself, things
would be easier; at least I would see the child. So I loaded myself up with presents and climbed on a jet, dead drunk. I passed
out as soon as I reached my seat and woke to a brilliant sunrise.
There were dark islands below—the Hebrides, I suppose—and
the eastern sea was on fire. From that altitude, the world looked
calm and vivid and possible. But by the time we landed at Prest-
wick the clouds were down like the black cap on a hanging
judge. We waited and waited hopelessly on the runway, the
rain drumming on the fuselage, until the soaking fog lifted at
London Airport.

When I finally got home, hours late, no one was there. The
fires were blazing, the clocks were ticking, the telephone was
still. I wandered around the empty house touching things, frightened, expectant. Fifteen minutes later, there was a noise at the

front door and my child plunged shouting up the stairs into my arms. Over his shoulder I could see my wife standing tentatively in the hall; she, too, looked scared.

"We thought you were lost," she said. "We went down to the terminal and you didn't come."

"I got a lift straight from the airport. I phoned but you must have left. I'm sorry."

Chilly and uncertain, she presented her cheek to be kissed. I obliged, holding my son in my arms. There was still a week until Christmas.

We didn't stand a chance. Within hours we were at each other again, and that night I started drinking. Mostly, I'm a social drinker. Like everyone else, I've been drunk in my time, but it's not really my style; I value my control too highly. This time, however, I went at the bottle with a pure need, as though parched. I drank before I got out of bed, almost before my eyes were open. I continued steadily throughout the morning until, by lunchtime, I had half a bottle of whiskey inside me and was beginning to feel human. Not drunk: that first half-bottle simply brought me to that point of calm where I usually began—which is not particularly calm. Around lunchtime a friend—also depressed, also drinking—joined me at the pub, and we boozed until closing time. Back home with our wives, we kept at it steadily through the afternoon and evening, late into the night. The important thing was not to stop. In this way, I got through a bottle of whiskey a day, and a good deal of wine and beer. Yet it had little effect. Toward evening, when the child was in bed, I suppose I was a little tipsy, but the drinking was merely part of a more jagged frenzy which possessed us all. We kept the hi-fi booming pop, we danced, we had trials of strength: one-arm press-ups, handstands, somersaults; we balanced pint pots of beer on our foreheads, and tried to lie down and stand up again without spilling them. Anything not to stop, think, feel. The tension was so great that without the booze we would have splintered into sharp fragments.

On Christmas Eve, the other couple went off on a skiing holiday. My wife and I were left staring at each other. Silently and meticulously, we decorated the Christmas tree and piled the presents, waiting. There was nothing left to say.

Late that afternoon I had sneaked off and phoned the psychotherapist whom I had been seeing, on and off, before I left for the States.

"I'm feeling pretty bad," I said. "Could I possibly see you?"

There was a pause. "It's rather difficult," he said at last. "Are you really desperate, or could you wait till Boxing Day?"

Poor bastard, I thought, he's got his Christmas too. Let it go. "I can wait."

"Are you sure?" He sounded relieved. "You could come round at six thirty, if it's urgent."

That was the child's bedtime; I wanted to be there. "It's all right," I said, "I'll phone later. Happy Christmas." What does it matter? I went back downstairs.

All my life I have hated Christmas: the unnecessary presents and obligatory cheerfulness, the grinding expense, the anticlimax. It is a day to be negotiated with infinite care, like a minefield. So I fortified myself with a stiff shot of whiskey before I got up. It combined with my child's excitement to put a glow of hope on the day. The boy sat among the gaudy wrapping paper, ribbons, and bows, positively crowing with delight. At three years old, even Christmas can be a pleasure. Maybe, I began to feel, this thing could be survived. After all, hadn't I flown all the way from the States to pull my marriage from the fire? Or had I? Perhaps I knew it was unsavable and didn't want it to be otherwise. Perhaps I was merely seeking a plausible excuse for doing myself in. Perhaps that was why, even before all the presents were unwrapped, I had started it all up again: silent rages (not in front of the child), muted recriminations, withdrawals. The marriage was just one aspect of a whole life I had decided, months before, to have done with.

I remember little of what happened later. There was the usual family turkey for the child and my parents-in-law. In the evening we went out to a smart and subdued dinner party, and on from there, I think, to something wilder. But I'm not sure. I recall only two trivial but vivid scenes. The first is very late at night. We are back home with another couple whom I know only slightly. He is small, dapper, cheerful, an unsuccessful poet turned successful journalist. His wife is faceless now, but him I still see sometimes on television, reporting expertly from the more elegant foreign capitals. I remember him sitting at our old piano, playing 1930s dance tunes; his wife stands behind him, singing the words; I lean on the piano, humming tunelessly; my wife is stretched, glowering, on the sofa. We are all very drunk.

Later still, I remember standing at the front door, joking with them as they negotiate the icy steps. As they go through the gate, they turn and wave. I wave back. "Happy Christmas," we call to each other. I close the door and return to my wife.

After that, I remember nothing at all until I woke up in the hospital and saw my wife's face swimming vaguely toward me through a yellowish fog. She was crying. But that was three days later, three days of oblivion, a hole in my head.

It happened ten years ago now, and only gradually have I been able to piece together the facts from hints and snippets, recalled reluctantly and with apologies. Nobody wants to remind an attempted suicide of his folly, or to be reminded of it. Tact and taste forbid. Or is it the failure itself which is embarrassing? Certainly, a successful suicide inspires no delicacy at all; everybody is in on the act at once with his own exclusive inside story. In my own case, my knowledge of what happened is partial and secondhand; the only accurate details are in the gloomy shorthand of the medical reports. Not that it matters, since none of it now means much to me personally. It is as though it had all happened to another person in another world.

It seems that when the poet-journalist left with his wife, we had one final, terrible quarrel, more bitter than anything we had managed before, and savage enough to be heard through his sleep by whoever it was who was staying the night in the guest room above. At the end of it, my wife marched out. When she had returned prematurely from the States, our own house was still let out to temporary tenants. So she had rented a dingy flat in a florid but battered Victorian mansion nearby. Since she still had the key to the place, she went to spend the night there. In my sodden despair, I suppose her departure seemed like the final nail. More likely, it was the unequivocal excuse I had been waiting for. I went upstairs to the bathroom and swallowed forty-five sleeping pills.

I had been collecting the things for months obsessively, like Green Stamps, from doctors on both sides of the Atlantic. This was an almost legitimate activity since, in all that time, I rarely got more than two consecutive hours of sleep a night. But I had always made sure of having more than I needed. Weeks before I left America, I stopped taking the things and began hoarding them in preparation for the time I knew was coming. When it finally arrived, a box was waiting stuffed with pills of all colors, like Smarties. I gobbled the lot.

The following morning the guest brought me a cup of tea. The bedroom curtains were drawn, so he could not see me properly in the gloom. He heard me breathing in an odd way but thought it was probably a hangover. So he left me alone. My wife got back at noon, took one look, and called the ambulance. When they got me to the hospital I was, the report says, "deeply unconscious, slightly cyanosed, vomit in mouth, pulse rapid, poor volume." I have looked up "cyanosis" in the dictionary: "A morbid condition in which the surface of the body becomes blue because of insufficient aeration of the blood." Apparently, I had vomited in my coma and swallowed the stuff; it was now blocking my right lung, turning my face blue. As they say, a morbid condition. When they pumped the barbiturates out of my stomach, I vomited again, much more heavily, and again the muck went down to my lungs, blocking them badly. At that point I became—that word again—"deeply cyanosed"; I turned Tory blue. They tried to suck the stuff out, and gave me oxygen and an injection, but neither had much effect. I suppose it was about this time that they told my wife there wasn't much hope. This was all she ever told me of the whole incident; it was a source of great bitterness to her. Since my lungs were still blocked, they performed a bronchoscopy. This time they sucked out a "large amount of mucus." They stuck an air pipe down my throat and I began to breathe more deeply. The crisis, for the moment, was over.

This was on Boxing Day, December 26. I was still unconscious the next day and most of the day after that, though all the time less and less deeply. Since my lungs remained obstructed, they continued to give me air through a pipe; they fed me intravenously through a drip tube. The shallower my coma, the more restless I became. On the evening of the second day the airway was removed. During the afternoon of the third day, December 28, I came to. I felt them pull a tube from my arm. In a fog I saw my wife smiling hesitantly and in tears. It was all very vague. I slept.

I spent most of the next day weeping quietly and seeing everything double. Two women doctors gently cross-questioned me. Two chunky physiotherapists, with beautiful, blooming, double complexions, put me through exercises—it seems my lungs were still in a bad state. I got two trays of uneatable food at a time and tried, on and off and unsuccessfully, to do two crossword puzzles. The ward was thronged with elderly twins.

At some point, the police came, since in those days suicide was still a criminal offense. They sat heavily but rather sympathetically by my bed and asked me questions they clearly didn't want me to answer. When I tried to explain, they shushed me politely. "It was an accident, wasn't it, sir?" Dimly, I agreed. They went away.

I woke during the night and heard someone cry out weakly. A nurse bustled down the aisle in the obscure light. From the other side of the ward came more weak moaning. It was taken up faintly from somewhere else in the dimness. None of it was desperate with the pain and sharpness you hear after operations or accidents. Instead, the note was enervated, wan, beyond feeling. And then I understood why, even to my double vision, the patients had all seemed so old: I was in a terminal ward. All around me, old men were trying feebly not to die; I was thirty-one years old and, despite everything, still alive. When I stirred in bed I felt, for the first time, a rubber sheet beneath me. I must have peed myself, like a small child, while I was unconscious. My whole world was shamed.

The following morning my double vision had gone. The ward was filthy yellow and seemed foggy in the corners. I tottered to the lavatory; it, too, was filthy and evil-smelling. I tottered back to bed, rested a little, and then phoned my wife. Since the pills and the booze hadn't killed me, nothing would. I told her I was coming home. I wasn't dead, so I wasn't going to die. There was no point in staying.

The doctors didn't see it that way. I was scarcely off the danger list; my lungs were in a bad state; I had a temperature; I could relapse at any time; it was dangerous; it was stupid; they would not be responsible. I lay there dumbly, as weak as a newborn infant, and let the arguments flow over me. Finally, I signed a sheaf of forms acknowledging that I had left against advice and absolving them from responsibility. A friend drove me home.

It took all my strength and concentration to climb the one flight of stairs to the bedroom. I felt fragile and almost transparent, as though I were made of tissue paper. But when I got into pajamas and settled into bed, I found I smelled bad to myself: of illness, urine, and a thin, sour death-sweat. So I rested for a while and then took a bath. Meanwhile, my wife, on orders from the hospital, phoned our National Health doctor. He listened to her explanation without a word and then refused, point blank, to come. Clearly, he thought I was going to die and didn't want me counted on his, no doubt already prodigious, score. She banged down the receiver on him in a rage, but my green face and utter debility frightened her. Someone had to be sent for. Finally, the friend who had driven me home from the hospital called in his private family doctor. Authoritative, distinguished, unflappable, he came immediately and soothed everyone down.

This was on the evening of Thursday, the twenty-ninth. All Friday and Saturday I lay vaguely in bed. Occasionally, I raised myself to perform the exercises which were supposed to help my lungs. I talked a little to my child, tried to read, dozed. But mostly, I did nothing. My mind was blank. At times I listened to my breath coming and going; at times I was dimly aware of my heart beating. It filled me with distaste. I did not want to be alive.

On Friday night I had a terrible dream. I was dancing a savage, stamping dance with my wife, full of anger and mutual threat. Gradually, the movements became more and more frenzied, until every nerve and muscle in my body was stretched taut and vibrating, as though on some fierce, ungoverned electrical machine which, fraction by fraction, was pulling me apart. When I woke, I was wet with sweat, but my teeth were chattering as if I were freezing. I dozed off almost at once and again went through a similar dream: this time I was being hunted down; when the creature, whatever it was, caught me, it shook me as a dog shakes a rat, and once again every joint and nerve and muscle seemed to be rattling apart. Finally, I came awake completely and lay staring at the curtains. I was wide-eyed and shuddering with fear. I felt I had tasted in my dreams the death which had been denied me in my coma. My wife was sleeping in the same bed with me, yet she was utterly beyond my reach. I lay there for a long time, sweating and trembling. I have never felt so lonely.

Saturday night was New Year's Eve. Before I even arrived back from the States, we had arranged a party; there seemed no point now, despite everything, in calling it off. I had promised the doctor to spend it in bed, so for a while I held court regally in pajamas and dressing gown. But this was an irritating, self-important posture. Friends came up to see me out of a sense of duty—they had been told I had had pneumonia. Obviously, they were bored. The music and voices below were enticing, and, anyway, I had nothing now to lose. At ten thirty I got up, just to see in the new year, I said. I got back to bed at six the following morning. At 10 a.m. I was up again and went down to help clean the house while my wife slept on. The debris of that New Year's binge seemed to me like the debris of the monstrous life I had been leading. I set to work cheerfully and with a will, mopping up, polishing, throwing things away. At lunchtime, when my wife staggered down, hung over, the house was sparkling.

A week later, I returned to the States to finish the university term. While I was packing, I found, in the ticket pocket of my favorite jacket, a large, bright-yellow, torpedo-shaped pill, which I had conned out of a heavily insomniac American the day I left. I stared at the thing, turning it over and over in my palm, wondering how I'd missed it on *the* night. It looked lethal. I had survived forty-five pills. Would forty-six have done it? I flushed the thing down the lavatory.

And that was that. Of course, my marriage was finished. We hung on a few months more for decency's sake, but neither of us could continue in the shadow of such blackmail. By the time we parted, there was nothing left. Inevitably, I went through the expected motions of distress. But in my heart, I no longer cared.

The truth is, in some way I *had* died. The overintensity, the tiresome excess of sensitivity and self-consciousness, of arrogance and idealism, which came in adolescence and stayed on and on beyond their due time, like some visiting bore, had not survived the coma. It was as though I had finally, and sadly late in the day, lost my innocence. Like all young people, I had been high-minded and apologetic, full of enthusiasm I didn't quite mean and guilts I didn't understand. Because of them, I had forced my poor wife, who was far too young to know what was happening, into a spoiling, destructive role she had never sought. We had spent five years thrashing around in confusion, as drowning men pull each other under. Then I had lain for three days in abeyance, and awakened to feel nothing but a faint revulsion from everything and everyone. My weakened body, my thin breath, the slightest flicker of emotion filled me with distaste. I wanted only to be left to myself. Then, as the months passed, I began gradually to stir into another style of life, less theoretical, less optimistic, less vulnerable. I was ready for an insentient middle age.

Above all, I was disappointed. Somehow, I felt, death had let me down; I had expected more of it. I had looked for something overwhelming, an experience which would clarify all my confusions. But it turned out to be simply a denial of experience. All I knew of death were the terrifying dreams which came later. Blame it, perhaps, on my delayed adolescence: adolescents always expect too much; they want solutions to be immediate and neat, instead of gradual and incomplete. Or blame it on the cinema: secretly, I had thought death would be like the last reel of one of those old Hitchcock thrillers, when the hero relives as an adult that traumatic moment in childhood when the horror and splitting-off took place, and thereby becomes free and at peace with himself. It is a well-established, much-imitated, and persuasive formula. Hitchcock does it best, but he himself did not invent it; he was simply popularizing a new tradition of half-digested psychoanalytic talk about "abreaction," that crucial moment of cathartic truth when the complex is removed. Behind that is the old belief in last-moment revelations, deathbed conversions, and all those old wives tales of the drowning man reliving his life as he goes down for the last time. Behind that again is an older tradition still: that of the Last Judgment and the afterlife. We all expect something of death, even if it's only damnation.

But all I had got was oblivion. To all intents and purposes, I had died: my face had been blue, my pulse erratic, my breathing ineffectual; the doctors had given me up. I went to the edge and most of the way over; then gradually, unwillingly, and despite everything, I had inched my way back. And now I knew nothing at all about it. I felt cheated.

Why had I been so sure of finding some kind of answer? There are always special reasons why a man should choose to die in one way rather than in another, and my own reasons for taking barbiturates were cogent enough, although I did not recognize them at the time. As a small baby, I had been given a general anesthetic when a major operation was performed on my ankle. The surgery had not been a great success and regularly throughout my childhood the thing gave me trouble. Always the attacks were heralded by the same dream: I had to work out a complicated mathematical problem which involved my whole family; their well-being depended on my finding the right answer. The sum changed as I grew, becoming more sophisticated as I learned more mathematics, always keeping one step ahead of me, like the carrot and the donkey. Yet I knew that however complex the problem, the answer would be simple. It merely eluded me. Then, when I was fourteen, my appendix was removed, and I was once again put under a general anesthetic. The dream, by then, had not recurred for a year or two. But as I began to breathe in the ether, the whole thing happened again. When the first sharp draft of gas entered my lungs, I saw the problem, this time in calculus, glowing like a neon sign, with all my family crowding around, dangling, as it were, from the terms. I breathed out, and then, as I drew in the next lungful of ether, the figures whirred like the circuits of a computer, the stages of the equation raced in front of me, and I had the answer: a simple two-figure number. I had known it all along. For three days after I came round, I still knew that simple solution, and why and how it was so. I didn't have a care in the world. Then gradually it faded. But the dream never returned.

I thought death would be like that: a synoptic vision of life, crisis by crisis, all suddenly explained, justified, redeemed, a Last Judgment in the coils and circuits of the brain. Instead, all I got was a hole in the head, a round zero, nothing. I'd been swindled.

Months later, I began to understand that I had had my answer after all. The despair that had led me to try to kill myself had been pure and unadulterated, like the final, unanswerable despair a child feels, with no before or after. And childishly, I had expected death not merely to end it but also to explain it. Then, when death let me down, I gradually saw that I had been using the wrong language; I had translated the thing into Americanese. Too many movies, too many novels, too many trips to the States, had switched my understanding into a hopeful, alien tongue. I no longer thought of myself as unhappy; instead, I had "problems"—which is an optimistic way of putting it, since problems imply solutions, whereas unhappiness is merely a condition of life which you must live with, like the weather. Once I had accepted that there weren't ever going to be any answers, even in death, I found to my surprise that I didn't much care whether I was happy or unhappy; "problems" and "the problem of problems" no longer existed. And that in itself is already the beginning of happiness.

It seems ludicrous now to have learned something so obvious in such a hard way, to have had to go almost the whole way into death in order to grow up. Somewhere, I still feel cheated and aggrieved, and also ashamed of my stupidity. Yet, in the end, even oblivion was an experience of a kind. Certainly, nothing has been quite the same since I discovered for myself, in my own body and on my own nerves, that death is simply an end, a dead end, no more, no less. And I wonder if that piece of knowledge isn't in itself a form of death. After all, the youth who swallowed the sleeping pills and the man who survived are so utterly different that someone or something must have died. Before the pills was another life, another person altogether, whom I scarcely recognize and don't much like—although I suspect that he was, in his priggish way, far more likable than I could ever be. Meanwhile, his fury and despair seem improbable now, sad and oddly diminished.

The hole in my head lasted a long time. For five years after the event I had periods of sheer blankness, as though some vital center had been knocked out of action. For days on end, I went around like a zombie, a walking corpse. And I used to wonder, in a vague, numb way, if maybe I had died, after all. But if so, how could I ever tell?

In time, even that passed. Years later, when the house where it had happened was finally sold, I felt a sharp pang of regret for all the exorbitant pain and waste. After that, the episode lost its power. It became just so much dead history, a gossipy, mildly interesting anecdote about someone half-forgotten. As Coriolanus said, "There is a world elsewhere."

As for suicide: the sociologists and psychologists who talk of it as a disease puzzle me now as much as the Catholics and Muslims who call it the most deadly of mortal sins. It seems to me to be somehow as much beyond social or psychic prophylaxis as it is beyond morality, a terrible but utterly natural reaction to the strained, narrow, unnatural necessities we sometimes create for ourselves. And it is not for me. Perhaps I am no longer optimistic enough; I assume now that death, when it finally comes, will probably be nastier than suicide, and certainly a great deal less convenient.

MORE "ABNORMAL" PEOPLE

Alan A. Stone and Sue Smart Stone introduce their book *The Abnormal Personality Through Literature* (Prentice-Hall, 1966) with a poem by Emily Dickinson:

> Much madness is divinest sense
> To a discerning eye:
> Much sense the starkest madness.
> 'Tis the majority
> In this, as all, prevails.
> Assent, and you are sane:

Demur, — you're straightway dangerous,
And handled with a chain.

This is but a sample of the collection of excerpts from the literature of the world to be found in the Stones' book. Each excerpt is chosen to illustrate some facet of the human personality. The interested student might find this approach useful in identifying psychological principles in other literature he encounters.

If you found the case history of Georgia M. intriguing, you will wish to read all of Elton McNeil, *The Quiet Furies* (Prentice-Hall, 1967). Another collection of stories, this time first-person accounts of personality disturbance, is to be found in Bert Kaplan (Ed.), *The Inner World of Mental Illness* (Harper and Row, 1964). Some of our students have read this book and have found it fascinating. As one student wrote, "The essays are surprisingly well-written and give a real feel for what it is like to be mentally ill and treated as such."

Letters From Jenny, by Gordon W. Allport (Harbinger, 1965), is another book students have found useful in furthering their understanding of the abnormal personality. One student wrote of it, "*Letters From Jenny* is a good book and one well worth the time spent reading it. The letters portion of the book is easy reading, but the analyses are more difficult. Presenting several different methods of analysis applied to the same situation is a good way to compare and contrast them."

Robert Lindner, *The Fifty-Minute Hour* (Bantam, 1954), also intrigued student readers: "This collection of five psychoanalytic stories taken from Dr. Lindner's experiences with actual patients is fascinating to read." However, a few students disagreed with Lindner's psychoanalytic method: "Already doubting the value of psychoanalysis as an effective therapy for deviant behavior, *The Fifty-Minute Hour* moved me to question it even further."

This is the one area of psychology which seems both to attract the greatest reader interest and to provide the most literature to feed that interest. One of the real best sellers is Hannah Green, *I Never Promised You a Rose Garden* (Holt, Rinehart & Winston, 1964), a true account of the experiences of a schizophrenic girl who eventually recovered.

Part Fourteen

Creativity:
A Healthy
Addiction

Experience, by its very nature, is highly personal. Every experience is essentially new. It is the first time the person has had that particular experience. But some experiences are more nearly unique, more novel, than the everyday, run-of-the-mill sort. Creativity is the production of something that is essentially novel *to the person doing the creating.*

It may seem just a little strange to begin a chapter on the subject of creativity with an article on religion. But this is not an article about religion, as such, about religion as a doctrine or a dogma. It is a discussion of the nature of religious experience, of what having an experience of this type does to and for the person involved.

It would seem that a deep religious experience is an example of genuine creativity. In this next selection, the writer speaks of "something happening in the personalities of eminent men and women of history. . . ." What happened?

Something that can be noticed about creative people is their enthusiasm, their commitment to the activity which is absorbing their time and energy. Religious experience seems to involve this combination of creativity and commitment. The commitment may be so great as to be justifiably called an addiction. Is it a healthy addiction?

45

THE PSYCHOLOGY OF RELIGIOUS EXPERIENCE
WALTER HOUSTON CLARK

A few years ago an inconspicuous member of one of my classes sought me out. The mother of a family, she told me about a religious experience of a mystical nature, a story she had confided to no other living person. Not understanding it, except in its general nature, I listened sympathetically but gave no advice. But the incident seemed to set in motion a psychological and religious process of surprising proportions. Shortly afterward she became more active in her church. Now others seek her out to take leadership in discussion groups, and, to her embarrassment, church members refer problems to her that, more appropriately, should go to the pastor. Besides being much more forceful, she is more attractive, and she herself is amazed to find that she is becoming a positive force for good in the community and in her family instead of just another aging housewife.

Source: Reprinted from *Psychology Today* Magazine, February, 1968. Copyright © Communications/Research/Machines, Inc.

This is an illustration in a commonplace, contemporary person of the influence that religion may have in the transformation of personality. I have seen and studied such phenomena in ordinary men and women, and in many persons undergoing a religious experience under psychedelic drugs. The psychological study of religion is as fascinating as man himself, and as compelling as his fascination with God.

We have records of something happening in the personalities of eminent men and women of history—Socrates, Moses, the Buddha, St. Paul, St. Francis, Teresa of Avila, the French mathematician Pascal, John Wesley, and Jesus. In large part, it was to seek the source of this power in scores of intense souls that William James wrote his great treatise, *The Varieties of Religious Experience*, certainly the most notable of all books in the field of the psychology of religion and probably destined to be the most influential book written on religion in the twentieth century.

It is a paradox that, in view of such evidence, modern psychologists should be so incurious about the dynamics involved and so neglectful of a force in human nature with the influence religion has for both good and evil in human personality and human history. Since the time of William James, the psychological study of religion has fallen on dull days. In our day, its prestige has gradually begun to revive, but the conventional psychologist still tends to observe it warily as a subject that he is not quite sure belongs in his field.

And this is not hard to understand. In the 1920's, behaviorism was obtaining a firm grip on psychology. The aim of shaping psychology into another natural science still seemed to be within reach if all psychologists would only agree to neglect the mind and to confine themselves to a study of environmental stimuli and its resulting behavior.

But religion, particularly if one wishes to probe its depths and make sense of it, requires the study of the inner life more than almost any other human activity. With its close associations to theology and philosophy (more universally acknowledged in William James' day, incidentally), considering the psychology of religion as a natural science seems far from ideal.

By far the most interesting, instructive, and yet puzzling phenomenon of religious experience is the mystical one. I would agree with William James that "personal religious experience has its root and center in mystical states of consciousness." This characteristic seems to me to separate religious consciousness from other forms of consciousness. All other aspects of the religious life have their counterparts in man's secular life. A mystical state alone is *sui generis* and is so different from any other psychological state that subjectively it is seldom mistaken for anything other than religion. A mystical state produces a particular kind of perception involving what is probably the most intense positive psychological experience known to man. It may be compared to romantic love. Yet mystics, in order to serve God, have been known to desert their possessions, their previous ways of life, and those whom they love. It is the very differentness of mysticism that causes trouble for the mystic. He finds no words to explain exactly what he has experienced unless he is talking to other mystics. Thus the mystic is often a lonely person, keeping within himself the expression of his pearl of great price, the thing that gives meaning to his life.

The psychologist, unless he is a mystic himself (which he seldom is), is forced to rely on the words of the mystic to describe the experience, though he also notes the sharp changes in behavior that frequently accompany mystical states. The feature most often reported and which seems to be at the core of the experience is a perception of unity, accompanied also by a sense of timelessness, of holiness, and by the feeling that one has directly encountered ultimate reality accompanied by a sense of great peace. It would be easy for the psychologist to pass off this strange state of ecstasy as just another aberration, were it not for the wholesome changes of personality that often follow it. Certainly, even if such transformations do not occur every day, one might suppose that a thorough study of them at least would throw some light on the nature of personality change and human creativity.

In the study of religious experience and personality change, I will venture to mention a controversial but incomparable tool for the study of this elusive area—psychedelic drugs. Formerly I was extremely critical of the religious value of the drugs. However, I have experimented on myself and have had an opportunity to participate with others in research. My conclusions were not unlike those of William James after he had tried nitrous oxide, the psychedelic of his day. He said:

One conclusion . . . is that our normal waking consciousness, rational consciousness as we call it, is but one special type of consciousness, whilst all about it, parted by the filmiest of screens, there lie potential forms of consciousness entirely different. . . . We may go through life without suspecting their existence; but . . . no account of the universe in its totality can be final which leaves these other forms of consciouseness quite disregarded. . . . My own experiences . . . all converge towards a kind of insight to which I cannot help ascribing some metaphysical significance.

Certainly if the psychedelics do not release genuine religious experiences, then the differences are so subtle that even religious experts cannot tell the difference, apart from knowing that a drug has been involved. The experiment that did the most to convince me that the psychedelics triggered mysticism was the following: Dr. Walter N. Pahnke, in a Harvard doctoral study, set up nine criteria of mystical experience using principally those of Princeton's expert, W. T. Stace, and William James. He then gave 30 milligrams of psilocybin to ten theological students, and to ten others he gave a placebo. None of the 20 were informed which they had received. All of them then attended the same Good Friday service. In their descriptions after the service, nine of the ten who had been given the drug reported unmistakable characteristics of mystical phenomena, while only one who had taken the placebo did, and his reaction was very mild.

What further supports many psychedelic experiences as being religious is that, when the subject reports a religious experience, therapeutic results are often more marked. This was the case with pioneer experiments in which massive doses of LSD were given to hopeless alcoholics in Saskatchewan by Humphrey Osmond and Abram Hoffer. After five years, half of the sample of 60 cases were still found to be nonalcoholic. "As a general rule," Hoffer reported, "those who have not had the transcendental experience are not changed; they continue to drink. However, the large proportion of those who have had it are changed."

There also has been experimentation with criminals in Europe and the United States. In order to find out for myself what the results had been, I studied several convicts to whom Dr. Timothy Leary had given psilocybin and who, according to his report, had encountered religious experiences of a life-changing nature. Some of these convicts definitely had fallen by the wayside—through lack of follow-up after the controversial Leary project collapsed.

But I discovered a rather remarkable phenomenon. Those who had remained in jail had started what they called the "Self-Development Group," a very successful AA type of self-rehabilitation that continued on a nondrug basis. One middle-aged armed robber, serving a twenty-year term, in a drug session had seen a vision of Christ. Shortly afterward, he said, "All my life came before my eyes, and I said, 'What a waste!'" Now, five years later, this man, a group leader, is considered by the authorities to be completely rehabilitated.

The point of these experiments is that not only do subjects, after psychedelic therapy, talk like religious people but religion for them has had the effect of radically changing their values and attitudes. The drugs seem to do what the churches frequently only *say* they do in their talk of salvation, redemption, and rebirth. All this is not to minimize the real dangers and problems of the drugs, but to call attention to certain facts that have not appeared often in the news media and to point out the connection of the drugs with religion.

The psychologist of religion faces some formidable problems. Even the definition of religion is a matter of great dispute. Several years ago I asked a number of experts in the field of the scientific study of religion to define what they meant by the word *religion*. Of 68 replies, no two were exactly alike, and even when replies were grouped, the categories differed. This is hardly a happy situation for a discipline making any pretense to being a science.

Yet the psychology of religion is beginning to emerge from its long period of exile. Strangely enough, this discipline of psychology owes its emergence in no small measure to another genius who held religion in much lower esteem than did James. That man was Sigmund Freud, who was able to seduce large numbers of modern scientific psychologists through his own scientific background and through his insistence, which at least in his early days seemed completely sincere, that he was strictly a scientist and nothing more.

Actually, to an extent that Freud himself did not realize, he was an artist of the human soul. While his observations involved close study of the lives of his patients, his intuitions and speculations went far beyond pedestrian reports of stimuli and responses to them—the responses, of course, and some of the stimuli as well, being merely the products of his patients' inner lives. Aided by a clarity of style hardly matched in such a complex field, Freud opened the doors for many behaviorists to the study of man's subjectivity, whose studies and writing were thereby enriched. As examples I might mention the followers of the Yale behaviorist Clark Hull—men like John Dollard, Neal Miller, and O. Hobart Mowrer.

More directly, Freud set an example through his own writings on religion—through books like *Totem and Taboo*, *The Future of an Illusion*, and *Moses and Monotheism*. He dealt with religion as merely the search for a father image and as "the universal neurosis of mankind." But he wrote more about religion than any other single subject except sex. That this interest may have had its roots in the connection of his forebears with Jewish mysticism is suggested in a volume by David Bakan. Then Freud occasionally alarmed some of his close followers after conversations lasting into the early hours when he said he had times when he could almost bring himself to believe in many things, even "der liebe Gott!" Certainly this interest has led many Freudians and neo-Freudians to think and write of religion.

One of the most influential of the latter was the Swiss psychiatrist Carl G. Jung, whom Freud at one time had designated as his successor. Though a more obscure writer than Freud, Jung was more positively and openly religious. It was he who declared that, among his patients over the age of 35, there were none whose problems did not have their roots in religion. Like Freud he found the principal roots of religion in the unconscious, especially in what he called the racial unconscious, by which he explained the universal aspects of much religious symbolism.

Somewhat nearer to the orthodox academic psychological tradition in America have been several scholars, all presidents of the American Psychological Association in their day, who have written on the subject, though none has worked in the psychology of religion as his major field. The list includes Gardner Murphy, the late Gordon Allport, O. Hobart Mowrer, and Abraham H. Maslow. Of these, perhaps Allport did most toward making the subject academically respectable, through his volume of lectures, *The Individual and His Religion*. Maslow includes religion among the "peak experiences" that are the fruits of what he calls B-cognition, the source of human creativity.

A somewhat different influence on the psychology of religion, one especially strong in theological schools and churches, has been exerted by clinical pastoral psychology. This movement in the United States has had an interesting history.

In the early 1920's a middle-aged clergyman, considering his life a failure, was hospitalized with the diagnosis of catatonic schizophrenia. Through his stay in the hospital, he became convinced of the need of many mental patients for adequate pastoral care. On his recovery, after some difficulty with conventional administrative ideas as to the value of religion for mental patients, he persuaded Dr. James A. Bryan, Superintendent of Worcester State Hospital in Massachusetts, to appoint him the first chaplain at a mental hospital in this country. Shortly after his appointment, the chaplain persuaded several theological students to study the ministry to the mentally ill under his direction.

Thus started the clinical pastoral counseling movement in the theological schools, a training now required in at least one-third of the Protestant theological schools and in some form optional with most other seminaries, including many of the Catholic and Jewish seminaries as well. The clergyman who started it all was Anton T. Boisen, who died a few years ago at the Elgin State Hospital in Illinois, where he was Chaplain Emeritus, honored and lamented by thousands of students and patients.

About the time that Boisen began his ministry to the mentally ill, one of the first of a long line of volumes in the field of religion and mental health appeared—*Pastoral Psychiatry and Mental Health*, by James Rathbone Oliver, both a psychiatrist and a clergyman. One of the most articulate contemporary writers in this field is Seward Hiltner of Princeton Theological Seminary.

However, recently authors in religion have multiplied themselves in so many volumes that they have become increasingly repetitive and even boring.

There has been a fringe benefit, however, in enrichment for clinical psychology. Theologians usually not noted for their attention to the practical or empirical have been forced to take some notice of mental health and of the fact that the clinician may often lead his patient to consider matters of "ultimate concern." The best-known theologian to encourage dialogue with therapists was the late Paul Tillich, particularly in his book, *The Courage to Be.* And the greats in psychology all have responded to his dialogue. There are recordings of conversations with Carl Rogers, Hobart Mowrer, Erich Fromm, and with the man who perhaps was Tillich's closest friend, Rollo May.

But let us look again at Anton Boisen in another way. One of the striking facts in the lives of many great religious leaders has been abnormality, which sometimes has grown into full-blown psychosis. Ezekiel's visions of complicated flying beasts and "wheels within wheels" are only darkly understandable, while some of Jeremiah's words and actions mark him as, at the very least, a peculiar fellow. At one time Jesus' family and friends spoke of him as "beside himself," while George Fox, founder of the Society of Friends, probably would have been hospitalized in this day and age. William James discusses this subject in the first chapter of his *Varieties.* Of Boisen's psychic instability there is no doubt. He acknowledged it himself, and the records of the diagnosis and his stay still remain at Worcester State Hospital in Massachusetts.

His sickness gave him an incomparable opportunity to observe a psychosis from the inside. In addition to this, having a scholarly cast of mind, as he recovered he had an opportunity to observe his fellow sufferers and to reflect on his observations. The result was his *Exploration of the Inner World,* a contemporary minor classic filled with original observations on the nature of schizophrenia and on the value of religion as a dynamic aspect of many cures. He regarded catatonic schizophrenia, from which he suffered, as the presentation to the patient of a crisis in his life so profound as to drive him into a panic. The very profundity of the problem offered religious dimensions to be coped with only by a radical religious decision.

Thus, the crisis tended to "make or break" the individual, leading either to rapid cure or to continued deterioration. For this reason Boisen saw religion as an essential therapeutic tool for many patients, one that might make the difference between sickness and health, and out of which strength might come. In this way he explained the power of George Fox and other unstable religious leaders. Psychologists have acknowledged the originality of Boisen's theories, and while they would not for the most part generalize them to the extent that he did, most would grant that at least they fit his own case very aptly.

The relationship between religion and mental illness suggests a paradox with respect to religion and mental health, and thus leads to two schools of thought. On the one hand are those who see religion as a positive force leading to a sense of well-being and optimism, tending to reduce morbid human attitudes and to maximize healthy-mindedness. On the other hand are those who make much of the association between religion and mental illness. Psychiatrists in the latter camp frequently stress the fact that there are some patients in whom the very consideration of religion will touch off a psychosis, and the fact that almost any mental hospital can display a varied assortment of self-styled messiahs and Jesus Christs. An interesting example of three such personalities is found in Rokeach's *Three Christs of Ypsilanti.*

Actually, the situation is much too complex for either of these views to be the whole truth. It is worth mentioning William James' two famous types of religion, the "religion of healthy-mindedness" and that of the "sick soul." James sees them simply as two differing expressions of religion usually associated with differing types of temperament or life style, though these may alternate within a single personality. The healthy-minded person expresses his religion in a context of exuberance and joy. He minimizes the tragedies of life and may even systematically deny the existence of sickness and evil, as in Christian Science, according to James. James points out that this way of dealing with life works well for some people and thus empirically demonstrates its core of truth.

But there are others who cannot turn away from life's tragic elements, its sicknesses, strife, injustices, and its suffering. Men are not born equal with an equal chance in life, and death is the only leveler. An honest facing of such facts leads to a much deeper probing of the meaning of life than "the religion of healthy-mindedness," even though it may not produce cheery apostles. The title of one of Kierkegaard's books is *The Sickness Unto Death,* and one must acknowledge that this particular gloomy Dane produced some of the most searching religious observations of the last century. James, at least when he wrote *The Varieties,* looked on the sick soul as one who recognized a truer dimension of religion and life.

If one looks at these two religious styles, he may see them not as mutually exclusive but as two roads to religious growth. There are none of the great religious faiths that do not provide for the expression of both. The greatest literary production of the Hebrew Bible—and indeed one of the great pieces of world literature—is the Book of Job, a consideration of suffering and its relation to evil. But the same Bible is filled with an account of the triumphs as well as of the disasters of the Children of Israel. The theme of Death and Resurrection is a universal one in religion, derived from the depths of human nature. It is significant that the Passion of Christ's Crucifixion is followed by His Resurrection. Good Friday is linked with Easter. This symbolizes that alternation in human destiny, that dialogue of opposites, through which religious development takes place.

This search for understanding of the process of religious growth will bring any religious psychologist worth his salt to the delicate and fascinating field of religious experience. I say *delicate*, for the churches have widely differing but nevertheless very positive convictions in the area. One runs the risk of offending some people no matter what one says or how carefully one phrases one's research and thought. This is one reason that psychology is somewhat gun-shy about religion. But such subjects as conversion, mysticism, possession, and prophecy need to be dealt with not only by the psychologist of religion but by any psychologist who pretends awareness of the total man.

It is an oversimplification, of course, but we can see religious life as containing two interrelated but very different psychological functions. Rudolf Otto, in *The Idea of the Holy*, has termed them the *rational* and the *nonrational*. If we liken the religious pilgrim to a ship in voyage, we might designate as the rudder the critical, directive, rational, and reasonable parts of the pilgrim's nature; the ship's propulsion then would be the nonrational, the feeling and intuitive elements, providing energy, liveliness, and movement. Perhaps in this respect religion is simply a special case of all of life. But we might note that a boat, no matter how strong its rudder, would get nowhere without an engine, while a rudderless ship with a powerful engine would be a hazard to itself and to all navigation. Thus religion through the ages has needed the prophet, the convert, the seer, the martyr, and the saint as well as the theologian and the priest.

This well may be why the more dynamic forms of religion often deprecate the scholar and the rationalist. It also helps explain why churches so often have been afraid of religion in its livelier forms. The church develops the conservatism typical of any institution, and it prefers saints to be dead before it begins to worship them.

Partly because the churches at about the turn of the century made more of the phenomenon of conversion, James (and E. D. Starbuck, his predecessor in the field of the psychology of religion) devoted many pages to this phenomenon. The bad name which conversion has acquired among scholars is due partly to the fact that some churches have forced on their members a highly emotional experience of unsettling shallowness, which has obscured the significance of many a sudden conversion of life-saving proportions. The founders of Alcoholics Anonymous are an outstanding example. Against a background of brain-washing and Pavlovian theory, William Sargant gives some reasons for the power of sudden conversion, both for good and for ill, in *Battle for the Mind.*

It seems to me that religion at its best can be illustrated well by contrasting the two great psychologists, Gordon Allport and William James. In *The Individual and his Religion,* Allport speaks of "mature religion" as self-critical and as possessing its own motivational force; as consistent in its moral consequences; as comprehensive and integrative; and, finally, as eternally questing.

James tries to define what he sees as religion at its best in the chapter "Saintliness," in *The Varieties.* He defines the best thus: (1) "A feeling of being in a wider life than that of this world's selfish little interests; and a conviction, not merely intellectual, of the existence of an Ideal Power." (2) "A sense of the friendly continuity of the ideal power with our own life, and a willing self-surrender to its control." (3) "An immense elation and freedom as the outlines of the confining selfhood melt down." (4) "A shifting of the emotional center towards loving and harmonious affections, towards 'yes, yes,' and away from 'no' where the claims of the non-ego are concerned."

James is not uncritical of some of the excesses of saintliness. Yet, when we compare his view of high religion with Allport's, we sense a wide gap. Allport is the rationalist.

Most college students take to Allport—the rudder. But some prefer James. These tend to be the more sensitive, more emotional ones, those who may have experienced the aesthetic and the mystical in their own lives, and who may be scorned a bit by their more rational classmates. Perhaps this is reminiscent of the situation on the Harvard campus in James' day, when his colleagues shook their heads at the vagaries of their attractive colleague.

We can trace this difference in emphasis to roots in James' own nature—half artistic and half intellectual, with mystical sensitivities of a profound nature, heightened through his experience with nitrous oxide and other experiences of which he spoke only to his intimates. Thus, we can bring these two students of religion into dialogue and take from each his characteristic contribution to theory as we derive from them the rational and nonrational components in religion at its best.

But, taken as a whole, the psychologist's contribution to religion is mainly a rational one. The psychologist is like the music critic, who can analyze and therefore help the hearer to appreciate. And so, as a psychologist of religion, I work to understand when I can. But ultimately I must stand in awe before what, as a psychologist, I cannot match—the authentic religious life. This is the subtlest, most profound, yet puzzling and paradoxical, of the achievements of the human spirit. It is religion *par excellence,* which has the power to transform human life and so give it meaning, and it is for these reasons that the religious consciousness is the most fascinating object of study of all human phenomena. At least, that is how one psychologist of religion sees it.

Edwin H. Land of the Polaroid Corporation is, himself, a highly creative man. He presented a lecture on his experiences in creative activity when he received the Seventh Cosmos Club Award in Washington, D.C. The next selection is the text of that lecture.

Mr. Land speaks of the *wonders* of certain experiences, of *yearning* for a deep insight, of a strange *intuitive* program, of *mystery,* of *excitement.* He might be discussing a religious experience. No! An experience with drugs? Not that either. Mr. Land is, as he says, addicted—to scientific experimentation, addicted to a form of creativity.

46

ADDICTION AS A NECESSITY AND OPPORTUNITY
EDWIN H. LAND

Last Christmas, while riding through London, I found that in spite of my delight in the galleries, libraries, and concerts, there was within me a deep and insatiable need. I found myself saying to our driver, "Green, did you know that I am an addict?" He is of the old school so that he did not turn his head. "No, sir, I did not know that." "I am addicted to at least one good experiment a day—sometimes I can arrange it by telephone. When I cannot, the world goes out of focus, becomes unreal." Possibly somewhat disappointed, but clearly relieved: "I see, sir."

And then last month I was participating in a student seminar at one of our great universities. We were in the professor's room. We sat on the floor, and the boys and girls sat in a circle

Source: From *Science,* 1971, *171,* 151–153. Copyright © 1970 by the Cosmos Club. Reprinted by permission.

around me. The men, including the professor, wore magnificent long hair and, of course, the whole variety of handsome beards. It was rather hard for the women to compete with the colorfulness of the men. Furthermore, the women seemed somewhat restive, with an inner concern about the relationship to reality to the new world they were all trying to create together. As we all talked, I found myself describing the wonders of the scientific experience. I told of the way in which one yearns for a deep insight in some domain; of the strange intuitive program of collecting observations; of the mystery of formation of hypothesis within one; of the competence of the mind-body system to select the crucial experiment; of the excitement of interaction between experiment and hypothesis; of the sense of relief and even of nobility when the hypothesis is proven true by the experiment and the stage set for the next hypothesis. I remarked on the sense of awe that one could be the instrument of this process, as if input had flowed into one and significant outputs emerged from one. I was pleased to note the comprehension on one of the bearded faces. He turned to the neighboring girl and said with firm conviction, "Why, it's just like heroin, isn't it?"

And, finally, a few weeks ago, sitting with the board of a foundation, I shared in the sense of helplessness and impotence, confronted with the problem of how to use money to block the sweep of drugs across our nation. As an inveterate hypothesis maker I had an insight into the nature and function of addiction, and it is that insight I should like to examine with you tonight.

Some years ago, talking to a group of brilliant high school students about the life of a scientist, I said, "My own recollection of your age is a curious alternation which, I think, goes on through life for the scientist. It is alternation between the one mood and attitude of feeling part of the race as a whole, part of the family, part of the neighborhood; the mood of being in love with friends, women, men, people all over the world; the mood of being in love with what is great in music and art—all that on the one hand and then, quite suddenly, a separateness from all that—a separateness that comes during the preoccupation with a particular scientific task. There is a need, a transient need, a violent need for being just yourself, restating, recreating, talking in your own terms about what you have learned from all the cultures, scientific and non-scientific, before you and around you. During that period you want to be almost alone, with just a few friends. You want to be undisturbed. You want to be free to think not for an hour at a time, or three hours at a time, but for two days or two weeks, if possible, without interruption. You don't want to drive the family car or go to parties. You wish people would just go away and leave you alone while you get something straight. Then, you get it straight and you embody it, and during that period of embodiment you have a feeling of almost divine guidance. Then it is done, and, suddenly, you are alone, and you have a need to go back to your friends and the world around you, and to all history, to be refreshed, to feel alive and human once again. It is this interplay between all that is richly human and this special, concentrated, uninterrupted mental effort that seems to me to be the source, not only of science, but also of everything that is worthwhile in life."

In examining this description I want to avoid both the obvious cliches of drug-taking terminology and the professional characterizations of Freudian categories. I suggest that this description deals with two different modes of relationship between the individual and the world around him. In the first, the social mode, a perfectly normal and healthy mode, the individual is not at all an integrated single being. A thousand as yet unnamed and unisolated components of personality interplay with analogous fragments in the people around him. Except for his image in the camera, he has really vanished to become part of the composite creature, a social group. Through this group entity, feelings, thoughts, hopes and speculations travel from boundary to boundary, resonating and reflecting within its confines. Most vicarious participation in music and sports involves this mode of existence. Talk programs on radio, the nationally shared entertainment on television, a poker game, the committee on pollution, the mad ecstasy of riots, the Easter parade, traffic jams, Mylai murders—all these are not groups of individuals in aggregations of units, but examples of the non-unity of the components of an individual when those components are intermixed with the components of other individuals to form the biological unit, the multiple-man. The multiple-man can be grand, or trivial, or elegant, or decadent, or noble. He moves through our bodies leaving them rejoicing or desperate, helpless participants in this mode of human existence. The interests of multiple-man are only in feeling, affect, emotion, conquest, discovery, victory, vast inchoate revelation. When the great symphonies of multiple-man echo through us, our individual conditioning, background and predispositions introduce only trivial variations on a main theme.

Before we go on to singular-man we should note what a horrible problem for him multiple-man is. For while multiple-man is richness, vastness, glory and triumph, multiple-man is interested in intellect only as a tool for power, joy, conquest, and the delights of monumental destruction. For him, indeed, war is an extension of politics and, more seriously, politics is an extension of war. Multiple-man can never analyze except for aggrandizement or rejoicing. Facts are slaves for his amusement, to be toyed with, savored, destroyed, distorted. Life is a game with ever-changing rules, a game of glorious pretensions for good or evil, as the winds may blow. The multiple-man is not a vast, racial, historic composite. Multiple-man is three people, or seven, or fifty, or a thousand, or sometimes a nation. As our world is organized, the government, the universities, the scientific society, the committee, the group of neighbors, all are multiple-man who uses reason and intellect only as one of the most delightful pawns in the electric game of group living. During the time that the components of our personality are part of multiple-man, they exist in that mode.

As I talk I wonder if that mode may not be the only one for animals. My thesis is that for us another quite different mode is frequently possible. This is the mode in which the components of the individual's personality are integrated with each other instead of being cross-integrated with those of the group. In this mode, which we might call singular-man, talents, aptitudes, senses, competences of the individual, serve an entirely different set of purposes. Although the product of this activity may have inestimable significance for the race, again for good or evil, the first function of the total activity of singular-man is to serve himself. The intellect, when it serves himself, can be enjoyed for what it is, a tool for analysis, synthesis, speculation, a tool for hypothesis and experiment. For singular-man, emotion can be controlled, utilized, enjoyed, at his will. He can discover for discovery, learn for learning, be ethical for ethics, be moral for morality, be noble for nobility. He can discover causes and create effects. He is a god in his freedom for self-integration and controlled search. Often his independence and freedom are unbelievably poignant, frequently terrifying, and the trip from singular-man to multiple-man can be as agonizing as that from Jekyll to Hyde. The ready transition between modes is the deepest of human needs, for without it man is either animal or derelict, and yet the transition, as with so many human needs, is not practiced intuitively. Success for an individual may be an accident in the profligacy of evolution. When I was talking with the students, both in high school and in college, about the scientific experience—it could as well have been any newly created aesthetic experience—I was talking about one technique for making the transition. Presumably, there are many. The important point is that the bona fide transition from multiple-man to singular-man involves the full integration of the components of the individual for a singleness of purpose and for ends of no interest to multiple-man—the purpose, the ends, must be real if singular-man is to survive. The "drug," the "addiction," is the pursuit by singular-man of this real purpose—a purpose, the achievement of which provides continuous interaction and satisfaction, feedback if you will, for the integrative process.

My suggestion is that the need for the transition to singular-man is so great that if an individual has been unfortunate enough not to learn bona fide healthy techniques for the transition, if he has not been able to find objectives in the real world to which he can relate in this mode of living, then he will seek escape from permanent entrapment in the mode of multiple-man—he will seek escape from multiple-man to singular-man through artificial means such as drugs. My hypothesis for the evening is that the expansion of consciousness through drugs is merely a synthetic production of integration in the mode of singular-man. Drugs in this concept serve not as an escape *from* one's self but rather as an escape *to* one's self. The use of drugs is a shortcut, which presumably is also a blind alley, for there is no feedback between the produce and the integrative process. In the bona fide situation, the interplay between the integrative process and the artistic or scientific product leads to a strengthening of the integrative process and to increased mastery of the technique of willful transition between the multiple and singular modes. With drugs, tragically, the first phases of integration are achieved along with the wonderful sense of relief of being a singular human rather than part of an animal group, only to find that because of the lack of feedback the process is not self-supporting and self-strengthening. Obviously, we are much too far away from understanding the biochemical differences between the bona fide situation and the synthetic one to hazard any analysis of why one is constructive and the other destructive. The lesson from the hypothesis, however, is that unless we can provide the bona fide techniques of transition, unless we can provide the healthy addictions, disaster will eventuate. Individuals may stay too long in the multiple mode, where in addition to enjoying the rich variegation of the world of feeling, they will also substitute, permanently, the important irrational absurdities of politics, committees, and boards, for the discerning rationality that can exist only in the mode of the singular-man. Even if they do not become drug addicts, they are in danger of becoming habituated to the slap-happy excesses that are as valid for the multiple-man as are magnificence and grandeur.

It occurs to me as we explore, there are indeed many lonely souls trapped in the second mode, the mode of singular-man. I suspect that alcohol enables many of them to make the transition to the first mode of multiple-man. In the few days during which these ideas have been crystallizing, I have found them very useful in understanding the mysteries of the Iagos and the

Judases; the astonishing number of small betrayals by men of honor; the eternal paradox of the politician as a man of honor at one moment and of low credibility at the next; the deadly conclusions of decent souls when they gather together to make decisions; the alternations between inspired insight and unbelievable stupidity of a handful of brilliant scientists en masse; the magnificent elation that we can feel together; the kind of transcendency that we can achieve when we are a group, and the evil that we can perpetuate—all this is an antithesis not between God and the devil, but between singular-man and multiple-man, both of which we are and between which we must learn early in life to migrate skillfully.

We have said that we are not going to provide you with all the answers, but prefer to induce you to ask questions. However, Mr. Land has suggested some answers. Do you agree with them? Suppose that you had been present when this address was delivered. Suppose there were then a question period. What are some of the questions you might have asked him?

Perhaps you, too, would like to become a creative scientist. Certainly, not all people who work in scientific settings are called upon to be creative. Many tasks are imitative and repetitive. But there are opportunities for creative invention and for discovery. No matter how well-known something may be to almost everyone else, he who experiences it for the first time is truly a discoverer. When we first viewed the Pacific Ocean we felt as truly the experience of discovery as had Balboa many years before. It is so with creating. Creativity is a personal experience.

Becoming a creative scientist depends much on the characteristics of the person involved. In the next selection, Anne Roe describes the personality patterns of "truly creative" scientists. If you fail to measure up to all of them, don't be too easily discouraged. She is describing the ideal. Certainly there are many people who are making worthwhile contributions to science who are not perfect. But her article does point a direction and provide a standard for evaluation.

THE PSYCHOLOGY OF THE SCIENTIST

ANNE ROE

Science is the creation of scientists, and every scientific advance bears somehow the mark of the man who made it. The artist exposes himself in his work; the scientist seems rather to hide in his, but he is there. Surely the historian of science must understand the man if he is fully to understand the progress of science, and he must have some comprehension of the science if he is to understand the men who make it.

The general *public* image of the scientist has not been and indeed is not now a flattering one, and at best it certainly is not an endearing one. Characterizations of scientists almost always emphasize the objectivity of their work and describe their cold, detached, impassive, unconcerned observation of phenomena which have no emotional meaning for them. This could hardly be further from the truth. The scientist as a person is a nonparticipating observer in only a very limited sense. He does not *interact* with what he is observing, but he does participate as a person. It is, perhaps, this fact—that the scientist does not expect, indeed does not want, the things that he is concerned with to be equally concerned with him—that has given others this impression of coldness, remoteness, and objectivity. (The social scientist is in a remarkably difficult position since the "objects with which he is concerned" are people, and both they and he may be more than a little ambivalent about this matter of interaction. But this is a special problem which I will by-pass here, noting only that in many ways the social scientist differs from the natural scientist in terms of personality and motivations.)

The truth of the matter is that the creative scientist, whatever his field, is very deeply involved emotionally and personally in his work, and that he himself is his own most essential tool. We must consider both the subjectivity of science and what kinds of people scientists are.

THE PERSONAL FACTOR   But first we must consider the processes of science. Suppose we take the scientist at the time when he has asked a question, or has set up a hypothesis which he wants to test. *He* must decide what observations to make. It is simply not possible to observe

SOURCE: From *Science*, 1961, *134*, 456–458. Copyright 1961 by the American Association for the Advancement of Science. Reprinted by permission of the author and the publisher.

everything that goes on under a given set of conditions; he must choose what to observe, what measurements to make, how fine these measurements are to be, how to record them. These choices are never dictated entirely by the question or hypothesis (and anyway, that too bears his own particular stamp). One has only to consider how differently several of his colleagues would go about testing the same hypothesis to see that personal choice enters in here.

But this is just the beginning. Having decided what is to be observed, and having set up the techniques for observing, the scientist comes to the point of making the actual observations, and of recording these observations. All the complex apparatus of modern science is only a means of extending the range of man's sensory and perceptual capacities, and all the information derived through such extensions must eventually be reduced to some form in which man, with his biological limitations, can receive it. Here, too, in spite of all precautions and in spite of complete honesty, the personal factor enters in. The records of two observers will not dovetail exactly, even when they read figures from a dial. Errors may creep in, and the direction of the error is more likely than not to be associated with the observer's interest in how the findings came out. Perhaps the clearest evidence on this point comes from research on extrasensory perception. A scientist who is deeply committed to a hypothesis is well advised to have a neutral observer if the import of an observation is immediately apparent. Often, of course, such errors are minor, but they can be important, not only to the immediate problem but to society. I have wondered to what extent the disparity in figures on radioactive fallout may reflect such factors. Very few scientists, including psychologists, who have demonstrated selective perception as a laboratory exercise, take account of the phenomenon in their own work.

Once the observations are recorded, other questions are asked: When is the evidence sufficient to be conclusive, one way or the other? How important are discrepancies? What degree of generalization is permissible? Here, again, we may expect personally slanted answers. Taxonomy offers a very clear illustration of the effect of personality: One biologist may classify a given set of specimens into a few species, and another may classify them into many species. Whether the specimens are seen as representing a few or many groups depends largely on whether one looks for similarities or for differences, on whether one looks at the forest or the trees. A "lumper" may honestly find it impossible to understand how a "splitter" arrives at such an obviously incorrect solution, and vice versa. Such differences cannot be resolved by appeal to the "facts"—there are no facts which cannot be perceived in different ways. This is not to say that the facts are necessarily distorted. The problem of the criterion exists in all science, although some scientists are more aware of it than others.

The matter of personal commitment to a hypothesis is one that deserves more consideration than it usually receives. Any man who has gone through the emotional process of developing a new idea, of constructing a new hypothesis, is to some extent, and usually to a large extent, committed to that hypothesis in a very real sense. It is his baby. It is as much his creation as a painting is the personal creation of the painter. True, in the long run it stands or falls, is accepted or rejected, on its own merits, but its creator has a personal stake in it. The scientist has more at stake than the artist, for data which may support or invalidate his hypothesis are in the public domain in a sense in which art criticism never is. It may even be because of this that scientists customarily check their hypotheses as far as they can before they state them publicly. And, indeed, the experienced scientist continues to check, hoping that if errors are to be found, it will be he who finds them, so that he will have a chance to make revisions, or even to discard the hypothesis, should that prove necessary. He finds it less difficult to discard his hypothesis if, in his efforts at checking, he has been able to come up with another one.

The extent of personal commitment to a hypothesis is a prominent factor in the historical interplay between scientists. The degree of this commitment varies in an individual with different hypotheses, and varies between individuals. One very important factor here is the scientist's productivity. If he has many new ideas he will be less disturbed (and less defensive) if one fails to pan out. If he has very few ideas, an error is much harder to take, and there are many historical instances of errors which the author of the idea has never been able to see himself. I think many scientists are genuinely unaware of the extent, or even of the fact, of this personal involvement, and themselves accept the myth of impersonal objectivity. This is really very unfortunate. It is true that only a man who is passionately involved in his work is likely to make important contributions, but the committed man who knows he is committed and can come to terms with this fact has a good chance of getting beyond his commitment and of learning how to disassociate himself from his idea when this is necessary. There is little in the traditional education of scientists to prepare them for this necessity, and there are many who are still unaware of it. The extent of a scientist's personal involvement in a theory can now be a matter of grave public concern. Scientists who become advisers on political or other policy have an extraordinarily heavy responsibility for achieving some detachment from their own theories. How many of them realize this?

But once one hypothesis is found acceptable, this is not the end of it. One hypothesis inevitably leads to another; answering one question makes it possible to ask other, hopefully more precise ones. And so a new hypothesis or a new theory is offered. How is this new theory arrived at? This is one expression of the creative process, and it is a completely personal process. It is personal regardless of whether one or more individuals is involved, for in every advance made by a group, the person contributing at the moment has had to assimilate the contributions of the others and order them in his own personal way.

THE CREATIVE PROCESS   There have been many millions of words written about the creative process, few of them very illuminating. The reason is not hard to find. The process is intimate and personal and characteristically takes place not at the level of full consciousness but at subconscious or preconscious levels. It has been inaccessible to study largely because we have not yet found any means for controlling it. Many effective scientists and artists have learned a few techniques which may reduce interference with it, but no one to my knowledge has discovered any means by which he can set it in motion at will.

It is probable that the fundamentals of the creative process are the same in all fields, but in those fields in which an advance in knowledge is sought, there is an additional requirement—or rather, one requirement receives particular emphasis. This is the need for a large store of knowledge and experience. The broader the scientist's experience and the more extensive his stock of knowledge, the greater the possibility of a real breakthrough.

The creative process involves a scanning or searching through stocks of stored memories. There seems to be a rather sharp limit to the possibility of very significant advance through voluntary, logical scanning of these stores. For one thing, they vary enormously in their accessibility to conscious recall and in the specificity of their connections, so that reliance upon conscious, orderly, logical thinking is not likely to produce many results at this stage, however essential such procedures become later in verification. This scanning is typically for patterns and complex associations rather than for isolated units. It may be, however, that a small unit acts as a sort of key to a pattern. What seems to happen, in creative efforts in science as well as in every other field, is that the individual enters a state in which logical thinking is submerged and in which thought is prelogical. Such thought is described as random largely because it typically tries seemingly illogical and distantly related materials, and it often makes major advances in just this way. It is not fully random, however, because it is goal-directed and because even in this preconscious work there is appropriate selection and rejection of available connections. This stage of the creative process is accompanied by generally confused or vague states of preoccupation of varying degrees of depth; it is well described as "stewing." It is this stage which apparently cannot be hurried or controlled.

Although termination of this stage (finding a solution, or "getting insight," as it is often called) quite frequently occurs in a moment of dispersed attention, it apparently does not help to induce a state of dispersed attention in the hope of provoking a quicker end to the process. It should be added that, while insights do frequently occur "in a flash," they need not do so, and that the process is the same whether or not the insight turns out to have validity.

To acquire the necessary store of knowledge requires long and difficult application, and as science advances, the amount of information to be assimilated becomes greater and greater, despite increasing generalization in the organization of the data. Obviously, as more experience is stored and as the interconnections become better established and more numerous, the scanning becomes more effective. Such interconnections develop more and more readily as the process of acquiring experience takes on significance in the light of theory. This process requires not only the basic capacity to assimilate experiences but very strong motivation to persist in the effort. Strong motivation is also required if one is to continue with a search which may for a long time be unproductive. Motivation of this kind and strength derives from the needs and structure of the personality. Its sources are rarely obvious, although they can sometimes be traced. They do not necessarily derive from "neurotic problems," although they frequently do. It is no cause for dismay when they do. The ability of the human being to find in a personal problem motivation for a search for truth is one of the major accomplishments of the species.

If past experiences have brought about a compartmentalization of the storage areas, so that some portions are partially or wholly inaccessible, obviously the scientist is limited in his search. Compartmentalization of particular areas may result from personal experiences of a sort that lead to neurotic structures generally, or it may result from specific cultural restrictions, such as political or religious indoctrination. The extent to which such indoctrination will inhibit creative effort, however, depends upon how close the inaccessible areas are in content to the problems at issue. We have fairly conclusive evidence that political indoctrination need not interfere with inquiry into mathematical and physical science. Religious indoctrination can interfere strongly at any point, as history has documented very fully for us. The conclusion is no different from the basic principle of therapy: the more areas of experience there are accessible to conscious and preconscious thought, the better are the prospects for creativity.

Once an apparent answer to the scientist's question has been found, there is still a long process of pursuing and checking to be gone through. Not every man who can produce new ideas is also good at the business of checking them, and of course the reverse is also true. It is in the utilization of such personal differences as these that a "team approach" can make sense.

THE CREATIVE SCIENTIST
This, then, is a brief review of what little we know of the process of creation. What do we know of the characteristics of scientists who can use this process effectively? Many lines of inquiry have demonstrated that the range of characteristics that are associated with creative productivity in a human being is very wide. These characteristics fall into almost all categories into which personal traits have been divided for purposes of study—abilities, interests, drives, temperament, and so on.

To limit our discussion to scientific productivity, it is clear to start with that there are great variations in the amount of curiosity possessed by different people. Curiosity appears to be a basic drive. I suspect it may vary consistently with sex, on either a biological or a cultural basis, but we have as yet no idea how to measure such drives. No one becomes a scientist without a better-than-average amount of curiosity, regardless of whether he was born with it, was brought up in a stimulating environment, or just did not have it severely inhibited.

Intelligence and creativity are not identical, but intelligence does play a role in scientific creativity—rather more than it may play in some other forms of creativity. In general, one may summarize by saying that the minimum intelligence required for creative production in science is considerably better than average, but that, given this, other variables contribute more to variance in performance. It must also be noted that special abilities (numerical, spatial, verbal, and so on) play somewhat different roles in different scientific fields, but that ability must in no case be below average. A cultural anthropologist, for example, has little need for great facility with numbers. An experimental physicist, on the other hand, does require facility with numbers, although he need not have great facility with words.

A number of studies have contributed to the picture of the personality patterns of productive scientists, and it is rather striking that quite different kinds of investigations have produced closely similar results. These can be briefly summarized in six different groups, as follows:

1. Truly creative scientists seek experience and action and are independent and self-sufficient with regard to perception, cognition, and behavior. These findings have been expressed in various studies in such terms as the following: they are more observant than others and value this quality; they are more independent with respect to cognition and value judgments; they have high dominance; they have high autonomy; they are Bohemian or radical; they are not subject to group standards and control; they are highly egocentric.

2. They have a preference for apparent but resolvable disorder and for an esthetic ordering of forms of experience. They have high tolerance for ambiguity, but they also like to put an end to it in their own way—and in their own time.

3. They have strong egos (whether this derives from or is responsible for their independence and their tolerance for ambiguity is a moot question). This ego strength permits them to regress to preconscious states with certainty that they will return from these states. They have less compulsive superegos than others. They are capable of disciplined management of means leading to significant experience. They have no feeling of guilt about the independence of thought and action mentioned above. They have strong control of their impulses.

4. Their interpersonal relations are generally of low intensity. They are reported to be ungregarious, not talkative (this does not apply to social scientists), and rather asocial. There is an apparent tendency to femininity in highly original men, and to masculinity in highly original women, but this may be a cultural interpretation of the generally increased sensitivity of the men and the intellectual capacity and interests of the women. They dislike interpersonal controversy in any form and are especially sensitve to interpersonal aggression.

5. They show much stronger preoccupation with things and ideas than with people. They dislike introversive and affect-associated preoccupations, except in connection with their own research.

6. They like to take the calculated risk, but it must involve nature, not people, and must not depend on simple luck.

CONCLUSIONS How do these personality characteristics relate to the creative process in science as I have discussed it? An open attitude toward experience makes possible accumulation of experience with relatively little compartmentalization; independence of perception, cognition, and behavior permit greater than average reordering of this accumulated experience (the behavioral eccentricities so often noted are consistent with this). The strong liking for turning disorder into order carries such individuals through the searching period which their tolerance for ambiguity permits them to enter. The strong egos, as noted, permit regression to prelogical forms of thought without serious fear of failure to get back to logical ones. Preoccupation with things and ideas rather than with people is obviously characteristic of natural scientists, and even of some social scientists. This characteristic is not directly related to creativity, I think, but rather to the content of it.

I need not add that such statements as these are generalizations and that any individual case may be an exception. We may go farther, however, and generalize differences among men who follow different branches of science. That a man chooses to become a scientist and succeeds means that he has the temperament and personality as well as the ability and opportunity to do so. The branch of science he chooses, even the specific problems he chooses and the way he works on them, are intimately related to what he is and to his deepest needs. The more deeply engaged he is, the more profoundly is this true. To understand what he does, one must try to know what his work means to him. The chances are that he does not know or care to know. Indeed, he does not need to know. We do.

We have drawn our examples of creativity from two areas of interest, religion and science. It is probable that the nature of the creative experience is the same in all fields: music, graphic art, architecture, literature . . . whatever. Creativity would seem to demand a commitment. Creativity would seem to be an addiction. Insofar as creativity contributes to the development of the individual, to the development of society, to either or both, it is a healthy addiction.

Creativity, however, is not without its difficulties. Lewis A. Dexter, writing about innovating leadership, cautions that "the innovator, the prophet, the reformer, the originator, are rarely essentially well adapted to society."[1] Creative people

---

[1] Lewis A. Dexter in A. W. Gouldner (Ed.), *Studies in Leadership.* New York: Harper & Row, 1950, p. 592.

are not usually conformers. Society, it seems, can tolerate innovation—creativity—at only a limited rate.

As we write, someone elsewhere in the house is playing a recording of "Fiddler on the Roof" and a few words suddenly stand out. It is Tevye saying, "Without our tradition our lives would be as shaky as the fiddler on the roof."

Think of a number of outstandingly creative people in the development of human culture. How many are there whose ideas were accepted immediately? How many were persecuted for ideas that have later been accepted? We recall a comment by a clergyman years ago: "Did you ever stop to think that every conservative is worshipping at the grave of a dead radical?"

MORE EXPERIENCES WITH CREATIVITY

Suggestions for additional reading regarding religious experience have been given you in Clark's article. We, too, have found that many of our students are interested in reading Gordon Allport, *The Individual and His Religion* (Macmillan, 1950), and some of them, particularly those with a deep religious commitment, are attracted to William James, *Varieties of Religious Experience* (Longmans Green, 1902).

There are many good discussions of creativity. Some students have read with interest J. W. Getzels and P. W. Jackson, *Creativity and Intelligence* (John Wiley and Sons, 1962). A very different approach will be found in Arthur Koestler, *The Act of Creation* (Macmillan, 1964).

If you are interested in more of Land's ideas, he has another article on the subject: Edwin H. Land, "The Role of Invention in Organized Society" (*Product Engineering,* March 2, 1964). And Anne Roe has an entire book, *The Making of a Scientist* (Dodd, Mead, 1964).

For a general review of literature on creativity (including an extensive bibliography) see Norman H. Mackworth, "Originality" (*American Psychologist,* 1965, *20,* 51–66).

Part Fifteen

Social Psychology: Interdependence

Social psychology is concerned with people (and animals) in groups. Social psychology is sometimes defined as the study of the behavior of the individual in society. We need to add this second definition, unless we understand what we mean by a group. A group is not just a collection of people in a limited physical space. A group, as we shall use the word, is formed by two or more individuals who interact for purposes of satisfying one or more of the needs of the individuals involved. A group grows out of *interdependence.* Social psychology, then, is concerned with individuals who are interdependent.

We might examine the structure of many groups. We could look for those factors found in common among them. We should then have discovered some basic principles of social psychology. That, of course, is just what social psychologists do.

Social psychologists are concerned with groups of all sizes. But they do find that sometimes there are many, many people who are motivated by the same factors. What begins as a group becomes a social movement. We cannot, here and now, examine a large number of either small groups or social movements. We can, however, examine one such group or movement as an example of social movements in general.

As we shall see, the factors involving human group membership—or non-membership—are so important to the people involved that they are frequently emotionally loaded. If we are going to be objective we need to study a group to which no one now belongs and regarding which no one has any strong feelings. We need to look at a social movement that, for some reason or another, has run its course. To do this, we are going back between thirty-five and forty years. Two experienced social psychologists then made a study of such a social movement. It all happened long enough ago that today's students may not even have heard of it. Unfortunately, for the sake of complete objectivity, it may still carry some emotional loading, for it concerns black people. Both blacks and whites in our society still have *feelings* about race. Even those who think that racial factors really don't exist, or at least should be ignored, even these people tend to feel strongly about their position.

The skin color has nothing, directly, to do with the phenomena in this study. It does, indirectly, because certain, perhaps most, of the motivating factors were related to skin color.

This article has also been published as a chapter in a book, *The Psychology of Social Movements* (Wiley, 1941), by Hadley Cantril. In introducing this particular chapter in his book, Cantril says:

Father Divine's kingdom serves as a prototype of those social movements we know as 'cults'—organized actions, generally rather restricted and temporary, in which the individual zealously devotes himself to some leader or ideal. The fact that we shall be concerned with Negroes is merely accidental. It just happened that the writer had an opportunity to study this particular cult; it just happened that his cult had Negroes as members. Cults are found among individuals of various colors, nations, and classes, and within almost every society. No one 'race' as such is more prone to join a cult than any other.

This is about as close as we can come to objectivity. So, do the best you can, as you read this selection, to look for the basics involved. Why did these people behave as they did? What were the human drives or needs, otherwise neglected, that this movement satisfied?

48

THE KINGDOM OF FATHER DIVINE
HADLEY CANTRIL AND MUZAFER SHERIF

THE KINGDOM
AS A
MICROCOSM

"Father Divine is God!"

Whether whispered, spoken, sung or shouted hysterically, these words are believed by hundreds, even thousands, of people. They may be heard almost any afternoon or evening at the main kingdom of heaven, housed in an ordinary brick structure forming part of a crowded street in the center of New York's Harlem. During the past few years the street has been more crowded than ever, for now Father Divine's cars and busses with their placards of "Peace," "We thank you, Father," and "Father Divine's peace mission" are lined along the curbing. Nearby laundries, cafeterias, and small shops, otherwise like most of their kind, display signs of "Peace," "Special attention given to FATHER DIVINE children. I thank you." On Saturday and Sunday afternoons and evenings moving crowds fill the sidewalk in front of kingdom headquarters. Sooner or later most people are inside.[1]

SOURCE: From *Journal of Abnormal and Social Psychology,* 1938, *33,* 147–167.

[1] More complete biographical accounts of the Reverend M. J. Divine and both historical and descriptive accounts of his movement may be found in R. A. Parker, *The Incredible Messiah* (Boston: Little, Brown, 1937); John Hosher, *God in a Rolls Royce* (New York: Hillman-Curl, 1936); and S. McKelway and A. J. Liebling, "Who is this King of Glory?" *New Yorker,* June 13, 20, and 27, 1936.

The doors of the kingdom are always open. In the small corridor leading to the upstairs assembly hall we face a brightly colored sign: "The relaxation of your conscious mentalities is but the reconception of God's omniscience." The hall itself is filled with believers sitting on simple wooden benches. Most of them are negroes, with a sprinkling of whites. White visitors are easily recognized. They are given seats or ushered to the platform at the front of the hall.

The room is filled with crude banners. High overhead are stretched in silver letters "Father Divine is Dean of the Universe." The followers (or "children," as they call themselves) are singing the verse:

> Father Divine is the captain
> Coming around the bend
> And the steering wheel's in his hand.

The song has five verses. Singing is accompanied by a small brass band. No one officially leads the "children." It is unnecessary. A few already know the song, and the rest soon catch the simple rhythm. The crescendo increases with each verse. At the end of this song, a large, middle-aged colored woman testifies how Father cured her bad knee, which specialists had been unable to help. Some listen, others close their eyes and moan. Shouts of "Isn't it wonderful!" "He's so sweet!" and "We thank you, Father!" are frequent. One or two hysterical negroes walk around dazed and shouting, occasionally falling. The testimony ends with the first line of another song, sung with great feeling by the testifier. It is immediately picked up by others. The band catches the tune. Soon all are singing:

> One million blessings,
> Blessings flowing free,
> Blessings flowing free,
> There are so many blessings,
> Blessings flowing free for you.

As the song continues (substituting "billion" and "trillion" for "million"), some begin to sway; shouting becomes more frequent, a white man jumps up and down praising Father, the rhythm is emphasized by the clapping of the children. Still no one is leading them. This song ended, there is another testimonial. A man castigates himself for his former sins. He was an adulterer. He had stolen food and money. He had been a drunkard. Someone told him about Father. He came to hear him and was immediately cured of his evil ways. He intersperses his testimony with "I do thank you, Father. You are so wonderful."

Other children confirm his belief. They listen intently to his confession. He talks for about ten minutes, exhausting himself with the vitality of his speech. He sits down, wipes his face, puts his head on his knees. Someone begins to sing:

> Now don't let me say it, unless I mean it.
> Oh! Don't let me say it, unless I mean it.
> For I know it will manifest just as I've seen it,
> Since you are here, Sweet Father.

It has eleven verses and a chorus. The last verse is sung loudly, with clapping and many outbursts, some of the children tap dancing, some crying, some laughing.

This spontaneous flow of songs and testimonials continues for hours on end. There is perfect freedom to do what one wants—to sing, shout, cry, sway, jump, meditate, testify, or dance. Frequently the eyes turn to the many banners on the wall where home-made signs tell us:

Father Divine is God Almighty. The same one that John said, "There would come one greater yet and I will baptize you with the holy ghost and fire."

Out of one people Father Divine made all men, therefore races, colors, creeds, distinction, divisions, nationalities, groups, segregation, nicknames, classes, and all such abominations must come to an end. All these things are of the flesh and no flesh shall glorify itself in the presence of the almighty Father Divine. Man's day is done. God alone shall reign. This is his day of reign. Thank you Father.

Our justice and truth is called in the expression of the Father. Peace.

Peace, peace, peace! Father Divine is the wonderful counsellor, Prince of Peace. At his name all war shall cease.

We turn to our colored neighbor and ask him when Father Divine is coming. He looks at us blissfully and says, "He's here." "Where?" He points at random: "He's there, there, everywhere. He's in your heart." Another follower notices our dilemma and advises us to go downstairs to the banquet table. Father speaks there, if he speaks at all. Many have already gone down. It is about 11 p.m.

The banquet hall is filled. A large horseshoe table takes up most of the space, and around it are seated about a hundred children. Another hundred or more are standing in the crowded spaces nearby. There is one conspicuously vacant place at the head of the table, near which sit several well-dressed negroes and one white. We are told they are Angels. They seem more self-possessed, more patient, more intelligently alert than the rest. On the table in front of the Angels are great platters of turkey, chicken, cold cuts, fruit and bread. The air is close and sticky.

This room, too, is lined with banners, proclaiming such sentiments as:

Father Divine is the only redemption of man.
Father Divine is God and a little child shall lead them.

In general the group downstairs is more orderly, more unified than it was upstairs. Still there is no leader present. Yet here is a self-contained microcosm, bound together by a common set of norms.

FACTORS CREATING AND SUSTAINING THE MICROCOSM
The testimonials which continue show that within the microcosm basic needs are satisfied. Children who live outside the kingdom also tell how Father has provided for them. One woman says, "I thank you, Father Divine, God almighty, for what you have done for us since coming in contact with the Peace Mission. Thank you, Father. My brother was ill and suffering pain and covered with sores. In two weeks time he was able to work without pain or sores. Truly there is nothing to do but to thank you, Father." Another ends her testimonial in song:

Father I thank thee, Father I thank thee,
Father I thank thee, for what You've done for me.

The testimony of Life Dove—a pretty young negress—is received enthusiastically: "People have been talking about God for many years, but today, a God whom you can't see or never have any personal contact with just doesn't fill the bill. A promise of some home far beyond the clouds, with milk and honey flowing freely, really isn't what it takes to keep going down here, on terra firma. If God can't take care of me here and now, then how can I know or even believe He'll do so very much after I'm dead and gone. . . . Now, all in all, I ask you, what more of a God do you want, than one who'll give you shelter, food to eat, clothes to wear and freedom from sickness, worry and fear? Now isn't that wonderful!" [2]

In return for the benefits they receive, supposedly everything the children have is Father's—their money, their services, their thought, their love. Those who come to live in one of the numerous kingdoms give Father their property, their insurance, their extra clothes, their savings—everything. Most of those who live outside the kingdoms give him something after providing minimum needs for themselves.

Even more important for the unity of the microcosm is the common "positive attitude" Father has inculcated in them. They

[2] *The Spoken Word*, August 18, 1936, 21. This is a semi-weekly publication of the Peace Mission. Weekly magazines are *The World-Herald* and *The New Day*. The kingdom's newspaper, *The New York News*, is published each Saturday.

are told constantly "to visualize Him, so they can realize Him, so they can materialize Him." "If you concentrate your thoughts and your energy and your mentality in the Positive direction you must produce and receive the results of the POSITIVENESS, which will be SUCCESS and PROSPERITY and HARMONY, where the negative direction will cause the result to be the expression of negation with all of its expressions and from all of its angles. You see, that is the Mystery." [3]

The effect of the positive attitude—constantly thinking of Father and thanking him—is to cause the thought to enter "the sub-conscious mentality so that your very sub-consciousness got it, then and there, you had it. Now isn't that wonderful? As you had it, so you have it. By this, you can speak the Words into 'tangibilization' or outer expression 'visibilated' and cause mankind to observe that which you have been thinking. This is a beautiful thought, is it not—the great Universal Brotherhood of man and the conscious recognition of the FATHERHOOD of GOD, and the realization of the PRESENCE of both it and them—of both HIM or HE and them." [4]

To protect the "positive attitude" and to make it easier to cultivate, Father has strictly forbidden his children to have any direct outer contact with possible sources of "negative attitudes" —those which would shift concentration from him to something else. The children are forbidden to read any newspapers or magazines except those published by Father. They must read only the books Father or his Angels recommend. They must listen to no radio programs except when Father broadcasts. They are not allowed to attend moving picture shows. Their senses, as well as their services and thoughts, are Father's.

The unity of the microcosm is further preserved and emphasized by the almost complete break most of the children in the kingdom have made with the outer world. For one thing, all dates appearing in any publications are followed by the letters ADFD—Anno Domini Father Divine, although some of the followers interpret the letters more simply as "Always Divine Father Divine." The new frame of reference is further established by the rebirth of the follower. Since he is "reborn" when he enters the kingdom, his age is reckoned from that date. He gives up, furthermore, his former name and identity, receiving another name by revelation and thereby severing a whole host of past associations, personal and social values. The new name is a "kingdom" name which fits the pattern of the new world: Quiet Devotion, Glorious Illumination, Crystal Star, Job Patience, Celestial Virgin, Fineness Fidelity, Flying Angel, Rolling Stone, Quiet Love, Wonderful Devotion.

[3] Hosher, *op. cit.*, 167 f.
[4] *The New Day*, July 9, 1936, 4 f.

With the disappearance of the old identity goes all thought of race, color, or vocation. "All God's children are equal." "In God's sight there is no difference in color." No one is allowed to use the words "black," "white," or "negro" in the kingdom. One speaks of "A person of the darker (or lighter) complexion."

A new vocabulary has been created to express the wonderfulness of Father. Father sets the pace in coining words and phrases; the children imitate him. Another extract from one of Father's messages shows some typical "kingdom" words. "It is a privilege to realize GOD as INFINITE, EVER-PRESENT and OMNIPOTENT, and YET INCARNATABLE and REPRODUCIBLE and RE-PERSONIFIABLE, as HE has been PERSONIFIED. GOD would not be OMNIPOTENT, the same today, yesterday and forever, if HE were not REINCARNATABLE. GOD would not be the same today, yesterday and forever, if HE were not RE-PERSONIFIABLE. Now isn't that wonderful?" ("Truly wonderful!" assert the children.)

Parents who join the kingdom are separated as man and wife. They generally leave their children behind in the outer world to fend for themselves. More frequently a single parent (usually the mother) enters the kingdom, forgetting and giving up completely children and spouse. Worldly habits such as smoking and drinking are taboo. There is no co-habitation in the kingdoms. The general positive attitude is sufficiently dynamic to overcome these specific, worldly behavior patterns. All signs of bodily afflictions, such as glasses, trusses, or crutches are thrown away. Ailments are forgotten. No medical or dental attention is allowed.

The isolation achieved by the follower when he breaks thus from the outer world in his change of name, his reckoning of time, his contacts, his habits, his thoughts, and his close personal associations, makes it possible for him to form a new frame of reference very similar to that of the other children around him. The deliberate cultivation of the "positive attitude" keeps the children psychologically united. During the meetings they are kept overtly together by the simple words of the songs, the simple melodies of their particular variety of spirituals, and, above all, by the simple rhythms which instill the behavioral accompaniments of clapping and swaying and often lead to a more exaggerated physical activity.

INDIVIDUAL DIFFERENCES AND CONFLICTS WITHIN MICROCOSM

But within the boundaries of this small world are still found differences and conflicts characteristic of any group of people. An observer will notice the differential enthusiasms of the followers: a few are hysterical, many are excited, some are calm and deliberate. Inquiry reveals that there are differential sacrifices: though most of the children give all they possess and earn, some withhold a small portion, while others keep their material things to themselves. The testimonials, too, reflect varying degrees of enthusiasm and sacrifice. Father's rewards are meted out unequally because of his realization that different children have different values for his purposes. One finds within the kingdoms individuals seemingly possessing no more personality traits in common than one would expect from any group of similar size chosen at random. A high degree of intelligence is displayed by some of the followers; a few are obviously below the average. In short, we may hazard the guess that within the microcosm the psychologist would probably find an almost normal distribution curve for any measurable trait or capacity.

Rivalries and schisms develop in heaven as they do elsewhere. Jealousy is often shown by those who are not so close to Father as some others. An Angel sitting at the right hand of God is envied by all. Father's alleged sexual intrigues with certain Angels create friction among those intimately acquainted with the machinations of the kingdoms. More obvious rivalries and potential schisms develop in some of the meetings when a controversy ensues over the interpretation of Father's words. One follower may preach Father's gospel in a way which is inconsistent with the meaning another follower has derived. If a quarrel seems imminent, an Angel will intervene and point out, "Father wants only praise. Preaching is His exclusive right," or, "It is Spirit that makes you praise Father this way or that way." Hereupon the controversy stops; all seem satisfied with the explanation and the Angel sings, "Father writes on the wall," temporarily dissolving dissension.

To avoid sectarianism within the kingdoms, Father teaches his children to tell all their secrets to him alone. His chief Angels spread the doctrine of peace and serve as spies. For example, a possible rupture in the Los Angeles kingdom was prevented by Faithful Mary ("Angel No. 1"), who went from New York as Father's personal missionary. To these western brethren she explained: "Father says when you write something about his works and criticize, you are trying to knock him and he will expose you. Because whenever you have anything you want God to know personally, you will tell God alone. You may know when you are writing up something and putting it in the paper you want everyone to know about it. Now if you loved Father, in the mortal consciousness, and you had a sister who got pregnant, or broke a leg, as we called it in the South, don't you know you would not have it established in the paper, because you wouldn't want anyone to know it?" [5]

[5] Hosher, *op. cit.*, 153 f.

Father is well aware of the dangers of controversy, against which he warns his children. They must align themselves with "cosmic forces" or the cosmic forces will destroy them. "God will express dissatisfaction, or dissatisfaction in what you are doing, if you will reflect or manifest dissatisfaction. Now, isn't that Wonderful—for the reaction of your thoughts and actions may be manifested in the atmospheric conditions of the weather. It is indeed Wonderful! This has been the experience of all Religions. The Cosmic Forces of Nature through the Ages, worked according to the conscious mentality of the people. When their minds were antagonistic and conflicting one with the other, the atmospheric conditions would be exhibited from that angle of expression. Now isn't that Wonderful!" [6]

The cosmic forces are all on Father's side. He can turn them against dissenters, who thus are caused to sicken and to die. "If man works inharmonious to Me we believe the Cosmic Forces of Nature will destroy him." [7] These mysterious forces are the causes of wars, floods, tornadoes, race riots, storms, pain, and disease. They can be brought under the control of the individual to work for his personal satisfaction and happiness only when there is "harmony in his conscious mentality."

POLARIZATION AROUND CONCRETE SYMBOL
Father's children, then, are likely to quarrel individually or in groups during his absence. The "cosmic forces" may tend to catapult some of them away from the kingdom's center of gravity. But as the time for Father's appearance approaches, all differences dissolve. The developing crescendo of the songs in the banquet hall downstairs and the general increase in excitement indicate that personal identity is being submerged in a common value. All thoughts are centered on Father. All eyes are searching for a concrete focal point—found in the empty chair at the head of the table. The songs themselves reflect the intense need for the symbol of this common feeling:

Father, I love you, Father I do.
Father, I love you, Father I do.
Father, I love you, Father I do.
Father, I love you, Father I do.
Father, I love you, Father I do.
Father, I love you, Father I do.

Father arrives. His entrance is greeted with an uproar. He is an unusually short, well-dressed negro about 60 years old, though he looks younger. He sits down. Dishes of hot food are

[6] *The Spoken Word*, August 11, 1936, 5.
[7] Hosher, *op. cit.*, 121.

brought him which he blesses by starting on their way around the large table. Sometimes Father pours coffee. All the while there is more singing, interspersed with more testimonials. Father seems unmoved by all of this turmoil. He pays absolutely no attention to the praises heaped upon him. The most glowing testimonial fails to excite him. He knows that it is unnecessary to respond to each song or testimonial. He knows that he is already the idol of the people, a symbol already created by their intense feeling. And since the idol is strong in the minds of the children, it needs no support from the outside. He eats and chats with his neighbor though he may somewhat nervously drink many glasses of water while undergoing this bombardment of adoration. Those at the table eat heartily as Father has told them to do. When one person finishes his meal, another takes his place. After an hour or so of eating, most of the children are happily replete.

Now that Father has satisfied their hunger, the followers appear blissfully content. Satiety has further dulled all critical processes. The unity of their attitudes, their full stomachs, and their fatigue make them more suggestible than ever. Their testimonials and songs show that all ego identities have broken down. They are one with God.

Father rises to speak. His opening words sustain the identity in the minds of the children. "Peace, everyone." "Peace, Father," shout the children. "Here you are and there I am, there I sit and here you stand, and yet I sit and stand as well as sit in the midst of the children of men. As you are so am I and as you may be, so am I that you might be partakers of the Nature and the Characteristics of Christ." [8] Or "Here we all are again, just the way we should be, just as I am. When I say, 'Here we all are again,' it means nothing less than the consciousness of the Allness of God in the likeness of man, and the nothingness of man, where such a recognition stands. Now isn't that wonderful? A place wherein you can stand, where all the Allness of God and the nothingness of matter will be a reality to you." [9]

For several minutes he directly sustains their belief that he is God and that they are part of him: "Oh, it is a privilege to live in the Land of the Living, where God Himself according to the Scripture, shall be with us, and shall be your God and you shall be His People, for the Mouth of Spirit is Speaking. Oh, it is a privilege to realize, every positive spoken word can and will be materialized if you will allow such to be, by the sacrifice of your life for that which you have spoken." [10] There is no doubt in the minds of the children that they are face to face with God. "We

[8] *The Spoken Word*, August 18, 1936, 17.

[9] *Ibid.*, May 30, 1936, 17.

[10] *Ibid.*, July 7, 1936, 17.

believe every word you say, Father," they shout from time to time. Father reassures them in their belief, explaining that "by your intuition you know it is true."

The message may last an hour. The delivery of the message, like the testimonials and the singing, is dramatic. But Father's exit, like his entrance, is business-like, in spite of the praises which follow him to his car outside or to his office on the top floor of heaven.

Father's mysterious movements add to his divinity. He has a private airplane to speed him through the heavens. One never knows when or where he will appear. The statement that he was never born, but was "combusted" in Harlem about 1900 is generally known to the children.[11] His letters, which they read in their papers and magazines, are the letters of no ordinary individual. All of them have the same ending: "This leaves ME as I hope you are and all who are concerned may also be, Well, Healthy, Joyful, Peaceful, Lively, Loving, Successful, Prosperous and Happy in Spirit, Body and Mind, and in every organ, muscle, sinew, vein and bone and even in every atom, fibre and cell of MY Bodily Form." At the 1936 International Righteous Government Convention it was moved and passed that "Father Divine is God." There were no dissenting votes.[12]

Since he is God, all are under his power—city, state and federal officials, kings, premiers, and popes. His publications reproduce his letters to Mayor LaGuardia, President Roosevelt, the Pope, Gandhi and other celebrities. Occasionally city or state officials come to speak at his meetings, but Father, as would be expected, always steals the show. If Divine has not yet demonstrated his control of individuals outside his microcosm, at least those within it are acting under his direction. Before the 1936 presidential election Father repeated in sermon after sermon that his followers should not vote until he had told them how to vote. "Hold your HANDS. I say, STAY your HANDS, until you find the man that will stand for RIGHTEOUSNESS, TRUTH and JUSTICE for 'He that waits upon the Lord shall renew his strength.' Now isn't that wonderful! Now I know you are enthusiastic, and filled with the spirit of Politics for RIGHTEOUSNESS, yet I believe every one of you will HOLD YOUR HAND; will STAY your HAND, until you get the Command."[13] "Yes Father," cry the children. "Since," as Father said, "not one of the major parties, officially and nationally or conventionally, has come to me and accepted of my righteous government platform, we must stay our hands."[14] His command—repeated hundreds

[11] Hosher, *op. cit.*, 259.
[12] *Ibid.*, 238.
[13] *The Spoken Word*, June 20, 1936, 5.
[14] *New York Times*, November 4, 1936.

of times—was apparently effective, for the Harlem polls were virtually deserted on election day.[15]

IMPACT OF
EXTERNAL
WORLD ON
MICROCOSM

The world that Reverend Divine has created, the world in which he is God, the world in which his commands are obeyed is essentially a microcosm within a larger world organization. It has its own standards, its own norms. Yet even in the moments of greatest frenzy, in the geographical center of the Kingdom of God, *the realities of the outside world may be seen to intrude.* One notices that the testimonials of white children are listened to more attentively than those of the negroes. When a white visitor enters, or wants to pass in the crowd, children of the darker complexion politely make way for him. The class consciousness and servility of the negro have become so ingrained that they pervade a heaven where one of the strongest tenets is that there shall be no thought of race or color.

Because of the glaring discrepancies between the beliefs and standards of the kingdom and those of the harsher world outside it would be expected that a follower's exit from the former world and his entrance into the latter would be fraught with difficulties. Most of the children spend their week days working in a society where Father Divine is not God, where there are rigid differentiations regarding color, race, and class. What happens when the devout follower leaves the kingdom on Sunday night?

Father is aware of the possible difficulties arising from the fact that he demands all of a follower's love and thought and also commands him to do his work well. "Do your job conscientiously but think constantly of me." Both of these tasks can be accomplished simultaneously, says Father, "if you don't let your right hand know what your left hand is doing." Those who have menial or routine jobs are apparently quite able to think about one thing while doing another. The discrepancies between the two world orders are not seen by the more ignorant believers. But anyone in a responsible position requiring concentration and intelligence finds it almost impossible to visualize Father and at the same time to perform efficiently. Happy Star, a trusted housekeeper in a family to which she is devoted, was completely unable to reconcile the two duties successfully. She reported, "It drove me almost crazy to try to plan a dinner for the family and guests and at the same time relax my conscious mentality. And sometimes when Mr. X (head of the house) would ask me something, I would say 'Peace. Thank you, Father.' This embarrassed me to death. I did not know what to do. I tried to resist Father's hypnotic powers and kicked myself for going to the kingdom and giving up my salary. But I kept going."

[15] *Ibid.*

A responsible butler reported that he found it difficult to be alert in his duties and at the same time to think always of Father. Furthermore, his teeth were aching, his eyes were bad, and he was constantly constipated. Since Father had forbidden any medical or dental attention as well as the use of drugs, and since the butler was giving Father all of his monthly wages, he could do nothing to remedy his condition. And yet, though he became skeptical of the movement, he did not leave for several years.

Why is it difficult for intelligent children to escape Father's influence? They all give the same answer—fear. Father is all-powerful. He has told them that the cosmic forces are on his side, that he has power of life and death. Several incidents have served to strengthen this belief. In June, 1932, Judge Smith sentenced Father to jail. Three days later the judge died. When asked about this Father said, "I hated to do it." Will Rogers made some unfavorable remarks about Father in a radio broadcast. His airplane crash soon followed. Huey Long refused to see one of Father's Peace Mission delegations. A few days later he was assassinated.[16]

This fear of Father pervades the kingdom. Blessed Life, who finally left heaven, had been one of Father's chief Angels until Father got all his money. Then he was gradually moved from the head to the foot of the table. Soon he had a very menial position in the kingdom, and Father no longer paid attention to him. He grew skeptical. Sores developed on his legs. He was not able to speak to his wife when they met at the meetings. Why could he not talk to her as to any other sister? He was lonesome and desperately unhappy. The bed-mate, with whom Blessed Life had been sleeping for weeks, died of tuberculosis. His wife finally communicated with him secretly, helped him overcome his fear, and the two escaped. But many in the kingdoms have no outside connections, no money, no job, and remain in agony.

This condition may partially account for some of the psychopaths taken from the kingdoms to the Bellevue Hospital. It certainly accounts for the fact that one is likely to remain a follower even with rapidly growing doubts. The only people who remain happy are the poor and the ignorant who have lost nothing by the transfer of allegiance.

INCOMPATIBILITY OF THE TWO WORLDS

Some of the more courageous and intelligent children do leave the kingdoms. For them adjustment is difficult. Happy Star finally left but admitted later that it was eighteen months before she realized that no harm would come to her. Although a conservative, refined negress she said it was hard to "hold myself

[16] Hosher, *op. cit.*, 177.

in" when she was no longer under Father's spell. She wanted to do in excess all that Father had forbidden—smoke, drink, have sexual relations with her husband. Mrs. Y. is also a backslider. For Father she had given up her small savings, her family, her friends, her reputation as a reliable cook. When she left the kingdom she had nothing to depend on. Her husband would not take her back. Penniless and worried, she realized that she had "been a fool" and didn't know where to turn next. She must make a new life for herself. She does not like to talk about her days in the kingdom. She is filled with her hatred of Father, "not for what he did to me," she says, "but for what he is doing to all the poor souls in there now."

These cases could be multiplied. They all illustrate the complete incompatibility of Father's microcosm and the world of reality. One collapses when the other is entered. Compromise is impossible. Behind this fact lies the explanation of Father Divine's following. His children are people who want to escape the world of reality, where their needs are not satisfied, and enter into a new world, where they will have material and psychological comfort.

Here are some typical biographical snatches gathered at random from conversations with children in the kingdom:[17]

Mrs. A. (negress about 35). "I'm happy now, but while I was down yonder in Alabama, I was bowded with trouble. My children give me so much trouble, I just liked to worry myself to death, but since I been living in this consciousness, I know that Father is God, and he takes care of his own. They wan't my children nohow; they was God's all the time, so I've give them up mentally, cause I know God will take care of them. Two boys and a girl. The boys by my first husband and the girl by my last. Them boys was all the time getting in trouble, and the white folks is so mean down there, 'til it kept me worried. But they ain't like that in the kingdom. It's just wonderful. Everybody is the same. . . . I didn't know about Father down there, that is not 'til I come to New York, but he caused me to come here to him. One day I just pitched down everything, and left, and I got work and a woman on the job told me about Father and I came and been coming every since. I don't worry bout nothing now. Thank you, Father."

Mrs. I. (negress about 40). "I made up my mind that I was going to New York, where I could see God in the flesh. I told Jim that I was going to leave California. He didn't want to come, so I left him. He wan't no good nohow, but I had been living with him a long time. We was supposed to be married by the laws of the world, but according to God's law we was living in adultery. . . . No, I don't miss him none. He wan't nothing but a worry all the time. When we left Florida with

---

[17] The writers are indebted to Miss Esther V. Brown, a colored student who mixed freely with the "children" in the kingdom and gathered many case histories.

our whitefolks, I had to do most everything, then when I got sick, he acted like he was mad cause I had to stop working. Men don't mean you no good in this world, and the sooner you find that out the better off you are. Put your trust in God, and he will give you everything, or else he removes it from your consciousness."

Many of the songs suggest past or present troubles:

> Father's going to save this soul of mine:
> Yes, He is, I know He is.
> Father's going to heal this body of mine:
> Yes, He is, I know He is.
> Father's going to feed me all the time:
> Yes, He is, I know He is.

Others express conscious gratitude for the escape:

> I have found Heaven, Heaven at last.
> I leave behind me all of my past.
> I come to rest on his sacred breast.
> I thank you Father.

REASONS FOR EXISTENCE OF MICROCOSM

1. Escape from material hardships. It is not difficult to see why Father Divine should flourish in Harlem, famous for its congestion, poverty, high rents and general squalor. "In many tenements basic sanitary facilities are unknown. Open fireplaces are used to heat congested railroad flats. In 1931 the death rate from tuberculosis was three times as high in Harlem as in New York City as a whole. The infant mortality rate in central Harlem was the highest for any district in Manhattan. Other diseases were disproportionately high. The National Urban League reported in 1932 that in a single block in Harlem 70% of the tenants were jobless, 18% were ill, 33% were receiving either public or private aid and 60% were behind in their rent. There were practically no recreation facilities for the children, except on the streets. In 50 cases picked up at random only one was found to have contact with organized recreation. In three years the ownership of Harlem real estate by negroes had decreased from 35% of the total to 5% of the total." [18]

Bewildered and hopeless souls living under these conditions readily surrender to a god who literally provides them what they have always craved—food, shelter, peace, security. They are anxious to believe and to follow a god who says, "I am lifting you, and all humanity out of the ruts, the mirks, and mires, out of human superstition, out of lacks, wants and all human limitations, out of all the depressions and off of the welfares and other

[18] Hosher, *op. cit.,* 88 f. See also, Parker, *op. cit.,* 34–59.

public charities into the reality of God's PRESENCE, where there is a FULL and a PLENTY for all of His Children." [19]

When they compare their days in the kingdom with their days outside, the contrast appears heavenly indeed. Father encourages the children to believe that heaven is on this earth, not on another one. "Men have used Religion to keep you in poverty! They used Religon to bind you in Slavery! But I have come to break their bands and set the prisoner free. . . . All that they have surmised and all that they have striven to get you to visualize, I have brought down from the sky. We are not studying about a God in a sky. We are talking about a God here and now, a God that has been Personified and Materialized, a God that will free you from the oppressions of the oppressors and free you from the segregations of the segregators. . . ." [20] To the poor, the oppressed, and the segregated these words are an answer to life-long prayers and needs, momentarily bringing the individual's level of accomplishment and performance up to his level of aspiration.

2. Meaning provided. The provision of a certain material comfort, the promise of security, prosperity, and health, are explanation enough for the faith of many followers. One finds in the kingdoms, however, some children who even before coming to him have had material comforts, security, health, and comparative freedom. The desires Father satisfies in them are somewhat less elemental but none the less real. For one thing, Father gives meaning to the environment in which they live. Complexity, confusion, hopelessness, and purposelessness are changed into simple understanding, peace, happiness, and a faith in the abstract principles embodied in the person of Father. A middle-aged white fisherman from the coast of Oregon, Humble by name, has crossed the continent several times to spend a few days in the main kingdom. He already had food, shelter, security, the material comforts of the middle class. But the state of the world had troubled him. He could make nothing out of changing economic and social conditions. Somehow he heard of Father. Now he says, "As you study this movement more and get to know Father better, you will become convinced, as I am, that Father has the only solution for all political, economic, and social problems of the present day. I believe Father is God in the same sense that I would call a man who knew the laws of mathematics and was able to control mathematical formulas and equations, a mathematician. Father knows the laws of the universe and is able to control cosmic forces,—something that only God can do. Therefore, Father must be God." For Humble and

[19] *The Spoken Word,* August 18, 1936, 29.
[20] Hosher, *op. cit.,* 233.

many others of his class, Father provides an escape from a tortuous mental confusion caused by complex, conflicting circumstances. He gives meaning to the individual life and to the world. It is perhaps largely for this reason that one finds in the movement so many "joiners"—people, many of them whites, who have been Baptists, Holy Rollers, Christian Scientists, and Theosophists before coming to Father. Their search for a solution to the meaning of life leads them from one formula to another.

3. Status raised. Even more important in explaining the adherence of many middle-class followers, especially negroes, is the fact that in Father's movement they are given a status which they have always craved and which has always been denied them in spite of their comparatively large bank accounts. A well-paid, healthy cook of the darker complexion related how Mother Divine [21] called for her with her big car and chauffeur and how Father called for her husband with his Rolls Royce and chauffeur. "We felt like we were big shots," the wife confessed. Their status was raised from that of servant to that of their employer or anyone else who might ride behind a chauffeur. They were, furthermore, riding with God and the wife of God.

The Reverend M. J. Divine is sincere and aggressive in his fight for negro equality. His "righteous government" platform demands legislation in every state "making it a crime to discriminate in any public place against any individual on account of race, creed, or color, abolishing all segregated neighborhoods in Cities and Towns, making it a crime for landlords or hotels to refuse tenants on such grounds; abolishing all segregated schools and colleges, and all segregated areas in Churches, Theatres, public conveyances, and other public places." It further demands "legislation making it a crime for any newspaper, magazine, or other publication to use segregated or slang words referring to race, creed, or color." [22]

This elevation of social status, even if temporary, is a sufficient reason for many people to follow Father's movement. For where else can the servile negro or the outcast white so easily find a real democracy? Who else is so openly fighting for negro equality? Only the Communists, for whom Father directed his followers to vote in 1932 but from whom he has now severed all relations.

Father encourages self-respect by familiar devices. He makes good use of *prestige suggestion*. For example, in the *World Her-*

---

[21] Mother Divine occasionally appeared with Father as his wife, although she was generally kept in the background. She recently died in a charity hospital, apparently forsaken by Divine, who will not admit that sickness and death can come to a real follower.

[22] *The Spoken Word*, June 20, 1936, 11 ff.

ald we read: "FRENCH COUNTESS VISITS FATHER DIVINE.
Joining the *ever increasing* list of *celebrities* and *important figures* from *every* walk of life that have visited FATHER DIVINE
since HE has made HIS Head-quarters in New York, is the
'Comtesse Roberte de Quelen.' The tall, stately, *blond* Countess,
on an extended vacation from her Chateau Historique de Surville
in Montereau, France, was one of FATHER DIVINE'S guests,
Monday night. Finally overcome by the Wonderful SPIRIT of
FATHER, and the beautiful singing and enthusiastic testimonies
of the Angels, plus the sumptuous banquet, the Countess arose
and literally beaming, said 'I love this place, and I love you
all!' " [23] Such words from foreign, white nobility obviously en-
hance the egos of followers with circumscribed environments
and limited opportunities.

The *impression of universality* is maintained in sermons, publications, and slogans. On the back cover of every *Spoken Word*
(a semi-weekly publication) the Kingdom Peace Missions are
listed. We find that there are 13 in Harlem, 25 throughout the
rest of New York state, 90 others scattered over the United
States, and 22 in other parts of the world, including Australia, British West Indies, Canada and Switzerland. Significantly
enough, at the end of the list we read, "Because of the unknown
number of FATHER DIVINE connections throughout the world,
the above is but a partial list for reference." A banner in the
banquet hall assures the children—"20,000,000 people can't be
wrong. We thank you Father." In a parade held in January, 1936, a large banner informed spectators that there were
22,000,000 people in the movement. By September of that year
the number had increased to 31,000,000. The actual number
of the following is almost impossible to ascertain. Estimates
range from 3,000 to 25,000.

Whatever the exact membership of the group may be, there
is no doubt that the norms of the kingdom are accepted by
thousands of individuals. An official investigation of the movement, ordered by a New Jersey judge, summarized as follows the
reasons for its growth:[24]

1. Search for economic security.
2. Desire to escape from the realities of life and improverished
   conditions.
3. Search for social status.
4. Instinctive search for God and assurance of a life hereafter.

[23] *The World-Herald*, January 7, 1937. Italics ours.
[24] Committee report to the Honorable Richard Hartshorne, Judge, Court
of Common Pleas, Essex County Court House, Newark, N.J., December
11, 1933, 35.

The first three of these conclusions are similar to those outlined above as basic causes for the movement's appeal. The
Committee's fourth conclusion, however, will not withstand psychological scrutiny. It would be more accurate to substitute for
the phrase "instinctive search for God" the idea that individuals
are constantly seeking to give meaning to their environment, and
that when a meaning rooted in the realities of the world cannot
be found, the individual either creates and reifies for himself a
symbol that will satisfactorily resolve his conflicts or accepts
from his culture some preëstablished symbol around which to
relate his environment meaningfully.[25] The last phrase of the
Committee's conclusions—"assurance of a life hereafter"—does
not seem to square with actual facts. Father Divine, as we have
seen, preaches that the Kingdom of Heaven is on this earth, not
beyond it, and that those who completely align themselves with
cosmic forces will have everlasting life.

THE MICROCOSM
AS A PROTOTYPE

This interpretation of the cult allows it to serve merely as one
example of a great variety of escape mechanisms now observable
among individuals of various nations, colors, and classes who
seek an easy resolution of their own mental conflicts—some clo-
sure from free-floating, incomplete meanings. Father Divine's
movement is similar, serves the same psychological function as
Theosophy, Buchmanism, the Townsend Plan, Nazism, and other
such mass movements.[26] It differs only in content, and in the
particular conditions that have created the confusion and suffering from which the followers seek an escape. An observer of the
Oxford Group, for example, confirms this impression with his
statement: "They (the Buchmanites) seem to have been struggling with the complexities of life rather than with any distortion
of their own souls. They are relieved to transfer to God this
struggle with a complex civilization. The more complete the
surrender to God, the more complete the escape from worry
and fear. In this escape, lies the great attraction of the Oxford
Groups." [27]

Dr. Buchman, in turn, advocates Fascism, another variation

[25] Cf. C. K. Ogden, *Bentham's Theory of Fictions*, New York: Harcourt
Brace, 1932; H. Vaihinger, *The Philosophy of "As If,"* New York: Harcourt
Brace, 1925; T. W. Arnold, *Symbols of Government*, New Haven: Yale
University Press, 1935.

[26] For an account of several recent movements, see L. Whiteman and
S. L. Lewis, *Glory Roads*, New York: Crowell, 1936; also C. W. Ferguson,
Fifty Million Brothers, New York: Farrar & Rinehart, 1937.

[27] Hugh O'Connor, "The Oxford Groups," *New York Times Magazine*,
July 18, 1936.

of the same theme. "The world needs the dictatorship of the living God. . . . Human problems aren't economic. They're moral. . . . They could be solved within a God-controlled democracy, or perhaps I should say a theocracy, and they could be solved through a God-controlled Fascist dictatorship. . . . I thank heaven for a man like Adolf Hitler." [28] And the Nazis sustain a similar fiction that "there is something mystical, inexpressible, almost incomprehensible, which this unique man (Hitler) possesses, and he who cannot feel it instinctively will not be able to grasp it at all. We love Adolf Hitler, because we believe deeply and unswervingly that God has sent him to us to save Germany." [29]

The disparities between any microcosm and the larger world macrocosm become more acute as the discrepancies increase between basic and derived needs satisfied in the two worlds. We have already noted the collapse of Father Divine's microcosm when a follower reënters the world of reality. The same phenomenon is apparent when one observes the disillusionment of a former Buchmanite, Townsendite, Theosophist, Christian Scientist, or Nazi. Frictions between microcosm and macrocosm will continue until one of two things occurs. Either the microcosms themselves must be patterned to fit the needs of an individual living in our modern world, or the conditions in the larger macrocosm must be changed to provide the satisfactions and meanings now artificially derived in the microcosms.

[28] *New York World Telegram*, August 26, 1936.
[29] Quotation from a speech by Hermann Göring, reported in F. L. Schuman, *The Nazi Dictatorship*, New York: Knopf, 1935, 122.

As we have studied Father Divine's Kingdom we have been concerned, principally, with those factors which made this movement possible. Now, look at contemporary social movements. We hesitate to name any; they change so fast. By the time you read this they may no longer be contemporary. But there have been the "hippie" groups, the back-to-nature communes, the "Jesus Freaks." These are only a few. They involve the younger age group. But the elders have "movements" too. Identify as many such groups as you can, then ask: Do the reasons given by Cantril and Sherif for the existence of the Kingdom apply in each case?

Is escape from material hardship involved? (Remember that Father Divine's Kingdom existed during the Great Depression.) In many cases this will not apply. In others, yes. Look at the Communist movement in China as a huge example.

Does joining the movement provide or seem to offer to provide a meaning to life? Does this need any comment to young people today? But, are there not "over thirty" people involved in a search for meaning, too?

Does belonging to the movement raise the status of the individual? This may be more important for some people than for others. We suspect that possibly the more the movement provides *meaning* the less it needs to provide *status*. Do you think that this is so?

Not all groups are formed in just this way. We belong to some groups because of the neighborhood in which we live, the school we attend, the church to which our parents have taken us. Some groups are formed voluntarily, some accidentally, some by varying degrees of coercion.

For whatever reason the soldier gets into the army, he soon finds himself in an interdependent relationship with others in a like predicament. He brings with him a language that has proved adequate for most situations up to now. But now he must add some words and phrases. He must do this because he needs new expressions to cope with the new objects and new situations in his life. He also needs to belong to the group. One way of belonging is to speak the same language as the others. Each person in the group lets everyone else know that he is a part of that particular group—by his language.

There are other ways in which members of groups identify themselves. One of these is clothing. We have a feeling that, if Uncle Sam did not require his soldiers to wear a certain uniform, the men themselves would adopt one of their own. Different, yes, but a uniform.

But right now we are concerned with uniformity in language. In reading this selection you may get the idea that the writer is more than a bit stodgy. Keep in mind that it was originally published in 1946 and that there have been, since then, many changes in what is permissible in print. Rather than blame the writer, try to understand the society in which he lived. Actually, he was probably being very brave in being as open in expression as he was.

49

THE SOLDIER'S LANGUAGE
FREDERICK ELKIN

1 This paper discusses the soldier's language in so far as it relates to certain social-psychological aspects of his adjustment to Army life. It is hoped, further, to present a picture of distinctive expressions which a soldier employs when among his fellows.

Considered as "soldier expressions" are: (1) those expressions not known in civilian society and therefore distinctive of Army life and (2) those expressions, employed in small sections of civilian society and generally understood by civilians, which in the Army become much more frequently and openly expressed. Both these groups of expressions are understood in all Army society, and every soldier, at some time or another, employs some of them. They are spoken of as distinctive of the Army, although actually many are common to the Navy, Marines, and Air Forces as well. Not being familiar with these services and their distinctive languages, however, I do not attempt to discuss their unique expressions.

That soldiers among themselves tend to speak differently from civilians, in both the expressions employed and the manner of expression, is generally known; but the actual expressions used and their significance in understanding the soldier have received but little attention. The popular lists and numerous references to soldier language in newspapers and magazines give a false picture. The lists, first of all, are generally full of phrases, especially substitute names for objects, which are not only rarely, if ever, heard, but of which many soldiers do not even know the meaning. For example, combining expressions from two such sources,[1] we find the following substitute expressions for "coffee": blackout, tar water, paint remover, solvent and boiler compound, battery acid, bootleg, black strap, blanko water. We find the following for "cook": belly robber, hashburner, slumburner, greasepot. There are few soldiers who could identify these. Coffee is generally called "coffee," and a cook is generally called a "cook." The substitute expressions are much less common in the Army than such references indicate.

Popular articles, furthermore, give a false picture in that they

SOURCE: From the *American Journal of Sociology*, 1946, *51*, 414–422. Reprinted by permission of the author and the publisher, The University of Chicago Press.

[1] Park Kendall, *Dictionary of Service Slang* (New York: M. S. Mill Co., Inc., 1941; reprinted 1944); Albert A. Ostrow, "Service Men's Slang," *American Mercury*, November, 1943.

omit all obscene terms, a most significant proportion of the soldier's language. Such terms, used by themselves or in combination phrases, are in almost every sentence a soldier says, sometimes with their literal meaning but more often with a meaning of an altogether different nature.

To many a recruit the constant and crude use of obscenity by the older soldiers comes as a shock. The recruit was often not aware of the extent and the range of subjects to which this language was applicable. In time, however, with constant exposure to such language, the shock lessens; and eventually, to a greater or lesser degree, practically all soldiers adopt it.

It is assumed throughout this discussion that the language adopted by a soldier is functional. Had the new expressions not in some way satisfied a need or a disposition of the soldier, they would not have been adopted, and the soldier would have spoken as he did in civilian life. Obviously, there is no invariable relationship between an expression and a function. In any given attempt at understanding, the analysis will vary with the language and the unit under study. But there are certain more general patterns that seem applicable throughout the Army, and we shall employ a few of them as a framework for our language discussion.

II   Before we begin the discussion of the expressions of more social-psychological interest, it seems advisable to eliminate what we designate as "convenience expressions." These include abbreviations and designations which denote phenomena having no counterpart or which could be expressed only cumbersomely in civilian language. Their prime function being convenience, they tend to be of less interest to the social psychologist. Examples of "convenience designations" are:

sun-tans . . . . . . cotton, khaki uniforms
latrine . . . . any toilet, and sometimes washing, facilities
burp gun . . . . . .a given type of German machine gun
short arm . . . . . medical genital inspection
jeep . . . . .a given type of ¼-ton vehicle

Examples of "convenience abbreviations" are:

OP . . . . .observation post
CQ . . . . .charge of quarters
CO . . . . .commanding officer
SP . . . . self-propelled
CDD . . . . certificate of disability for discharge

The adoption and diffusion of such designations generally does not require elaborate explanation. From our point of view the designations were adopted primarily because they were convenient and made for ease of expression. Some, such as "CDD," are authorized Army abbreviations; some, such as "SP," easily come to mind; some, such as "sun-tans," "latrine," and "jeep," are expressions of perhaps unknown origin, which were convenient and appropriately designated the new phenomena.

The objects of reference for such "convenience expressions" are generally objects toward which, per se, a soldier is neither attracted nor repelled. They tend to be expected physical details of living, military objects, routinized Army jobs, or accepted Army phenomena.[2] Since the objects of reference are relatively neutral in tone, so, too, are the expressions. They do not designate unique types of persons to whom one must adjust, nor do they connote individual or group values. A CO is the given person, no matter what kind of person he may be, who commands the unit. A short arm becomes an expected physical examination.

To the sociologist the most significant feature of such expressions is that, once diffused, like all other soldier expressions, they give the soldier a unique universe of discourse which helps distinguish him, and thus they become a binding in-group force. This tends to give him a greater feeling of freedom among other soldiers, for he can speak the expressions which more easily come to his mind, many of which would not be understood or must consciously be avoided when he is among civilians.

Employing the language of soldiers for source material in the study of a given problem has the two following merits: (1) the language has, for the greater part, been unconsciously learned, and (2) the language is "dynamic."

A new recruit may rather deliberately say "what's for chow" or "look at that f——ing line" in order to reflect an image of himself which manifests his assimilation in the Army. But in most cases the learning is completely unconscious. A soldier hears an expression, unconsciously learns its meaning in context, and soon employs it himself. Even for the more deliberate recruit, the expressions soon become his unconscious normal way of speaking.[3]

[2] The soldier, in actuality, adjusts relatively easily to such new physical situations or to such routinized ways of doing things. It may be inconvenient and unpleasant at first, but, when necessary, a soldier soon takes for granted that he must have a CO, that he must use an outside latrine, that he must wait in pay line and salute, that he must set up pup tents or even live in foxholes. To have an unpredictable or favor-currying first sergeant, however, or to take orders from an immature and cocky lieutenant are adjustments never so readily or so satisfactorily made.

[3] A plausible explanation of how such learning comes about is given by Ellsworth Faris in *The Nature of Human Nature* (New York and London:

As we have noted, we assume the expressions are functional; had they not met the requirements of the soldier, they would not have been adopted. That a soldier, therefore, so readily and unconsciously adopts these expressions bespeaks their appropriateness in his changed way of life. Further, since in the soldier's expressions we find implied attitudes and values, we can derive therefrom a spontaneous reflection of his reactions to Army life.

Another pertinent characteristic of soldier language is that it is "dynamic," it does not remain constant. As new situations are met, new adjustments are made: old expressions are discarded or used with new meanings, and new expressions become popular. Were there no changes in language, the adjustment would probably be unsatisfactory. In the same way that a sulking, maladjusting person does not tend to develop or adopt new slang expressions, neither would a sulking, maladjusting Army unit.

III   The distinctive language of the soldier may be roughly divided into two categories: (1) habitual expressions, those more deeply absorbed expressions that are learned by all soldiers and are heard constantly throughout their Army careers, and (2) fashion expressions, those found in local units or throughout the Army for relatively short periods of time.

Likewise, corresponding to certain styles which do not become popular with the public, so, too, there are expressions in the Army heard only a few times and then not at all.

The expressions discussed in this paper are primarily the habitual expressions; but it seems pertinent to give a brief discussion of the fashion language of the soldier because this registers the adjustment of a given unit.

Many expressions are fashion among those who have only recently been inducted into the Army. Some of the expressions found in lists of soldier slang, such as "armored cow" for canned milk, "tin hat" for helmet, "topkick" for first sergeant, are among these. So, too, is "hit the deck" at reveille. These are often the expressions of the new soldier who wants to present an image of cleverness or of assimilation into the Army.

The most common "fashion expressions" are those which became popular in foreign countries. In England, many soldiers came to speak of "torches," "queues," and "Piccadilly Commandos." In France in their everyday language, they used *beaucoup, fini, combien, parti,* and *tout de suite.* In Italy, soldiers spoke of *vino, grazie,* and *come sta.* When the soldiers entered Germany, the French and Italian phrases, save for *beaucoup* and *vino,*

McGraw-Hill Book Co., 1937), wherein he speaks of "unconscious imitation."

tended to be forgotten, and soldiers soon learned to say *kaput, prima, was ist los? nichts gut, Fräulein,* and others.

Other fashion expressions were adopted from miscellaneous sources. From the comic strip "Dick Tracy," Gravel Gertie came to mean any very homely girl. From the issue of a style of jacket which Eisenhower wore, soldiers spoke of "Eisenhower jackets." Extending the meaning of Army-publicized designations, soldiers used "liberating" to mean any kind of appropriating and looting, and "fraternizing" to mean meeting civilians of any kind for social reasons.

Many expressions became fashionable in given groups, befitting their unique experiences. In one unit of former academic men, all doing details of various sorts, "Ph.D." came to mean "post-hole digger." German planes which always strafed at a given time at night were called, in certain groups, "Bed-check Charlie." In one unit, soldiers said to a person who interrupted a conversation, "Who pulled your chain?"

Many such fashion expressions refer to officers of men within the given unit. In a tank destroyer battalion, for example, a lieutenant who especially sought pillboxes to destroy became known as "Pillbox Mullhall." A mess officer in one unit became the "Commissioned KP." Mimicking an officer who once told his men to "chop down those wooden trees," the men placed "wooden" before the name of any wooden object they had occasion to mention. A soldier who always "angles" to buy and sell at a profit may be called "shady Robbins" or "BTO" for "big time operator."

These expressions manifest an adjustment to new phenomena and new situations. Likewise, through creating a common universe of discourse to refer to their common experiences, the fashions create a greater solidarity among the men. Often the expressions evidence a cryptic humor in accepting uncomfortable situations, or a certain satisfaction in characterizing superiors, e.g., "Commissioned KP." In all cases they build up new interests which help prevent the men of the unit from psychologically "getting into a rut."

We have noted, then, two characteristics of the soldier's language: it is unconsciously learned, and it is "dynamic." However, since the language on which we shall focus comprises the more permanent soldier expressions, the latter characteristic will be less relevant.

IV   We shall discuss the soldier's language from two perspectives: (1) in so far as it reflects his image of himself and the image of himself he wishes to portray to others and (2) in so far as it reflects his attitude toward the authoritative situation.

The image he has of himself and the image he wishes to present to others—primarily other soldiers—tend to be the same, and unless we state otherwise, we shall so assume.[4] For certain features of personality this soldier image is no different from that of civilian life—for example, in the recognition of success and cleverness. In part, however, the soldier has developed new images to which he responds and by which he judges his own actions and the actions of others. Of the new emphases in his total self-image, we select the following for further discussion: (1) the image of solidarity with other men in the Army, (2) the image of freedom from certain restraints of civilian society, and (3) the image of strength and virility.

The image of solidarity.—The soldier from the very beginning of his Army life feels there is a bond between himself and those whom Fate has placed in a similar situation.

As already observed, many a recruit, in order to picture himself as an assimilated member of the Army, deliberately adopts Army expressions. In time, however, as he becomes more accustomed to feeling that he is a soldier, he does not deliberately have to present this role of himself, and the language mirrors a more unconsciously adopted image.

The soldier feels that he belongs to groups at various Army levels and cross-sections. It may be a squad, a division, a branch, a training camp, a battle area, a zone occupied, or the entire Army itself. On all these levels and cross-sections, expressions may develop, but generally these are what we have called "fashion expressions." The expressions, besides manifesting the unique experiences of each group, both mirror and reinforce the sense of solidarity. For the study of a given group, these "fashion expressions" are most important. Our emphasis, however, is on those more habitual expressions which have become diffused throughout the Army and which manifest the image of one's self in solidarity with all other soldiers.

Most common of these expressions is "GI," when it designates the American enlisted man. Stemming from "government issue," "GI" has become the soldier's term for himself and his fellow-soldier and, despite the implications of its derivation, is said with a sense of pride. "GI" links the men together and distinguishes them from officers, civilians, British soldiers, or any other group in question. The use of "GI" indicates that a soldier is expected to feel the bond, and claims for help are made on this basis. The driver who does not pick up a hitchhiking soldier or the cook

[4] For a study of a given person or group in which this distinction might be relevant, the different images may be partly weighted by acute observation of "expressive behavior." Whether a given expression, for example, is said with confidence, with caution, or with "daringness" betrays in the speaker something of the function it is serving for him.

who refuses to give a visiting soldier a meal are condemned in that it is a "dirty trick" not to help out a GI.

Another such expression, used more personally, is "Joe" or sometimes "Mac." One asks a strange soldier, for example, "What time ya got, Joe?" It is an expression with a friendly connotation, evidencing a solidarity among all soldiers. Until shown otherwise, it is expected that a fellow-soldier is one like you, with whom you can be friendly.

Also common is the term "buddy." Sometimes "buddy" refers to a close friend, sometimes just to any fellow-soldier. A soldier may speak of a buddy from his home town in the Eighty-third Division or a buddy with him in a foxhole, meaning any member of his company. "Buddy" does not necessarily refer to someone in the Army, but its use in the Army and in reference to fellow-soldiers is most common. It is ordinarily with a sense of pride that one uses the term "buddy." All these expressions indicate the soldier's self-image of belonging to an Army consisting of men like himself, who undergo experiences like himself. They indicate that he has absorbed feelings of solidarity with other American soldiers, no matter who they are or where they may be. The soldier likes this image of himself and feels a certain security within it.

Freedom from social restraint.—Soldiers have the reputation of assuming less responsibility toward society's ideals and values. In the American Army the soldier often comes not only to realize this reputation but to accept it as a prerogative. Depending on a combination of numerous factors, this feeling of prerogative becomes, to a greater or lesser degree, imbedded in his mind. The expression of this self-image manifests itself in his thoughts, his behavior, and his language.

In his image of himself, then, the soldier tends to feel a freedom from civilian society's taboos and controls. This image would, in most cases, never exist in an isolated individual; it is a feature of the crowd. In a group of similarly minded men these expressions are no longer taboo; on the contrary, they are often the conventional way of speaking. In his own mind, however, the soldier is aware that he is expressing what was formerly a taboo and is thus freer from social restraint. The expression of this soldier self-image is primarily in profanity.

The expression of obscenity obviously gives the soldier certain indulgences. Violating the taboos of language gives feelings of courage and freedom; it is in itself satisfying. It seems, however, that more can be derived from the given expressions than the mere fact that the soldier obtains indulgences, for each expression manifests something of a repressed sphere. In most respects, however, this is a field of study for the psychoanalyst.

Strength and virility.—This is the most obvious image of

much of his slang. In great part this language is no different in either vocabulary or principle from the language of construction crews, poolroom crowds, dock workers, and other units of men where virility is a value. Its significance in the Army derives from its quantitative increase; so many more men, of varied upbringings, constantly employ this language.

The self-image of strength is evidenced in both the manner of expression and the expressions used. That the expressions may be more clever, more picturesque, or more obscene than civilian equivalents is not relevant here; it is only relevant that to the soldier they are stronger ways of saying things and so manifest the image of a stronger self. Most of such expressions are obscene, but some are not. Some examples of the latter are:

to be on the ball . . . . to be alert, prompt, or "sharp"
to blow one's top . . . . to become angry
to sweat out . . . . to wait anxiously for something over which one has no control
to bitch . . . . to gripe or strongly complain
to take off . . . . to leave
to hit the sack . . . . to go to bed
to be snowed under . . . . . . to be overwhelmed with work, advice, etc.
to shack up . . . . to spend a night, or longer period of time, with a girl

A common group of obscene expressions are carry-overs from civilian conversation. In the Army, however, they are more frequently expressed. Under this classification come the literal meanings of the tabooed four letter words. Soldiers tend to use the crude, less euphemistic terms rather than more polite substitutes.

In the Army, as in other male societies, e.g., the work gang, the sporting and gambling worlds, the college fraternity, these vulgar words for physiological functions and the sex act enjoy a greatly extended and exaggerated role. They are applied to situations and experiences of crucial importance to the person but which are apparently devoid of sexual connotation. They are merely expressive of the conception of virility, masculinity, and freedom from social restraint characteristic of an exclusively male world. As obscene terms come into such universal and seemingly indiscriminate usage, they tend to lose their original sexual significance. As casually spoken by soldiers, obscene expressions do not mean that the users actually are thinking on the sexual level; they are merely speaking the language of their social group.

Other soldier profane expressions are in part "convenience

expressions" in that there are no adequate substitutes and a soldier finds it almost necessary to adopt them to explain given situations. Such, for example, is the common obscene expression which has the meaning in some way or another to bungle a job or to make a bad choice. There are numerous occasions in the Army when such an expression is pertinent. There are a few acceptable substitutes such as "screw up" or "mess up," but these do not have the emphasis value of the obscene equivalent. Interestingly, the expression "snafu," derived from this, "Situation normal, all f———ed up," is coming into general civilian use.

The interchangeability of vulgar terms is such that they have no distinct meanings of their own. Generally the reference is negative, but it may be positive or with no emotional overtone.

v   The language of the soldier, besides being studied in its own right, may also be studied for the light it throws on other problems of sociological interest. More specifically, we shall select for discussion some of the expressions which reflect the soldier's attitude toward, and his adjustment to, authority.

The principles underlying military authority, although they are rarely explicitly expressed to the soldier, come to be vaguely apprehended and understood. The new soldier learns that, theoretically for the sake of efficiency, there is rule by impersonal hierarchy in which problems are resolved and decisions made according to rank. He learns that rank is all pervading in the Army and that even for men of equal grade there are criteria for deciding which is the superior and which the subordinate. He learns by innumerable instances his own low position in the hierarchy. The regulations of authority, he further learns, regard him impersonally and have little respect for his individuality. This is impressed upon him from the very beginning of his Army career—if not in the speeches, then in the experiences he undergoes. He is crowded into trucks with hundreds of other men. He stands in seemingly endless lines to take a physical examination, to sign his service record, to receive immunization shots, and for dozens of other such details. He is further made to feel the impersonality and lowliness of his position when he moves into a barracks with fifty beds and finds a complete lack of privacy in the latrine. He further feels it when he is commanded to pick up cigarette butts and matches in the street. The Army's image of him does not correspond to his own image of himself. He sees himself as a person with preferences, dislikes, pride, and sensitivities; not so the Army. The soldier vaguely understands that some theory of efficiency underlies this.

There may be indulgences for the soldier in the adventure, anonymity, and irresponsibility of his new Army life, but mostly there are deprivations; and if he is to adjust, he must develop a new conception of himself which allows for his subordinate position.

That many would not be able to or cannot adjust to military service of which this authority is such an important factor is manifested in the number of men rejected and discharged for psychological reasons. The others do generally tend to develop satisfactory and more or less common conceptions of themselves which better enable them to adjust. And to characterize aspects of the authority and their relations to it, they develop and adopt new language expressions. This language reflects what he expects of the authority; it reflects an attitude toward those who do not adjust well, toward those who sacrifice their individuality to adjust, and the like. For our purpose it is not relevant how a given expression originated or in what manner it diffused; it is only relevant that it is pertinent, commonly used, and has a generally accepted significance among Army men.

We shall discuss the soldier expressions concerning authority under two headings: (1) attitude toward authority and (2) adjustment to authority.

First, the attitude toward authority. No matter what the soldier's feelings toward the Army may be, in accordance with his hazily comprehended principles of military authority, he expects to find certain rules and regulations to govern his behavior. Representing these expectations, the soldier employs the adjective "GI." Having, depending on its context, numerous meanings, it signifies in this usage an expected degree of personal control. It tends to be a neutral expression signifying the adherence to the rules. An officer who is "GI" is, per se, not abusive of his position. To the authority-disliking soldier, the officer may be "too Goddamned GI"; to another soldier, he may be "GI, but a good egg."

The standard of what is GI does not remain constant. Strong discipline, acceptable in a training camp, would not be so in combat or after the end of the war when soldiers believe that discipline serves less purpose. As the situation varies, so do the expectations of the soldier and the connotations of "GI."

However, the expected authority is often exceeded. The authority perhaps demands excessively polished buttons, is unduly strict on saluting, demands clean areas in the midst of shelling, punishes too strictly for minor offenses, or in other ways attempts under the given circumstances to regulate with too much discipline or in too great detail. In this case the authority exceeds being GI, it becomes "chicken s———," sometimes abbreviated to "CS" or "chicken."

In the soldier's language, however, we find no common expression implying that the regulations of authority are good.

This does not indicate that soldiers see no necessity of authority or do not find indulgences in being subordinate; it does indicate, however, that authority is not a direct positive value. In public one can only deprecate the need for the authority.

We may more indirectly learn of soldiers' attitudes to authority by observing how they view one another in relation to it. We may note, for example, how soldiers conceive of (1) those who fight authority, (2) those who readily accept authority, and (3) those who do not adjust well to the authority.

In reference to those who fight authority, we note that there is little stigma to the expression "f—— off" applied to their acts, such as when a man gets away with something against the Army by evading a detail of hauling beds or a talk on military courtesy, or in some other way avoids an Army requirement. Such action is considered legitimate and is generally spoken of with pride.

In reference to those soldiers who readily accept authority, we note a strong stigma. It is considered that such a soldier is disloyal to his friends and is sacrificing his individuality and self-dignity. We find these attitudes implied in "asslicker" or, with a more limited meaning, "bucker." The term "asslicker" is applied to a man who readily adopts and acts the role of the subordinate, in order that he may be more highly thought of by his superiors and be given special consideration, or else through mere weakness of character. "Bucking" always connotes trying to get ahead.

That these terms sometimes imply individual weakness is seen in their application to the superior who too obviously curries the good will of subordinates. Even though there are numerous "asslickers" and "buckers" in the Army and even though they be unconsciously envied for those characteristics which enable many to be successful, it is still of pertinence that this is not an ideal. To be a bucker is a condemnation. One is hurt and annoyed to be considered such by his fellow-soldiers.

Thirdly, we learn of soldier attitudes to authority by noting the sympathy for those who are not successful in adjusting but are "f——ed up." A soldier is often not proud of being so labeled, for it may connote inability or inefficiency. But he is not stigmatized, rather he is viewed sympathetically.

Expressions implying such sympathy are "8-ball" and "sad sack," the latter being more common. A "sad sack," derived originally from "sad sack of s——," and popularized as the cartoon character in *Yank*, is the lowest soldier in the Army hierarchy. He symbolizes the civilian who is completely lost in the Army, gets bad breaks, and makes only pathetic adjustments. He is only a cartoon, but there are often unique personalities in the Army, perhaps very fat or with other distinctive physical features, who do approach the ideal. Such people are viewed sympathetically. In part this may be due to feelings of superiority when a sad sack is present, but in part also it seems a sympathy for the person who cannot make the grade in his struggle with authority.

As expressed in the language, then, the attitude toward authority is negative. It is accepted but considered as something of a necessary evil. But most soldiers, no matter how they feel toward the authority, accept it and adjust more or less satisfactorily to it. What can we learn of his adjustment from his expressions?

We have already noted in the adjective "GI" that there is a certain acceptance of authority and of the soldier's position within it. We find acceptance also in the expression "sweating it out." "Sweating it out," like "GI," connotes nothing positive or negative; it again indicates the acceptance of an overhead control toward which the soldier himself is powerless.

There are certain obscene expressions which manifest an acceptance of one's position in the hierarchy with more negative connotations. Such, for example, are the obscene expressions, "to be s—— on," or to "take s—— from someone." They often imply an injustice against which the soldier, because of his subordinate position, can do nothing; they express a rather bitter acceptance.

Under this general heading also are the expressions "to have one's ass chewed" or "to have one's ass reamed," referring to reprimands by superiors. These, however, do not per se have such a bitter connotation, and the soldier often feels that he deserves the reprimand.

Some obscene expressions indicate adjustment with serious, reluctant acceptance of one's subordinate role. There are other expressions, however, which indicate a realization of one's position and a smiling resignation toward it. The soldier views his position in the hierarchy, accepts, and even laughs at it.

One such expression is "TS" or "tough s——." For example, a soldier is told that he deserves a promotion but that his officer is not authorized to recommend him; or he is on temporary duty and cannot or will not thereby be placed on a furlough list. There are innumerable such occasions in the Army when the soldier is told that nothing can be done to help him in his given situation. This in the Army is "TS," resigned acceptance, said with a bitter smile. It is an accepted resignation to an unhappy situation in which the soldier is powerless but at which nevertheless he may smile.

There are other expressions which better illustrate this conception in which one recognizes one's position and smiles or jokes at it. Examples, such as "GI," and "snafu," are actually caricatures of the Army's authority and of one's own position within the authority.

A soldier is a "GI," a "government issue," a standardized Army article like a pair of socks, a cake of soap, or a vehicle. As an adjective in this context, "GI" refers to the Army method of doing things, such as learning to fire or setting up tents—a method standardized and routinized. Obviously, the soldier does not see himself in this image; he has merely caricatured this image of how the Army authority views him. That he takes a certain pride in this characterization of himself, however, implies that he tends to accept readily the role of the "government issue," and he assumes with it some of the anonymity and irresponsibility which the term connotes.

Another such caricature expression is "dog tags," used to indicate the identification tags a soldier wears around his neck. This, too, caricatures the Army's conception of him—he is the animal who does not think and has need of a tender.

When a soldier has to urinate at night or when a convoy stops for a "break" on the road, the soldier designation is "piss call." The new soldier is very soon made aware of the Army routine. He learns not only of reveille, retreat, and taps, but also of mess call, church call, drill call, pay call, school call, and sick call. So the soldier extends this Army routine over his personal life a little further and speaks of "piss call."

"Snafu" is a caricature of Army direction. The soldier resignedly accepts his own less responsible position and expresses his cynicism at the inefficiency of Army authority.

The caricaturing of both the Army and himself evidences an adjustment in which the soldier accepts his subordinate position in his own mind but does not completely adopt the subordinate role. It bespeaks a satisfactory adjustment; a completely subjugated or a sensitive brooding group of soldiers would hardly adopt such caricatures.

From this discussion of expressions manifesting attitudes and adjustment to Army authority, we can derive no profound conclusions. We can only generalize that (1) authority is accepted as essential, (2) authority, per se, has a negative value, (3) the soldier adjusts to authority with varying degrees of bitterness, resignation, and caricaturing acceptance.

These are not of themselves very illuminating; but from the unique expressions we do obtain a certain understanding of the types and variations of the soldier's adjustments.

What are the factors in society that make it now the custom to use certain words in print when a few years ago this was "just not done"? Why did Elkin write "f---" when he meant "fuck"? Why was his behavior *then* a kind that seems prudish and hypocritical *now*?

Why did we include so out-of-date a selection? Simply because we feel that you can be more objective as you look back on something in the past than you can in relation to something now. You are living in the middle of "now" and have all kinds of *feelings* regarding it.

You have looked at a study that concerns the soldier's adjustment to the army in the early 1940's. Use that as a basis for comparison. Are the problems of the soldier's adjustment now the same as then? Or are they different? How?

What about the individual's adjustment to other groups: the work group, high school, college? What expressions do you use now that you did not use before you came to college? Does the language used by various groups reflect anything about the roles of the individuals in those groups or at least the way each of them sees his role?

What groups do you know that have "languages" of their own? There is the jargon of space technology. Some years ago someone coined the word "pedaguese" for the language of teachers (pedagogues). What about the "hippie" culture? The "third world" groups? What does each of these languages tell us about the concept the individual member of the group has in relation to the rest of society?

We have seen in the "Chitling Test," in a previous chapter, a sample of a language developed by the blacks. What are some of the words and phrases used by black groups that are not ordinarily used by whites? Do these words have any special significance? What might we learn from a study of the language of the ghetto or the barrio that would tell us something significant about present-day social psychology?

IF YOU WOULD READ MORE ABOUT INTERDEPENDENCE

Both Cantril and Sherif have written many other works about social movements. Old, but of value in gaining an objective view of how social movements come to be, is Hadley Cantril, *Psychology of Social Movements* (Wiley, 1941). Somewhat of a classic in its field is Muzafer Sherif, *The Psychology of Social Norms* (Harper and Row, 1936). Not only do groups form around their interdependencies, but they often come in conflict with other groups. The nature of conflict as it involved two groups of boys is discussed by Sherif in "Experiments in Group Conflict" (*Scientific American,* November, 1956). An expansion of this theme will be found in Muzafer

Sherif, *In Common Predicament: Social Psychology of Intergroup Conflict and Cooperation* (Houghton Mifflin, 1966). In this book Sherif is particularly concerned with the prevention of wars.

A group, by its very nature, places social pressures on its members. The effects of social pressure on judgment are discussed and illustrated in Solomon E. Asch, "Opinions and Social Pressure" (*Scientific American,* November, 1955).

The selection on "The Soldier's Language" is one of several articles in an entire issue of the *American Journal of Sociology* (March, 1946) devoted to the topic, "Human Behavior in Military Society."

Most of us have long been aware of the existence of stereotypes in the thinking of the members of one group about members of another. Many of these stereotypes are related to minority groups within our own country. Others pertain to the people of various other nations. Many people have been trying very hard to get rid of stereotypes of this sort. We seem to believe that, in general, there has been a change, a change toward fewer of these stereotypes. We seem to believe that each new generation of college students either comes to college or, at least, leaves college with fewer stereotypes.

In 1932 D. Katz and K. W. Braly did a study, "Racial Stereotypes of 100 College Students" (*Journal of Abnormal and Social Psychology,* 1933, *28,* 280–290), in which they found that their sample of Princeton undergraduates did subscribe to the stereotypes and prejudices in our culture.

In 1950 G. M. Gilbert, "Stereotype Persistence and Change Among College Students" (*Journal of Abnormal and Social Psychology,* 1951, *46,* 245–254), repeated the study. He again used Princeton students and used the same checklist Katz and Braly had used to see whether or not there had been any change in the tendency to stereotype. He did find a change, a change in the direction of fewer stereotypes.

We would suggest that this would make a good special project for a few students, or even a project for an entire class. Use the same technique as was used in the Princeton studies and try to determine the extent of racial stereotypes on your campus. You cannot, of course, do a completely controlled experiment, for you have two independent variables, campus and year. But you might compare men with women, fraternity and nonfraternity, freshmen and seniors, students in different majors.

If you like doing experiments of this sort, here is another you might try. See Jay M. Davis and Amerigo Farina, "Humor Appreciation as Social Communication" (*Journal of Personality and Social Psychology,* 1970, *15,* 175–178). It is concerned with the role of humor in communication between two people.

Which provides us with a beautiful lead-in to the next part —"Communication."

Part Sixteen

Communication: Is Anybody Listening?

We have been discussing interdependencies. But isn't this communication? We cannot really separate them. Communication is one aspect of social psychology. To understand the total person we must view him in his surroundings, understand his interactions with people. These interactions involve communication.

More than twenty years ago William H. Whyte, Jr. wrote a book which he called *Is Anybody Listening?* (Simon and Schuster, 1952). We liked the title so well we borrowed it to use in our part heading. The book is about "How and why U.S. business fumbles when it talks with human beings." You may wish to read it, particularly if you are interested in business management. Probably most of what it has to say about business communication—or the lack of it—is still true, not only in business, but elsewhere, too.

In most discussions the people involved are *not* listening. They are too busy thinking of what they are going to say when they get the floor. So the discussion ends with each person more convinced of his own position than he was before.

How well do you listen? If you would like to find out, here is a technique to use. It will help you, and others who take part, to listen better.

50

THE TEST OF LISTENING
THOMAS GORDON

Because we can never be sure that we have completely understood another person, it is important to test the accuracy of our listening. Unfortunately, in most situations involving an attempt to communicate with others, we rarely put our understanding to a test. Consequently, we often misunderstand others or distort their meanings. One of the best ways of minimizing this misunderstanding and distortion is for the listener to try to restate in his own language the expression of the speaker and then to check to see if the restatement is acceptable to the speaker. This is essentially what the group-centered leader is continuously doing throughout the initial stages of the group's development. He calls it "reflection of feelings or meanings," to

SOURCE: On pages 179–180 of *Group-Centered Leadership.* Copyright 1955, by Thomas Gordon. Reprinted by permission of the publisher, Houghton Mifflin Company.

convey that he is trying to mirror the speaker's expressions so accurately that the speaker himself is satisfied that he has been understood.

This is an extremely difficult thing to do, even momentarily. The reader who is interested enough to test out the accuracy of his own listening will find the following experiment both interesting and revealing:

> Choose a situation in which you have become involved in a controversial discussion or argument with another person. Suggest to the other that you both adopt a ground rule and follow this strictly throughout the discussion. The rule: Before either participant can make a point or express an opinion of his own he must first reflect aloud the statement of the previous speaker; he must make a restatement that is accurate enough to satisfy the speaker before he is allowed to speak for himself.[1]

This little experiment, if it is seriously carried out, will demonstrate, first, that it is very difficult to adopt another's frame of reference. Second, it will give the participants a new kind of experience in which they will find that emotions tend to drop out and differences become minimized. Furthermore, each participant will discover that his own views are changing and will admit that he has learned something new from the other.

[1] Suggested to the writer by S. I. Hayakawa, the semanticist.

Just listening to other people is not all of the communication process. Much of the information we receive comes to us by means of a nonhuman device of some kind. People receive information from telephones, televisions, and typewriters. Do they listen? Meaningfully? Can they understand all of the information input designed for human consumption?

People provide input to machines. Machines transfer information to other machines. And then there are computers! All of this embodies what we have come to call (with apologies to women's lib) man-machine systems. Since human behavior is involved, psychologists get involved. They answer to various names, but we increasingly think of those psychologists who work with problems of this sort as *engineering psychologists.*

The writer of our next selection is an engineering psychologist. He asks the question: What do we need to know to build a computer that can communicate? This leads, naturally, to another question: What is involved in human communication? For, if we are to design a computer that can simulate man, we must first understand man.

We have said that communication is a necessary aspect of person-to-person interaction. Just how necessary? Just how important is the communication function in our daily lives? An attempt to answer these and other related questions should help us understand at least two things. First, what are the requirements of a really good computer? Second, and far more important, what is the nature of the human communication process?

PRELUDE TO 2001: EXPLORATIONS IN HUMAN
COMMUNICATIONS
ALPHONSE CHAPANIS

"It is the thesis of this book that society can only be understood through a study of the messages and the communication facilities which belong to it; and that in the future development of these messages and communication facilities, messages between man and machines, between machine and man, and between machine and machine are destined to play an ever-increasing part [Wiener, 1950, p. 9]."

In the science fiction film *2001: A Space Odyssey* and in the book based on that film (Clarke, 1968), one of the principal characters is a computer called HAL. HAL is quite a remarkable gadget. It directs and plots the course of an enormous vehicle traveling through deep space. It computes courses, speeds, and trajectories for satellite vehicles that leave and return to the mother ship. It monitors continuously the various subsystems of the space ship and displays the information it senses in a variety of forms. In anticipation of emergencies and equipment failures, it alerts the astronauts and suggests expedient courses of remedial action. It controls the physiological condition of astronauts who are in hibernation for the duration of the trip, as well as those who are in a normal physiological state and on duty. When the astronauts are bored, it plays chess with them and engages in other intellectual diversions upon request. Indeed, HAL even has some primitive human emotions and motivations, and it is those that eventually lead to a catastrophic end of the mission.

SOURCE: From *American Psychologist*, 1971, *26*, 949–961. Copyright ©
1971 by the American Psychological Association, Inc. Reproduced by permission.

All these things that HAL did in the film are more fact than fiction, for computers today already do all the things enumerated or are at least capable of doing them. Computers guide space vehicles. They monitor complex assemblages of men and machines and warn of emergencies that are beyond human capacities to sense and comprehend. Computers keep watch over the physiological states of astronauts as well as comatose patients in intensive-care units. Computers play tolerably good games of chess and poker, and never lose in games of tick-tack-toe and matching pennies. Finally, most people who work with computers are convinced that they have personalities with some of the same perverse traits one can find in emotionally unstable persons.

What is unusual about HAL is the way in which it interacts with its human counterparts. The astronauts can and do insert data into the computer through pushbuttons and similar manual devices, much as we do today. That primitive kind of interaction, however, is the exception rather than the rule. HAL more typically interacts with the astronauts in humanlike terms. For the most part, HAL and the astronauts converse orally in idiomatic English, and what contributes to the eventual destruction of most of the crew is that HAL can even read lips.

That, you say, is pure fiction, and indeed it is—today. Still, some very able minds do not see it as unattainable fiction, but as a prophecy of things to come. Even if you do not believe that such things are possible, I ask you to go along with the fiction for a little while.

WHAT DO WE NEED TO KNOW TO BUILD A COMPUTER LIKE HAL?

The question I would like you to keep constantly before you while you read this article is the following: What do we need to know to build a computer that would communicate like HAL? Many of you will probably think immediately that this is a matter of engineering technology and not a psychological question at all. I do not agree. Engineers are very clever people, and it is axiomatic in engineering that if you can describe any phenomenon in precise quantitative terms, an engineer can build a machine to simulate it. Think about that for a moment. If we could specify in precise, quantitative terms exactly how we hear and recognize speech, engineers would have no difficulty in building a speech-recognition machine to do what we do. As psychologists, we believe that all human behavior is lawful, orderly, and measurable. But it is our inability to describe our behavior fully in exact mathematical terms that is the chief obstacle standing in the way of our attempts to design conversational computers. So, you see, my question really is a psychological one. If we *really* knew how people communicate, we would be able to build a computer like HAL.

Purpose of My Talk Communication between computer and man is the focus of research efforts in my laboratory at the present time. I am happy to say that I think we have been able to make some significant inroads into this virtually unexplored area. Still, I am not going to give you many results. My purpose is rather to pose some questions and, in so doing, to show you how questions about an important practical problem can at the same time be fundamental ones about human behavior. In a more general way, the reason I would like you to consider my question about what we need to know to build a computer like HAL is that it provides us with a convenient vantage point, a hilltop, from which to see how some of us look at life, behavior, and the world in which both occur. I want to introduce you to an area of applied psychology that some of you may recognize only by name. I would like to try to convince you that problems in this area of applied psychology are at least as stimulating as, and often much more difficult than, those in basic areas of psychology. Finally, I would like to show you that trying to solve a practical problem can lead you to ask exciting basic questions, questions that might not otherwise be asked.

Philosophical Stance The history of man is littered with labels that have been attached to various stages of it. You surely recognize the age of enlightenment, the age of reason, the golden age, and the roaring twenties. The years in which we find ourselves at present will in some future time, I suppose, be called the age of relevance. All of a sudden, psychologists are raising serious questions and entertaining nagging doubts about the relevance of their science. As an engineering psychologist, I do not have these doubts, because, you see, we have always been relevant. To be sure, you might not be excited by the things we have been relevant about, but we have been relevant.

Although I have just identified myself as an engineering psychologist, I also answer to the name of human factors engineer or ergonomist, depending on where I am and to whom I am talking. These contemporary labels are, however, not quite as descriptive of my philosophical position as a considerably older title that has now, unfortunately, been gradually dropping out of use. There was a time, you see, when I called myself an experimental psychologist, albeit a special sort of experimental psychologist, an *applied* experimental psychologist. Indeed, my first book written with Garner and Morgan (Chapanis, Garner, & Morgan, 1949) over 20 years ago coined the term applied experimental psychology.

As an applied experimental psychologist, or, if you will, as an engineering psychologist, I have little patience with most so-called theoretical or basic experimental psychology, a substantial amount of which I find trivial, turgid, and an appalling misuse of scarce and precious resources.[1] I say this not because I am opposed to basic research per se, but rather because I am completely unimpressed by certain kinds of basic research. You see, it is my firm belief that the best basic work in psychology starts not with psychological theory, but with attempts to solve questions posed by the world around us. The history of psychology is full of examples: reaction-time studies started with a practical problem in astronomy; the field of mental testing started with a problem put to a French elementary school teacher; the field of speech communication and its measurement started from some problems raised and first attacked by telephone engineers; information theory started from attempts to understand complex switching networks; and some of the best work in color vision has been done to construct a usable system of specifying colors for engineering, business, and industry.

So one of my purposes in writing about communication between computers and people is to try to convey to you some of the challenge and the excitement of starting with a practical problem and attacking it with all the intellectual skills you can bring to bear upon it. I mean to imply by that statement a much broader view of the science of psychology than is currently taught in many graduate schools. Basic and theoretically oriented experimental psychologists typically spend a great deal of time playing intellectual games, called experiments, in their laboratories. Because laboratory experiments today are often elegantly formulated, intricately designed, and meticulously executed, it is easy to assume that they are thereby useful and powerful. This does not follow. In a recent methodological paper (Chapanis, 1967), I have called attention to the many technical, statistical, and philosophical difficulties one encounters when he tries to extrapolate from laboratory research to the solution of practical problems. The applied experimental psychologist, on the other hand, is not bound by an undeviating dedication to laboratory experimentation. He has in his repertoire a great many techniques of investigation, of which laboratory experimentation is only one. The object of his game, you see, is not to be elegant, but to be right.

Now that I have stated my biases and my reasons for writing this article, I suspect that I have either delighted or antagonized you. I doubt that you are neutral. Whatever the state of your affect at the moment, I hope that at he very least I have been able to capture your attention. If I have done so, perhaps I will be able to show you how some of us in psychology try to be relevant.

The starting point for an engineering psychologist is not a

[1] A point of view shared even by some basic experimental psychologists (see, e.g., Tulving & Madigan, 1970).

deduction from someone's theory or a self-generated hypothesis, but a real-world question, a question such as people asked some 10 years ago. What do we need to know to put men on the surface of the moon? or the question I am asking today: What do we need to know to build a computer that would communicate like HAL?

COMMUNICATION AS A FIELD OF PSYCHOLOGICAL INQUIRY

Having framed a question, the engineering psychologist next usually wants to know, Is it an important question? One thing that is characteristically different about our outlook on life as compared with that of the typical experimentalist is that we want our answers to make a practical difference. It is not enough that our results be statistically significant. We want them to be practically significant as well. Basic research scientists are fond of pointing out the difficulties of making judgments about the importance of any particular research question or any area of research. Although I certainly agree about the difficulty of making such judgments, I do not admit that they are impossible. As a practical matter, the resources available for research in this country, and the time and talent that can be dedicated to this kind of activity, are not sufficient for us to undertake research on anything and everything with equal commitment or justification. Like it or not, the research administrator, and the research man himself, is forced to make value judgments about the comparative importance of problems and programs. We recognize implicitly that we should not fritter away our time on problems that do not or will not make much difference. Life is too full of big things that need doing for us to waste our time in that way.

How important is communication as a subject for psychological study? Not very, if we were to judge from the amount of work that has been devoted to it by psychologists. After all, the word started to appear regularly in the index to *Psychological Abstracts* only with Volume 16 (1942). Even then, entries under the heading of *communication* were sparse until Volume 23 of the *Abstracts* appeared in 1949.

The situation has changed since that time, to be sure. The semiannual index of the *Abstracts* for the first half of 1970 contains 171 entries under the word communication. This means that communication has finally nosed out dissonance, eyelid conditioning, galvanic skin response, paired-associates learning, and parapsychology. Still, it is by no means as popular a topic as conditioning, rat, and reinforcement. Indeed, there are well over 1,000 entries under *rat* in that index. To keep things in their proper perspective, too, one should bear in mind that the 171 communication entries are only 1.8% of the total of 9,485 items abstracted during the period I am considering.

A substantial fraction of the current and recent literature one finds under the heading of communication is concerned with what has come to be called communication theory or information theory. That literature is essentially useless for our purposes. I have yet to find a single instance in which psychological research on communication theory has contributed to the solution of any practical psychological problem. For one thing, the bits, bytes, or chunks of communication theory are like mouthfuls of sawdust. They are as mindless as they are tasteless. Communication theory is concerned only with the randomness or, conversely, with the statistical organization of messages. It ignores completely their sense or content. The kinds of communication we are concerned with when we talk about men and computers are meaningful communications.

The impressions I have tried to convey about the relative importance of communication as a psychological process are supported by what one finds in contemporary textbooks of psychology: A survey of some of the most popular books in the field reveals that communication has been, and still is, a topic of some minor interest to psychologists.

An Activity Analysis of a Work Day

Is this as it should be? In worrying about communication, are we indeed concerned with a kind of behavior that occurs only infrequently in life? Not at all. Klemmer [2] and his associates at the Bell Telephone Laboratories recently completed a careful activity analysis of how clerks, secretaries, technicians, professional people, and supervisory personnel spend their time. Observations were made on over 3,000 persons at carefully chosen intervals throughout the work day. Some of Klemmer's findings are summarized in Figure 1. On the average, the people in Klemmer's study spent over two-thirds of their time in some form of communication.

However surprising these figures may be, they are almost certainly not atypical. Other smaller studies by Burns (1954) on four managers in a single manufacturing company, Hinrichs (1964) on chemists and chemical engineers, and Stewart (1967) on 160 managers in several British companies all agree in showing that technical and supervisory personnel spend considerably more than half their time in some form of communication activity.

Communications in Our Society

If we look at communications in a slightly different way, it is clear that efficient networks of communication are as vital to a modern society as the nervous system is to a livng body. Even a partial breakdown of communications, such as occurs during a newspaper or telephone strike, can cripple a society as effec-

[2] E. T. Klemmer, personal communication, March 20, 1970.

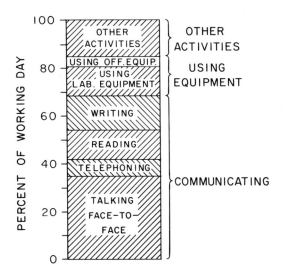

Figure 1. Proportion of the working day spent in various activities by clerks, secretaries, technicians, professional people, and supervisory personnel. (E. T. Klemmer, personal communication, March 20, 1970.)

tively as a crushed nerve can cripple a man. Wars have been lost and empires destroyed by poor communications. Indeed, communication problems of one kind or another seem to be at the root of what many of us see as the disintegration of our contemporary way of life. Therein lies a kind of paradox, for communications are so much a part of everyday living that it is easy for us to forget how pervasive and extensive they really are.

Take, for example, postal communications. No official estimates are available on the total amount of work done by the United States Post Office Department prior to 1847, but in that year the service handled some 124 million pieces of mail. That was only a trickle. In the following century the volume of mail increased over 100 times (see Figure 2). It is expected to reach 84 billion pieces this year and to increase another 50% by the end of the decade. When the data are converted to pieces of mail handled per person, the rate of growth is no less impressive.

Postal communications are, of course, concerned primarily with the transmission of written, printed, or hard-copy messages. Telephonic communications, by contrast, are almost exclusively concerned with the transmission of oral messages. Despite this important difference between them, certain statistics for the two kinds of communication parallel one another very closely. From the time of the introduction of commercial telephones in 1884, the yearly volume of telephone conversations

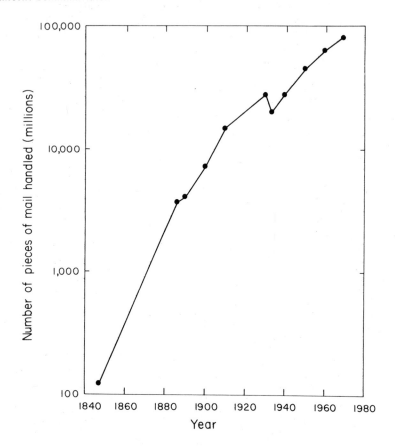

Figure 2. Selected data on the yearly volume of mail handled by the United States Post Office Department from 1847 to the present. (Sources: United States Department of Commerce, 1960, 1970.)

in the United States has grown to a total that is about as far beyond our ordinary comprehension as is the national debt. In Figure 3, I have plotted the average number of telephone calls per day made in the United States from 1880 to 1969. For comparison, I have plotted population figures for the United States on the same graph. Especially dramatic is the way in which the divergence between the slopes of the two curves is increasing decade by decade.

On the Flood of I could now turn to still another kind of communication and tell
Written you about the total number of different printed pieces of writing
Communications available to an avid reader today. Since Licklider (1966) among others has already described the situation dramatically and since I myself have written about this elsewhere (Chapanis, 1965), let me make just one observation about the volume of literature in

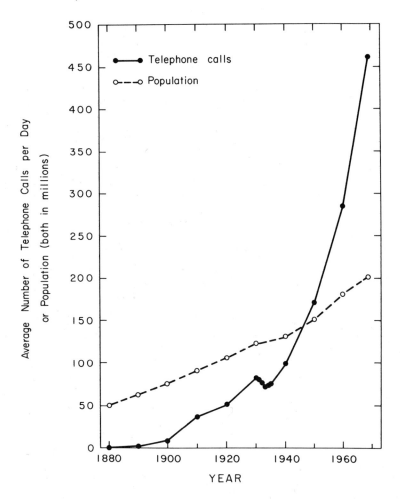

Figure 3. Selected data on the average daily number of telephone calls made in the United States from 1880 to the present and population figures for the same period. (Sources: United States Department of Commerce, 1960, 1970.)

my own highly specialized subfield of psychology. A compulsive, well-versed engineering psychologist would have to read, I estimate, somewhere on the order of 30–40 articles, books, theses, and technical reports every day of the year merely to keep abreast of the current literature, much less catch up with things that have been published in the past. This is a communication problem of staggering proportions. And the worst is yet to come!

Communications and Computers In writing about these aspects of communication, perhaps I have been able to convey to you my feeling that communication is a central problem in our society and that it will continue to be so for the indefinite future. Never in the history of society has communication been so abundant, so freely available, and so much used. Yet on all sides we hear that the major faults of society can be traced to insufficient communication. I submit that the reverse may be true. We have too much communication; that is, we have far more communication than it is possible for mortal man to assimilate by himself. In coping with these problems of communication we shall need, among other things, to make use of the enormous information-handling capacities of modern computers. I see no other rational alternative. The ways in which computers are harnessed for our use is what I am concerned with today.

ON COMPUTERS AND PEOPLE

One of the most dramatic and impressive developments in the technology of American society during the past 20 years has been the growth in the number of computers and in the uses to which they have been put. In fact, it would probably be more economical to list those areas in which computers have not been applied than it would be to list those in which they are being applied. So far, government agencies, business and industrial organizations, and large scientific laboratories have been the chief beneficiaries of these advances. Most of us still have little direct contact with computers. Nonetheless, they already affect our lives in varied and often unexpected ways. Not only do computers prepare our utility bills, credit card bills, and bank statements, but they also control our traffic, assist us in making travel and theater reservations, and help diagnose our bodily ills.

Although most computers still require an intermediary between the ultimate user and the computer, the advent of time sharing and other interactive computer systems is almost certain to produce a radical change in current practices. The physician concerned with proper drug dosages and side effects, the student needing help on some math homework, the young couple trying to decide how to spend an infrequent night on the town, and the householder ordering merchandise from a large mail order house, all may soon rely for help on a computer and do so directly through their own terminals.

Even though modern computers admittedly have many limitations, the last two decades have already seen a fantastic increase in the number of computer users. Computer users today are, however, different from those who have been the principal companions to computers during their childhood and adolescence. These new users are not computer programmers, nor are they interested in computer technology per se. This new breed of users sees the computer as a tool, a terribly expensive and complicated tool, to be sure, but a tool nonetheless. They are interested primarily in what the computer can do for them, and not in how the computer does it. The typical user today is no more interested in understanding or getting into the guts of a modern computer than he is in tearing down the engine of his high-powered automobile. He wants both machines to do what he asks them to do, when he asks them to do it, in the way he wants the job done. Trying to find out how best to meet these human demands is at the heart of the question about how we could build a computer like our fictitious HAL.

On the Nature of Man-Computer Interactions

The interactions between man and modern computers may, in a manner of speaking, be thought of as conversations. They are characterized by commands, statements, questions, answers to questions, and sundry other messages that go from man to computer and vice versa. These conversations are all carried out in one of several different foreign languages called programming languages. This means that the computer user has to learn a foreign language with all of the difficulties associated with that learning task. To be sure, programming languages are continually being improved in attempts to develop those that are most convenient for the user and most efficient for the computer. At the present time, programming languages compromise between the requirements of man and machine, and even computer experts admit freely that it is the user who has to adapt to the computer rather than vice versa.

For all practical purposes, these interactions are all written or, to be more precise, typewritten. Although significant attempts are being made to broaden the channels of communication between man and computer, the fact remains that the bulk of the messages that go from man to computer, or vice versa, are printed messages produced by some sort of a keyboard device. When messages are not printed, they are often painted onto television-like screens, but however you describe them, the channels of communication between man and computer are, at present, highly limited.

It is also important to recognize that for all the successes we have had with computers, we can probably find equally impressive and expensive failures. No one likes to talk about failures, and there is no incentive in writing them up for posterity to see in print. Still, it is not hard to find examples of computer systems and applications that have scarcely survived their conceptions. Very often these failures are not due to any defect in the mechanical or electrical features of the machine itself, but are instead due to a failure to match the computer to the needs of the people who need and want to use it. However apt it may be to say that the interaction between man and computer is a conversation, we have in all fairness to add that most of these conversations are stilted, esoteric, and frustrating. Perhaps even more important, communication with computers requires thought patterns and processes that are, at best, unfamiliar for most people and, at worst, unnatural.

If we are to know how to build computers so that they can converse with their human users in efficient, human-like terms, we need to know first how people naturally communicate with each other. When we can describe how people communicate with each other most effectively, we will then be able to formulate general principles that can be used in the design of truly conversational computers for the future.

Let me tell you two reasons why I see the problem this way. The first has to do with a fanciful way I think about computers. In my mind's eye, I sometimes think of a computer as a huge, compliant, and versatile slave from another planet. The slave has arrived and is here waiting to serve me. Unfortunately, his whole life, from birth to adulthood, was spent alone on a space ship. As a result, this poor chap has never had the experience of communicating with earth people and, indeed, he does not even know how one goes about the business of communicating. It is my job to teach this underprivileged fellow the language of conversation. But, even more important than the mere language itself, I have to teach him the rules of conversation. And there is the rub: Before I can teach him how to communicate, I have to understand how I myself carry on conversations with my fellow man. I have to be able to describe the rules, the essence of human communication.

My second reason for saying that we need to know first how people communicate is a more realistic one. You know, of course, that no one teaches computers anything. Computers are just pieces of hardware, designed, built, and programmed by people. Human communication is often characterized as having intent, or intention. Messages from computers have no intent. Whatever intent is there is the intent of the man who built and programmed the computer. So, if we want to have truly conversational computers, we have to be sure that the people who design, build, and program these computers know and understand the rules of human communication. This is entirely a psychological problem. As psychologists we have to be able to describe human communication in precise terms and convey the rules of human communication to other people—the people who are ultimately responsible for the computers with which we will interact. Indeed, let me put that last statement even more strongly. Unless we psychologists tell engineers and technicians how to design computers, they will go about the job as they have in the past, using their own intuitions, hunches, and guesses. If that happens, and if we later grumble because computers are badly designed for human needs, we should remember that we have only ourselves to blame.

On the Value of Interactive Communications Systems

Why do I place so much emphasis on computers that will converse in human-like ways? Or, more generally, is it really important to have communication systems that respond to us in our terms? I think so, and there is some evidence to support my opinion. Kinkade and his colleagues recently investigated a number of variables that affect the human use of an information clearinghouse (Kinkade, Bedarf, & Van Cott, 1967; Kinkade & Bedarf, 1967). For their studies, they set up a specialized information retrieval system in cooperation with the Federation of American Societies for Experimental Biology. In one study, the subjects were 50 biological scientists working in universities in the Washington, D. C., area; 46 of the same scientists served as subjects for a second study.

The procedure was straightforward enough. Scientists with questions were invited to telephone their requests to a central office where the requests were recorded. Answers were returned to the initiators of the request at a later time. In one experiment, requests were received either by a biologically trained scientist or a tape recorder. Requests were tape-recorded in all instances, but the presence of the biologically trained receptionist in half the trials provided human feedback and interaction with the requester. The users of the system were free to choose either the human or the machine receptionist, and they knew precisely when each would be on the channel. Figure 4 shows the results obtained throughout the 22 days during which the system was tested. It seems clear that, given a choice, users of this information retrieval system more often preferred to interact with a human rather than an impersonal machine.

In another study, scientists had the option of telephoning their requests to a scientifically trained receptionist or to an intelligent, but scientifically unsophisticated receptionist. Both receptionists provided human interaction and feedback, but the scientifically trained one could, of course, interact more meaningfully with the originator of the request. The results of this study, conducted over a period of 30 days, yielded curves something like those in Figure 4 with the scientifically trained receptionist receiving the greater number of calls.

As you see in Figure 4, however, there were some exceptions to these general findings. Some scientist users deliberately chose to communicate with what you might regard as the less desirable kind of receptionist. The data from these exceptions are, in some ways, as interesting and as informative as the data from those who were in the majority.

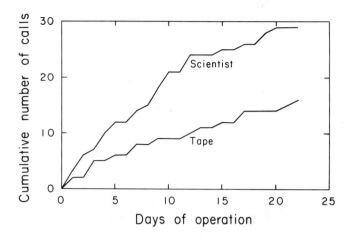

Figure 4. Cumulative number of requests telephoned to a biological information clearinghouse when the receptionist was either a biologically trained scientist or a tape recorder. (Adapted from an article by R. G. Kinkade and E. W. Bedarf from American Institutes for Research Technical Report No. 3. Copyrighted by the American Institutes for Research, November 1967.)

Users had to work harder when they placed their requests with the machine or with the less sophisticated receptionist. Requests had to be more precise, and the requesters had to spend more time organizing their questions before they reached for the telephone. Relatively simple, structured requests—such as a request for a specific document—were placed about equally with the untrained and trained receptionists. In both studies, scientist users preferred scientifically trained receptionists for more complex queries, for bibliographic searches, and for requests that were less well structured. Indeed, for these more complex kinds of requests, users made conscious efforts to telephone into the more knowledgeable receptionist.

To conclude, then, there is some evidence that human, or human-like, interaction in information retrieval systems is desirable. As is true of most things, that simple statement does not tell the whole story. People prefer to communicate with people, or people-like systems, when the information to be communicated is complex or unstructured. Moreover, the communications themselves take on different forms depending on the purpose of the communication. This, I think, leads us naturally into my next question.

WHY DO PEOPLE COMMUNICATE? Some of the most basic questions we might ask about human communication are: Why do people communicate? and What function does communication serve? Why? is such a fundamental question that you might suppose people would have spent a great deal of time searching out answers to it. Oddly enough, that is not the case at all. To be sure, most people who write about communication have some general things to say about why we communicate: such as, to persuade or to convey information. What I have in mind, however, is something much more detailed and precise. What I am looking for is a kind of taxonomy of communication much like the one that Miller (1969) tried to provide us for problem solving.

A precise statement of the *why* of human communication has not only great significance for the understanding of human behavior itself, but relevance to the design of computers as well. Briefly, communication serves different human purposes, and to serve these several purposes, the very nature of communication takes on different forms. We had a glimpse of this in the results of the Kinkade studies to which I have just referred. I would like now to amplify that theme. In so doing, we shall see, I think, that communication for some purposes is easily served by interactive computers; other purposes are not so easily adapted to intelligent machines.

Human conversations and communications run the gamut from the sublime to the ridiculous, from the profound to the silly, from the formal to the intimate. In the most general sense, I suppose one could say that we engage in communication to impress, cajole, threaten, influence, inform, shape, deceive, conceal, alert, warn, question, query, explain, demonstrate, argue, and perhaps a few hundred other things as well. As far as I know, no one has ever made a comprehensive catalog or a sensible grouping of all the reasons why we communicate with our fellow man. Most of the purposes implied in the verbs I have listed above suggest an interpersonal relationship between two particular people, one of whom is trying to impress, cajole, threaten, influence, etc., the other through his communications. The very large, impersonal purpose of communication—and the primary general purpose for which computers are being designed —is the transmission of factual information. In confining our attention to this more circumscribed purpose we can exclude things like gossip, lovers' quarrels, family conversations, psychiatric interviews, and what are generally referred to these days as "meaningful dialogues."

Communications whose sole purpose is the transmission of factual information still include a very large group of functions that have never been systematically catalogued, described, or investigated. Let me talk about a couple of such functions to illustrate the kind of thing I have in mind.

Perhaps the most obvious function served by factual communication is the transmission of very specific information in response to simple inquiries. In some cases, you may not only phrase the inquiry, but you may also find your own answer. You do this when you consult a timetable to find out about plane schedules from one city to another, when you consult a newspaper to find the feature times of a movie you want to go to after dinner, or when you thumb through a dictionary for the definition of a word.

In other cases, you may phrase the inquiry but obtain the answer from another communicator or a machine. This is what happens when you consult the central directory service for a telephone number, when you call your broker for the latest quotation on your favorite growth stock, or when you telephone a machine to find out the exact time of day.

Who? When? Where? How long? How many? are some of the forms that simple inquiry may take. The objects of these inquiries may be any of the thousands of entities with which we come in contact during our daily lives or about which we need to know. They include such things as stock numbers, model numbers, stock quotations, selling prices, departure times, transit times, arrival times, route numbers, flight numbers, names, addresses, distances, sizes, and weights.

Although many inquiries and communications require highly sophisticated communicators and are technical in content, they are still classifiable as simple communications. Examples are the following: What is the product-moment coefficient of correlation between these two sets of numbers? What is the chemical formula for chlorpromazine? What is the simplest diode transistor logic circuit for representing "Not (A and B and C)"? Understanding these questions requires a considerable amount of technical sophistication. Nonetheless, I still call them simple inquiries. To the person who understands each question, there is a simple, direct, and unequivocal answer. In response to the first question, one has merely to insert the numbers into the appropriate formula and do the computations correctly. In the case of the latter two questions, one has merely to consult the appropriate books, documents, or files, or, perhaps, the memory of a sufficiently knowledgeable human communicator.

Since speed is one important requirement of this kind of communication, it is probably better served by the auditory rather than the visual channel. Spoken requests are easier to make than written, printed, or typewritten requests. Similarly, spoken replies are usually quicker to make and easier to assimilate unless the reply is so complex that it might exceed the immediate memory span of the listener. A time of arrival, flight number, or route numbers is probably best conveyed through the auditory channel. Even a coefficient of correlation is probably best communicated that way. On the other hand, if the reply is a 15-digit stock number or a circuit diagram, the reply may be better communicated in some other way.

Computers can generally do a superb job at this kind of communication because they can search rapidly through enormous files of data for precisely the information that is desired. Further, communications of this kind usually involve no hidden assumptions, ambiguities, or judgments to complicate the reply.

Free Browsing   Free browsing is, in a manner of speaking, at the other end of the continuum from simple inquiry and the communication of simple facts, for in browsing you are generally not looking for anything in particular. When you pick up the morning newspaper and scan the headlines, you are usually searching for things that satisfy an exceedingly vague criterion: The items must pique your curiosity, stir your imagination, or otherwise excite your interest. Some articles may be read thoroughly, some skimmed lightly, and others passed over entirely. The particular set of items that falls into each of these categories will differ for each reader according to his profession, his level of education, his avocations, and his idiosyncratic interest patterns.

For all its indefiniteness, browsing is probably an extremely important form of intellectual activity. You browse through the new book offerings in a bookstore or at professional meetings to find out what is new in your field. You browse through the titles of papers in professional journals to get ideas for new research projects. You browse through advertisements to get ideas about the latest in fashions, automobiles, and houses. You browse through exhibits of garden equipment, boats, camping equipment, and machine tools for much the same reason. Although no one appears to have made any attempt to measure the amount of time that is consumed by browsing, I suspect that it is a highly productive source of new ideas and of catching up with the world.

The psychological requirements for communications that can be used in effective browsing are quite different from those that are used for the communication of simple facts. For one thing, the material to be scanned has to be grouped in some sort of organizational scheme. Although any one person's browsing is a free-ranging activity, it is bounded. Some people never look at the business and financial pages of a newspaper, others never look at the sports section, while still others have no interest in the women's section. Neither physician nor physicist has enough time to browse through all the medical and physical journals available to him. So free browsing is both free ranging and selective. Other characteristics undoubtedly occur to you.

As far as I can tell, there has been almost no psychological research on free browsing. The problems here are sufficiently numerous to support at least a dozen doctoral theses. For example, we seem to do most of our free browsing visually, but I know of no studies to show this sensory channel to be either better or worse than the auditory channel. Suppose one were to use the auditory channel for free browsing, how could material be best presented? How should material for visual free browsing be most effectively organized? Are the free-browsing habits of scientists different from those of lawyers, businessmen, government officials, and other citizens? What are the constellations of interest patterns that characterize these various groups of individuals, and how can browsing material be selected to make them match those interest patterns? How could a computer like HAL best assist us in free browsing? Other questions I leave to you.

Other Functions of Communication

I do not have time to enumerate all the other functions served by communication, nor, indeed, am I entirely sure how many other functions there are. Let me merely mention a couple of others.

Directed browsing is considerably more restricted than free browsing. Directed browsing is what a scientist does when he compiles a bibliography or what a patent attorney does when he searches patent files. There is browsing, to be sure, but the browsing has a much more definite goal.

Briefing and status reporting are important functions of communication in such things as weather reporting, reviewing the state of the economy, monitoring patients in hospitals, and planning military campaigns. Briefing and status reporting are, in a sense, much more complicated than any of the functions I have enumerated above because in presenting a report on the status of the weather, business, a patient in an intensive-care unit, or a battle, there always has to be some selection and condensation of data. Insuring that the condensation does not at the same time bias or distort the status report is something that not even psychologists know how to do at the present time. How then are we to instruct HAL to do this kind of communicating?

ON CHANNELS OF COMMUNICATION

Repeatedly throughout what I have said so far, I have had occasion to refer to channels of communication. This is a general area in which our own studies at Johns Hopkins have been primarily concentrated. To be sure, people were studying information transmission through various media long before the advent of the computer. For example, questions that educators raised about effective teaching methods have stimulated over the years a very large number of experiments comparing aural and visual forms of presentation. Almost without exception, all this earlier work has treated the human subject as a passive recipient of information. None of it has been concerned with truly interactive communication of the kind that characterizes human conversation or man-computer communication such as our fictitious astronauts engaged in with HAL.

Let's start with fundamentals and ask about how many different kinds of communication skills are common and widespread enough to be serious candidates for man-computer communication. The list is surprisingly short. Almost everyone can speak and understand one of the natural languages—perhaps not correctly, but fluently. In addition, most people these days seem to know how to write, at least in some rudimentary way. Many people know how to type, and those that do not know how to type can almost intuitively peck out acceptably comprehensible messages. But there the list ends.

The aim of our research so far has been to describe what happens when people communicate naturally through each of these several channels. Briefly, our subjects are asked to solve complex problems by communicating with one another. As you might expect from my professional orientation, our problems are real problems; that is, they are problems of the kind that already have been, or could be, programmed into computers. Our communication channels, or "modes" as we have been calling them, do not simulate any particular system but rather model computer systems that are, in a certain sense, ideal ones.

As so often happens with research, after you see the data, the findings seem obvious. We have to force ourselves to recall the predictions that we and other people made before our experiments to recapture the feelings of surprise we experienced as our summary tables and graphs took shape.

Figure 5 gives some results from one of our experiments. It shows the times required to solve our problems in four different modes of communication. In the typewriting mode, subjects communicated through special slaved typewriters. Whatever one subject wrote on one machine appeared simultaneously on his partner's in an adjoining room. In the handwriting mode, subjects wrote messages back and forth to one another. In the voice mode, subjects were able to talk freely but were not able to see each other. In the communication-rich mode, subjects sat side-by-side and were able to converse naturally using voice, gestures, and handwriting.

I call to your attention first the range of the differences represented in these data. In the typewriting mode, subjects took, on the average, about two and one-half times as long to solve problems as in the communication-rich mode. This is a difference

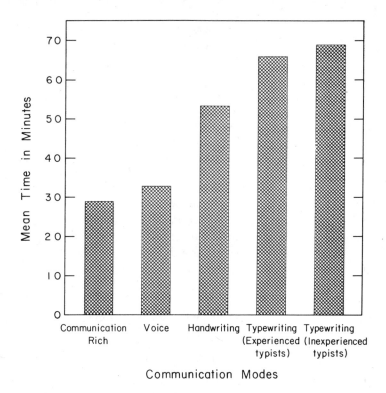

Figure 5. Average times required by teams of subjects to solve complex problems using various modes of communication.

of some considerable magnitude. One of our first surprises was the small difference between the results for our experienced and inexperienced typists. For the kinds of communication we are concerned with, typing skill seems to make much less difference than we and most other people assumed it would. Our second surprise was the small difference between the communication-rich and the voice modes. Gestures, facial expressions, and handwriting appear to contribute little extra to pure oral communication.

One of our biggest surprises, when we first saw the data, is illustrated in Figure 6. This shows the number of messages that subjects exchanged in the solution of problems. A message is a single uninterrupted utterance, or written or typewritten sequence of words. The data in the preceding figure become all the more impressive in the light of these. The voice and communication-rich modes, which turn out to be so fast, are also characterized by an enormous number of interchanges, or messages. One's first inclination is to guess that the lengths of the messages must also be different. I do not have data on that point to show

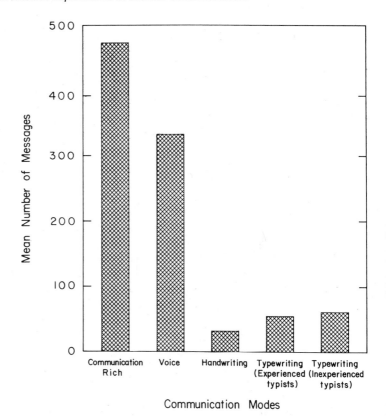

Figure 6. Average number of messages exchanged by teams of subjects in solving complex problems using various modes of communication.

here, but let me say that the story is not quite that simple. Typewritten messages do indeed tend to have somewhat more words per message than do voice messages, but this is true only of the sophisticated typists and at that the differences are surprisingly small. If you count the total number of words exchanged in the solution of problems, the data look almost exactly like those in Figure 6, except for a change in the numbers along the ordinate.

Another surprise came out of another study for which I do not show data. Feedback is such an important concept in psychology, we felt sure that problems would be solved much more efficiently if we allowed a subject to interrupt freely, rather than forcing him to wait until his partner had completed an utterance of message and released the communication channel to him. Not so. This is one of our variables that has no demonstrable overall effect.

On the Style of   One of our biggest surprises, and the one with which I would
Communication   like to close, is something that I think we knew intuitively but
never really appreciated until we looked closely at our data. Almost all linguistic and psycholinguistic research today is being
done with what I would call "immaculate" prose. Immaculate
prose consists of messages that are grammatically pure and correct. They are sentences like:

> John hit the girl with a ball.
> It is true that I have two arms.
> The man treats the boy and the girl in the park.

These are messages that have been carefully laundered, sanitized,
starched, and pressed. Every word, phrase, and punctuation mark
has been carefully selected, set into place, and then ironed out
firmly on the printed page or writing tablets. It is literally immaculate writing.

When one looks at the typewritten protocols of what happened in our communication-rich and voice modes, one's first
and almost immediate reaction is, What in the world were they
talking about? At first glance, natural interactive communications between people convey the impression that they follow no
grammatical, syntactical, or semantic rules. And yet obviously
there are rules, for meanings do get across and problems do get
solved. If we are ever to have computers that behave like HAL,
we must somehow try to formulate those rules. Do you want to
have some real scientific fun? Join us in our attempts to unravel
this important practical problem.

REFERENCES

Burns, T. The directions of activity and communication in a
departmental executive group. *Human Relations*, 1954, 7,
73-97.

Chapanis, A. Words, words, words. *Human Factors*, 1965, 7, 1-17

Chapanis, A. The relevance of laboratory studies to practical
situations. *Ergonomics*, 1967, *10*, 557-577.

Chapanis, A., Garner, W. R., & Morgan, C. T. *Applied experimental psychology.* New York: Wiley, 1949.

Clarke, A. C. *2001: A space odyssey.* New York: The New
American Library, 1968.

Hinrichs, J. R. Communications activity of industrial research
personnel. *Personnel Psychology*, 1964, *17*, 193-204

Kinkade, R. G., & Bedarf, E. W. *Science information requirements of scientists: The need for an interacting request receiver in an information clearinghouse.* (American Institutes
for Research Tech. Rep. No. 3) Silver Spring, Md.: American
Institutes for Research, 1967.

Kinkade, R. G., Bedarf, E. W., & Van Cott, H. P. *Science information requirements of scientists: The need for a scientific request receiver and processor in an information clearinghouse.* (American Institutes for Research Tech. Rep. No. 2) Silver Spring, Md.: American Institutes for Research, 1967.

Licklider, J. C. R. A crux in scientific and technical communication. *American Psychologist,* 1966, *21,* 1044–1051.

Miller, R. B. Archetypes in man-computer problem solving. *Ergonomics,* 1969, *12,* 559–581.

Stewart, R. How managers spend their time. *Management Today,* 1967, 92–160.

Tulving, E., & Madigan, S. A. Memory and verbal learning. *Annual Review of Psychology,* 1970, *21,* 437–484.

United States Department of Commerce, Bureau of the Census. *Historical statistics of the United States, colonial times to 1957: A statistical abstract supplement.* Washington, D.C.: United States Government Printing Office, 1960.

United States Department of Commerce, Bureau of the Census. *Statistical abstract of the United States, 1970.* Washington, D.C.: United States Government Printing Office, 1970.

Wiener, N. *The humane use of human beings: Cybernetics and society.* Boston: Houghton Mifflin, 1950.

Chapanis ends his article with a challenge to the reader. Few, if any, of you will be in a position to conduct formal research studies on communication, but, still, you might be someday. If you have time for a special project, there could be one or more here. We shall not design an experiment for you this time. You should, by now, be able to state a problem, control all variables except the independent variable, and measure the dependent variable or variables. Various modes of communication could be compared. . . . It's your problem!

MORE WORDS ABOUT COMMUNICATION

Another article by Alphonse Chapanis, "Words, Words, Words" (*Human Factors,* 1965, 7, 1–17), deals with "the language and the words that are attached to the tools, machines, systems, and operations with which human factors engineers are concerned." It might also give you some ideas for a project.

Did you ever try to assemble a bicycle, or a lawn mower, or even a simple garden cart? You follow the printed directions that come with a box full of pieces. That is, you *try* to follow them. Or can you read better than we can? Perhaps there is a project here.

Another source of information is T. M. Higham, "Basic Psychological Factors in Communications" (*Occupational Psychology,* 1957, *31,* 1–10).

For more information about the relationship between people and computers, we suggest Ulric Neisser, "The Imitation of Man by Machine" (*Science,* 1963, *139,* 193–197). He discusses the possibilities and limitations of an "artificial intelligence." "The deep difference," Neisser states, "between the thinking of men and machines has been intuitively recognized by those who fear that machines may somehow come to regulate our society. If machines really thought as men do, there would be no more reason to fear them than to fear men. But computer intelligence is indeed 'inhuman': it does not grow, has no emotional basis, and is shallowly motivated."

Part Seventeen

Animal Behavior: Comparisons

There seems to be no really good reason why there could not be an animal psychology devoted solely to understanding animals; a study of animals for no reason other than an interest in animals. But most people who study the behavior of animals seem to do so for other reasons. They wish to know more about human behavior. In fact, most of the psychologists who work with animals don't even call their field of study "animal psychology." They prefer to call it "comparative psychology."

Harold E. Burtt, in his book *The Psychology of Birds,* states that the psychologists' "interest in the lower animals, including birds, is to quite an extent due to the way studies of animal psychology contribute to the better understanding of human psychology. Many of the theoretical principles which govern human behavior were worked out with laboratory animals." [1]

Jane van Lawick-Goodall, who studies animals in their natural environments rather than the laboratory, also sees this study as contributing to the understanding of man. In her book *In the Shadow of Man,* she says: "Eventually the detailed understanding of chimpanzee behavior that will result from our long-term research . . . will help man in his attempts to understand himself." [2]

When the understanding of animal behavior is the primary purpose of a study or of a research program, even then its potential benefit to mankind seems usually to ride along. We humans have an absorbing interest in our own behavior. At the same time, we tend to think of ourselves as being distinctively different from animals—something entirely apart from them. So, when we see our own behavior mirrored in the behavior of an animal, it becomes something remarkable. This is particularly so if it is a behavior we have always considered distinctly human.

While Jane van Lawick-Goodall is best known for her studies of chimpanzees, she has recorded a story of some observations of birds. On this occasion she and her husband were on an expedition to photograph wildlife in the Seréngeti National Park in northern Tanzania.

[1] Harold E. Burtt. *The Psychology of Birds.* New York: Macmillan, 1967, p. 3.

[2] Jane van Lawick-Goodall. *In the Shadow of Man.* Boston: Houghton Mifflin, 1971, p. 259.

52

TOOL-USING BIRD: THE EGYPTIAN VULTURE
JANE VAN LAWICK-GOODALL

But our attention was abruptly riveted by an extraordinary action among the vultures.

"He's using a tool!" Hugo and I exclaimed almost with one voice.

Amazed, we watched an Egyptian vulture, a white, yellow-cheeked bird about the size of a raven, pick up in his beak the stone he had just thrown down. The bird raised his head and once more threw the stone at the ostrich egg lying on the ground before him.

It was true! We were watching that seldom-recorded phenomenon—the use of a tool by an animal. And we were, as far as we know, the first scientifically qualified witnesses to this extraordinary talent of the Egyptian vulture.

Gradually we sorted out the different vultures. The company included the usual gathering of white-backed vultures and Rüppell's griffons, some hooded vultures, a few huge lappet-faced vultures, and just two of the small white Egyptian vultures.

As we watched, the second Egyptian vulture picked up a stone in his beak and moved toward an egg. With excellent aim the bird threw the stone with a forceful downward movement of head and neck. He pecked at the shell, as though feeling for a crack, then picked up the stone again and flung it. This time he missed the egg, but the third time he scored another hit. Three minutes later a direct hit cracked the shell, and after a few more throws, the vulture buried his beak in the rich, nutritious yolk as it spilled onto the ground.

Three of the larger vultures immediately rushed in and drove the stone-thrower away. Others joined them, and soon the egg was lost beneath a mass of feathers. In a few moments there was nothing left save the broken shell and a damp patch on the earth.

As for the provider of the feast, he was walking toward another egg, head in air, stone in beak. "Crack!"—the sound told us of the success of his first throw.

NO OTHER SPECIES SEEN CRACKING EGGS   We soon noted that only the Egyptian vultures were able to fracture the ostrich eggs. Even the lappet-faced vultures, despite repeated efforts with their strong beaks, failed to crack the

SOURCE: From the *National Geographic Magazine*, May, 1968. Pp. 631–633 reprinted by permission.

shells, which are a sixteenth of an inch thick and extremely tough.

The two stone-throwers eventually opened all the eggs, though they never got more than a couple of beakfuls of food before their larger cousins chased them away.

When the vultures dispersed, we drove back to our camp at Seronera. We were greeted by Hugo's brother Michael, who was visiting with us.

"See anything interesting today?" he asked.

Our words tumbled over each other as we told of our discovery.

"Surely someone else must have seen that," said Michael.

While agreeing that the local Masai tribesmen might have, we expressed confidence that we were the first trained observers of the astounding event. Such a notable occurrence could not have escaped the spotlight of publicity if it had been scientifically observed.

We got into a discussion of the use of tools by animals in general. Michael knew about the chimpanzees we had studied at the Gombe Stream Game Reserve—how they use sticks and bits of grass to fish for termites and ants, and how they clean themselves with leaves, as humans use toilet tissue.

"They also crumple leaves in their mouths," I told him, "making a sort of sponge to sop up water from hollows in trees, when they can't reach it with their lips."

We knew that chimps in the west African country of Cameroon had been observed poking sticks into an underground bees' nest. Another, in Liberia, had been seen using a rock to pound open a palm-nut kernel.

Hugo and I told Michael of other mammals that occasionally use tools—a report of a gorilla using a crooked stick to pull fruit within reach, an Indian elephant seen scratching itself with a stick. But except for the chimp, the only mammal habitually using tools is the California sea otter: It lies on its back at the surface of the water, puts a flat rock on its chest, and breaks shellfish by beating them on the "anvil" with its paws.

Tool using! Fantastic! But we can accept it. In all cases the tools are very simple; behaviors that each species may have come upon by accident. But the same writer has another story to tell us. This time it concerns the chimpanzees whose behavior she has observed so painstakingly and written about so engagingly.

53

TOOLMAKING BY CHIMPANZEES
JANE VAN LAWICK-GOODALL

It was within two weeks of this observation that I saw something that excited me even more. By then it was October and the short rains had begun. The blackened slopes were softened by feathery new grass shoots and in some places the ground was carpeted by a variety of flowers. The Chimpanzees' Spring, I called it. I had had a frustrating morning, tramping up and down three valleys with never a sign or sound of a chimpanzee. Hauling myself up the steep slope of Mlinda Valley I headed for the Peak, not only weary but soaking wet from crawling through dense undergrowth. Suddenly I stopped, for I saw a slight movement in the long grass about sixty yards away. Quickly focusing my binoculars I saw that it was a single chimpanzee, and just then he turned in my direction. I recognized David Graybeard.

Cautiously I moved around so that I could see what he was doing. He was squatting beside the red earth mound of a termite nest, and as I watched I saw him carefully push a long grass stem down into a hole in the mound. After a moment he withdrew it and picked something from the end with his mouth. I was too far away to make out what he was eating, but it was obvious that he was actually using a grass stem as a tool.

I knew that on two occasions casual observers in West Africa had seen chimpanzees using objects as tools: one had broken open palm-nut kernels by using a rock as a hammer, and a group of chimps had been observed pushing sticks into an underground bees' nest and licking off the honey. Somehow I had never dreamed of seeing anything so exciting myself.

For an hour David feasted at the termite mound and then he wandered slowly away. When I was sure he had gone I went over to examine the mound. I found a few crushed insects strewn about, and a swarm of worker termites sealing the entrances of the nest passages into which David had obviously been poking his stems. I picked up one of his discarded tools and carefully pushed it into a hole myself. Immediately I felt the pull of several termites as they seized the grass, and when I pulled it out there were a number of worker termites and a few soldiers, with big red heads, clinging on with their mandibles. There they

SOURCE: On pages 35–37 of *In the Shadow of Man*. Copyright © 1971 by Hugo and Jane van Lawick-Goodall. Reprinted by permission of the publisher, Houghton Mifflin Co.

remained, sticking out at right angles to the stem with their legs waving in the air.

Before I left I trampled down some of the tall dry grass and constructed a rough hide—just a few palm fronds leaned up against the low branch of a tree and tied together at the top. I planned to wait there the next day. But it was another week before I was able to watch a chimpanzee "fishing" for termites again. Twice chimps arrived, but each time they saw me and moved off immediately. Once a swarm of fertile winged termites —the princes and princesses, as they are called—flew off on their nuptial flight, their huge white wings fluttering frantically as they carried the insects higher and higher. Later I realized that it is at this time of year, during the short rains, when the worker termites extend the passages of the nest to the surface, preparing for these emigrations. Several such swarms emerge between October and January. It is principally during these months that the chimpanzees feed on termites.

On the eighth day of my watch David Graybeard arrived again, together with Goliath, and the pair worked there for two hours. I could see much better: I observed how they scratched open the sealed-over passage entrances with a thumb or forefinger. I watched how they bit the ends off their tools when they became bent, or used the other end, or discarded them in favor of new ones. Goliath once moved at least fifteen yards from the heap to select a firm-looking piece of vine, and both males often picked three or four stems while they were collecting tools, and put the spares beside them on the ground until they wanted them.

Most exciting of all, on several occasions they picked small leafy twigs and prepared them for use by stripping off the leaves. This was the first recorded example of a wild animal not merely *using* an object as a tool, but actually modifying an object and thus showing the crude beginnings of tool*making*.

Previously man had been regarded as the only tool-making animal. Indeed, one of the clauses commonly accepted in the definition of man was that he was a creature who "made tools to a regular and set pattern." The chimpanzees, obviously, had not made tools to any set pattern. Nevertheless, my early observations of their primitive toolmaking abilities convinced a number of scientists that it was necessary to redefine man in a more complex manner than before. Or else, as Louis Leakey put it, we should by definition have to accept the chimpanzee as Man.

Perhaps there is unity in all life. Perhaps the arbitrary barrier between mankind and all other living things will one

day disintegrate. There are indications of some movement in the Western world in the direction of Oriental thought. Will this in any way affect our thinking about animals?

There is much room here for discussion—for disagreement. We have learned much from the use of animals in laboratory research. Animal research has taught us a good share of what we know about the nervous system, about genetics, about the learning process. Animals have been used and sacrificed in developing cures for numerous diseases. Animals have preceded man into space.

It may be that the relation of mankind to other living beings is more in the realm of philosophy than psychology. But it certainly has its psychological aspects. Without the white rat, the pigeon and the chimpanzee, psychology would not be what it is today.

We have mentioned previously the *ethologists,* students of animal behavior. Ethologists, unlike experimental comparative psychologists, make most of their observations of animals in the wild state, with maximal freedom of motion for the animals. Outstanding among this group of naturalists is Konrad Lorenz. Julian Huxley has said of Lorenz that he "has given himself over, body and soul, to his self-appointed task of really understanding animals, more thoroughly than any other biologist-naturalist that I can think of."

We may be able to come closest to capturing the point of view of this man through the give-and-take of conversation. We can't all do this ourselves but the next best thing is a report of such a conversation.

54

CONVERSATIONS WITH KONRAD LORENZ
EDWARD R. F. SHEEHAN

Professor Lorenz came downstairs wearing an old windbreaker, corduroy leggings, and a pair of rubber boots. Not even a costume as casual as that could diminish the distinction of his appearance, his rich white mane and bearded chin themselves sufficient to persuade the visitor that he walked with a wise man. The Professor carried a bucket of barley grain and cursed his

Source: From *Harper's Magazine*, May, 1968. Copyright 1968 by Edward R. F. Sheehan, reprinted by permission of the Harold Matson Company, Inc.

aching tooth; as we pursued the gravel path past the gray lake a helicopter chopped across the drizzly heavens. "Damned airplanes!" he exclaimed. "They scare the geese!"

He unlocked a rusty gate; we trod in the raw Bavarian mist over rolling autumn meadows by a forest of pine until we reached a large clearing; the Professor picked up a metal megaphone standing in the field, pointed it in the direction of his Institute, and shouted, *"Komm! Komm-komm! Komm!"* We waited, but the geese did not come. Through the drizzle of the darkening afternoon I could perceive only the distant buildings of the Max-Planck Institute for the Physiology of Behavior, all constructed in the style of Bavarian peasant houses and half-hidden among clusters of birch and willow trees, where colleagues of Dr. Lorenz were working with computers to decipher the song patterns of bullfinches, the smelling mechanisms of butterflies, the cybernetics of praying mantises. The Institute is situated well off the main road in a forest at Seewiesen, at least an hour's drive from Munich, but its remoteness has not prevented it from becoming a place of pilgrimage for naturalists from all over the world.

"Komm!" In a while we heard a wild honking from afar, until, at a high altitude, some of the geese began to glide above the meadow. Eventually a few graylags landed; the Professor dug into his bucket, scattered some barley grain about, and started to scribble notes. More and more geese, scores of them, glided toward the ground, hovering like helicopters just before they landed—graylags, Canadians, barheads, white-fronted geese. "At present I'm studying communal fighting between families," Dr. Lorenz remarked. Some snow geese waddled up to the Professor; bending over, he fed them from his bucket. "I call these 'my five,' " he said. "They are very unpopular because I hand-reared them and I pamper them. There, see them snap at those graylag ganders. Now, we walk away from them and—just as the son of a rich man gets a beating when he is caught without his big brother—the graylags attack my five."

"How is rank established among geese?" I asked.

"By previous fighting, of course. Geese are great status seekers. They have their own language and signal codes. Families always stick together. *Komm! Komm-komm!* I just made a magnificent observation. Those two families of graylags there, A and B let's call them, just ganged up and vanquished family C. Then family C met family A alone and beat them. The joke is that they all know it. Look at the older gander there—he's lost an eye. His wife is very courageous. She may even be a gander."

"A gander!"

"I'm not quite sure, but homosexual pairs do occur and such an alliance is always very high-ranking, because no man and wife can stand up against two ganders. Homosexual pairs try to engage in the sex act but they can't. They both try to mount, but nothing functions. Nevertheless, they remain together for a long time. Here come a couple of mallards. They're sexually perverted."

"Homosexuals?"

"No, they think they're geese. They were reared with geese and will respond only to geese."

"What lesson do you draw from that?"

"There's no *lesson*. We're just curious. What we've found may be of interest to psychopathologists: the fact that even in birds early childhood experiences may cause a permanent kink. There's a gay little goose: she's trying to steal someone's husband. Look at his wife go after her—peck as she might, she can't get that flirt to go away. Geese can be great flirts, but in principle they are monogamous. There are divorces—sometimes gradually, sometimes sudden and dramatic."

We were surrounded now by nearly two hundred noisy geese; presently we were joined as well by three lovely fräulein, assistants of Dr. Lorenz, who proceeded to dictate data on goose behavior into tiny tape recorders. Dr. Helga Fischer, another of his colleagues, emerged from the misty grass of an adjoining meadow; just as she did she lost her footing and fell to the ground, quite harmlessly. But the geese were terrified; in an instant, in an eerie honking chorus, they all took flight. We ducked, or rather I did—Professor Lorenz was well-splattered with goose *merde*. "Come on," he said. "Let's go home. You have learned nothing today."

As a layman, I imagined that I had already learned a great deal, for if any living scientist was qualified to interpret the bellicose behavior of the goose—and of man—it was Konrad Lorenz. Among many other things he is a biologist, zoologist, and a psychiatrist; probably no contemporary empiricist knows more about the kingdom of animals and its parallels to human action. Dr. Lorenz has been described by Sir Julian Huxley as "the father of modern ethology," a branch of the "new biology" which may be defined in its most elementary sense as the study of the behavior of animals in their natural environment, with particular regard to the role of instinct. This definition conveys no notion of the ethologist's sophisticated techniques, which in Arthur Koestler's words "make the classical naturalist look hopelessly old-fashioned."

Until two years ago Konrad Lorenz possessed a modest but enthusiastic body of admirers in America and Britain as the author of *King Solomon's Ring* (1952), a charming account of the comportment of various beasts, birds, and fishes; *Man Meets Dog* (1955), an equally delightful sequel to his earlier work; and

Evolution and Modification of Behavior (1965), a highly technical critical study of the concepts of "innate" and "learned" elements of behavior. It was not until 1966, however, with the publication in English of *On Aggression*, that Dr. Lorenz displayed to a wider audience the full scope of his scientific insights and literary skill, combining a remarkable gift for anecdote and humor with awesome empirical erudition—all of which made very credible his declaration that "I have something to teach mankind that may help it to change for the better."

The argument of *On Aggression* proceeds from a base of almost pure Darwinism to expound what amounts to a revolutionary view of the instinct of aggression in beasts and man, an instinct which Dr. Lorenz defines as being primarily "intra-specific—predominantly directed against members of the same species. It is only in man that the aggressive urge becomes disruptive. In animals, it often serves an extremely constructive purpose which is essential to the preservation of the species. Aggression, quite to the same degree as the drives of hunger and sexuality, is an innate aptitude in its own right. In coral fish, for example, by balancing the distribution of individuals over the available "territory," by selecting the most rugged members to do the reproducing, and by defending the young, innate aggression helps to propagate and protect the species. Furthermore, evolution and natural selection have endowed many animals with special mechanisms and rituals which derive from aggression but which in the nick of time inhibit and redirect the instinct from lethal use against members of the same species. This applies not only in the "triumph ceremony" of the relatively harmless graylag gander, when the gander symbolically vanquishes an imaginary competitor for the edification of his goose and his gosling; the more savagely armed the beast—the wolf, for one—the stronger his built-in barriers to intra-specific slaughter.

Moreover, in a remarkable paradox, only aggressive animals are capable of close personal relations and the bond of love, since it is precisely from the aggressive instinct and from its inhibiting rituals that these emotions are phylogenetically derived. But unlike other animals, man has developed the powers of conceptual thought and verbal speech, faculties which have enabled him to invent weapons so effective that his instinctual inhibitions against killing fail to master the dangers arising from his inventions. Indeed, Dr. Lorenz postulates that "an unprejudiced observer from another planet, looking upon man as he is today, in his hand the atom bomb, the product of his intelligence, in his heart the aggressive drive inherited from his anthropoid ancestors, which this same intelligence cannot control, would not prophesy long life for the species."

Dr. Lorenz makes an ardent plea that the insight which natural science provides into the causes of aggression in animals may endow us with the power to modify its effects in man. But first we must understand that man himself *is* an animal, perhaps first and foremost, and that—before it is too late—the analogous behavior of animals must be recognized by other disciplines as indispensable to any sane effort to analyze and thus to temper the errancies of human conduct. As Dr. Lorenz has written elsewhere: "It is high time that social and group psychology began to occupy itself with the physiological side of behavior and more especially with the innate processes. Hitherto it is only the demagogues who seem to have a certain working knowledge of these matters."

Dr. Lorenz's diagnosis is dazzling; he is much less convincing when he proposes remedies which would sublimate and redirect—not eliminate, since that is impossible—man's aggression against his fellow. He suggests an accentuation of peaceful competition between nations in sport and space, the exchange of more students between diverse cultures, the rechanneling of "militant enthusiasm" for the benefit of the young, the disavowal of jingoistic nationalist ideologies, and so on. He admits the inadequacy of such measures and expresses the hope that natural selection will favor the evolution of a higher and better being whose built-in inhibitions against aggression will be stronger than those we presently possess. Perhaps "the long-sought missing link between animals and the really humane being is ourselves!"

Such are the bare bones of Dr. Lorenz's argument, which is of course virtually bottomless in its moral and philosophical implications—implications which prompted me to return with him to his goose field on several subsequent afternoons to engage in leisurely chats. His books are stimulating—but not as stimulating as an hour of his conversation.

ANALOGIES
FROM A
SQUID'S EYE

Question: *Your probings into the depths of instinct seem to possess a certain affinity to the studies of Jung and his theory of "the collective unconscious."*

K.L.: I've tried to read Jung. He was a genius, and his thoughts contain a great amount of truth. But then I lose him in a labyrinth of mysticism. I miss in him the desire to provide a natural physiological explanation for his conclusions. We are far from being able to bridge the gap between neurophysiology and the behavioral sciences. But at least the approach ought to be from the side of the natural sciences, and that's where I feel much more in sympathy with Freud than with Jung. These symbols of Jung's, the mandalas and so forth—I refuse to accept them. I just don't grasp them. I think they're eyewash, honestly. That's speculative philosophy—neither susceptible to proof nor to falsification. One has to be able to *disprove* an hypothesis.

You mentioned Freud.

K.L.: If he had discovered nothing else but the dynamics of drives he would have to be considered a great man. Freud discovered from an entirely different basis and approach that drives, or instincts, are sources of motivation which without any outward stimulation actively impel the organism to do something. In other words, he discovered spontaneity, for which we now think we have physiological explanations, and although I don't agree with all of present psychoanalytic doctrine I do consider Freud to be a great discoverer. He depended upon empirical evidence, even if it was one-sided.

Didn't he overemphasize sexual motivation?

K.L.: I couldn't give a simple answer to that. I wouldn't know. He may have been quite right. I do know more about animals than Freud or Jung did—that's my business—and more about evolution. I think that the problem of behavior, motivations, and the like can be approached only by strictly scientific methods, ones which have been used in the science of evolution in the days since Darwin. What Jung says about archetypes is very brilliant speculation, but on the whole it's not scientific.

Some of your critics contend that you push your own conclusions too far. Arthur Koestler, for example, accuses you of offering us an "anseromorphic view" [anser = goose] of man, of taking flight on the treacherous wings of analogy by exaggerating the parallels of behavior between the goose and human beings.

K.L.: I don't think I go too far. They harp that I draw false analogies. False analogies do not exist. An analogy of form or function can go more or less far, can be more or less detailed. If in an octopus or a squid I find an eye, with lens, an iris, a nerve—I need not even observe the animal—I need only to state these formal analogies to know it is an eye, which has evolved to see with. It has the same formation as my eye, my vertebrate eye, which has evolved independently of the octopus eye, but a detailed similarity informs me it has the same function, and nobody balks at calling it an eye. If I find some much more specialized forms of behavior, which presuppose a sensory and nervous organization which is infinitely more complex than that of a mere eye, then my assertion is perfectly justified that this behavior, which evolved independently in two entirely different groups of vertebrate animals, must indubitably serve the same function. Construct a computer model of an animal being jealous —one system having a social relationship with another, resenting a third one doing the same and interacting with both and trying to break up their relationship. This function would presuppose an enormous complication, much more so than the functioning of an eye. You can speak of jealousy with respect to dogs and ganders, certainly. Assertions that these are false analogies or anthropomorphizations betray a lack of understanding of functional conceptions. To call the animal jealous is just as legitimate as to call an octopus' eye an eye or a lobster's leg a leg.

So much for jealousy. How far can you go in predicting animal and human behavior?

K.L.: In certain respects you can predict how man will act. If you put a certain number of boys together in a classroom, you can predict there will be some striving for supremacy. You can predict the "pecking order." Some boys will be respected and dominant, others will be picked on and underdogs. This always happens when you put together five boys, five cockerels, five canary birds, five cichlid fish—you can see the same phenomenon. There is no doubt about the analogy of this behavior. When I gave a lecture on aggression at Honolulu University recently, I started by reading three or four pages of *Tom Sawyer*. Tom meets a new boy. "I can lick you," he says. One might call this syndrome "I-can-lick-you" behavior. This kind of behavior represents not merely a reaction to environment, it has the spontaneity of a true instinct, just like sex, which can be proved experimentally.

This was something Freud was perfectly aware of despite his theory of the death-drive, which incidentally I agree with only in part. What I mean is that repressed aggression may result in self-destructive behavior. It is now known to psychiatrists that a great number of suicides result from repressed aggression. Freud didn't really think so. But when he was in a depressed mood himself, he said that aggression was a self-drive originally and primarily directed at one's own self, deflected on one's own self, and then redirected against one's social environment. In my opinion, it's the other way around. Repressed aggression may turn back on one's own self and result in self-destructive behavior. My example of the death-drive is the man who is himself driving his automobile too fast in dense traffic, gets angry because others are inconsiderate, and drives still faster, endangering his own life.

Freud had a good excuse for his opinion because his model of an instinct is the sexual drive, which is really directed primarily at the self and then reflected outwards; no doubt there is some truth in that. But this does not apply to aggression. What Freud says generally about sex contains much truth—I don't believe that the sexual drive is quite as important as Freud contends; there are other drives we must contend with as well. But at least Freud knew that a drive is something that wants out.

The repression of a drive requires a constant supply of energy. A better way of dealing with an unassuaged drive is to sublimate it. Man's great struggle today is to find the correct and most constructive sublimation for his aggressive drives. My suggestions as to how he should proceed are anything but comprehensive, and to imply that I have pretended so is an unfair reproach of me. I have no pretensions to a universal system. I never said I was Doctor Know-It-All.

But there is a cult growing up around your writings.

K.L.: Such a cult would be a dangerous thing. I'd be the first to discourage that. A scientist may have pupils, but the most dangerous thing for a discoverer is to have disciples instead of pupils. Psychoanalysis, one of our most promising branches of science, has suffered because some of Freud's pupils turned into disciples.

SCIENCE AND "FREE WILL"
Speaking of your disciples, what is your opinion of Robert Ardrey's The Territorial Imperative, *which has been all the rage?*

K.L.: Ardrey started with an interesting theory and then went out and found convincing evidence for it, rather than the other way around, which would have been the more scientific. I admired his *African Genesis*. But in *The Territorial Imperative* he pushes his deductions too far and explains several things on the basis of territorial aggression. I found myself always saying "Yes—but." You can't explain everything in terms of territory. Geese, for example, except for defending a tiny nesting area before and during incubation, manifest no territorial behavior. But Ardrey is much more scientific than Arthur Koestler, because he confines himself to the popularization of what he really knows. Koestler, in his *The Act of Creation*, is guilty of several crude misrepresentations of my own and other people's work. At least Ardrey quotes me accurately.

What of the impact of your discoveries about aggressive drives, in animals and humans, on the classical conceptions of free will?

K.L.: I don't know anything about free will. The problem of free will is one that cannot be approached scientifically. I can observe myself when I am making a decision out of my own free will. I cannot doubt the reality of my own act, but I can only describe this as a phenomenologist, and how subjective phenomena correlate with physiological phenomena is a problem that cannot be solved by science.

But as a scientist I am absolutely convinced that everything I do is physically determined. I wouldn't necessarily say *causally* determined because the science of physics has lost its belief in the absolute applicability of causality everywhere. Causality loses its meaning in atomic physics. But the unpredictability of atomic events is not in my opinion an acceptable explanation of free will, nor is quantum physics. It is certainly possible that the sudden decision to some act could be the result of a quantum jump. A quantum jump cannot be predicted by causality but only statistically. However, to explain human acts in that light would give us only the freedom of chance, of the falling dice— just as has been proposed by the great German physicist and philosopher Pascual Jordan.

Aren't members of an advanced culture intellectually freer of compulsive behavior patterns than primitives are?

K.L.: Freer than primitives? Hardly. We of technological Western society are bound up intellectually in our taboos, cultural rights, culturally determined norms of behavior, habits of thought, probably no less inescapably than the savages of the forest. Our norms and taboos are so much a matter of course with us that we don't notice them as we do the habits of strange cultures. Your "primitive" is a happily lazy man who would probably find the compulsions of structure in our culture very crazy. We are much more in danger than they. We are certainly nearer to self-extinction, to cultural suicide, than any primitive people ever were.

You seem pretty much of a determinist.

K.L.: In science I'm strictly a determinist. I see the evidence for free will only in myself. It would be ridiculous to deny it. To say that my perception of color is only subjective, an illusion, is stupid. All our supposedly objective knowledge comes to us through subjective experience. That others have the same free will proves it exists—practically it does. Philosophically there are objections. Solipsism—the belief that everything is a dream, that only *I* have existence—can't be disproved. On the other hand philosophers who profess not to believe in the reality of the extra-subjective world admit the existence of other men and that they have the same subjective experience as themselves. Physiologically you cannot find any proof that your brother man has a soul. Nevertheless, you end up by accepting as truth many things which command no scientific evidence.

I am confronted with two facts: One, I have to regard myself as a physical mechanism as strictly determined as physics are, as anything in the physical world is, otherwise I cease to be a scientist. Two, I have to face the fact that inside, subjectively, I experience free will. Am I exercising free will when I make a decision on the side of morality? This free will of the highest order is not the freedom of arbitrariness, it's a freedom to obey some very predetermined and complicated laws which are the laws of ethics. This is a description, not an explanation of free will. In any event, it is probably predetermined that I believe in my free will.

But I do not at all believe in what some theologians and philosophers call "fallen man" and "fallen nature." I believe in rising nature. Plato is the perfect believer in fallen nature. Like many Eastern philosophers, he yearned for man to rise again to a perfection he supposedly once possessed. I reject the doctrine of original sin. Sin signifies a deviation from the progressive development of man.

I do have a great sympathy for some of the ideas Teilhard de Chardin. He sees redemption in the progress of evolution, which is aimed upwards. In a way, Christianity's belief in redemption makes it the most evolutionary and biological religion I know of because it believes in the rising of man. On the other hand, human history has been too brief to indicate definitely whether or not it represents an appreciable evolutionary progress. The span of written human history is really awfully short, and in terms of evolution it may represent an unhappy period. In fact, for all my optimism, man may be on the downgrade at this moment. Man hasn't really evolved that much within the period of recorded history, and neither have animals—unless dogs have, perhaps. But on the whole, taken from the beginning, evolutionary history is indubitably progressive. The higher animals have more essential value than lower ones. I think we can see some progress in human history but I don't think we can prove it. Man *is* subject to progressive evolution.

Many Christian theologians would of course object that you miss the point of the doctrine of original sin. They call it the felix culpa—*the starting point for man's drive upwards toward redemption.*

K.L.: I only object to the doctrine of *re*-demption. I believe in *demption*, if I may mint a word, not re-demption. Furthermore, I object strongly to all the cyclic theories of history: the idea that the rhythm of history is a constant repetition of the same inexorable patterns. History never repeats itself; it is sometimes similar to the past in its development but it is also constantly new and changing in its progress. What is utterly unique in human history during the last few centuries is the knowledge explosion, and all of science has participated in that.

Of course the life cycle repeats itself.

K.L.: It does indeed, but not exactly. Were it not for the little deviations from exact repetition, there would be no evolution. Evolution is slower than cultural development by powers of ten —a million times slower, perhaps. Cultural development progresses quickly, but its very speed is dangerous. Thus the great question is: will man gain sufficient knowledge of himself before he destroys himself? We are witnessing a race between self-knowledge and self-destruction. I don't accept any appreciable genetical differences between peoples and races. The barbarism of the Nazis could have happened anywhere. It was a sort of mass psychosis, like burning witches, or war itself, which I regard as absolutely pathological. The "territorial imperative" does much to explain the causes of war, such as the Arab-Israeli dispute, which I consider almost purely territorial. In a review of *On Aggression*, Margaret Mead made an excellent criticism of my work. As regards human aggression generally, she said, poor Lorenz forgot that there is also a strong element of predatory instinct. Human aggression cannot be explained simply in terms of territory. The predatory instinct is neither territorial hunger nor pure aggression. And to that I say, yes indeed, Margaret Mead is right; I forgot about that.

In your earlier work, Evolution and Modification of Behavior, *you made a searching distinction between the concepts of "innate" and "learned" behavior. Evidently you believed that a great many of the modern psychologists badly needed to be put in their place.*

K.L.: Yes, I consider *Evolution* my most important book, and I hoped it would settle the argument. Some psychologists believe that everything in human and animal behavior is "learned" and can therefore be controlled by nurture. Marx made the same error. He didn't consider the instinctive side of human nature. He thought in terms of stimulus and response, believing that if only we could remove cruelty and oppression—and all the other stimuli that supposedly produce aggression—man would turn into an angel. He was wrong, because aggression doesn't depend on stimulus or environment. It's built in. Man is programmed that way.

In that case can we hope that man will find some way to avoid destroying himself?

K.L.: Only if he discovers more intelligent and less harmful outlets for his innate aggression. Much more clever and effective techniques of sublimation can be evolved; don't ask me exactly what or how. But the answer is more complicated than just having all of us go out and play some football. For example, consider "redirected activity." If a furious woman smashes crockery instead of hitting her husband—that's not sublimation, that's redirected activity, which can be very useful and at times even necessary. If you want proof, consider the notion of "non-frustration" children: the belief that by never frustrating a child you will produce a non-frustrated man. This was a disastrous experiment. The "non-frustration" hypothesis caused incalculable damage to mental health. Struggle is necessary for everyone. You cannot achieve success without working hard for it, which always involves some frustration. Imagine the angry child who draws only a placid response from his parents at all times: this is the greatest frustration of all, and it's dangerous.

Speaking of aggression, I'd like to hear a little of your experi-

ences during the last world war. Perhaps you'd prefer to start even earlier.

K.L.: You mean about my career?

Yes.

K.L.: My greatest debt is to Darwin. I learned my Darwin from a Benedictine priest in high school in Vienna, the city of my birth. I was fifteen when the first world war ended, and after spending a few months studying biology at Columbia in New York I entered the University of Vienna, where I studied medicine and acquired my medical degree. I was qualified as a comparative anatomist but I didn't practice as an M.D. until the second world war. Zoology was what interested me, and I started studying that. In 1935 I was offered an unpaid lectureship in comparative anatomy and comparative psychology at the Zoological Institute of Vienna. Daringly I chucked my paid job at the Anatomical Institute of Vienna to take the lectureship. Incidentally, my wife—who is a physician, too—held a paid position as a gynecologist in a hospital. I was very successful as a lecturer.

At the Zoological Institute I collaborated for a time with Professor Niko Tinbergen, and between the two of us we founded the science of ethology. I was good with intuition, hunches, and observation, but he was the experimenter *par excellence*. We complemented each other perfectly, and we still do. He's now at Oxford, and still my closest friend. In 1940, one year after the war came, I accepted an appointment as professor of psychology at the University of Königsberg, the citadel of Kantian philosophy. At Königsberg I acquired a deep admiration of Kant but a hatred of German idealistic philosophy. The consequences of that philosophy were so unfortunate. It contributed to Germany's ills, particularly the notion that history has a *purpose*— that it's not causally determined—and a mission. Then I was drafted into the army. For me the only good thing about the war was that it forced me into psychiatry.

Hadn't you ever met Freud earlier in Vienna?

K.L.: No, never, and I repent it deeply today. I could have met him so easily! But at the time I was a very intolerant young scientist and I despised Freud for his inexactitude. Freud was slightly demagogic. On page five he would present some speculation. On page fifteen he would say of the same thing, "As we have shown to be probable." On page twenty, it would become, "As we have already proved." I distrusted him. Even though he was right there in Vienna I never attended his lectures. What a pity, for his style was so crystalline, and no one could write better German than Freud, not even Thomas Mann, the acknowledged master of the language. It wasn't until I got deeper into my own behavioral work and realized the parallels that I

really became interested in Freud. I started reading him inten-
sively just before the war, and by that time he had fled to London. Even during the war—when I was a prisoner of the Russians—I managed to get some of his books. This was a feat,
because the Russians hated Freud as much as the Nazis did.

How did you happen to practice psychiatry during the war?

K.L.: I was recruited into the German army in 1941 from my
professorship at Königsberg. I was thirty-eight years old. They
made me a common G.I. It was overlooked that I was an M.D.
At first I was employed as a motorcycle dispatch rider in East
Prussia—I'd done a lot of motorcycle racing in my younger days.
Then it was discovered that I was a medical man, and I was assigned to a hospital in Poznan as a psychiatrist and neurologist.
I worked there from 1942 to 1944, when they sent me to the
Russian front as an army doctor with the grade of sergeant; I
never became an officer. I was taken prisoner three months later
in June 1944 near Vitebsk in White Russia.

The Russians put me to work as a prisoner-doctor in one of
their military hospitals. I was the neurologist in charge of six
hundred hospital beds. I went on to become camp doctor in
thirteen different prisoner camps ranging from White Russia to
near the Urals to the Upper Viataka River, down to trans-Cau-
casia—Armenia—and back to Moscow before I was liberated.

AN ARISTOCRACY
OF GANGSTERS

*What were the main lessons you learned from your experience
in Russian camps?*

K.L.: One of them was that a POW camp was such a remarkably self-contained model of human society. There you could
observe crystallized the whole range of human weaknesses. You
had a status system, a rigid ranking order as in geese, an aristocracy of gangsters. At its best it could serve as an ideal of
human society, at its worst a grotesque caricature. And I can
assure you that at all times it was far from being a classless
society.

During the war, very many of my patients were hysterics,
schizophrenics, and psychotics. The term "shell shock" was unknown then; we called them "breakdowns." In many of my
camps I saw men dying of starvation. That's the softest and
least painful death you can imagine: the men die in their sleep.

*Some of the saints have told us that starvation can induce
mystical experience. Aldous Huxley agreed, and attributed this
to chemical changes in the body brought on by the starvation
process. Did you see any evidence of that?*

K.L.: The mystical phase is experienced only by the well-fed
man who is starved suddenly. But when a man is gradually
starved, in the initial and middle phases he becomes by turns

absolutely bestial, asocial, apathetic, irascible, and completely egotistical. So Huxley's observation is not true of gradual starvation. No one could care less for mysticism than a man experiencing the final phases of prolonged starvation. He even ceases to care for eating.

When were you liberated?

K.L.: Not until 1948. I returned to Vienna, where I started a small private institute and continued my ethological studies. Later the Max-Planck Gesellschaft invited me to establish my present institute, at first in Westphalia, and, since 1955, here in Bavaria.

I'd like to pursue a few more implications of your writings since then. In On Aggression, *you state that the expert teaching of biology is the* one and only *foundation on which really sound opinions about mankind and its relation to the universe can be built. Isn't this claiming a bit too much for biology? Can't others learn as much about mankind in their own disciplines and perceptions?*

K.L.: No, this isn't claiming too much for biology. Ordinarily, intelligent people must learn more about the essential biological facts, in order to acquire the proper perspective with which to assess themselves and others as human beings. The younger generation today tends to be very irreverent, and this is a dangerous state of affairs. A general lack of reverence toward the deep traditions of a culture, and even toward the order of the universe, such as we witness so much of presently, means a blindness to real values. If you bring up a young man in a big city where he sees only man-made things, he senses how impermanent it all is, how easily it can be destroyed and built up again. Tear down that old building there, get rid of that rusty Cadillac—better ones are being made. Young people in urban society are bored to tears because they observe nothing in the world that's really worthwhile; they are ignorant of a whole universe of life and order and values which deserves their veneration. But if you were to teach young men and women biology in the interesting manner it merits—and not just to impart technical knowledge—you might awaken their subconscious sense of beauty.

Can't art do that?

K.L.: A real education in art or music might produce similar results. In fact, gifted young artists are about the only young people today who are not irreverent. But there are many people who have no aptitude for art. My point is that if you take a child out into the woods far from the city, and teach him about nature, you'll never get a Teddy-boy. In biology the quests for beauty and knowledge go so splendidly hand in hand.

You've also written that the danger to modern man arises not so much from his power of mastering natural phenomena as from his powerlessness to control sensibly what is happening today in his own society. I certainly agree with that—particularly in view of the Vietnam war and the urban riots in America last summer—but then you go on to say that this powerlessness is entirely the consequence of the lack of our insight into the causation of human behavior. I wonder. Isn't this the same sort of hyperbole that Freud and some of his disciples have practiced? I really wonder whether it's enough to know what's wrong in order to achieve a cure. A great many of us know what is wrong within ourselves—but we don't change because we don't really want to change.

K.L.: I am simply insisting that even with the highest moral principles you cannot manage human sociology without knowledge. The recognition of what's wrong in man and his society does not remove the evils there, but scientific evidence and precise data are prerequisites for doing something about them. I don't know, with believers perhaps prayer can achieve the same result.

IF THERE IS A GOD . . . *In your writings you've disavowed the belief that man is "nothing but" an ape; you add that he is essentially more. Without getting into the scholastic conceptions of the soul, as between apes and men do you at least see any room for the intervention of a divine spark?*

K.L.: Yes. Every step of evolution is the divine spark. Every step of evolution is of a different dimension and importance—but behold the spark, spark, spark all the time. Admittedly the spark which intervenes between anthropoids and hominids is one of the bigger sparks, but even that is not half as interesting or as much a riddle still as the origin of life itself. As for who or what God is, I do not try to conceive of Him. If there is a God, He exists entirely beyond the power of human conception.

Nehru once remarked that the more we discover of the forces of nature and the universe, the less we look for supernatural causes.

K.L.: That is an entirely mistaken conception of religion. It is a fundamental error to believe that even a complete explanation of the universe would have any dismantling influence on the philosophy of values and religions. That notion of Nehru's was something which is typical of German idealism: the belief that you dethroned God by explaining nature. All of the sciences put together couldn't constitute a convincing argument to push out the possibility of God. But I say that it's a very primitive belief to think that God, if He exists at all, exists only in miracles and not in natural phenomena. Confining God to events in which the laws of nature are suspended or don't even apply is the worst possible blasphemy. He needn't suspend the laws of nature; if He did, He would contradict Himself. I think He would contradict Himself if He really made the Eucharist His own body and blood. The idea of the Eucharist wasn't *meant* to mean that in the beginning; I'm convinced that it was intended only to be a symbol, but it was taken too literally. One mustn't treat the statements of mystical writers as if they were the pronouncements of a modern physicist.

I know that you agree with G. K. Chesterton that—to a considerable extent—the religion of the future will be based on humor. And I agree with you that we do not as yet take humor seriously enough.

K.L.: Humor somehow enforces absolute honesty with oneself. A humorous man cannot be pompous, or take himself too seriously. This is very fundamental to the scientist's honesty and to the ethics of science generally. One must always be ready to say ha-ha-ha when one is proved entirely wrong.

Have you ever been proved entirely wrong?

K.L.: Yes. I was totally mistaken when I believed that all behavior, all instinct, was based on chain reflexes, which is what I was brought up on. I still believed that in 1936, when I wrote a paper on the conception of instinct.

You've stated somewhere that you intend to tell the life history of a goose in one of your future books. A whole book about one goose?

K.L.: No, I don't intend to write a whole book about one goose. I might write one whole chapter, or one whole nice short story with some embroidery and fantasy—or one could make one novel out of one goose.

The Zen philosophers have a saying, "The wild geese do not intend to cast their reflection. The water has no mind to receive their image."

K.L.: That's beautiful. It's true that geese don't see their reflection in the waters. They don't look for it. Perhaps some primates do.

Could it be that the reflection does not exist at all—unless there's a man there to see it?

K.L.: Poor fellow—you're a solipsist if you believe that.

Even Lorenz, the ethologist, does not content himself with the study of animals for their own sake. On the basis of his studies of animals he develops a theory of aggression which he carries over to a discussion of human aggression. But he has studied humans, too.

Several issues are raised in this conversation. One is the ever-present heredity-environment debate. Compare Lorenz's attention to the physiology of behavior and his emphasis on the innate processes with the behavioristic approach of B. F. Skinner's type of psychology.

The student who has come to take the ideas of Freud and other psychoanalysts for granted may be surprised to find so much criticism of Freud, Jung, and psychoanalysis in general. One of the weaknesses of these men, important as they have been in psychology, was that they allowed cults to be built around their contributions. They then attracted a following that has extolled their virtues uncritically and has prevented their being considered in proper perspective. Note Lorenz's reaction to the idea of attracting disciples.

MORE ANIMAL STORIES

Chimpanzees, being so much like humans in so many ways, have intrigued many researchers. To discover just how much humanlike behavior chimps can be taught, attempts have been made to get chimps to learn a language. Most such attempts have been to teach the animal to vocalize simple words, as used by humans.

Allen and Beatrice Gardner, "Teaching Sign Language to a Chimpanzee" (*Science,* 1969, *165,* 664–672), have started with the fact that the most common natural communication among chimpanzees is by gesture. They have taught their pupil, Wahoe, to use the sign language used by the deaf. Their success has been fantastic.

David Premack, "The Education of Sarah" (*Psychology Today,* September, 1970), also taught his chimpanzee, Sarah, a nonvocal language. He used plastic symbols that varied in shape, size, color, and texture and Sarah was able to learn and use more than 120 words in two-way communication.

There are two books, each recounting the experiences resulting from taking an infant chimpanzee into the home of a psychologist and rearing it as one would rear a human child. In one of these, W. N. and L. A. Kellogg, *The Ape and the Child* (Hafner, 1967; originally published by McGraw-Hill, 1933), the Kelloggs had a child of their own the same age as the chimpanzee. In the other, Cathy Hayes, *The Ape in Our House* (Harper and Row, 1951), the chimp was an "only child."

The student who becomes interested in animal behavior is fortunate. For him study can readily become pure joy, for so many of the books in this area are delightfully written.

We have already drawn your attention to *In the Shadow of Man,* by Jane van Lawick-Goodall, and to one of her occasional contributions to the *National Geographic Magazine.* And the "Conversations" article has mentioned Lorenz's books, among them *King Solomon's Ring* (Thomas Y. Crowell, 1952), *Man Meets Dog* (Penguin, 1953), and *On Aggression* (Harcourt Brace Jovanovich, 1963).

We have also mentioned, in other contexts, Vincent Dethier, *To Know a Fly,* and Moyra Williams, *Horse Psychology.* Another good source is the beautifully illustrated book by Niko Tinbergen and the Editors of *Life, Animal Behavior* (Time, Inc., 1965).

We can sometimes look at behavior more objectively if we see it in an animal. Perhaps the animal, being a less complex organism than man, can be seen as a whole more readily. It is really doubtful that man is intelligent enough ever to understand, completely, his own intricacies. Perhaps he can understand a jackdaw, a dog, a horse, even a chimpanzee. When he can come to see one of these, not as a collection of fragments of learnings, perceptions, emotions, and motivations, but as an integrated whole, he might come closer to an understanding of himself.

Part Eighteen

Reading Psychology: Integrations

You are not going to learn all of the psychology you ever will learn from one book or from one course. Nor, for that matter, from many courses. What you come to know about psychology, about the behavior of people and of animals, will grow as you continue to have experiences with them.

Man long ago learned that he could not reexperience, directly, all of the experiences of those who came before him. Primitive man learned that if he were to be aware of the collective experiences of the tribe he must listen to the stories told by his elders. Since man invented writing, we have access to the accumulated knowledge of the race (or as much of it as we care to and have time to read).

You recall that, when we discussed perception, we found that sensory input has to be given meaning for it to become a perception. Present sensations are integrated with past experiences to develop something meaningful. This is true of the assimilation of all knowledge.

To discuss how this process of integration can involve you and your learning, we call on one of our favorite writers, our colleague, Virginia Voeks.

55

YOU COULD INCREASE YOUR ABILITY TO SEE INTERRELATIONSHIPS
OF ALL KINDS AND MAKE NEW, MORE MEANINGFUL INTEGRATIONS
VIRGINIA VOEKS

"Integration" refers to a synthesis of materials. It is a sort of tying together of the concepts, data, methods, and ideas available from one source with those available from other sources—from other courses, books, and magazines, from newspapers, movies, and plays, from one's life in general.

With skill in making integrations, each new fact or concept makes old ones more meaningful and comprehensible. All aspects of the world are enriched whenever one discovers anything about any aspect of the world. To a person of such facility, a knowledge of literature contributes to his understanding of individual behavior (psychology), to his understanding of group characteristics (sociology), to his understanding of the areas of his world most extensively considered by philosophers, anthropologists, political scientists, economists. Similarly, an understanding of psychology or sociology, philosophy or anthropol-

SOURCE: From *On Becoming an Educated Person*, Third Edition. Philadelphia: W. B. Saunders, 1970. Pp. 8–12.

ogy, economics or political science can enable one to read literature with deeper appreciation and comprehension. Through making integrations, your fund of concepts and facts becomes valuable and useful.

The concept of "integration" is fairly simple. The process is not. To illustrate the integrations you could make and the effect of seeing these interrelationships, let us consider some parts of psychology and one bit of literature, Flaubert's *Madame Bovary*.

In that book, Flaubert paints certain episodes from Emma Bovary's childhood and adolescence. Suppose you understand many of the facts and principles of psychology and are skilled in making integrations. Then these portrayals take on deeper color for you. You go between and beyond the lines and see vividly, deeply the effects of these experiences on Emma. You put these together with your knowledge of psychology and get new views of the world about you. The effects of her impoverished home, devoid of beauty to Emma, but providing materials from which the child created elaborate dreams of life-to-be— these you would see keenly. No longer are those pages stuffy descriptions, dull background information. They are laden with gripping drama—when you know and use your knowledge of psychology. You understand more fully what is resulting from Emma's creation of that world of fantasy and from daydreaming as an habitual response to frustration. Much else too you see more clearly and understand more deeply: how Emma responds to the discovery that the dashing prince she married is neither a prince nor dashing—and never will be . . . how the world strikes her when she finally does get a home of her own . . . how her husband (and life) look to her when she moves into this "new" home, the home which was to be a sort of castle, elegant, exciting, and peaceful, but which actually is shabby, despicably ordinary. How these later experiences affect Emma, you foresee and appreciate more keenly when you know the common results of living in fantasy and integrate this knowledge with the material of the novel. If you add to this an understanding of the relationship between frustration and aggression, you will understand with greater acuity the murderous actions to which Emma later resorts. You understand better, also, the world in which you live.

This is the merest hint of how a book takes on added significance and richness when you integrate a knowledge of psychology with the portrayals of a novel. Through such integrations, you catch more of the author's ideas; you build more ideas of your own; you notice more aspects of the world described; and you see more completely what is happening in your own world. You read with deeper appreciation and enjoyment than you otherwise could, for new dimensions have been added.

Literature becomes more meaningful when you integrate it

with your knowledge of psychology. Similarly, psychology becomes more meaningful when you integrate it with your knowledge of literature. You can better comprehend psychological concepts, principles, and facts if you have read reflectively such a book as *Madame Bovary* and have developed skill in seeing interrelationships. To illustrate this, let us look at a sentence from a psychology textbook.

"One's vocational and marriage choices are based, in large part, on fantasy." [1]

Now there is a statement which looks trivial, almost puerile —until you start to think about it and relate it to your other knowledge. Suppose in the course of your thinking, you recall Emma Bovary and *her* marital choice based on fantasy. How did that work out? You remember how she repeatedly compared her husband with her dream and found Charles always sorely lacking, the dream always better, far better. You remember her disappointed bitterness when the dream exploded. You recall the way she spoke and acted after she discovered her husband was no gallant knight, no extraordinarily gifted man. You recall how she humiliated and taunted him, goading him for years to try the near impossible; and you recall how Charles became, as a consequence, ever less like her dream. You remember Emma's ensuing conquests, her ruthless exploitation of other men—men who might be princes, but never were.

"One's . . . marriage choices are based, in large part, on fantasy." [1] Do we have clues here concerning an underlying difficulty in many homes? Could this account perhaps for some of the disrupting flashes of rage, the damaging onslaughts, we have often witnessed but seldom understood? The sentence from the psychology text *combined* with a knowledge of "Madame Bovary" gives one new leads concerning the nature of the world. That is one result of "making integrations."

"One's vocational . . . choices are based, in large part, on fantasy." [1] If one chooses a vocation in terms of a dream of the job, would not the results resemble those so tragically illustrated in Emma Bovary's marriage? Does this give some clue to why many people are sorely disappointed by their vocations, rebellious toward their employers, beset by feelings of betrayal? With similar bases for their choices and for Emma's, we should expect similar results. This may afford new insight concerning one way to avoid the disillusioned bitterness and conviction of betrayal common in our world.

The foregoing does not mean we can prove the statements in a text by finding parallels in literature. One cannot do that, but what one can do is truly remarkable. By integrating materials from literature and other fields of life with text materials, you can illustrate the statements in the text. You can bring out their meanings. You can see more of the possible implications. Dry facts become alive; new ideas are born.

REFERENCE

1. Symonds, P. The Dynamics of Human Adjustment. New York: Appleton-Century-Crofts, 1946, p. 495.

What Voeks has done in integrating *Madame Bovary* and a basic psychological concept can be done with many novels. A well-known psychologist recently wrote to us: "I learn more about human behavior from reading Proust, Dostoevski, and Kafka than I do from reading psychology journals."

Another psychologist, in a correspondence regarding books for psychology students, suggested that we include "works by the truly great psychologists, Dostoevski, Hesse, Pirandello, Leo Rosten, Philip Roth and, if you have to add an academic, Nietzsche."

Certainly you will modify these suggestions; you will have your own favorite authors from whom you may learn much about human behavior. There is, however, a necessary caution. You can learn about human behavior from a novelist, provided only that his portrayal of behavior is accurate. We must constantly keep in mind that the novelist is not at all limited to describing what people actually do. He *creates* people.

As an example, suppose we look at a book that you have very likely read, William Golding, *Lord of the Flies* (Coward-McCann, 1954). Students sometimes assume that the story is descriptive, that they now know how a group of boys behaves under these circumstances. Not at all! These boys are not and never were real. If Golding knew boys sufficiently well, he might have created a situation in which they acted as real boys would. At least one critic doesn't think he did. Kenneth Rexroth says of *Lord of the Flies:* "The boys never come alive. They are merely the projected annoyance of a disgruntled English schoolmaster. . . . Certainly this is not a picture of the juvenile delinquency that has swept over the world from Jakarta to Reykjavik." [1]

Of course, many readers think that Golding did not intend to describe the behavior of boys; that he created a novel situation to symbolize certain aspects of society.

How, then, is the student to know what stories are psychologically valid? No doubt this will always be, to a great

[1] Kenneth Rexroth. "William Golding." *Atlantic,* May, 1965, p. 97.

degree, a matter of opinion. But it is a part of the teaching function. It becomes the teacher's obligation to the student to aid him in finding reading materials that are adequate representations of behavior. Many of these books should be broad in scope. At least some of them should deal with the whole person, or with animals, in such a way that students will be aided in the process of integration. They should assist the process of making this knowledge of psychology a functional part of the self.

To do this with a broad range of fiction is something we dare ask of no more than a small handful of psychology professors. There is a book that attempts this type of guidance to a limited degree: Caroline Shrodes, Justine Van Gundy, and Richard W. Husband (Eds.), *Psychology Through Literature: An Anthology* (Oxford University Press, 1943). It contains selections from writers ranging from William Shakespeare to James T. Farrell; mostly, but not quite all, fiction.

While we do not mean to underestimate the value of novels and short stories as adjuncts to more formal psychological literature, we do feel that we are treading on more solid ground when we get into the realm of nonfiction. This may be an illusion, for there are books on the market that pretend to be good psychology that would do credit to any novelist for sheer invention. There would seem to be no substitute for the judgment of qualified psychologists in evaluating the validity of novels and other general books as teaching aids in psychology. But don't expect them always to agree.

For an account of one attempt to find books that were valid as psychology and also interesting to the student, we present a selection by another of our favorite writers.

56

PSYCHOLOGICAL THRILLERS:
PSYCHOLOGY BOOKS STUDENTS READ WHEN GIVEN
FREEDOM OF CHOICE

IVAN N. MC COLLOM

Psychology as a topic of general interest is possibly more popular with the general public than is psychology as an academic

SOURCE: From *American Psychologist*, 1971, *26*, 921–927. Copyright © 1971 by the American Psychological Association, Inc. Reprinted by permission.

subject-field with college students. Furthermore, the content of the general interest psychology is probably quite different from the content of a college course. What is there about the "good" psychology of the classroom that is less enticing than the "inferior" popular brand?

Is it possible that academic psychology is designed solely for potential professional psychologists and that the professors purposely ignore the interests of other students?

I once heard a very well-known professor say, in an obviously unguarded moment, that the principal purpose of the first course in psychology was "to proselyte the bright students and let the pigs go where they may." Unfortunately this, though extreme, may well represent the feelings of many who plan and conduct such a course.

But there is another point of view. George A. Miller (1969), in his APA Presidential Address, deplored the alienation of people "from a society in which a few wise men behind closed doors decide what is good for everyone [p. 1074]" and suggested that "psychological principles and techniques can be usefully applied by everyone [p. 1073]" and that "psychological facts should be passed out freely to all who need and can use them [p. 1070]."

The proponents of general education as a significant aspect of higher education have long held to this position. It is most encouraging that so prominent a leader in the field of psychology has come to this way of thinking, but discouraging that it has taken so long.

General education in psychology, the process of freely passing out psychological facts, requires good teaching to be effective. Good teaching involves the process of assisting students to become self-educative. Rather than attempt to *cover* the subject, the instructor of an introductory course may well attempt to aid the student in gaining some basic knowledge; help him to identify competent sources of additional information; and arouse his interest sufficiently so that, long after completion of the course, he will continue to add to his knowledge.

A few studies (Anderson, 1956; Ogdon, 1954; Spencer, 1961) have shown the low levels of readability and human interest of the reading materials typically presented to students in the beginning course in psychology. Prescriptive reading of materials written at a high level of reading difficulty and, all too frequently, carrying little that is intrinsically motivating is, we know, not a sound method of inducing learning.

Some people seem to have known for quite some time that this system does not work. Howells (1895) wrote that "The book which you read from a sense of duty, or because for any reason you must, does not commonly make friends with you [p. 42]."

Boswell quoted Samuel Johnson (Hill, 1934) as having stated

the concept just a bit more positively: "A man ought to read just as inclination leads him; for what he reads as a task will do him little good [p. 428]."

While it is not so, just because these people have said so, experience would indicate that there is much truth in what they say. Is there not, then, a workable method of inducing students in introductory psychology classes to read desirable material, yet to do their own selecting of what is to be read?

In a recent *Saturday Review* editorial, Bowser (1970) said that

too many people actually believe the canard that science is a cold, clanking affair, flatly opposed to humanity, beauty and wonder. Why don't more science teachers make it a point to show youngsters the glowing, psychedelic beauty of ordinary crystals, as seen through the polarizing microscope [p. 26]?

Paraphrasing this, can we not truthfully say that too many people who emerge from a beginning course in psychology actually believe that psychology is a set of rules for behavioral conditioning, mostly derived from the study of rats, and multi-syllabic names for personality characteristics discovered in institutions for the seriously disturbed? Why not show our students overall patterns of behavior of people in a living society, expressed in the beauty of well-written prose?

Why not allow time within the course structure for reading from available materials that (*a*) are good, sound psychology, (*b*) cover topics that have an inherent interest for the students involved, and (*c*) are written in such a style that they hold the interest of the student reader. Is it at all possible that there are books that will do all this and will, as well, actually thrill the student? Can we create a list of *psychological thrillers?*

There will be no single, fixed list, no list of books that will do all things for all students. But if the available titles are sufficiently numerous, and if they offer a sufficiently broad choice of areas within the field of psychology, there will be something there for everybody.

This "cafeteria" type of supplementary reading program will not appeal to some who attempt to instruct young people into the organized mysteries of psychology, simply for the reason that it is not organized sufficiently. But like the "cafeteria" feeding studies of young children, might the student eventually work out his own balanced fare? Even if he doesn't, who knows exactly what are the essentials for a beginning student? No two textbooks, no two instructors, agree. Are we not—at least should we not be—more concerned with arousing the student's interest in psychology than with an abortive attempt to "pour in" prechosen facts for regurgitation on examinations, no matter how well those facts may be organized?

DEVELOPMENT
OF AN
"HONORS"
READING LIST

For some years I have been teaching a one-semester course in general psychology to selected "honors-at-entrance" students. These students represent the highest 5% of high school graduates, all of them probably ranging upward of 130 on the familiar IQ scale.

Psychology has been a general education requirement for all students, generally taken in either semester of the first college year. These particular students thus represent, in terms of major fields of academic interest, a cross section of the entire campus. Many of them have not yet firmly decided on a major. The honors class, as conducted, is designed as a general education course, and no conscious attempt has been made to recruit psychology majors. It is true, however, that psychology gets more than its fair share of majors from the students who have been in these honors classes.

I have long been searching for supplementary books for beginning psychology students, books that have a high level of intrinsic merit and that students will read not because they are required reading, but because the students find in them something of interest and value. Although this search has not always been highly productive, some such books have been discovered. Beginning with this brief list of titles, suggestions were solicited from colleagues and from students.

In general, I desired books that were of a reasonable length. The reinforcement that comes with having finished reading a book should be relatively frequent.

It does not always seem possible to predict with a high degree of accuracy just what will appeal to college students. But a suggested list of supplementary books was presented at the beginning of a term. The members of the class were asked to select and read one or two books from the list. In later semesters, this was increased to a minimum of three. Some read more. And students have told me a year or more after completing the course involved that they were still reading books from that list.

After reading a book, each student wrote a brief report in which he had been requested to state "what you think of the book, how you feel about it, whether or not it should have been included in the list [and] your recommendation to other members of the class as to investing time in reading it."

The list was composed at any one time of about 12–15 books. A title remained on the list for subsequent semesters only if it were both read frequently and highly praised. The decision to retain or delete a book was made on the basis of student judgments.

Now and then new titles were added, for the search continued. Students in the classes could, and did, nominate books for the list. But to win an initial listing, a book must be sound psychology. This I reserved the right to judge, a right that the students seemed quite willing to respect.

Over a period of several semesters, 34 titles appeared on the list. Fifteen of them have survived. Of the 19 casualties, a few were dropped because the students found them too difficult, some because they were reported to be uninteresting, a couple because students thought them too simple. Two had to be dropped because they were out of print, and the few available copies could not stand the traffic. A few books interested occasional readers but were considered too specialized for the general reader. A few suffered from neglect, probably because of a combination of circumstances. Informal communication among students seems to have been an important factor in the continued popularity or the unpopularity of books on the list.

STUDENT REACTIONS

Brief reports written by 304 introductory psychology students have been retained and reread. In addition, about 60 students, representing a variety of academic major fields, have been enrolled in an upper-division-level honors course in psychology. Most, but not all, of these people had been in the introductory honors course. These students were allowed free choice in selecting books to be read within the broad limits of the area of psychology. They each read, on the average, 10 books in a semester. The diversity of selection was extremely great. Many read from the introductory course list books that they had not read previously. Their written reports of this reading are included in the analyses, along with those of the beginning students.

Some kind of numerical rating of these "psychological thrillers" seems called for at this point. However, it is not possible to secure a truly objective summary of the students' appraisals. The number of people reading a given book might be considered an index of student interest. In this case, this is true only to a very limited degree. Some titles have been on the list of suggested books for several semesters, others have been added along the way, some quite recently; nor were all books equally available. Paperback books tend to be popular. Yet often books become paperbacks because of demonstrated popularity.

Nearly 800 student reports were read and independently evaluated by the writer and by a graduate student. [1] On the basis of our pooled judgments, the titles are placed in the order of the overall evaluations made by these students. This ranking is certainly only an approximation, but it does give some idea of the relative interest shown by the students in these books.

[1] The author expresses his gratitude to Susan Johnson, whose contribution is gratefully acknowledged.

"PSYCHOLOGICAL
THRILLERS"

Axline, V. *Dibs: In search of self*. Boston: Houghton Mifflin, 1964. (Paperback, Ballantine edition) (82) [2]

Lorenz, K. *King Solomon's ring*. New York: Thomas Y. Crowell, 1952. (Paperback, Apollo edition) (57)

Green, H. *I never promised you a rose garden*. New York: Holt, Rinehart & Winston, 1964. (Paperback, New American Library, Signet) (76)

Adcock, C. J. *Fundamentals of psychology*. Baltimore: Penguin, 1964. (Paperback, Pelican edition) (21)

Voeks, V. *On becoming an educated person*. (2nd ed.) Philadelphia: Saunders, 1964. (81)

Wilson, J. R. (Ed.) *The mind*. New York: Time, 1964. (38)

Skinner, B. F. *Walden two*. New York: Macmillan, 1948. (120)

Blatz, W. E. *Human security: Some reflections*. Toronto: University of Toronto Press, 1966. (23)

Hesse, H. *Siddhartha*. New York: New Directions, 1951. (16)

Dethier, V. F. *To know a fly*. San Francisco: Holden-Day, 1962. (43)

Allport, G. W. *The individual and his religion*. New York: Macmillan, 1950. (Paperback, Macmillan edition, 1960) (42)

Grier, W. H., & Cobbs, P. M. *Black rage*. New York: Basic Books, 1968. (Paperback, Bantam, 1969) (27)

Cantril, H., & Bumstead, C. H. *Reflections on the human venture*. New York: New York University Press, 1960. (26)

Neill, A. S. *Summerhill*. New York: Hart, 1960. (30)

Hall, C. H. *A primer of Freudian psychology*. Cleveland: World, 1954. (Paperback, New American Library, 1955) (92)

STUDENT
REPORTS

The reports that students wrote about these books have been summarized by weaving together characteristic statements in such a way, hopefully, as to provide overall statements that reflect the students' appraisals of the books they read.

These summaries, I think, yield two kinds of information. First, they tell us something about the books, what they are about, and what there is about them that appeals to students. Second, and perhaps more important, these reviews yield information about the students who wrote them, about their interests, about the kinds of information they are seeking, about aspects of life that are meaningful to them.

Dibs: In Search of Self, by Virginia Axline, seems to be the most thrilling of our thrillers. Many students found the book "deeply moving" and repeatedly stated that they literally could not put it down until they finished reading it. Negative comments were rare.

[2] The numbers in parentheses indicate the number of times each book was read and reported on.

Young people identified with Dibs. As one student expressed it: "Even though this book is written about a five year old, it does have a significance to a college student who is trying to find himself and his place in the world." And another: "Although deprived of love and a feeling of self worth during his first years of life, Dibs was able, through the help of 'Miss A.' to discover his self and become a person, strong, real, and loving."

King Solomon's Ring, by Konrad Lorenz, "is an excellent book for all students of psychology to read . . . a rich and interesting and often amusing account of Lorenz' experiences and experiments with animals."

The book has three distinct appeals. As literature: the word "fascinating" kept popping up in the reports—"an aesthetic experience . . . poetry." As a source of knowledge of animal behavior: "This has got to be the best way to learn about methods of studying animal behavior." It "illustrated many points in my psychology textbook." As an opportunity to become better acquainted with a unique personality: "The charm of the book lies as much with the author as with the subject." "Lorenz has communicated the enthusiasm and affection he feels for animals." "When the book ends, far too soon, you are left with the urge to run right out and obtain a new friend of the nonhuman species to share life with." Out of reading this book comes learning at the feeling level.

I Never Promised You a Rose Garden, by Hannah Green, is another book that students found "difficult to put down." They became deeply involved and found it not only interesting but "inspiring," "so vivid it is almost frightening." "It gives the reader a tremendous insight into the struggle between the conflicting forces of insanity and sanity . . . almost as if he were experiencing the confusion, fear, and frustration himself."

"A fantastic book from which to gain an understanding of the nature of mental illness and mental institutions . . . the story of sixteen-year-old Deborah's fight to become a member of the participating world of people, to come out from the sidelines and the private world of her own creation."

C. J. Adcock's *Fundamentals of Psychology* was liked by students in the introductory class as "a good introduction to the basic principles of psychology," and they also found it "extremely valuable as a general review." While no one indicated that he stayed up half the night to read it, it was reported to be "far more interesting than . . . anticipated," a book that "can be read for enjoyment as well as information," "a really good book." They said such things about it as: "My interest was captured and held." "Illustrations from everyday life add interest to the material."

Students seem often to get lost amid the mass of detail in a comprehensive general psychology textbook. Adcock's *Funda-mentals* provides a brief and interesting account of the field as a whole.

On Becoming an Educated Person, by Virginia Voeks, has a very great appeal to most students, particularly freshmen. They commonly indicated that they have recommended it to their friends, that it should be read by all freshmen, and some went so far as to suggest that it be required reading for all college-bound high school seniors or first-year collegiates. "If more incoming freshmen would take the time to read this book, college would be a much more enjoyable and rewarding experience for them." "It would save them a lot of time, tears, and traumatic experiences." Student reports bear an interesting resemblance to old-fashioned patent medicine testimonials. "Since reading this book I have changed a few of my habits." "I got rid of some of the anxiety."

There was, for these students, a certain compulsiveness about this book. It seems to help them do, and do better, things they feel they should do. "Once you start reading it your conscience won't let you stop." Repeatedly, students said that it was "valu-able," "helpful," "worthwhile," as well as "interesting" and even "exciting."

The Mind, edited by John Rowan Wilson (a Time-Life Science Series volume), was recommended "because of the interest it creates, interest in several specific areas . . . which I plan to study more in detail." There was some initial suspicion of a picture-book approach, quickly dispelled on reading the book. Of particular fascination was the picture essay on "Strange Land-scapes from the Realm of Mental Illness." This includes a section on schizophrenic art with the Van Gogh sequence and the cats of Louis Wain.

The Mind, like Adcock's *Fundamentals of Psychology*, enables the student to stand on a high place and see the overall organi-zation of the material that lies ahead, supplying him with an outline map into which he can place the details as he plods more slowly through the specifics of subareas. Then, having collected a mass of detail, the student can, by reading the other of these two books, again stand on a promontory and see, as a whole, the territory he has traversed.

As I finished reading the 120 student reports on B. F. Skinner's *Walden Two*, I was reeling from the impact. They were filled with emotional expression all the way from "When can I join?" to "an infuriating, frightening novel." "*Walden Two* may arouse a variety of different emotions in its readers; the only certain thing is that it will arouse them." A few students were greatly attracted to the idea of the kind of utopian community that Skin-ner visualizes. Others see it as did one young man who said that

"Walden Two has a different race of man than the outside world. They don't fight, war, whore, get mad, yell, and may not even think." Far more were negative toward the idea of the kind of modern utopia depicted than were favorable. But while there was no agreement as to Walden Two as an institution, there was an extremely high degree of involvement in *Walden Two*, the book. It caused these students to think. Even more, it caused them to feel.

Through the reports students have written about *Human Security: Some Reflections*, by William E. Blatz, there ran a central theme. The book is thought provoking. "Blatz provokes his readers into thinking and learning." "It forced you to think, and that is the only real road to education." "Each chapter, each sentence, each word provokes questions . . . questions which only the reader can answer." "Although Blatz did not help me to make any decisions by telling me which side of a specific question is right and which is wrong," said one student, "reading this book did help me to discover the way in which problems should be faced." Blatz is not didactic, but these young readers perceived much in what he had to say with which they could identify in their reflections on their own security.

In recent years, the books of Hermann Hesse have attained a high level of popularity among college students, and their favorite is *Siddhartha*. Students who had previously read this "story of a young Indian boy who is searching for himself" have insisted repeatedly that *Siddhartha* should be on our reading list. Some of them grant that it may have more to do with philosophy than with psychology but state that it is "packed with psychological insight and understanding."

While professional psychologists may not agree that *Siddhartha* is psychology as the subject is conceived in the Western world, these young people see in it something for which they have been searching. "Hesse, eighteen years ago, wrote about what college students are searching for today." "Very timely, as it deals with . . . the finding of one's self." They are not too greatly impressed, anyway, with the prescribed boundaries of knowledge.

We shall include *Siddhartha* in our list of "psychological thrillers" simply because the *we* in this case includes the students who have read it, and they would have it so. Perhaps it is time we included in our Western studies something that, as one student wrote, "brought me closer to Eastern thinking and beliefs than I have ever been before."

Every student who read *To Know a Fly*, by Vincent F. Dethier, found it interesting, amusing, and enjoyable, in fact, "a MOST unusual book." One described it as "the cutest book I have ever read." For a few, it was just too cute, "too frivolous," "more enjoyable than scientific," "amusing and interesting in a trivial sort of way. . . . I question its worth as a supplement to a psychology course." These few students seemed unable to believe that any book so enjoyable, so completely humorous, could possibly contain anything seriously worth while. Yet for others, it made "learning something about science enjoyable," "an excellent combination of light humor and scientific knowledge." More positively, some saw it as "a valuable contribution to the student's introduction to the methods of experimental psychology," "a good example of how to conduct experiments, formulate hypotheses, fix up dependent-independent variable situations, and finally how to interpret the findings and come to conclusions." "The fun . . . was sugar coating for a well written explanation of how a scientist works." "Dethier makes learning a fun process and research sound very exciting." Perhaps a warning is in order! After reading the book, many students found it impossible to swat a fly.

Gordon Allport's *The Individual and His Religion* attracts only those readers already quite interested in the religious aspects of life. But it is read frequently, attesting that many students *are* interested in religion. Students with a deep religious commitment approached it with some suspicion, anticipating an atheistic or agnostic bias, but reported surprise at Allport's objectivity.

Not a recent book, *The Individual and His Religion* is actually as old or older than many of the students who read it. One of them said, "It's good, but dated." Yet another indicated that although it was "written twenty years ago it is still relevant to today's society." It does not seem to lead any of its readers to a rejection of religion, but does frequently lead to a reaffirmation, but at the same time a reinterpretation, a religion that is not in conflict with science. "It provides a rational basis for an individual to evaluate and improve his own religious philosophy." "Allport has enriched the concept that God is purely psychological. God is a hypothetical construct." There is a place for a student-centered book on psychology and religion. Allport's book is not the perfect answer, but until a better book is written it is providing something quite meaningful.

Many students became deeply involved in *Black Rage*, by William H. Grier and Price M. Cobbs, "a psychological study of the effects of racism on Black America" which "reveals many of the emotional conflicts of the American Negro." It "approaches the problems of racism and prejudice from the angle of . . . the manifestations of these problems in the psychological make-up of the Negro . . . considering the psychological problems peculiar to blacks which, through fear or pride, they were not able to show before." A few readers, themselves white, saw the book, written by two black psychiatrists, as biased. But the majority of those who read it saw it as "an important book," "tremendously enlightening."

A book that has great appeal to some students, particularly those with interests in literature and philosophy, is *Reflections on the Human Venture*, by Hadley Cantril and Charles H. Bumstead. This book "uses literature to illustrate concepts of psychology." It is "a book of quotations taken from the literature of the world and woven into one of the most comprehensive books on man that I have ever read. It shows man as a human, breathing, feeling animal, a picture of him that is somehow lost in the laboratory." "The kind of book you recommend to your friends so they, too, may see a little deeper into their own being."

If the goals for the teaching of psychology indeed include relevance to other aspects of life for the general student, this book does seem to accomplish this for many. Possibly because of its relatively greater length than most of the books discussed, this one was not read as often as some others, but most of those who read it seem to agree with the student who "emerged . . . with a deeper understanding of and respect for psychology as the analysis of human behavior."

Summerhill, by A. S. Neill, is a relatively recent addition to our list of suggested books. It was nominated by a student who had read it for an English class, and it has proved very popular. Of 30 reports at hand, only one "did not enjoy the book very much." While students commonly found themselves "turned off by his extreme Freudian views" and his "hang-up" with masturbation, and many doubted that Neill's program "would work anywhere except in a controlled environment such as his school," almost all of them agreed, essentially, with one who wrote: "I think that the kind of freedom that A. S. Neill is talking about would most certainly bring about a happy child and that what our society needs is more happy people."

Calvin S. Hall's *A Primer of Freudian Psychology* is the only title on our "thriller" list that frequently occurs on general psychology textbook lists of recommended additional reading. It is a very frequently read book, but, from the reports, one gathers that students read it mostly out of a combination of curiosity and a feeling that they really should know more about the ideas of this man Freud, whose name has become a household word. They did not dislike the book; it does supply some of the information they seek; but "it is more informative than entertaining." It did hold their interest, and sometimes it stimulated them to read more of Freud, to turn to Freud's own books. Never in reporting on it did any student express the sheer delight that is so characteristic of comments on some books, but because it is read so frequently it has remained on the list.

This becomes a good cutting point, and books evaluated with less enthusiasm by students cannot really be called "thrillers."

CONCLUSION   Here, then, is a list of books that have proved to be highly interesting to this group of students. Exact data are not available as to the residual effects of this type of reading. General observation, however, indicates that when students are given, as a part of their introduction to the study of psychology, interesting books to read, they are more likely than otherwise to continue reading psychological literature.

The search should continue for sound psychology books that are sufficiently well written that they will be read for their intrinsic interest. Perhaps better writing skills should be applied to the creation of psychology books. Perhaps, if interesting books are rewarded with increased readership, more "thrillers" will be created. At least there is some indication that the universal, or at least widespread, application of psychological principles and techniques will be facilitated by the availability of psychology books that provide some degree of excitement to their readers.

REFERENCES

Anderson, W. Readability of readers. *American Psychologist,* 1956, *11,* 147–148.

Bowser, H. Thinking with your blood. *Saturday Review,* 1970, *53*(38), 26.

Hill, G. B. (Ed.) *Boswell's life of Johnson.* Vol. 1. Oxford: Clarendon Press, 1934.

Howells, W. D. *My literary passions.* New York: Harper, 1895.

Miller, G. A. Psychology as a means of promoting human welfare. *American Psychologist,* 1969, *24,* 1063–1075.

Ogdon, D. P. Flesch counts of eight current texts for introductory psychology. *American Psychologist,* 1954, *9,* 143–144.

Spencer, D. S. Readability of references in introductory psychology. Unpublished master's thesis, San Diego State College, 1961.

There are two aspects of this study that we feel we must emphasize. One is the cooperative nature of the enterprise. The function of the psychology professor is to judge the validity of the material as psychology. He may make guesses as to how interesting certain books may be to students, but he won't always guess correctly. How much a book interests students, only students can tell. Many people who are teaching psychology courses have sent us lists of "popular" books that they suggest or assign to students. But, as far as we can tell, every one of these lists is instructor-made.

We join the "student rebellion" briefly at this point, for we think that all decisions should be made at the point where they can be made most effectively. To determine how well *you,* as a student, *like* a book is your prerogative. And while there will be many who will disagree, we hold firmly to our contention that liking a book makes it more meaningful.

The other point of emphasis. No list of books should ever be enshrined. It should be changing, constantly. The list in the last reading reflected the choices of those students, in that place, at that time. For example, the list includes Hermann Hesse's *Siddhartha.* That was in 1968 and 1969. In 1971 we read an article by John Wilkinson, "Heraclitus of Ephesus: In Today, Out Tomorrow" (*Center Report,* October, 1971), in which he says: "It is in the framework of the emporium theory of culture that I incline to interpret the astonishing rash of letters and verbal intimations I daily receive, all of which run more or less in accord with the formula: Heraclitus is definitely 'in' and Hermann Hesse is definitely 'out'."

The student culture changes, and with it the likes and dislikes of students. Old books become obsolete, new books are published. A few stay on, indefinitely. Interest and education seem permanently wedded.

One thing has surprised us: the tendency for students to be wary of anything humorously written. This has been mentioned in connection with Dethier's *To Know a Fly.* For a discussion of this subject look up the September, 1969, issue of *Impact of Science on Society.* It is devoted entirely to the subject, "The Science of Humour, the Humour of Science." In one of the articles, "Confessions of a Scientific Humorist," psychologist James V. McConnell tells the story of an attempt at humor that has grown into a regularly published journal, the *Worm Runners Digest,* which he edits. He also tells us that someone wrote in accusing him and his publication of "misleading students into thinking that science can be fun."

To which we respond with another quotation, this from Bud Schulberg, "The Chinese Boxes of Muhummad Ali" (*Saturday Review,* February 26, 1972): "Wise kings listened to inspired fools while foolish kings laughed at the exterior apparatus of their jokes."

Glossary

Abreaction: Relief of tension by expressing pent-up emotion; catharsis.

Antimony: Contradiction between two principles.

Ashram: Community organized to integrate meditation with working and playing together.

Attention: The focus of perception.

Au pair girl: Girl who performs domestic work for room and board, but little or no salary.

Black box: Any instrument that picks up input of one kind of energy and transforms it into output of another kind. Sometimes refers to human beings.

Catatonic schizophrenia: A psychosis characterized by an individual's lapsing into a rigid, unresponsive stupor.

Chronological age: Age in years and months; length of time passed since an individual's birth.

Classical conditioning: A form of learning wherein a neutral stimulus acquires, through association, the ability to elicit a response.

Cognitive: Pertaining to the process of becoming aware.

Compulsion: An irresistible urge to perform some act repeatedly.

Conditioned response (CR): A response attached, through learning, to a previously neutral stimulus.

Conditioned stimulus (CS): In classical conditioning, any event which through association acquires the ability to set off a response.

Control group: A group as nearly as possible equivalent to an experimental group. It shares all characteristics and treatments with the experimental group except for the independent variable.

Correlation: The degree to which two attributes are related; usually indicated statistically by a coefficient.

Cybernetics: Scientific study of control and feedback mechanisms.

Defense mechanism: An adjustment by which the individual prevents or reduces anxiety through self-deception or substitute behavior.

Deficit needs: External needs stimulated by such things as lack of food, safety, love, status, etc.

Dependent variable: Change which is a consequence of the independent, or experimentally controlled, variable. See *Independent Variable*.

Determinism: The theory that all events are natural consequences of events which have gone before them.

Dissonance: Motivation which grows out of the recognition of one's inconsistent thoughts and attitudes.

DNA: Deoxyribonucleic acid. Principal substance of the chromosomes.

Dualism: The assumption that there are two distinct kinds of phenomena, mental and physical.

Ego: The individual's concept of himself.

Emotion: A general term covering feeling states and their accompanying motor and glandular activities.

Empiricism: Philosophy which holds that experience is the source of all knowledge.

Engineering psychology (Ergonomics): The application of psychology to the study of man's relation to the equipment he uses.

Ergonomics: See *Engineering Psychology.*

Ethology: The study of animal behavior.

Eupsychian: Word coined by A. H. Maslow to mean "the good society."

Experimental group: Group of subjects whose behavior is observed under carefully specified conditions.

Galvanic skin response: Measurement of the electrical conductivity of the skin as an index of emotional arousal.

Genetic: Pertaining to that which is biologically inherited.

Gestalt psychology: Branch of psychology concerned largely with perceptual organization and emphasizing the study of whole patterns of behavior instead of analyzing its elements.

Gin: A snare or trap.

Growth needs: A term used by Maslow to indicate the inner need to develop one's capabilities; self-actualization.

Hallucination: An apparent perception without adequate external stimulus.

Homeostasis: Tendency of the body to maintain itself in a state of balance.

Hypothesis: Tentative explanation, based on previous observation, which is to be tested in an experiment.

Imprinting: Rapid learning which occurs at a critical period early in the life of an organism.

Incidental learning: Learning without formal instruction or intent, often without apparent motive.

Independent variable: The aspect of the environment which is changed systematically by the experimenter. See *Dependent Variable.*

Instrumental conditioning: Learning which takes place as the result of reinforcement of random behavior; so-called because the behavior is instrumental in obtaining the reinforcement.

Intelligence: A term covering the abilities to adapt to novel situations, to learn new information, to grasp abstract concepts; in general, to profit from experience.

Intelligence Quotient (IQ): The ratio of a child's mental age to his chronological age.

Interdependence: A mutual and reciprocal dependence among individuals.

Masochism: Pleasure, usually sexual, derived from experiencing pain.

Materialism: The philosophical view that matter is the ultimate reality.

Maturation: The orderly sequence of development of an organism resulting from its inherent nature and independent of its learning.

Mental age: A method of calibrating the intelligence level of children.

Molar approach: The study of behavior as the total, overt performance of the individual.

Molecular approach: The study of behavior concerned with analyzing its specific, often physiological, elements.

Morphological: Pertaining to form and structure.

Negative reinforcement: See *Reinforcement.*

Neuron: An individual nerve cell.

Neurosis: Psychological disorder characterized by excessive anxiety.

Obsession: Persistent and irresistible idea or emotion.

Organism: An individual animal.

Organismic principle: The concept that the whole is more than the sum of its parts.

Paradic: That which functions in accord with an inherent pattern or design.

Paranoia: Psychosis characterized by fixed and systematic delusions.

Parapsychology: Psychological study of extrasensory perception.

Pavlovian conditioning: See *Classical Conditioning.*

Percentile: Any of the 99 points which divide a rank distribution into 100 groups of equal frequency.

Perception: The individual's experience resulting from his interpretation of sensory input.

Phi phenomenon: The visual illusion of motion arising from stationary stimuli flashed in rapid succession.

Physiology: Study of the functioning of the organs of the body.

Placebo: An inert preparation given to subjects who believe they are receiving medicine.

Positive reinforcement: See *Reinforcement.*

Positivism: The doctrine that science is limited to observed facts and deductions from those facts.

Projection: Defense mechanism characterized by the attributing of one's own motives and attitudes to others.

Prophylaxis: Prevention of disease or disorder.

Psychedelic drugs: Drugs, such as LSD and mescaline, which often produce hallucinations and other disorganization of thought processes.

Psychiatrist: A physician who specializes in treating behavior disturbances.

Psychoanalysis: A theory of personality developed by Freud and his followers. Also, a special variety of psychotherapy based upon this theory.

Psychodynamics: Motivational system of the individual.

Psychology: Science of mental life; the organized study of experience and behavior.

Psychosis: Major mental disturbance involving disintegration of the personality and loss of contact with reality.

Psychotherapist: One qualified in the use of psychological treatment techniques. Includes psychiatrists, clinical psychologists, and psychiatric social workers.

"r": The symbol for coefficient of correlation. See *Correlation.*

Rationalization: A defense mechanism involving finding an acceptable explanation for one's thoughts and acts.

Reinforcement: In general, an attempt to influence the probability that a particular act will be repeated. *Positive reinforcement:* Increasing the likelihood of an act occurring by rewarding it. *Negative reinforcement:* Decreasing the likelihood of an act recurring by punishing it.

Repression: Defense mechanism which denies to consciousness unwanted thoughts or feelings.

RNA: Ribonucleic acid. Molecules which transfer information from the DNA to direct growth processes taking place in the body. RNA may also be involved in memory storage. See also *DNA.*

Satori: The ultimate state of consciousness sought in Zen Buddhism.

Self-actualization: See *Growth Needs.*

Sensation: The reception of energy by an organism through its sense organs.

Serendipity: The accidental discovery of something valuable while looking for something else.

Solipsism: The idea that a person can be certain of nothing outside his own experience.

Statistics: A mathematical means of handling the data resulting from measurement, for example, psychological measurement. A statistic is the individual mathematical datum.

Stereotype: A rigid set of greatly oversimplified beliefs about members of a group.

Stimulus: Any change in the environment, external or internal, which impinges on the organism through its sense organs.

Syntactic: Having to do with the way words are combined to form meaningful phrases, clauses, and sentences.

Tawsing: A custom, still prevalent in Scottish schools, of punishing pupils by whipping them with a tawse, a leather strap cut into thongs at one end.

Taxonomy: The orderly classification of plants and animals.

Therapy: Treatment of illness.

Unconditioned response (UCR): A response which occurs without learning.

Unconditioned stimulus (UCS): A stimulus which will automatically elicit an unlearned response.

Variance: Variability; a measure of the dispersion of an array of scores.

Volunteerism: The assumption that the individual by his own will may influence the course of events.

WASP: White Anglo-Saxon Protestant.

Zeitgeist: Spirit of the times.

Correlation of These Readings with Textbooks

CRM Books
PSYCHOLOGY TODAY (2nd ed.)
Communications Research Machines, 1972

Text chapter	Related readings	Text chapter	Related readings
1	1–6	13	
2	8, 9, 52–54	14	15–20
3–4	21–28	15	
5–6	1, 12–14	16	1, 7
7	11, 49	17	32–33
8	10	18–19	29–32
9	51	20	34–38
10		21–23	39, 40
11	14, 46, 47	24–29	40, 48–50
12		30–34	41–44

Dember & Jenkins
GENERAL PSYCHOLOGY
Prentice-Hall, 1970

Text chapter	Related readings	Text chapter	Related readings
1	1, 5, 6	11	21, 26, 27
2	2–4, 54	12	11, 51
3	34	13	14, 45–47, 52, 53, 55
4		14	34–38
5	7	15	32, 33
6		16	29–32
7	15–20	17	41–44
8		18	39, 40, 48–50
9	22, 23, 32	Concl.	55–56
10	24, 25, 28		

Edwards
GENERAL PSYCHOLOGY (2nd ed.)
Macmillan, 1968

Text chapter	Related readings	Text chapter	Related readings
1	2–6	10	40, 48–51
2	1, 8, 9, 29–32, 54	11	34–38
3	32, 33	12	39, 40
4	15–20	13	29, 32
5	20	14	41–44
6	22–25, 27, 28, 32	15	26–28, 50, 51, 56
7	12, 13, 21, 25–27	App. A	34, 35
8	11, 45–47, 52, 53, 55	App. B	7
9	8–14, 32, 49		

Gilmer
PSYCHOLOGY
Harper & Row, 1970

Text section	Related readings	Text section	Related readings
I	1–4, 55, 56	IX	21–28
II	8–14	X	32, 33
III	31, 39, 40	XI	10, 11, 14, 45–47, 51
IV	7	XII	1, 2, 28, 30, 31, 48, 49, 52–54
V			
VI	15–20	XIII	6, 11, 50, 51
VII	34–38	XIV	14, 31, 41–44
VIII	29–32		

Harrison
PSYCHOLOGY AS A SOCIAL SCIENCE
Brooks/Cole, 1972

Text chapter	Related readings	Text chapter	Related readings
1	1	9	34–38
2	2, 3, 4	10	41–44
3	5, 7	11	6, 48–50
4	15–28, 32	12	12, 13, 29–31
5	29–32	13	30, 31, 50
6	8–14	14	48, 49
7–8	39–40		

Hershey & Lugo
LIVING PSYCHOLOGY
Macmillan, 1970

Text chapter	Related readings	Text chapter	Related readings
1	31, 45, 46	7	15–20
2	21–28	8	39, 40
3	14, 45–47, 55	9	
4	8–14	10–11	41–44
5	29–32	12	55, 56
6	32–33		

Hilgard, Atkinson & Atkinson
INTRODUCTION TO PSYCHOLOGY (5th ed.)
Harcourt Brace Jovanovich, 1972

Text chapter	Related readings	Text chapter	Related readings
1	2–5	14	32, 33
2	7	15	34–38
3–4	8–14	16	1, 8, 9, 54
5		17	39, 40
6	15–20	18	
7		19	
8–10	21–28	20	41–44
11	11, 51	21	42, 43
12–13	29–32	22–23	6, 48–50

Hill
PSYCHOLOGY: PRINCIPLES AND PROBLEMS
Lippincott, 1970

Text chapter	Related readings	Text chapter	Related readings
1	2–6	8	10, 11, 14, 45–47, 52, 53
2	1, 7	9	34–38
3	21–28	10	39–44
4	29–33, 54	11	8–14
5		12	6, 48–51
6	15–20	13	2–5, 55, 56
7	26, 27		

Kagan & Havemann
PSYCHOLOGY: AN INTRODUCTION (2nd ed.)
Harcourt Brace Jovanovich, 1972

Text chapter	Related readings	Text chapter	Related readings
1	1–6	9	32, 33
2	21–25, 32	10	8, 9, 29–32, 54
3		11	41–44
4	12–14, 26–28	12	39, 40
5	11, 46, 47, 52, 53	13	
6		14	34–38
7	15–20	15	8–14
8	1, 7	16	48–51

Kendler & Kendler
BASIC PSYCHOLOGY: BRIEF EDITION
Appleton-Century-Crofts, 1971

Text chapter	Related readings	Text chapter	Related readings
1	1–5	9	10, 45–47, 51–53, 55
2		10	
3	15–20	11	34–38
4–5	12–14, 21–28	12	39, 40
6	8, 9, 29–33	13	41–44
7		14	6, 40, 48–50
8	11	App.	7

Kimble & Garmezy
PRINCIPLES OF GENERAL PSYCHOLOGY (3rd ed.)
Ronald Press, 1968

Text part	Related readings	Text part	Related readings
I	1–5	V	29–33
II	7–9, 54	VI	10, 14, 34–38, 45–47
III	15–20	VII	6, 39–44, 48–50
IV	11, 21–28		

Krech, Crutchfield & Livson
ELEMENTS OF PSYCHOLOGY (2nd ed.)
Alfred A. Knopf, 1969

Text unit	Related readings	Text unit	Related readings
1	1, 8, 9	36–37	7
2	5	38	
3	10–14	39–41	34–38
4	7	42–45	39, 40, 46, 47
5–18	15–20	46	54
19–22	21–28	47	41–45
23–27	10–14, 45–47, 52, 53, 55	48	
28–29	7	49	6, 30, 31, 48–50
30–32	29–32	50	5
33–35	32, 33		

Krech, Crutchfield & Livson
ELEMENTS OF PSYCHOLOGY, A BRIEFER COURSE
Alfred A. Knopf, 1970

Text unit	Related readings	Text unit	Related readings
1	1, 8, 9	15–16	14, 45–47
2	10–14	17–18	29–32
3	10	19–20	31, 32
4	11	21–22	41–44
5–7	35–37	23–26	39–41
8–11	15–20	27–29	48–50
12–14	21–28	30–31	7

Lana & Rosnow
INTRODUCTION TO CONTEMPORARY PSYCHOLOGY
Holt, Rinehart & Winston, 1972

Text chapter	Related readings	Text chapter	Related readings
1	1–5	7	14, 34–38, 45–47
2	7	8	39, 40
3	15–20	9	41–44
4	21–28	10	6
5	29–32	11	
6	6, 11, 50	12–14	30, 31, 48–50

Landauer
PSYCHOLOGY: A BRIEF OVERVIEW
McGraw-Hill, 1972

Text chapter	Related readings	Text chapter	Related readings
1	1–5	7	21–28, 54
2	6, 30, 31, 40, 48–50	8	11–14, 45–47, 52, 53, 55
3	34–40	9	8–14
4	41–44	10	7, 51
5	15–20	11	2–4
6	29–33		

Lindgren & Byrne
PSYCHOLOGY: AN INTRODUCTION TO A BEHAVIORAL SCIENCE (3rd ed.)
Wiley, 1971

Text chapter	Related readings	Text chapter	Related readings
1	1–6	11	35–38, 45–47
2	8–13	12	39–40
3	12, 14	13	41–44
4	21–25, 32	14	6, 48, 49
5	26–28	15	40, 48
6	7	16	11, 49–51
7	15–20	17	48
8	29–32	18	45–47
9	9, 29, 32, 33	19	30, 31, 34–36
10	34, 35	20	

McKeachie & Doyle
PSYCHOLOGY (2nd ed.) *
Addison-Wesley, 1971

Text chapter	Related readings	Text chapter	Related readings
1	1–5	10	14, 34–38, 45–47, 52, 53, 55
2	33, 37, 49	11	
3	7	12	39, 40
4	1, 8, 9, 54	13	10–14, 39
5	21–26, 32	14	41–44
6	15–20	15	30, 31, 48–50
7	29–32	16	6, 40, 50, 51
8	12–14, 27–29		
9	11, 49–51		

* The correlation of chapters to readings will be the same for *Psychology, The Short Course*, McKeachie & Doyle (Addison-Wesley, 1972).

McMahon
PSYCHOLOGY, THE HYBRID SCIENCE
Prentice-Hall, 1972

Text chapter	Related readings	Text chapter	Related readings
1	5	13	
2	2–4	14	34–38
3	1, 2, 5, 7, 8, 52–54	15	11, 14, 45–47
4	22, 23, 32	16	9
5	29–33	17	10–14, 27
6	15, 16	18	39, 40, 45
7	17–20	19	46
8	24, 28, 51	20	8, 33, 48, 49
9	21, 25–28	21	6, 50
10		22	40, 41
11		23	42–44
12	39,40	24	43, 44

Morgan & King
INTRODUCTION TO PSYCHOLOGY (4th ed.)
McGraw-Hill, 1971

Text chapter	Related readings	Text chapter	Related readings
1	1–5	11	39–40
2	8, 9, 13	12	41–44
3	12, 21–25, 28	13	41–43
4	21, 26, 27	14	40, 48–50, 54
5	9–11, 14, 29, 45–47, 55	15	6, 23, 43
6	29–32	16	30, 31, 34, 51
7	32, 33	17	1, 7
8	15–20	18	
9		19	7
10	34–38		

Munn, Fernald & Fernald
INTRODUCTION TO PSYCHOLOGY (3rd ed.)
Houghton Mifflin, 1972

Text chapter	Related readings	Text chapter	Related readings
1	1	12	8, 9, 29, 30
2	2–6	13	31, 32
3		14	32, 33
4	8–14	15	34
5	7	16	35–38
6		17	39, 40
7	15–20	18	41–44
8	21–25	19	42–44
9	26–28	20	6, 11, 49–51
10		21	48–50
11	14, 45–47, 52, 53	22	1, 54

Munn, Fernald & Fernald
BASIC PSYCHOLOGY (3rd ed.)
Houghton Mifflin, 1972

Text chapter	Related readings	Text chapter	Related readings
1	1	9	8, 9, 29, 30
2	2–6	10	31, 32
3	8–14	11	32, 33
4	21–25	12	39, 40
5	26–28	13	41–44
6		14	42–44
7	15–20	15	48–50
8	14, 45–47, 52, 53		

Resnick & Sachs
DYNAMIC GENERAL PSYCHOLOGY
Hobrook Press, 1971

Text chapter	Related readings	Text chapter	Related readings
1	1–4	9	12, 21–28, 32
2	7–9	10	14, 34–38, 45–47
3	10, 11	11	39, 40
4	34, 35	12	40
5	12–14	13	41–44
6	29–32	14	6, 30, 31, 39, 40, 48, 49
7	32, 33	15	12–14, 30, 31
8	15–20	16	55, 56

Ruch & Zimbardo
PSYCHOLOGY AND LIFE (8th ed.)
Scott, Foresman, 1971

Text chapter	Related readings	Text chapter	Related readings
1	5, 6	9	29–32
2	2–6	10	32, 33, 39, 46
3	1, 7	11	31, 34–40
4	8–14, 32	12	12, 48–50, 54
5	21–28, 32	13	1, 54
6	11, 15, 16, 55	14	41–44
7	15–20	15	41–43
8	7, 14, 45–47, 51		

Ruch & Zimbardo
PSYCHOLOGY AND LIFE (Brief 8th ed.)
Scott, Foresman, 1971

Text chapter	Related readings	Text chapter	Related readings
1	2–6	7	29–33
2	1, 7	8	12, 48–50, 54
3	8–14, 32	9	31, 34–40
4	21–28, 32	10	41–44
5	11, 51, 55	11	41–43
6	15–20		

Sanford & Wrightsman
PSYCHOLOGY: A SCIENTIFIC STUDY OF MAN (3rd ed.)
Wadsworth, 1970

Text chapter	Related readings	Text chapter	Related readings
1	1, 5, 6, 55, 56	11	21–25, 32
2	2–4	12	12–14, 26–28
3	8–14	13	10, 11
4	7	14	35–38, 45–47
5	34, 35	15	39–40
6	2–4	16	40, 48–50
7	29–32, 54	17	31, 38
8	32, 33, 41	18	32, 41–44
9		19	41–43
10	15–20		

Silverman
PSYCHOLOGY
Appleton-Century-Crofts, 1971

Text chapter	Related readings	Text chapter	Related readings
1	1–6	11	34–38
2	8–14, 52–54	12	39, 40
3		13	41–44
4	7	14	42, 43
5	21–25, 28, 32	15	48–50
6	7, 26, 27	16	6
7	15–20	17	12, 13, 26, 55
8	29–32	18	30, 31, 34, 35
9	32, 33	19	
10	10, 14, 45–47, 49, 55		

Stagner & Solley
BASIC PSYCHOLOGY
McGraw-Hill, 1970

Text chapter	Related readings	Text chapter	Related readings
1	1–6, 54	7–8	21–28
2	8–11	9	10, 11, 45–47, 52, 53, 55
3	32, 33	10	34–38
4	29–31	11	41–44
5–6	15–20	12	39–40

Telford & Sawrey
PSYCHOLOGY AS A NATURAL SCIENCE
Brooks/Cole, 1972

Text chapter	Related readings	Text chapter	Related readings
1	1–5	8	11, 14, 45–47, 52, 53
2	7	9	34–38
3–4	15–20	10	8, 9, 54
5–6	21–28	11	9, 29–32, 41
7		12	39, 40, 48–50

Thompson & DeBold
PSYCHOLOGY: A SYSTEMATIC INTRODUCTION
McGraw-Hill, 1971

Text part	Related readings	Text part	Related readings
One	1–5, 55	Five	11, 21–28, 32
Two	39, 40	Six	7–9, 54
Three	6, 48–50	Seven	14, 34–38, 45–47
Four	15–20		

Wertheimer, Björkman, Lundberg & Magnusson
PSYCHOLOGY: A BRIEF INTRODUCTION
Scott, Foresman, 1971

Text chapter	Related readings	Text chapter	Related readings
1	1–4	5	5, 6, 48–50
2	15–20	6	8, 9, 34–40
3	7, 29–33	7	34, 35, 41–44
4	10–14, 21–28, 54, 55		

Whittaker
INTRODUCTION TO PSYCHOLOGY (2nd ed.)
Saunders, 1970

Text chapter	Related readings	Text chapter	Related readings
1	1–6	11	14, 45–47, 52, 53, 55
2	7	12	
3	8–14, 32	13	34–38
4	48–51, 54	14	39, 40
5	29–32	15	
6	32, 33	16	41–44
7	21–25, 28	17	42–44
8	12–14, 26–27	18	6
9		19	48–50
10	15–20		

115412
CLG

150.8 MCCO

MAY 15 '85

FEB 1 4 1994

DISCARD